MW00669096

The International League

125 YEARS OF BASEBALL

BILL O'NEAL

EAKIN PRESS Waco, Texas

*Dedicated to the generations of players, executives,
and fans who have contributed to the longevity
and success of the International League.*

NOTE: Photos not otherwise credited are from the author's collection.

FIRST EDITION
Copyright © 2008
By Bill O'Neal
Published in the United States of America
By Eakin Press
A Division of Sunbelt Media, Inc.
P.O. Box 21235 ▱ Waco, Texas 76702
email: sales@eakinpress.com
▱ website: www.eakinpress.com ▱
ALL RIGHTS RESERVED.
1   2   3   4   5   6   7   8   9
ISBN 978-1-934645-56-7
Library of Congress Control Number 2008925696

Contents

*"I still have the box score of my first International League game,
played in Baltimore on April 22, 1914.
We met the Buffalo club and I shut them out with six hits...."*
BABE RUTH

*"We finished third and played Montreal in the International League playoffs.
They had Jackie Robinson and a heck of a club. We lost the series, and I lost my
head against the plate umpire, Artie Gore, on a close call at the plate."*
YOGI BERRA
Newark catcher, 1946

*"If I had a gun, I'd have shot the little pest [Berra] a hundred times.
Every time we played against Newark, they murdered us."*
BUCKY HARRIS
Buffalo manager

*"See, we had an easy-going club. Real loose. No rules.
No clubhouse meetings. It was a good life."*
LEFTY GROVE
Oriole ace, 1920-24

*"Jack Dunn was a very good loser. He wanted to win every game,
and eventually he instilled that same spirit in his ballplayers. If a ballplayer
loafed in a game or two, the rest of the team took care of him.
He wasted no time in getting rid of that kind of player."*
MERWIN JACOBSON
Oriole centerfielder

"Play ball!"
CAL HUBBARD
IL (and Hall of Fame) umpire, 1931-35

Foreword

As I sit down to write the foreword to this second book written by the International League's good friend Bill O'Neal, it is a daunting task to come up with the right words to preface this look at the League's 125-year history. I find myself stuck on where to begin and how to do justice to all of the individuals on and off the field that have allowed the League to become as successful as it is today. Any attempt to name names would result in failure to credit many who are deserving, so I won't venture down that path.

When Bill and Eakin Press produced *The International League—A Baseball History 1884-1991* back in 1992, I had been in the League President's position for less than two years. It is scary to think about how much I didn't know at that time and the limited perspective I had on the big picture of professional baseball at both the major and minor league levels. Having now been associated with the League for twenty-nine years and in the top administrative role for nineteen seasons, my perspective has obviously changed since I wrote the foreword in Bill's first book.

I have learned that the International League is about 125 years of people. Be it players, fans or administrators, it's all about the people. While we have faced challenges as a league and an industry during the past few decades, this period must truly be considered the golden age for Minor League Baseball. The challenges for those of us who entered the game during this period pale for the most part compared to those of our predecessors who routinely battled issues related to team and league survival. Thankfully, as a result of continued hard work and the foundation built by those before us, our experiences are filled with ever rising attendance totals and increased franchise values. It is overwhelming to think of the challenges and pressures the League faced during many its first century. Be it battles with other leagues for quality players, teams relocating from city to city during difficult times or the stress on communities during wartimes, the International League has endured and as a result can boast of being the second oldest league in all of professional sports, junior only to the National Baseball League. This incredible staying power hasn't happened by magic—it's all about the people.

To me, the characteristics the League should be proudest of during the past few decades are its stability and consistency. There is no equal in Minor League Baseball to the International for the stability and consistency of franchise locations, management, ownership and major league affiliation. These qualities have allowed the League to move forward steadily instead of constantly retrenching. Although some change is good for the sake of modernization and efficiency, nothing beats stable relationships, and that is at the core of the League's success on several different levels. Again, it's all about the people.

The most exciting aspect of the League's 125th anniversary celebration is the revival of the International League Hall of Fame. Begun in 1947 but dormant since the induction of 1963, the ILHOF again is inducting new members, thanks in large part to research conducted by former League employee Nathan Blackmon and current employee Chris Sprague. I can imagine no better way to recognize the storied history of the League than to honor those who have brought us to where we are today. The IL Hall of Fame helps us to realize that today we are all simply caretakers of the greatest game ever invented. One day we will be gone, but the game will continue on.

I hope that during the League's 125th season in 2008 and during many more to come, you have the opportunity to create lifelong memories with family and friends at an International League ballpark.

Please enjoy this book that Bill has prepared about the vibrant institution known as the International Baseball League.

—RANDY A. MOBLEY
International League President

Introducing the International League

Babe Ruth. Lefty Grove. Jackie Robinson. Yogi Berra. Satchel Paige. Iron Man Joe McGinnity. Rogers Hornsby. Nap Lajoie. Roy Campanella. Wee Willie Keeler. Tris Speaker. Bob Gibson. Wade Boggs. Curt Schilling.

For 125 years many of baseball's greatest players have flashed their formidable skills before International League fans. Baseball's oldest minor league was founded in 1884, just eight years after the National League and more than a decade and a half before the American League. Despite several name changes, the IL has achieved the longest continual history of any minor league, while a parade of nearly one hundred Hall of Famers has played and managed and umpired in IL ballparks. Many of the finest career minor leaguers, such as Ike Boone and Smead Jolley, also starred in the International League.

This book is a celebration of a century and a quarter of International League baseball. Almost sixty cities have hosted IL franchises, including communities in twenty of the United States, and—making the league truly international—six Canadian cities, as well as Havana, Cuba, and San Juan, Puerto Rico. From 1919 through 1925, Baltimore's IL Orioles won seven consecutive pennants, still the all-time championship run in professional baseball. Professional baseball's first unassisted triple play was an IL highlight. The Little World Series, pitting the champions of the International League against their American Association counterparts, was a minor league classic for more than four decades, while longtime IL executive Frank Shaughnessy devised the post-season playoff plan that became utilized by almost all minor circuits. The year before he famously broke the major league color barrier with the Brooklyn Dodgers, Jackie Robinson was the IL batting champ.

With a background that extends to the dawn of professional baseball, the International League boasts a rich chronicle of talented players and historic events. A look at the IL past is a unique baseball adventure.

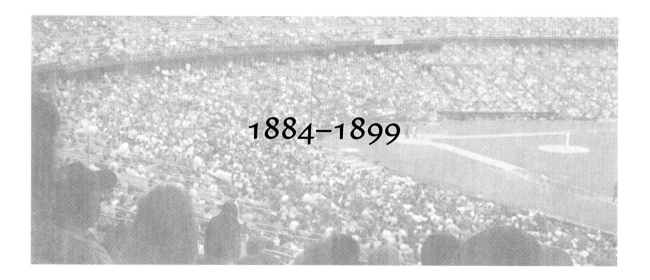

1884–1899

The International League originated during the outburst of athletic enthusiasm that surged across America late in the nineteenth century. Baseball in its primitive form was played in the cities of the Northeast prior to the Civil War, and Union soldiers from farms and rural communities learned the game in army camps throughout the long years of conflict. After the war these young veterans brought the sport home to a multitude of towns and villages. Baseball became America's first team sport: young men organized amateur nines to take on rival clubs; boys played ceaselessly on cow pastures and vacant lots; colleges and high schools established teams; and standout athletes began to be paid to play on semi-pro squads.

As baseball became America's first team sport, nine teams formed the National Association of Professional Base-Ball Players in 1871. Five years later this organization was superseded by an eight-team National League. In 1882 a second "major league" was founded, the American Association, and the Union Association was organized two years later. Three "minor leagues" commenced play in 1877, and by 1884, with three major leagues in operation, there were eight minor leagues.

Although most of the early minor leagues folded after one or two seasons, a circuit was formed in 1884 that would become a model of success and durability. An organizational meeting was conducted in Philadelphia on Friday, January 4, 1884. A native Philadelphian, 29-year-old Harry Diddlebock, agreed to serve as president of the new circuit, which initially would be called the Eastern League.

The original Eastern League commenced play with teams in eight cities: Richmond, Virginia; Baltimore, Maryland ("The Monumental Club"); Wilmington, Delaware; Allentown, Harrisburg, and Reading ("The Actives") of Pennsylvania; and Newark ("The Domestic") and Trenton of New Jersey. Richmond was the southernmost city, Harrisburg the westernmost, and Newark the northernmost. The league was compact, which eased travel expenses and scheduling: it was only 200 miles or so from Richmond to the Pennsylvania cities, and a little over 300 miles from Richmond to Newark, while other cities were neighbors and natural rivals. But with the cutthroat competition and constant player raids between the trio of major leagues, the inaugural season of the Eastern League IL proved to be an unsettled summer throughout the cities of the Northeast.

Eastern League teams with losing records and poor attendance began disbanding early in the season. The new circuit scrambled to find replacement cities, but two of the best

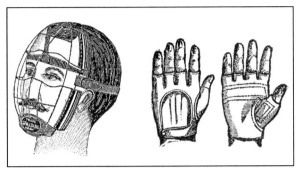

"Spalding's Special League Mask" was advertised for $3 in 1884, the first year of Eastern League play. These masks featured "extra heavy wire, well padded with goathair and the padding faced with the best imported dogskin...." The 1884 catchers "gloves" cost $2.50 a pair and were worn on both hands. "These gloves do not interfere with throwing," insisted Spalding's.

TIME OUT

A Rose By Any Other Name

The International League had several name changes during the formative decades, but the continuity of baseball's oldest minor league was unaffected. "International League" was first used during the circuit's third year of operation. Although other titles were tried in later seasons, the league returned again and again to "International League," which has remained the official label since 1920.

Eastern League	1884
New York State League	1885
International League	1886-1887
International Association	1888-1889
Eastern Association	1891
Eastern League	1892-1911
International League	1912-1917
New International League	1918-1919
International League	1920-

clubs, Richmond and Wilmington, were lured to the big leagues as replacement franchises. By August only five teams were left in the Eastern League, but these clubs gamely played to the end of a revamped schedule. Trenton was declared champion after posting the only winning record (46-38). Newark's J.W. Coogan won the batting crown with a .380 average, while the league's first no-hitter, a 2-1 victory by Trenton pitcher William Fox over Rochester, was posted on June 26.

The IL traditionally has claimed continuity since 1884 by including the New York State League of 1885, although there was a new president, a new circuit name, and no holdover cities from the Eastern League. The New York State League of 1885 was made up of towns from Albany, Binghamton, Oswego, Rochester, Syracuse, and Utica. Each of these cities would go on to enjoy an extended history in the IL, while Rochester and Syracuse maintain bellwether franchises in today's International League.

For 1886 the New York State League expanded into Canada, adding Toronto and Hamilton. Appropriately, the circuit was renamed the International League, which in time would become the league's permanent identity. All five New York teams which had completed the 1885 season returned for

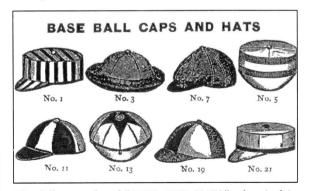

The different styles of "CAPS AND HATS" advertised in Spalding's Best Ball Guide, 1884. Selections available to the new Eastern league included "Chicago style" (No. 5) and "Boston shape" (No. 7 and No. 13).

1886, and an eight-team league was rounded out with the addition of the Buffalo Bisons, which had spent the past seven years in the National League.

Buffalo's ironman righthander Mike Walsh (27-21) pitched in 51 of 95 Bison games, recording more than half of this club's wins (50-45). All eight teams played nearly 100 games to the end of the schedule, a remarkable demonstration of league stability for the era. Admission throughout the International League was 25 cents for adults and 10 cents for children.

Rule changes were frequent throughout the 1880s. Beginning in 1887, for example, batters could no longer order up high or low pitches. In compensation, however, the number of strikes was increased from three to four, and walks were counted as base hits. The latter rule was dropped the following year, and the number of strikes permanently returned to three. Nevertheless, batting averages soared in 1887. Buffalo, for example, boasted an inflated team average of .335 (see diagram for the Buffalo lineup), and Bison kranks responded in large numbers to the offensive show. Although the Bisons lost the pennant to Toronto by three games, Buffalo owners enjoyed a comfortable profit of $4,000.

Buffalo righthander Mike Walsh posted an even better season in 1887 (27-9), and he had stellar support from workhorse John Fanning (28-21). The pitching feat of the year, however, was recorded by Newark southpaw George Stovey (35-14), who established an all-time IL record for victories. Another all-time league mark was set in 1887 by Toronto outfielder Mike Slattery, who stole 112 bases. The next year another Toronto outfielder, Ed Burke, led the league with 107 stolen bases in 111 games. (It should be pointed out that scorers credited runners with stolen bases when an extra base was taken, such as going from first to third on a single, so stolen base totals of the era were somewhat inflated.)

Newark's catcher in 1887 was 29-year-old Moses Fleetwood "Fleet" Walker. Thought to be the first African-American to play in the minor leagues, Fleet Walker began his professional career in 1883 with Toledo of the American Association. After playing for Newark in 1887, Fleet stayed in the IL with Syracuse in 1888 and 1889. But he only hit .170 and .216, and perhaps because of poor offensive production—or perhaps because of growing racial discrimination—Fleet Walker left professional baseball.

In 1888 Toronto hurler Al Atkinson, an experienced big leaguer, struck out 307 batters while walking only 79. But George Haddock of Troy lost 20 consecutive games, while Cornelius Murphy of Syracuse uncorked 47 wild pitches—both all-time IL records. Another record was set by Peter Weed of Hamilton, who hit

BUFFALO BISONS, 1887
65–40

Tobias Griffin .374
Charles Hamburg .345
John Galligan .333
John Remson .391
Harry Esterday .325
Frank Grant .366
John Reidy .333
Mickey LeHane .392

PITCHERS
Mike Walsh 27–9
John Fanning 28–21
Ed Green 16–18

John Chapman, Mgr.
Team BA — .335

Joe Kappel .368
Dan Dugdale .302

TIME OUT

Black Players in the Early IL

Despite blatant racial discrimination common to the period, there were several black players in the league during the 1880s. One of the best was Buffalo second baseman Frank Grant, who was spectacular in the field, and who hit .344 in 1886 and .366 in 1887. Also in 1887, Syracuse southpaw Robert Higgins posted a 19-8 mark, and another lefty, George Stovey of Newark, set an all-time IL record with 35 victories. But by 1888, racist factions attempted to drive all blacks out of the International League, although Buffalo countered with a proposal to limit each team to two black players. Frank Grant, who hit .366 with a league-leading 11 homers in 1888, was spiked so often that he moved to the outfield. His salary was lowered after he suffered an injury, and he never again played in organized baseball. Blacks soon vanished from IL playing fields, not to reappear until after World War II.

34 batters, although Frank Knauss of Detroit equaled this dubious mark the next year, when he went 27-9.

Syracuse, league champions in 1885, became the first city to claim a second pennant, with an outstanding 81-31 (.723) performance in 1888. But in 1889 Detroit, which had just completed eight years in the National League, joined the IL and won back-to-back championships.

Detroit's 1890 pennant came at the early end of the International League's only abbreviated season. Competition for quality players was especially intense in 1890, with 24 teams in the major leagues trying to outbid each other. (Two of these circuits soon disbanded, and from 1892 until 1901 the National League enjoyed a monopoly

The Syracuse Stars, champions of 1888. "Iron Man" Connie Murphy (second row, second from left) led the league with 34 victories and a 1.27 ERA, while the best hitters were shortstop Ollie Beard (.350—second row, far left) and outfielders Rasty Wright (seated between Murphy and George Hacket) and Lefty Marr (.342 with 83 steals—second row, far right). Catcher Fleet Walker (top row, far left) and pitcher Bob Higgins (bottom row, far left) formed a black battery, but blacks soon disappeared from the league until 1946. (Courtesy Onondaga Public Library, Syracuse)

as the only major league.) In 1890 six IL teams opened the season with less talent than local kranks were used to seeing. Two teams soon had to fold, and the remaining four finally called it quits on July 7—the only time in 125 years the IL has not finished a season. Indeed, after the Spanish-American War broke out in the spring of 1898, the subsequent wartime distractions caused many minor leagues to cease operations early, but the Eastern League (which had returned to its original name) struggled to the end of the schedule, then rebounded strongly in 1899.

During the 1890s IL kranks enjoyed performances by many talented players who were headed for the major leagues—such as 20-year-old batting champ Wee Willie Keeler (.373 in 1892)—or by former big leaguers who still boasted formidable skills—such as Hall of Fame first baseman Dan Brouthers, who set the all time IL batting mark (.415 in 1897) at the age of 39. This talent parade has continued throughout the long history of the IL. IL fans of every era have enjoyed many of baseball's most gifted young athletes as they played their way into the big leagues, while noted major leaguers have brought excitement to IL ballparks—including today's stars, sent down for brief rehab assignments.

Outfielder Steve Brodie played for Hamilton in 1889 (.302). Brodie moved up to the National League the next season, but after a 13-year big league career, he played for Baltimore and Montreal in 1903, Providence in 1905 and 1906, and Newark in 1906 and 1910)

As a 20-year-old rookie to pro ball, "Wee Willie" Keeler won the 1892 batting crown with Binghamton. He spent 19 seasons in the big leagues (.345 lifetime), then ended his Hall of Fame career in 1911 by returning to the IL with Toronto.

During 19 years in the big leagues, first baseman Dan Brouthers pounded his way to the Hall of Fame with five batting crowns and a .349 batting average. At mid-season of 1896, the 38-year-old slugger was cast loose by Philadelphia of the NL. But Brouthers caught on with Springfield and hit .400 in 51 games. In 1897 he played every game with Springfield and set the all-time IL season record with a spectacular .415 average, along with plenty of power and 21 stolen bases.

Albany's nineteenth-century Riverside Park was located east of downtown and overlooking the Hudson River. (Courtesy Albany Public Library)

During the early 1890s IL rosters comprised twelve players, including only three or four pitchers. When a hurler started a game he was expected to finish it, and a durable workhorse was the key to most pennant-winners. For example, in 1891 the Buffalo Bisons won the pennant behind Les German, who led the league in victories (34-11) and his team in hitting (.314).

In 1891 and again in 1892 merely eight players hit .300 or better. But pitching dominance ended in 1893, when the distance from home plate to the mound was extended from 50 feet to the present 60 feet, 6 inches. Throughout baseball pitchers faced a drastic adjustment, particularly with their curve balls. During the adjustment period batters thrived, fulfilling the intentions of owners who wanted greater offensive production in an effort to stimulate attendance.

In 1893 in the Eastern League/IL, 45 regulars batted over .300 and 16 hit over .340. The batting champ was Buffalo infielder-pitcher Jacob Drauby, who hit .379. The next season Quiet Joe Knight won the batting title with a .371 average, and in 1895 Toronto first-baseman Judson Smith batted .379 to claim the crown. During the 1895 season 52 players hit above .300, including 14 above .340. At Buffalo's opening game, on Sunday, May 9, Bison outfielder Billy Bottenus clubbed four home runs and a double to lead an 18-13 victory over the Wilkes-Barre Coal Barons.

Such fireworks brought fans to IL ballparks, and in 1896—for the first time in league history—every team returned from the previous year. As early as the late 1880s the IL was widely considered the "most powerful of all minor leagues." By the end of the next decade the IL had showcased quality pro ball in 40 cities in eleven of the United States and Canada.

At the close of the nineteenth century

baseball reigned supreme as the National Pastime, far surpassing in popularity football, newly-invented basketball, boxing, bicycling, or any other sport embraced by the American public. And the strongest and most respected minor circuit in professional baseball was the Eastern League/IL.

In 1895, 20-year-old outfielder Fielder Allison Jones hit .399 and scored 57 runs in 50 games for Springfield. Jones then enjoyed a long career as a big league player and manager.

TIME OUT

Quiet Joe Knight

During the 1880s and 1890s, no player was more familiar to IL kranks than hard-hitting outfielder "Quiet Joe" Knight. Born in Canada in 1859, Knight did not turn pro until he was 23. At first he was a left-handed pitcher, but his talent with a bat soon put him in the outfield on a daily basis.

Knight first appeared in the International League with Hamilton in 1886. He played three seasons for Hamilton, batting .335 in 1887 and leading the league in doubles in 1888. In 1889 he moved over to another Canadian franchise, London, where he hit .350 and was purchased by Cincinnati of the National League. Although he hit .312 in 1890, he returned to the IL the following season.

During the 1890s, Quiet Joe Knight roamed IL outfields for Rochester, Syracuse, Utica, Binghamton, Wilkes-Barre, Providence, Ottawa, and Buffalo. After batting .299 for Rochester in 1891, in successive seasons he hit .380, .389, .371, .363, 377, .335, and .338. Knight again led the league in doubles in 1892, he was the batting champ in 1894, and he enjoyed his best season in 1893, leading the circuit in hits and triples while batting .389 for Binghamton. In 1899 after hitting .360 in six games for Buffalo, the 40-year-old IL star retired, remaining in Canada until his death in 1938.

1900–1909

In 1900, the seventeenth season of the Eastern League/IL operation, the stable circuit retained the same eight cities from 1899. Providence won the 1900 pennant with a 16-man roster that included 11 players who were former or future major leaguers. The 1900 batting champ, run leader and home run titlist was Worcester first baseman Kitty Bransfield (.371, 115 R in 122 games, and 17 HR). Bransfield's 17 homers represented the highest total amassed by any professional in 1900, and he went on to a 12-year National League career. Indeed, 14 out of 15 men who hit .300 or better in 1900 had worn or would wear major league uniforms. "Wild Bill" Donovan, who pitched and pinch-hit for Hartsford in 1900, won 25 games for Brooklyn in 1901 and would play for 18 seasons in the big leagues.

The 1901 pennant was won by Rochester behind future—or past—big leaguers Ed "Battleship" Greminger (.343 as the third baseman), speedy outfielder George "Deerfoot" Barclay (.339), first-sacker and stolen base champ Harold O'Hagan (.320 with 51 steals), second baseman George "Heinie" Smith (.315), and run leader William Lush (.310 with 137 runs in 132 games). One of the primary reasons for the sustained success of the Eastern League/IL was the excellent quality of baseball that was played by star athletes day after day, season after season.

For 1901 Buffalo rejoined the league, replacing Springfield after an absence of two seasons. Buffalo had played in Ban Johnson's American League, but after the 1900 season Johnson announced that his new circuit would challenge the National League as a major league. Johnson unceremoniously shifted Buffalo's AL franchise to Boston. The Red Sox became a mainstay of the American League, and Buffalo became a mainstay of the IL for seven decades.

Unfortunately, Buffalo's 1901 club was a last-place outfit plagued by poor weather and the Pan-American Exposition (President William McKinley was fatally wounded by an anarchist while attending the Exposition on September 6, 1901). Owner Jim Franklin called his team the "Pan-Ams" and played a couple of games in Pan-American Stadium, but season attendance was so poor that he sold his club (and he died of a heart attack shortly thereafter).

Of consolation to Buffalo fans during this period was the play of outfielder Jake Gettman. Born in Russia in 1875, Gettman had played three seasons for Washington in the National League when he was purchased by Buffalo for $300 in 1900. He played seven seasons for Buffalo, then remained in the league through 1912 by wearing the uniforms of Toronto, Newark, New Jersey, and Baltimore. A familiar figure around the league for 12 consecutive years, Gettman enjoyed his best seasons in 1902 (.339), 1903 (.334), and 1912 (.344).

The impressive performance of the upstart American League during the 1901 season resulted in the momentous consequences for the minors, and the Eastern (International) League was in the van of change. Since 1884 (the inaugural season of the IL) the National League had abided by the National Agreement, which guaranteed the sanctity of player contracts and territorial rights for professional franchises. But with the loss of numerous stars to the rival American League, the National League declared all-out war in the competition of players, and by August 1901 the major leagues announced that the National Agreement no longer would be observed.

Minor league owners clearly understood the threat of losing their best players without compensation to a big league club. The president of the Western League, Thomas J. Hickey, wired every other minor league president, requesting an emergency meeting at Chicago's Leland Hotel on Thursday, September 5, 1901. Patrick Powers, the dynamic leader of the Eastern League, went to Chicago, along with the presidents of six other minor league circuits. The other four minor leagues sent proxies, and all eleven leagues agreed to form the National Association of Professional Leagues. The organization is still known as the National Association, and all member leagues were considered part of organized baseball. Thomas Hickey, who presided over the Chicago meeting, was asked to serve as president, but he was too deeply involved in organizing the league that would become the American Association. Pat Powers instead was elected; the Eastern League head served as first president of the National Association for eight years.

Another meeting was held on October 24 and 25 in New York City. Details for the National Association were hammered out, including a strict player contract system. Minor leagues were compartmentalized into Class A, B, C, and D classifications, determined by the size of member cities. Class D rosters were limited to 14 players, mostly rookies, while Class A clubs could carry 18 men. The Eastern League, of course, was awarded Class A status. (When Class AA was added in 1908, the Eastern League was promoted, along with the American Association and the Pacific Coast League. The AAA rating was created in 1946, elevating the circuit, now permanently termed the International League, once again.)

By the time the 1902 season opened, 15 leagues belonged to the National Association, and by 1903 membership had increased to 19. The American and National Leagues entered into an agreement with the united minor leagues, and an uneasy truce turned into a permanent peace (which would be increasingly dominated by the big leagues). Before the 1902 Eastern League season began, Buffalo's franchise was taken over by dapper George Stallings, a former big league manager who would lead Boston's "Miracle Braves" of 1914 to the NL pennant. A superb field manager and a keen judge of talent, Stallings put together a club on short notice. Behind Jake Gettman, third baseman Dave Brian (.335), outfielder-first baseman Myron Grimshaw (.318), and pitchers Cy Ferry (22-4) and Cy Hooker (22-9), Stallings moved the Bisons from the cellar to second place.

Toronto started poorly but rose to first by June 30, then battled back and forth with Buffalo before clinching the flag with a doubleheader sweep on the final day of the season. Clarence "Pop" Foster, an outfielder who played for both Providence and Montreal, led all minor leaguers with 14 home runs—the fourth time in five years that a slugger from the circuit had achieved this distinction. The batting champ was Bill "Jocko" Halligan (.351), a major league veteran who played or Jersey City.

Jersey City had rejoined the league, along with Newark, replacing Syracuse and Hartford. The two New Jersey cities were natural rivals and would strengthen the league for years. Jersey City, which finished third, boasted a new ballpark that was considered "the finest in the league, beyond question." Last-place Newark, however, had such a poor facility that *Spalding's Official Base Ball Guide* editorialized that "the owners never expected the fair sex to journey out to the park used at the present time." Fans of either sex could be excused from traveling out to the park, because Newark became the first team in league history to lose 100 games (40-100).

During a 17-year major league career that led to the Hall of Fame, catcher Wilbert Robinson spent 12 seasons with the Baltimore Orioles. In 1903 Baltimore was squeezed out of the American League and joined the Eastern League. "Uncle Robbie" stayed with the Orioles as manager and part-time player. At the end of the 1904 season Robinson, now 40, finally left Baltimore. His playing days were over, but for many years he was a coach or manager, primarily for the Giants and Dodgers.

TIME OUT

The First Unassisted Triple Play

The IL can claim the first unassisted triple play ever recorded in professional baseball. Al Buckenberger had managed the Rochester Bronchos to the 1901 pennant. Ed McLeon was the new manager, but with Rochester in sixth place he was replaced in August by Harry O'Hagan.

O'Hagan was a first baseman who had a cup of coffee with Washington in 1892, then bounced from Chicago to New York to Cleveland in 1902. With a lifetime average of .177 in 61 big league games, he wisely accepted the offer to be player-manager of the Bronchos.

He caught up with his new team in Jersey City on Monday, August 18, 1902, and promptly made baseball history. Early in the game, with no outs, Jersey City put George Shoch on second base and Mack Dooley on first. The Jersey City manager signaled for a sacrifice bunt, and the runners took off with the pitch.

But Jersey City catcher Johnnie Butler bunted toward first base in the air, and O'Hagan snagged the ball inches from the ground. O'Hagan then scrambled to first to double up Dooley. By this time Shoch, who apparently did not realize the ball had been caught in the air, had raced around third and was headed home. O'Hagan ran to second and stepped on the bag, ending the inning and helping the Bronchos to a 10-6 victory.

Worcester, with remote grounds located on the outskirts of the city, and Providence also were chastised for their ballparks. Prior to the 1903 season, however, Buffalo spent $10,000 to upgrade Olympic Park, adding another grandstand, bleachers, a ticket office and clubhouse.

The most impressive event of 1903 was the reenlistment of another franchise city from the American League, Baltimore, which played briefly in the IL's inaugural season, then went on to lasting baseball fame as the National League champions of 1894-95-96. Ned Hanlon's scrappy Orioles starred "Wee Willie" Keeler, Dan Brouthers, John J. McGraw, Hughey Jennings, and Wilbert Robinson. The Orioles joined Ban Johnson's fledgling American League, but after the 1902 season Baltimore was squeezed out of the AL in favor of New York. So Ned Hanlon bought American League Park for $3,000, then purchased Montreal's Eastern League franchise and moved to Baltimore. (Montreal did not miss a season, because local sportsmen acquired the shaky Worcester franchise.)

The 1903 pennant was won by Jersey City. Right fielder Moose McCormick (.362) won the batting title, and there was a superb pitching rotation of victory leader Pfanmiller (28-9), Mike McCann (26-8), and Jake Thielman (23-5). At the opposite end of the league, last-place Rochester's Frank Leary (8-29) tied George O'Keefe's 1888 record for losses. Buffalo's second-place club set a league attendance record with more then 305,000 fans, including a total of 30,000 for a morning-afternoon Memorial Day doubleheader.

George Stallings drove Buffalo to the 1904 pennant behind righthander Rube Kisinger (24-

11), just down from two seasons in the American League. With Buffalo Kisinger was a 20-game winner for three consecutive years, including another championship season with Stallings in 1906. Rube twirled a no-hitter in 1909, recorded 117 victories for Buffalo through 1910, and compiled a league record 31 career shutouts.

Another stalwart for Buffalo's 1906 champs was slugging outfielder Jimmy Murray, who spent nine seasons in his prime in the IL, including seven with the Bisons. Severely beaned during a game against Newark on June 27, 1908, Murray returned to action wearing a protective device, anticipating the modern batting helmet.

The minor league American Association had opened play in the Midwest in 1902. At the close of the 1903 league schedules, the American League and the National League champions engaged in a best-five-of-nine (soon to be four-of-seven) "World Series." Following the 1904 season the champs of the American Association and the Eastern League scheduled a "Little World Series." The playoff was curtailed by bad weather, with Buffalo

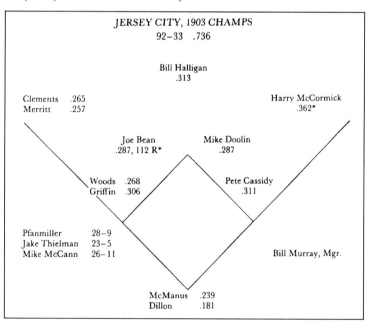

JERSEY CITY, 1903 CHAMPS
92–33   .736

Bill Halligan
.313

Clements   .265
Merritt   .257

Harry McCormick
.362*

Joe Bean
.287, 112 R*

Mike Doolin
.287

Woods   .268
Griffin   .306

Pete Cassidy
.311

Pfanmiller   28–9
Jake Thielman   23–5
Mike McCann   26–11

Bill Murray, Mgr.

McManus   .239
Dillon   .181

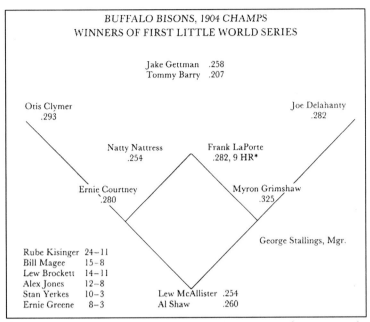

BUFFALO BISONS, 1904 CHAMPS
WINNERS OF FIRST LITTLE WORLD SERIES

Jake Gettman .258
Tommy Barry .207

Otis Clymer
.293

Joe Delahanty
.282

Natty Nattress
.254

Frank LaPorte
.282, 9 HR*

Ernie Courtney
.280

Myron Grimshaw
.325

George Stallings, Mgr.

Rube Kisinger 24–11
Bill Magee 15–8
Lew Brockett 14–11
Alex Jones 12–8
Stan Yerkes 10–3
Ernie Greene 8–3

Lew McAllister .254
Al Shaw .260

TIME OUT

Base Brawl

Today's hitters who charge the mound at every inside pitch are not the first baseball players willing to use their fists. Early-day baseball was noted for brawls, and feisty George Stallings presided over a typically pugilistic roster in Buffalo. On July 8, 1905, for example, Buffalo ace Rube Kisinger tangled with Rochester third baseman Jerry O'Brien, in a confrontation so vicious that both players were arrested and taken to the Rochester police station.

Back in Buffalo on July 13, Bison shortstop Nattie Nattress ripped the mask off the umpire, who promptly charged the irate infielder. The ump forfeited the game, and Nattress and Stallings were suspended. When the Bisons traveled to Newark, several players created a disturbance in a saloon. Two players were fined for public drunkenness, and when Stallings tried to protect his men he was arrested for interfering with the police.

In 1908 Stallings managed the Newark Tigers. Early in the year he wrangled during and after the game with umpire W.J. Sullivan, who later sued Stallings for $25,000. Sullivan claimed that the combative manager broke his arm and hit him in the head with a pool cue. "There was nothing to it," shrugged Stallings, "he wasn't even hurt."

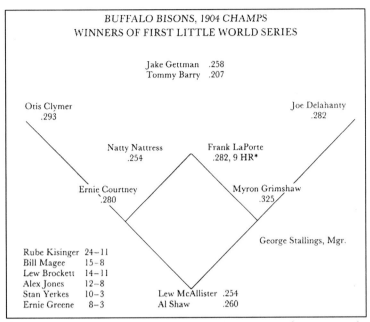

leading the St. Paul Saints, two games to one. The Little World Series was not played the next year, but the two leagues tried again in 1906, and in time the contest would become a minor league classic.

In 1905 32-year-old Jack Dunn became manager of the Providence Clamdiggers (earlier termed the Clam-Diggers). Dunn had worn the uniform of four big league clubs since 1897, playing as a pitcher, second baseman, shortstop, third-sacker, and outfielder. Player-manager Dunn (.301) promptly led the Clamdiggers to a pennant—the first of nine IL championships he would produce. Dunn's Providence pitching staff featured victory leader John Cronin (29-12 with a no-hitter) and Ed Poole (21-12).

Throughout the heyday of the national pastime, the season opener was a social occasion in baseball cities across the land. Schools and businesses closed early, dignitaries turned up to throw out the first ball, and festivities were highlighted with parades and bands and general celebration.

For example, the Eastern League opened the 1907 season on Wednesday, April 24, in Buffalo where 10,000 fans crowded into Olympic Park. Longtime league president Pat Powers tossed the first ball to Harry L. Taylor, who had filled in as president during the 1906 season.

The following day at Newark, uniformed players from both teams (Baltimore's Orioles provided the opposition) climbed into open carriages at two o'clock in the afternoon.

Player-manager Jack Dunn led the Clamdiggers to the 1905 pennant. Dunn hit .301, Hermus McFarland batted .319, John Cronin won 29 games, and Ed Poole added 21 victories.

Leaving from the Continental Hotel, the carriages were led to the ballpark by a brass band. At the stadium 8,000 fans cheered, as fluttering flags and the horns and drums of the band added to the excitement of the occasion.

In 1907 Toronto vaulted from the cellar to the pennant behind player-manager Joe Kelley, who had just completed 16 seasons in the major leagues. Toronto was the first of seven "worst to first" clubs in the IL (including Toronto again in 1960). The 1906 Toronto Canucks faced Columbus in the Little World Series. Although Columbus was appearing in its second consecutive postseason playoff, Toronto easily won, four games to one. The American Association had lost all three Little World Series, and the contest between the two leagues would not be played again until 1917. Boston of the National League hired Joe Kelley away from Toronto, and the defending champs dropped all the way to the cellar in 1907—last to first to last again.

Baltimore's manager in 1908 was the immensely capable Jack Dunn, who had won the

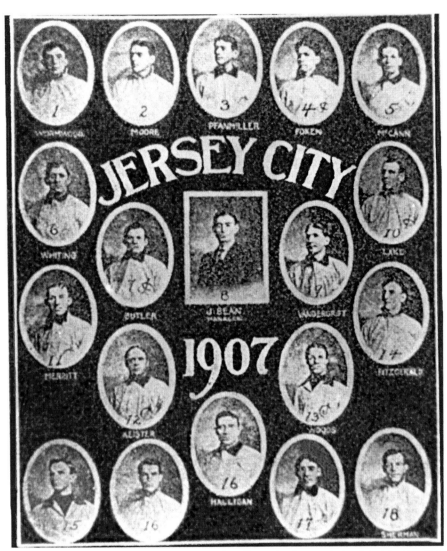

Jersey City's 1907 club boasted victory and strikeout leader Joe Lake (25-14, 187 Ks). Lake is No. 10 at right, while No. 12 (left of 1907) is William Keister, who was the stolen base champ in 1904 and 1905. Pfanmiller (No. 3 at top), led the league with 28 victories, while Bill Halligan (No. 16 below 1907) was the 1902 batting titlist (.351).

1905 pennant with Providence on the last day of the season in his first year as a field general. Dunn had made his home in Baltimore since playing as a pitcher and infielder for the American League Orioles in 1901. After serving the Clamdiggers as player-manager again in 1906, he took over the reins of the Orioles in 1907, bringing Baltimore its first Eastern League flag the next year. The 35-year-old

Dunn held down second base, and his best player was victory leader Doc Adkins (29-12). The Orioles clinched the pennant with head-to-head victories over second-place Providence in the last week of the 1908 season.

In 1909 the *Baseball Magazine* published an article about the Eastern League. The eight cities which comprised baseball's senior minor league boasted an aggregate population of nearly 2,500,000, "far and away next in importance to the two major league's largest circuits." Baltimore was the league's largest city (650,000); next was Buffalo (376,618), Newark (283,289), Montreal (267,730), Jersey City (232,699), Toronto (208,040), Providence (198,635()), and Rochester (181,672). Sunday games were permitted in most cities, and every franchise had drawn single-day crowds of 10,000 to 15,000 for weekend or holiday games. There had not been a franchise change in six years, and the league president still served as president of the National Association. The prestige of the Eastern League had never been higher.

An overflow crowd of 13,000 at Rochester's Bay Street Park looks on as the Hustlers down Providence, 6-4, on May 16, 1909. When a batted ball reached a roped-off fan section, the batter was awarded a ground-rule double. (Courtesy Rochester Public Library)

TIME OUT

Le b-r-r-r-r ...

Montreal and Toronto added a properly international flavor to the league from an early date, but the French Canadian population converted slowly to the American game. The June 8, 1907, issue of *The Sporting Life*, for example, pointed out that in Montreal a crowd of 12,000 attended a lacrosse match, while only 3,000 turned out for an Eastern League baseball game. But it was reported that the "Frenchmen are great ball fiends" and rooted for their team in broken English.

It often took dedicated "ball fiends" to endure Canadian conditions. Although the season always opened in the league's southernmost cities, weather conditions often were miserable in Montreal and Toronto. Temperatures hovered just above zero when the 1907 schedule opened in Montreal. The outfield was a sea of mud—not because of rain, but because of frost oozing out of the frozen ground! The outfield was so bad that fielders stood on planks. Balls hit into the outfield disappeared into the muck, while outfielders valiantly slogged toward the soggy sphere.

On Sunday, May 5, 1907, 5,000 fans turned out for a Montreal game. With the temperature in the twenties, though, players did not want to take the field. Management, however, was not about to refund 5,000 admissions. Some outfielders donned fishermen's hip boots, others wrapped bags around their feet, and the game proved to be a burlesque.

Toronto won the 1907 pennant behind player-manager Joe Kelley (center, dark suit). Canuck Stars included (top row, L to R.) catcher Rough Carrigan (.319), reliable hurler Baldy Rudolph, and two-time batting champ Jack Thoney (.329), while James McGinley (bottom row, second from left) was the team's leading pitcher (22-10).

Baltimore Orioles, 1908 champions. Player-manager Jack Dunn (center, No. 13) led his club to the pennant behind victory leader Doc Adkins (No. 11, 29-12).

1910–1919

Rochester produced the league's first dynasty, winning back-to-back-to-back pennants in 1909, 1910, and 1911. Following a last-place finish in 1908, Rochester owner-president C.T. Chapin reversed his club's fortunes by hiring as player-manager an experienced big leaguer, 35-year-old first baseman John Ganzel. For three years Chapin and Ganzel resourcefully put together winning lineups, and under Ganzel's hard-driving leadership the team earned the nickname "Hustlers."

Although Hustlers who attracted big league attention were sold by Chapin for profit, Chapin and Ganzel alertly watched big league rosters for experienced players who could bolster their Rochester teams. For example, southpaw Cy Barger led the 1909 pitching staff (23-13) before bring sold to Brooklyn, while righthander Ed Lafitte was the best hurler of 1910 (23-14), spurring a sale to Detroit. Conversely, righthander George McConnell was acquired from New York of the American League at midseason of 1909, pitching well for the Hustlers the rest of the year (9-3), twirling a no-hitter in 1910, and leading the championship drive in 1911 (30-8).

Ganzel drove the Hustlers to the 1909 pennant, the second worst to first finish in the league. In 1910 Rochester became the first city in league history to defend a championship successfully, and of course the Hustlers of 1911 made it three in a row.

Another historic performance was performed in Jersey City on August 9, 1910, when Buffalo righthander Chet Carmichael hurled the IL's first perfect game, outdueling Rube Kisinger—who had pitched a no-hitter the previous year—1-0.

Following the close of the 1910 season, Pat Powers stepped down after 15 years as league president (1893—1905, and 1907—1910). Powers, who would earn a niche in the Hall of Fame, had provided standout leadership and his shoes would be difficult to fill.

At the age of 42, Ed Barrow had been a manager, business manager, and owner in the Inter-State League and Atlantic League, and he had served as president of the latter circuit for three years. In 1900 he purchased a quarter interest in Toronto's franchise and became field manager, winning the Eastern League pennant in 1902. Then he went to Detroit as manager before reentering the Eastern League as manager of Montreal in 1905 and Toronto in 1906. He left baseball for three

The 1911 Hustlers brought a third straight pennant to Rochester. The team included catcher Frank Mitchell (No. 2 and .292), manager John Ganzel (No. 5), righthander George McConnell (No.6 and 30-8 in his best season), infielder Joe Ward (No. 8 and .309), and third baseman Hack Simmons (No. 19 and .319).

TIME OUT

Iron Man Joe McGinnity

In 1909 famed pitcher "Iron Man" Joe McGinnity had just concluded a major league career that would send him to the Hall of Fame. With the New York Giants in 1903 he was 31-20 with a league record 434 innings, and the next season he was 35-8 in 408 innings. Always willing to pitch doubleheaders, the Iron Man won both ends of three doubleheaders for the Giants in 1903.

McGinnity brought his signature durability and dominance to Newark. Pitching in 55 games, he was 29-16, setting all-time league marks with 422 innings and 11 shutouts. The next year, at 39, the Iron Man hurled 61 games with a 30-19 record and 408 innings. In both 1909 and 1910 he led the league in victories and in games and innings pitched. Because he was such a workhorse on the mound, manager McGinnity carried only six pitchers on his 18-man roster, allowing the luxury of extra position players.

A broken wrist in 1911 limited the Iron Man to a mere 43 games with a 12-19 mark, and in 1912—at 41—he was 16-10. McGinnity left the IL after four seasons, but he continued pitching in lower level circuits until he was 54, and twice during these twilight seasons he won 20 or more games

years, until accepting the presidency of the Eastern League. Barrow immediately impressed owners with "his tact, knowledge and unremitting attention to the duties of his office." After one season he succeeded in changing the name of the circuit back to the "International League," which has remained the label for nearly 100 years.

Rochester's bid for four consecutive titles was thwarted by veteran manager Joe Kelley, who directed Toronto to the 1912 pennant. The Maple Leafs led the IL in hitting and home runs, while boasting the league's only 20-game winner, righthander Dick Rudolph (25-10). Soon to become a National League star, Rudolph had gone 13-8, 23-14, 23-15 with a no-hitter, 18-11, and 25-

International League teams often held spring training in the South. In the spring of 1911 the Toronto Maple Leafs trained at Daisy Park in Macon, Georgia. When a circus came to town Maple Leaf players posed with elephants in front of the ballpark grandstand. (Courtesy Middle Georgia Archives, Washington Memorial Library, Macon)

International League executives in 1913. From left: Jacob Stein, Buffalo; Billy Manley, IL Secretary; Thomas Fogarty, Providence; James J. McCaffrey, Toronto; E.W. Wickes, Baltimore; Edward G. Barrow, IL President; J.C.H. Ebbetts, Jr., Jersey City; Jack Dunn, Baltimore; S.E. Lichtenhem, Montreal; H. Medicus, Newark; C.T. Chapin, Rochester.

10 since 1907—a 120-71 mark and an average of 20 wins a season for the Maple Leafs.

A far greater star was introduced to professional baseball through the International League two seasons later. Baltimore owner-manager Jack Dunn found the talented 20-year-old playing for a local Catholic boys' home. Although signed as a left-handed pitcher, the big youngster walloped a home run in his first spring training game, displaying an astounding hitting power that he continued to flash around the International League in 1914. During spring training veteran teammates ignored the unsophisticated rookie's first name and called him "Dunnie's Babe." By the time the club made it to Baltimore, he was known as Babe Ruth.

"I was a bum when I was a kid," recalled

George Herman Ruth, who spent most of his boyhood and adolescence at the home, which later became a reform school. Dunn signed him to a contract calling for $600 ($100 per month), but Ruth's performance was so impressive that he was raised to $1,200 in May, then to $1,800 in June. By early July Babe had forged a brilliant 14-6 record. But Jack Dunn was forced to dismantle his superb, league-leading Oriole roster at mid-season. One of the first players he sold, to the Boston Red Sox, was Babe Ruth.

Following his sale to the Red Sox, Ruth only pitched in two games (and two exhibi-

TIME OUT

Super-Ump

Bill Carpenter first umpired in the National League at the age of 23 in 1897. After a few seasons he found himself back in the minors, officiating in the Inter-State League, New York State League, and Southern Association. Carpenter was on the American League staff in 1904, returned to the National League in 1906 and 1907, then spent four more seasons in the Southern Association.

In 1912, at 38 and boasting a wealth of experience, Carpenter moved to the IL. He called 'em as he saw 'em for 21 years, the longest tenure of any ump in International League history. Carpenter was named chief of staff in the International League office in 1933. His duties included supervision of umpires and schedule-making, and he became so good at scheduling that many leagues began to employ his services. At the 1939 Baseball Centennial in Cooperstown, he was a logical choice as one of the umpires in the Minor League All-Star Game. In 1945 Carpenter was appointed chief supervisor of umpires for the National Association, a position he held until his death in 1952.

After running up a 14-6 record by July for Jack Dunn's 1914 Orioles, rookie lefthander Babe Ruth was sold to the Red Sox. But Ruth pitched only twice in seven weeks in Boston, and he was sent down to Providence for the pennant stretch. He went 9-2, turning in a 23-8 record in his only minor league season.

tions) for the next seven weeks. But Red Sox owner Joe Lannin also had purchased Providence, located just 40 miles away. After Baltimore sagged out of first place in August, Providence launched its pennant drive. Grays manager "Wild Bill" Donovan needed another good pitcher, and Ruth was sent down in time for a crucial series with Rochester.

Babe was greeted at Melrose Park by an overflow throng of 12,000, the largest crowd that had ever attended a game in Rhode Island. As customary, fans were placed behind ropes in the outfield, but there were hundreds of others on the hill behind the center field fence and perched on trees and electric poles. Babe knocked in the winning run with his second triple of the day, and he continued to win, going 9-2 and batting .300, with half of his hits for extra bases. For the season he was 23-8 in International League play, despite having missed seven weeks at mid-season.

The next year Ruth helped pitch the Red Sox into the World Series, but baseball's greatest star—indeed, the most memorable figure in the history of American sports—had his only minor league experience in the International League of 1914.

Why did Jack Dunn have to sell Ruth and other accomplished players in July, breaking up a team that was dominating the league? Because of the impact of the Federal League, a minor circuit first organized in 1913 outside the National Association. The backers of this outlaw league were entrepreneurs keenly aware of the growing popularity of baseball and of the success of Ban Johnson's American League. The 1913 season established the Federal League in several solid baseball cities, and owners determined to establish a third major circuit by upgrading ballparks and raiding big league rosters' top talent.

In 1914 the Federal League aggressively

The Providence Grays won the 1914 pennant after a tight race. Standouts included righthander Al Platte (No. 1, and .318) victory and percentage leader Carl Mays (No. 7, and 24-8), young Babe Ruth (No. 9), batting champ Dave Shean (No. 12, and .334), manager "Wild Bill" Donovan (No. 16), and rookie Eddie Onslow (No. 19, and .322 in the first of 17 IL seasons).

opened play with eight "major league" franchises in Baltimore, Buffalo, Brooklyn, Chicago, Indianapolis, Kansas City, Pittsburgh, and St. Louis. The Feds mounted a head-on challenge against existing big league franchises in four cities—and against International League clubs in Baltimore and Buffalo.

In Baltimore the Terrapins were backed primarily by Ned Hanlon, manager of the Orioles during their heyday in the 1890s. Hanlon was eager to bring big league baseball back to his beloved Baltimore, and the city excitedly welcomed him and his major leaguers. Terrapin Park was erected across the street from ramshackle Orioles' Park. Jack Dunn, who had bought the Orioles from Hanlon in 1909, determined to fight the Federals by building a superior team. Offering major league salaries and, in several cases, three-year contracts, he fielded a roster that included two pitchers and six regulars with big league experience (and the spectacular local rookie, Babe Ruth).

On opening day of 1914 the Terrapins jammed nearly 30,000 fans into 16,000-seat Terrapin Park, while across the street merely 1,500 gathered to watch the International Leaguers. The Orioles dominated the International League, winning thirteen consecutive games at one point. But on the thirteenth day of this winning streak only 150 fans turned out to see the International League leaders. Facing financial disaster, Dunn sold six of his eight position players and two of his best pitchers—vowing never again to sell one of his stars until he had a replacement ready. Somehow Dunn's dismantled team held on to their lead for a few weeks, then dropped to sixth place.

In Buffalo local investors organized the Buf-Feds and constructed a 20,000-seat stadium, opening their season before 14,000 fans. Attendance was weak for the International League Bisons, even though they finished second in the International League pennant chase. Bolstered by Babe Ruth from the Red Sox, Providence won the flag with a late-season surge.

Despite heavy financial losses, the Federal League was back in 1915, transferring the championship Indianapolis club to Newark in an attempt to strengthen the circuit in the greater New York area. In 1915, therefore, the International League would face the Federal League in three cities: Baltimore, Buffalo, and Newark.

In Newark the International League Bears were run out of town before mid-season by the "New Feds," transferring to Harrisburg, which had been a charter member of the league in 1884. Jack Dunn had no intention of bucking the Feds again, moving his club from Baltimore to Richmond. Buffalo's president, Jake Stein, also quailed at another year of locking horns with the Buf-Feds. Stein sold the Bisons to Joe Lannin, who already owned the Boston Red Sox and the Providence Grays.

For a second year the Federal League suffered severe losses. After the 1915 season major league magnates agreed to provide compensation to Federal League owners, and the costly experiment ended—to the relief not only of American and National League executives, but also to the International Leaguers.

When the Federal League disbanded, Newark owners moved their franchise from Harrisburg back to New Jersey. Now that the Terrapins were gone, Jack Dunn wanted to resume activities in Baltimore. But Richmond backers were delighted with International League baseball, so Dunn sold his remaining interest in the franchise and bought the last-place Jersey City club. Dunn paid $25,000 for Terrapin Park and renamed it Oriole's Park. For 1916, therefore, a new Orioles team

Terrapin Park, a 16,000-seat Federal League stadium built across the street from Jack Dunn's ramshackle Orioles' Park. The Terrapins ran Dunn out of Baltimore, but when the Federal League folded the Orioles moved into Terrapin Park.

At the age of 41 baseball's first superstar Nap Lajoie, was an important gate attraction around the IL in 1917 when he won the batting title (.380) as Toronto's manager-first baseman.

would return to Baltimore, Newark was back in the International League, but Jersey City was out.

Joe Lannin hired longtime major league player and manager Patsy Donovan to direct his Buffalo club, and Donovan led the Bisons to back-to-back pennants in 1915 and 1916. In 1917 Toronto won a close pennant race behind future Hall of Famer Nap Lajoie (.380), who won the International League batting title at the age of 42 and was given a $1,000 bonus. The postseason featured a week of profitable exhibition games and the first Little World Series since 1907. But Indianapolis of the American Association defeated the Maple Leafs, four games to one—the first time in four tries that the International League representative had not won the series.

The United States had entered the First World War at the start of the 1917 season. There were travel restrictions throughout the season, along with the loss of players to the armed services and declining attendance. Eight minor leagues folded during 1917, and several International League owners voted to suspend operations for 1918.

But baseball's oldest minor league only appeared to be dead. Jack Dunn, Joe Lannin, and other owners scrambled to protect their investments. Lannin backed franchises in Buffalo and Syracuse; Baltimore, Toronto, Rochester and Newark agreed to continue operations; and teams were placed in Jersey City and Binghamton, cities with an International League background. The reorganized circuit was renamed the New International League, and although a late starting date was necessary, an abbreviated 128-game schedule was opened on May 8.

Only eight other minor leagues opened play in 1918 (there were 42 in 1914), and the difficulties of arranging travel and keeping players caused one circuit after another to suspend operations. The American and National Leagues played out a shortened season and, with special permission from the government, conducted the World Series. In the International League there was constant player turnover and little fan interest. But the league staggered to the end of the schedule with Toronto earning a second consecutive pennant. And the New International League could claim the distinction of being the only minor league to finish the 1918 season.

When the war ended in November 1918, baseball men everywhere anticipated an exciting and profitable renewal of enthusiasm. In Baltimore Jack Dunn built an overwhelming team, led by batting champ Otis Lawry (.364) and pitchers Rube Parnham (28-12) and Harry Frank (24-6). The Orioles stormed to the 1919 pennant, becoming the first International League team to win 100 games (100-47). It was Dunn's first International League flag in a decade, but six more soon would follow.

The 1919 Orioles became the first IL team to win 100 games, as well as the first of seven consecutive Baltimore pennant-winners. Oriole mainstays included first baseman–pitcher Jack Bentley (No. 1), pitcher Rube Parnham (3), Jack Dunn (5), catcher Ben Egan (6), shortstop Joe Boley (10), left fielder Otis Lawry (11), center fielder Merwin Jacobson (17), second baseman Max Bishop (21), and third baseman Fritz Maisel (22).

Built in 1907, Lauer's Park in Reading hosted IL ball from 1919-1931.

1920–1929

During the early decades of the twentieth century, the focus of professional baseball, for many players and fans, was not upon the major leagues. There were then no telecasts of the most popular big league teams, and in all but 11 big league cities (there were two major league franchises in Boston, Chicago, New York, Philadelphia, and St. Louis) fan interest centered on the local minor league club. In Texas, for example, where the nearest big league was in faraway St. Louis, 103 cities and towns backed minor league teams through the years. Minor league owners could remain free of major league control, although from an early date big leagues attempted to arrange secret working agreements. (In the International League Joe Lannin, owner of the Red Sox and IL franchises in Providence, Buffalo and Syracuse, facilitated player development in the minors for his big league team.)

But independent minor league owners could choose not to sell their best players. The autocratic, penurious major league owners of the era tightly restricted the salary scale, and it was not uncommon for marginal players to enjoy greater earning power with just the right minor league club. Indeed,

Pacific Coast League players, who received more paychecks because of baseball's longest schedule, sometimes balked at "promotion" to the big leagues. An article in *Baseball Magazine* for February 1922 described the independent attitude of many Class AA owners (Double-A was the highest classification in the minors, shared by the International League, American Association, and the Pacific Coast League): "This word 'minor' is distasteful to the AA moguls for they contend they are not 'minors' and this contention is bolstered by several facts chief among which are that some of their cities are larger than some cities in the Major Leagues, that Sunday baseball is played by all, that their teams make money on the road, and that many of their players, the greatest majority of whom have seen service in the majors, draw higher salaries in the minor than they did in the major."

A minor league organization could build and maintain a roster of dynamic capacities. The Fort Worth Cats, for example, won six consecutive Texas League pennants from 1920 through 1925. Five players starred in all six of these pennant-winners, and several other athletes played through most of the championship run.

26

Jim Thorpe, football and Olympic champion, doubled up as a professional baseball player for 12 years. Thorpe started the 1915 season with John McGraw's New York Giants, but soon he was sent to Jersey City, and later the speedy outfielder moved to Harrisburg. In 96 IL games Thorpe hit .303. In 1920, now 34, Thorpe spent the season with Akron of the IL. He batted .360, the highest average of his baseball career.

Jack Dunn, Baltimore player, manager and owner, and architect of the minor leagues' greatest dynasty. (Courtesy IL)

Impressive as the Fort Worth dynasty was, one of even greater duration was built in Baltimore by Jack Dunn. A native of Pennsylvania, Dunn had made his home in Baltimore since playing for the Orioles since 1901. After eight years as a big league pitcher, infielder and outfielder, Dunn became a minor league manager with the Providence Clamdiggers in 1905. Intelligent, aggressive, and a superb judge of baseball talent, Dunn won the IL flag in his first season with Providence. He took over Baltimore in 1907, won a pennant the next year, and bought the club from Ned Hanlon in 1909.

During the ensuing decade the Orioles finished in the first division seven times, and by 1919, with the Federal League battles and wartime problems at an end, Dunn had put together a championship team. Stubbornly independent of big league ties, Dunn kept his best players and discovered more youthful athletes. Not until his replacement pool was rich in talent did he begin to sell to the major leagues, and only then for record-setting prices. With a strong nucleus of players and a steady supply of new stars, Dunn's Orioles reeled off seven consecutive International League championships.

Dunn drove his 1919 Orioles to 100 victories and the pennant, while his 1920 club was even more successful (109-44). In 1921 the IL schedule increased to 168 games, but the Oriole victory totals continued to be impressive: 119, 115, 111, 117, and 105. The 1921 Orioles established an all-time league record for victories, while the teams of 1920 (.712), 1921 (.717), and 1924 (.709) won at a clip exceeding .700.

The 1919 Orioles led the league with a .299 team batting average and 37 home runs. Each of the other six title teams hit .300 or better, leading the league in 1920 (.318), 1921 (.313), and 1923 (.310), while the other clubs finished second. Former Oriole Babe Ruth was blasting home runs in unprecedented numbers in the American League, exciting fans and transforming baseball from a pitcher-dominated, low-scoring game to a heavy-hitting, high-scoring game perfectly suited to the Roaring Twenties. Home run totals soared, and the Orioles of 1921 won the first of five straight team totals with steadily increasing numbers: 102, 112, 141, 166, and 188.

The Oriole offense during these years was overwhelming, bristling with dangerous hitters. Left fielder Otis Lawry won the batting title in 1919 (.364); center fielder Merwin Jacobson was the hitting champ in 1920 (.404); first baseman-pitcher Jack Bentley led the league in 1921 with an even more startling figure (.412, as well as a league-leading 24 homers); outfielder Clarence Pitt came over from Rochester during the 1923 season in time to bring another batting title to Baltimore (.357); and outfielder-second baseman Dick Porter became the fifth batting champ of the championship era in 1924 (.364).

Third baseman and team captain Fritz Maisel was the leadoff batter and shortstop. Joe Boley hit in the seventh spot in the order during all seven title seasons. Otis Lawry batted second for the first five (and part of the sixth) of these years, and Merwin Jacobson hit third for the first six seasons. Jack Bentley always batted fifth, even when he was on the mound, while second baseman Max Bishop hit in the six hole for the first five title years. Dunn always batted his catcher eighth. Regulars and their averages indicate the stress faced by opposing pitchers:

First baseman-pitcher Jack Bentley started for the first four Oriole championship clubs. His best season came in 1921, when he led the IL in batting, hits, doubles, homers, and winning percentage (.412, 24 HR, 12-1). Bentley played a total of nine seasons in the IL, as well as nine years in the big leagues.

Dunn consistently acquired players who were .300 hitters for one or perhaps two seasons. Maurice "Flash" Archdeacon, for example, adequately replaced longtime center

	1919	1920	1921	1922	1923	1924	1925
1. Maisel	.336	.319	.339	.306	.275	.306	.329
2. Lawry	.364*	.315	.352	.333	.299	.303	
3. Jacobson	.351	.404*	.340	.304	.328	.308	
4. Holden		.352	.302				
Walsh				.327	.333		
Porter			.321	.279	.316	.364*	.336
5. Bentley	.324	.371	.412*	.350			
Sheedy					.359	.298	.332
6. Bishop	.260	.248	.319	.261	.333		
7. Boley	.301	.308	.317	.343	.306	.291	.330
8. Egan	.314	.331	.270				
Styles		.299		.315	.316		
Cobb					.320	.320	.266

*league leader

fielder Merwin Jacobson in 1925 (.310); and outfielder Wade Lefler hit well in 1920 (.336) and 1921 (.316).

Defensively the club was solid and efficient, leading the league in fielding in 1922 and 1924, and finishing second or third each of the other title seasons. Maisel and Boley held down the left side of the infield for seven years. Bishop was the second-sacker for five of the pennant-winners, while Bentley and Sheedy were steady at first. In the outfield Jacobson was speedy in center for six seasons, and Lawry was a fixture in left for five years. Other outfielders came and went, however, and there was also a procession of catchers (during 1922 catcher William Styles appeared at all nine positions for the Orioles).

In a hitters' era, the quality of Oriole pitching was remarkable. All seven of the championship teams produced the league's victory leader, three times with more than 30 wins. Lefty Grove recorded four consecutive strikeout titles, including an IL record 330 Ks in 1923, while Rube Parnham and Tommy Thomas also led the league in Ks. No hurler was present in all seven of the title years, but

Grove was 109-36 over five seasons. The other notable southpaw, first baseman Jack Bentley, moved to the mound during three seasons, often in a relief role, and posted a brilliant 41-6 record.

Among the best Oriole righthanders, control artist John Ogden led the league in wins three years in a row, including 31-8 in 1921. Ogden was 146-56 during six championship years, he won a total of 195 games as an Oriole, and he posted the highest career winning percentage of any minor leaguer who was a 200-game winner (213-103, .674). Rube Parnham was 88-34 during three seasons and parts of two others, and he was the victory leader twice, including 33-7 in 1923. Harry Frank was 93-36 during the first five title years, and Tommy Thomas was 105-54 for the last Oriole champs, including 32-12 in 1925.

With a stable of excellent players, Dunn received numerous offers for his stars from big league clubs. He felt that the best way to make money was to fashion a consistent win-

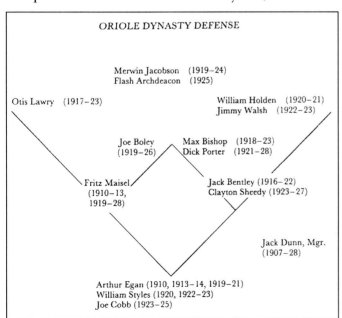

ORIOLE DYNASTY DEFENSE

Merwin Jacobson   (1919–24)
Flash Archdeacon   (1925)

Otis Lawry   (1917–23)

William Holden   (1920–21)
Jimmy Walsh   (1922–23)

Joe Boley
(1919–26)

Max Bishop   (1918–23)
Dick Porter   (1921–28)

Fritz Maisel
(1910–13,
1919–28)

Jack Bentley (1916–22)
Clayton Sheedy (1923–27)

Jack Dunn, Mgr.
(1907–28)

Arthur Egan (1910, 1913–14, 1919–21)
William Styles (1920, 1922–23)
Joe Cobb (1923–25)

Lefty Grove pitched for the Orioles champions of 1920 (12-2), 1921 (25-10), 1922 (18-8), 1923 (27-10), and 1924 (27-6). He led the IL in strikeouts the latter four seasons, fanning a league record 330 batters in 1923.

ner, but the attention his superb teams attracted swelled the offers to a level that no businessman could ignore. Dunn finally decided to sell his best players, but only for spectacular prices and at intervals that would permit the development of replacements. After winning four consecutive pennants, Dunn sold Jack Bentley, his superb first baseman-pitcher-slugger, to the New York Giants for $72,500—a record price for a minor leaguer. Following another championship in 1923, Dunn peddled second baseman Max Bishop to Connie Mack's Athletics for $25,000. (Bishop, a native of Baltimore and a splendid fielder, played in the American League for 12 seasons before returning to the Orioles in 1936. He then coached baseball at the Naval Academy from 1938 through 1961.)

Dunn's biggest sale followed the 1924 season, after Lefty Grove led the league in victories and winning percentage, and copped his fourth consecutive strikeout title. The 24-year-old "Groves," as he was known in the IL, was the best southpaw in baseball, but Dunn refused to sell him until Connie Mack agreed to pay $100,600 for his contract. "Babe Ruth was sold to the Yankees [by the Red Sox in 1920] for $100,000," related Mack, "so I raised the ante $600 for Grove." But in order to pay Dunn the record price for a straight player purchase, Mack had to ask for installment privileges. It was worth it: Grove won seven consecutive strikeout titles and 300 American League games. Grove, who was purchased for $3,200 by Dunn as a 3-3 rookie from Martinsburg of the Blue Ridge League, recorded a total of 412 major and minor league victories during his career.

Following the 1925 season Dunn sold longtime shortstop Joe Boley to Connie Mack for $65,000. Two years later, Dunn peddled slugger Dick Porter to Cleveland for $40,000, and ace righthander George Earnshaw to Connie Mack for $70,000.

From 1919 through 1925 the Orioles ran away from the rest of the league, except in 1920, when Toronto (108-46) offered Baltimore (109-44) the only serious challenge of the dynasty period. The Orioles reeled off 25 consecutive victories in 1920, then roared to a 27-game winning streak the next season. The Little World Series was resumed on an annual basis in 1920, but the Orioles only managed to win three of six series with the American Association champs.

It seemed as though the pennant string would continue in 1926. The Orioles were in first place as late as August and won 101 games. But late in the season Toronto surged

Orioles' Pitchers

	1919	**1920**	**1921**	**1922**	**1923**	**1924**	**1925**
Parnham	28*-12	5-0		16-10	33*-7	6-5	
Grove		12-2	25-10	18-8	27-10	27*-6	
Frank	24-6	25-12	13-7	22-9	9-2		
Ogden		27*-9	31*-8	24*-10	17-12	19-6	28-11
Bentley		16-3	12-1	13-2			
Thomas			24-10	18-9	15-12	16-11	32*-12
Earnshaw						7-0	29-11
Jackson						16-8	13-14
Knelsch	10-9	11-4					

*league leader

The Orioles of 1924, the last season Lefty Grove (No. 6) spent in the IL. Other key players included first baseman Clayton Sheedy (8), pitcher Johnny Ogden (9), pitcher Rube Parnham (10), third baseman Fritz Maisel (11), center fielder Merwin Jacobson (15), pitcher George Earnshaw (18), pitcher Al Thomas (20), shortstop Joe Boley (25).

George Earnshaw starred for Baltimore in 1925 (29-11) and 1926 (22-14), faltered slightly in 1927 (17-18), but moved up to a successful big league career the next year.

Attendance and Receipts for the Little World Series of 1921

At Louisville

Game	Attendance	Receipts
Wednesday, Oct. 5	3,253	$ 4,260.06
Thursday, Oct. 6	3,209	4,260.58
Saturday, Oct. 8	2,957	3,984.14
Sunday, Oct. 9	6,569	8,466.53
	15,988	$20,971.31

At Baltimore

Game	Attendance	Receipts
Thursday, Oct. 13	5,804	$ 6,882.88
Saturday, Oct. 15	7,841	9,297.40
Sunday, Oct. 16	12,545	14,515.89
Monday, Oct. 17	2,807	3,089.87
	28,997	33,786.04
Total for eight games:	44,985	$54,757.35

to the flag with the IL's best offense, then swept Louisville in the Little World Series.

Jack Dunn had prospered as an independent club owner-manager operating out of the largest city in baseball's oldest minor league. Although Dunn suffered a fatal heart attack on October 22, 1928, at the age of 56, his International League career proved him to be the greatest minor league operator in the history of the game.

But as Dunn's Orioles won pennant after pennant, other teams around the IL were less successful at the box office and more receptive to big league overtures. Major league clubs now were lining up affiliates throughout the minor leagues, and William Wrigley of Chicago bought Reading during the season. The most aggressive big league team was the St. Louis Cardinals, whose brilliant vice-president, Branch Rickey, was building a farm system that eventually would include 42 minor league clubs. The Cardinals already owned Syracuse, but Rickey now bought Rochester

and transferred the Syracuse players to Rochester. Warren Giles, a future Hall of Fame executive who had been placed in charge of the Cardinals' Syracuse club, was moved to Rochester, and he changed the name to the Red Wings. With the player pool that now became available through the Cardinal organization, Rochester now became the home of the next IL championship dynasty.

In 1928 the Red Wings, led by player-manager Billy Southworth (.361), challenged Buffalo, the 1927 pennant-winners. On the last day of the season Buffalo remained in first place by a few percentage points. But Rochester ace Herman Bell (21-8) pitched—and won—both games of a doubleheader with Montreal, allowing the Red Wings (90-74, .5487) to nose out the Bisons (92-76, .5476). It was Rochester's first pennant since the Hustlers won three in a row in 1909-1910-1911.

Toronto first baseman Dale Alexander was

Buffalo won 112 games and the IL pennant in 1927. The roster included shortstop Andy Cohen (No. 1, and .353), first baseman Del Bissonette (5, and .265, 31 HR, 167 RBI), right fielder George Fisher (7, and .320), pitcher Leo Mangum (9, and 21-7), outfielder Andy Anderson (12, and .328), pitcher Jack Hollingsworth (15, and 17-7), manager Bill Clymer (21), third baseman Bill Huber (23, and .334), center fielder Al Tyson (24, and .375), and left fielder Otis Carter (25, and .331).

the most spectacular player of 1928, recording the IL's first Triple Crown (.380, 31 HR, 144 RBI), and also banging out the most base hits, doubles, and total bases.

Rochester's 1928 pennant inspired the Cardinals to build a new stadium in the northern part of the city. At the home opener 14,000 fans were on hand to cheer the defending champs. The Red Wings responded to their new home by dominating the league, outdistancing second-place Toronto by 11 games. One of the Cardinals' best prospects, first baseman Rip Collins, led the IL in homers and RBIs (.315, 38 HR, 134 RBI).

Defensively, the Red Wings set a new record for organized baseball with 225 double plays (along with a pair of triple plays).

In 1929 41-year-old Tris Speaker, widely acknowledged as the era's greatest center fielder, came to Newark as player-manager. The "Grey Eagle" played occasionally and still flashed Hall of Fame batting skills (.348 in 55 games, and .419 in 11 games the next year).

Also closing a long playing career was first baseman Eddie Onslow, a six-foot lefthander who signed his first pro contract in 1911 at the age of 18. The next year he played 35

TIME OUT

Exhibition Games

During the early years of the IL, when league games were scheduled only three or four days a week, clubs staged exhibition contests on off-days against semipro teams or major leaguers who were traveling through on the railroad. During the 1880s, IL teams played as many exhibition games as championship contests.

Even in the twentieth century, when league games were played almost every day, exhibitions were squeezed in whenever possible. Professional players barnstormed together on postseason tours, often to the Southwest and Pacific Coast, where weather permitted baseball late in the year. Owners also arranged numerous exhibitions during spring training, and frequently minor league clubs squared off against big league teams. After breaking spring training camp in the South, major league teams would work their way north, earning revenue for the owners by playing in minor league parks, sometimes against rival big leaguers but more often against the local club. For years, while Blue Laws were still in effect, big league teams would visit a minor league city where games could be played before profitable Sunday crowds.

Minor league owners especially liked to showcase talented prospects in front of visiting big league owners and managers, hoping to negotiate a lucrative player sale. The minor leaguers, trying to impress, often beat the big leaguers, who diluted their exhibition lineups with reserve players. In the IL, Jack Dunn was especially fond of beating big leaguers, because the Baltimore owner-manager prided himself on building "a team that I believe is as strong as a second-division major league team, if not stronger." Dunn's splendid clubs frequently won exhibitions with major league teams.

On Friday, April 18, 1919, Dunn's Orioles hosted the Boston Red Sox in an exhibition won by the big leaguers. Babe Ruth, a former Oriole who was about to revolutionize baseball with his home run hitting, blasted four homers (he never hit four home runs during a regular season game). Four seasons later, on Sunday, September 30, 1923, Babe hit a grand slam out of Oriole Park when the New York Yankees came to town for an exhibition. The Yankees were about to win the World Series, but the Orioles had just taken their fifth consecutive IL title, and the minor leaguers beat the AL champs, 10-6, before an overflow crowd of 20,000. The winning pitcher was Rube Parnham, who went all the way in recording (unofficially, since it was an exhibition) his twenty-first consecutive victory.

games with the Detroit Tigers, but four tries at the big leagues totaled just 63 games.

Onslow found his baseball home in the International League. Beginning in 1913 he spent 17 seasons playing for five IL clubs. He was with Providence from 1913 through 1917, helping the 1914 Grays win the pennant (.322). Onslow moved to Toronto in 1918 (.318), his only other championship season.

He spent seven years with Toronto, before splitting 1925 between Providence and Rochester. Onslow was in Rochester the next two years, went to Baltimore in 1928, then finished his career with the Orioles and the Newark Bears in 1929 (.308 in 67 games). He compiled a .319 career average, hitting above .300 14 times in the IL. His best marks came in 1923 (.347), 1926 (.343), and his next-to-last year, 1928 (.346). Onslow's 17 seasons represent the longest tenure of any player in the International League, and he also established all-time career records for games played (2109), hits (2445), and triples (128).

The Rochester Red Wings of 1929 repeated as IL champs. The roster was loaded with men who would excel in the IL and big leagues: Paul Derringer (No. 1), Gus Felix (2), Tex Carleton (5), Herman Bell (8), George Watkins (9), Red Worthington (10), Ray Pepper (13), coach Ray Blades (17), president Warren Giles (18), player-manager Billy Southworth (19), Specs Torporcer (22), and Rip Collins (23).

1930–1939

By the end of the 1929 season the New York stock market had crashed, and before opening day of 1930 the American economy was in the grip of the Great Depression. Minor league baseball, like every other aspect of American life, would be profoundly affected. But the International League responded with its usual resilience.

"The ball mania is getting so bad that every city will soon have a mammoth structure like the Roman Colosseum to play in. This will be illuminated by electric lights so that games can be played nights, thus overcoming a serious objection at present existing." This prediction by the Rochester *Union and Advertiser* in 1877 proved premature by several decades, although the idea of night games as a gate attraction was tried in exhibition play as early as June 2, 1883, in Fort Wayne, Indiana. On July 23, 1890, Baltimore played an illuminated exhibition in Hartford, Connecticut. At Wilmington, Delaware, in 1896, manager Ed Barrow arranged an exhibition for his Paterson, New Jersey, team. These and other nineteenth century-contests were novelties played under temporary lighting, and the major leagues would not try this experiment until 1935. But the collapse of the economy in 1929 spurred minor league owners to embrace night baseball as a stimulant to attendance.

At the National Association winter meeting in 1929, Lee Keyser announced that his Des Moines Demons of the Class A Western League would play regularly under artificial light during the coming season. Keyser invested $19,000 in a lighting system and looked forward to the distinction of becoming the first club in organized baseball to stage a night game. But Des Moines opened on the road in 1930, and Independence, Kansas, of the Class C Western Association hastily rigged arclights and staged a night game against Muskogee on April 28. Four nights later, Des Moines played its first game under the lights, and within the next several weeks other clubs in other leagues followed suit, posting impressive attendance results.

In the International League, Buffalo owner-president Frank Offermann installed lights at Bison Stadium. On Thursday night, July 3, 1930, 11,262 fans gathered to watch the IL's first night game. Buffalo lost, 5-4, but crowds continued to be impressive. By the end of the season four more clubs had installed lights. More people could attend after

Baltimore first baseman Joe Hauser set an all-time IL record by blasting 63 homers in 1930. Three years later he hit 69 for Minneapolis of the American Association. Hauser was the first professional player to hit 60 home runs more than once.

working hours, and during the heat of summer fans could "cool off at the ballpark." Day games were mixed with the night contests, and players would complain that the irregular schedules hurt their performances. Hitters also grumbled that under the lights fastball pitchers had an important advantage. Simple economics overruled all complaints, however, as night baseball saved the minor leagues during the Depression.

Of course, there *was* truth in the charge that it was harder to see a good fastball under the primitive minor league lighting systems. (Some IL night games started as late as 9:00 P.M., because the lighting systems did not work as effectively until there was complete darkness.)

Dave Danforth was a lefthander who had logged 10 seasons in the American League (he was a Baltimore dentist in the off-season) and who pitched for Buffalo in 1930 (12-8). At the age of 40, his fastball still was good enough (161 Ks in 161 IP) to nearly win the strikeout crown from future Cincinnati star Paul Derringer (23-11 with 164 Ks). On Saturday night, September 20, Danforth mowed down 20 Rochester batters, establishing an IL strikeout record that would stand for 32 seasons.

In 1930 Baltimore acquired a 31-year-old left-handed slugger whose big league career had been wrecked by a leg injury. Although first baseman Joe Hauser had never hit more than 27 home runs in a season (with the Philadelphia Athletics in 1924), he assaulted minor league pitching from the friendly confines of Oriole Park. In 1930 the all-time home run record for a season was 62, set by Moose Clabaugh of the East Texas League in 1926; Tony Lazzeri of Salt Lake City had blasted 60 during the long Pacific Coast League season of 1925; and two years later Babe Ruth hit 60 for the Yankees. But Hauser exploded for an unprecedented 63 home runs, also leading the IL in runs (.313, 173 R, 175 RBI), as well as putouts and fielding percentage for first basemen. Hauser again led the league in homers the next season (.259, 31 HR, 98 RBI), but his production was so much lower that he was sold to Milwaukee at the

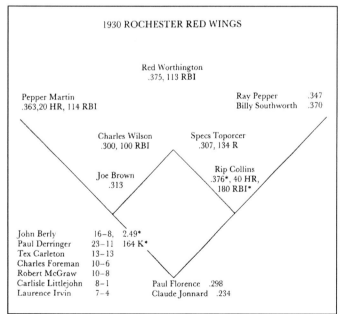

1930 ROCHESTER RED WINGS

Red Worthington
.375, 113 RBI

Pepper Martin
.363, 20 HR, 114 RBI

Ray Pepper   .347
Billy Southworth   .370

Charles Wilson
.300, 100 RBI

Specs Toporcer
.307, 134 R

Joe Brown
.313

Rip Collins
.376*, 40 HR,
180 RBI*

John Berly	16–8,	2.49*
Paul Derringer	23–11	164 K*
Tex Carleton	13–13	
Charles Foreman	10–6	
Robert McGraw	10–8	
Carlisle Littlejohn	8–1	
Laurence Irvin	7–4	

Paul Florence .298
Claude Jonnard .234

end of the season. He rebounded by leading the American Association with 49 homers in 1932—and 69 in 1933. Hauser was the first man ever to hit 60 homers in two seasons, and he last played for Sheboygan in the Wisconsin State League, batting .302 at the age of 43.

Rochester, the two-time defending champs, suffered a slow start in 1930, but the Red Wings moved into first place on July 13. Baltimore mounted a major challenge in August, and on Thursday, August 28, the Orioles came to Rochester for a crucial four-game series. On Sunday the Orioles left town, having lost all four games, and Billy Southworth's powerful Red Wings coasted to their third consecutive championship.

Southworth inserted himself into 92 games (.370), while the regular outfielders were Pepper Martin (.363, 20 HR, 114 RBI), Red Worthington (.375, 113 RBI), and Ray Pepper (.347). "Specs" Toporcer, who had played second base and served as team captain in all four pennant years, had his best season (.307 with 134 runs). Third-sacker Joe Brown again was productive (.313), and so was shortstop Charles Wilson (.300, 100 RBI). First baseman Rip Collins returned to win the batting title, and set the all-time IL RBI record (.376, 40 HR, 180 RBI, 165 R). Paul Derringer led the league in victories and strikeouts (23-11), while fellow righthander John Berley was the ERA champ (16-8, 2.49).

Fans turned out in large numbers to watch this exciting club, and Rochester set a league record with 328,424 paid admissions (all at day games—lights were not installed until 1933). Rochester had lost the Little World Series to the American Association champs in 1928 and 1929, but the Red Wings of 1930 downed Louisville, five games to three. Rochester was the first city to win three consecutive IL titles with the Hustlers of 1909-1910-1911, and now the Red Wings of 1928-1929-1930 had repeated the feat. The Red

Wings would make it four in a row in 1931, but the 1930 champs were the best of the four.

An overflow crowd of 19,006 turned out for the Red Wing opener in 1931, but Rochester barely won the fourth championship. Rip Collins, Paul Derringer, and Pepper Martin went up to the Boston Braves, John Berley went to the New York Giants, and three-year third baseman Joe Brown also was dealt away. But Billy Southworth had Specs Torporcer back at second, Paul Florence returned for his third year as catcher, and outfielder Ray Pepper came back to lead the team in hitting and the league in hits, runs, triples, singles, at-bats, and total bases (.356,

Ike Boone, the career minor league hitting leader (.370), played the last six years of his fabled 17-year career in the IL. With Newark the slugging outfielder won the 1931 batting title (.356). He was with Jersey City in 1932 (.320), before moving to Toronto in 1933 (.357) for his final four seasons. In 1934, at 37, he won his second IL batting crown (.372). The next year Boone still was effective (.350), but in 1936 he slumped (.254) and retired.

123 R, 121 RBI). The Cardinal organization restocked their Rochester roster with young talent such as hard-hitting outfielder George Puccinelli and righthander Ray Starr, who led the IL in ERA and winning percentage, as well as proven veterans, most notably legendary first baseman George Sisler. The 38-year-old future Hall of Famer (.340 lifetime average, including .407 in 1920 and .420 in 1922) played 159 games (.303, with just 17 strikeouts in 613 at-bats), and led all first basemen in assists.

Although Rochester drew 300,000 fans, Newark set a new attendance record with 335,000 and a team that was in first place for 80 days. Late in the season Rochester finally replaced Newark at the top of the standings. The Red Wings' last game was with Montreal, and the crucial contest remained scoreless until George Sisler ripped a line drive to the outfield. The ball caromed off the head of Royals' outfielder Jocko Conlan (the future Hall of Fame umpire spent eight seasons as an IL player), and Sisler raced around the bases with the only run of the game. The 1-0 victory clinched Rochester's fourth consecutive pennant, and the Red Wings then beat St. Paul in the Little World Series, five games to three.

Rochester now had won nine IL pennants, just ahead of eight for Baltimore, seven for Toronto, and six for Buffalo. The success of Rochester in the IL reflected the overall success of the parent Cardinals and their prototype farm system. Colonel Jacob Ruppert, owner of the New York Yankees, became convinced that he should emulate Branch Rickey and build a chain of farm clubs, despite advice to the contrary from Yankee GM Ed Barrow and other tradition-minded baseball men. Following the 1931 season, Ruppert began his farm system by purchasing the Newark Bears for about $350,000.

The Newark ballpark was renamed Ruppert Stadium and the Bears were attired in pinstripe uniforms like the Yankees. Future Hall of Fame executive George Weiss, who had been hired to run Baltimore after the death of Jack Dunn, was chosen to build the Yankee farm system and to lead operations in Newark. Weiss resourcefully began to stockpile talented players and to assemble a network of minor league clubs. A stream of fine athletes began to march into New York through Newark, producing pennant after pennant for both the Yankees and the Bears. From 1932 through 1942, Newark finished first seven times, reached the IL playoffs in each of the other four seasons, captured three playoff titles, won three out of four Junior World Series, and in 1937 showcased one of the greatest teams in minor league history.

Colonel Ruppert occupied a box seat at Ruppert Stadium on opening day in 1932. In 1932 the United States suffered through the worst year of the Great Depression, which hit industrial cities such as Newark especially hard. But more than 13,000 Newark fans joined Ruppert in 28-degree weather to welcome the 1932 Bears. Trailing the Toronto Maple Leafs 5-1 in the bottom of the ninth, the Bears rallied to tie with a grand-slam homer, then won the game in the tenth. "No World Series the Yankees ever won gave me a greater thrill," exulted Ruppert. "And they call it minor league baseball."

The Bears raced to a 13-4 start, then carried out a season record of 109-59, winning their first pennant in 19 years by 15 ½ games. Righthander Don Brennan led the league in victories, winning percentage, and ERA (26-8, 2.79). Also effective were Peter "The Polish Wizard" Jablonowski (11-1 in 12 games), starter-reliever James Weaver (15-6), and manager Al Mamaux (5-1, 2.56 ERA in 24 games). The Bears posted the league's best batting average (.304) behind infielder Marvin Owen (.317), who was voted the IL's

first Most Valuable Player, switch-hitting first baseman Johnny Neun (.341 with a league-leading 25 steals), shortstop Red Rolfe (.330), and outfielders Dixie Walker (.350 with 105 RBIs). Jesse Hill (.331 with 114 RBIs), and Woody Jensen (.345).

Newark won the first of three consecutive pennants in 1932. Starring for the Bears were victory leader Don Brennan (No. 3, and 26-8), future Yankee relief ace Johnny Murphy (5), second baseman Jack Saltzgaver (6, and .318), outfielder Jessie Hill (9, and .331), shortstop Red Rolfe (10, and .330), outfielders Dixie Walker (11, and .350) and Woody Jensen (13, and .345), MVP Marvin Owen (14, and .317), pitcher Peter Jablonowski (16, and 11-1), first baseman Johnny Neun (17, and .341), and manager and long-time IL pitching ace Al Mamaux (19, and 5-1).

Although Donie Bush, manager of the American Association titlist Minneapolis, brashly predicted victory in the renamed

TIME OUT

Shag

Frank J. Shaughnessy was born at Amboy, Illinois, on April 8, 1883. A long-time minor league outfielder, "Shag" played a total of nine American League games, with Washington in 1905 and Philadelphia in 1908. The following season he became player-manager of Roanoke, and promptly won the Virginia League pennant. After two more years at Roanoake, Shag moved to Fort Wayne in 1912, immediately producing a Central League flag. The next season he went to Ottawa, where he won three consecutive Canadian League championships (from 1913 through 1915). He spent 1916 with a troubled franchise in the Inter-State League, then managed Hamilton to back-to-back second-place finishes in the Michigan-Ontario League.

On July 30, 1921, Shag was appointed manager at Syracuse—the beginning of an International League tenure that would span 40 years. Syracuse was a perennial second-division club, and Shag was released on May 28, 1925. A week later, he signed on to manage Reading, but left after a miserable 1-8 start.

Shag coached at Detroit in 1928, then resurfaced in the IL in 1932 as GM at Montreal. A year later the league adopted his post-season playoff plan, and in 1934 he took over as field manager for 33 games. The next year he piloted Montreal to the IL pennant, his sixth flag in 14 seasons as a manager. Shag relinquished the managerial reins in August 1936 and was elected league president. He served as president of the IL until he retired in 1960, having established a length of stability unmatched by any other league.

Shag died in Montreal on May 15, 1969 at the age of 86.

Junior World Series, the Bears polished off the Millers, four games to two.

The 1932 batting champ was Rochester outfielder George Puccinelli (.391, 28 HR, 115 RBI), who went up to the Cardinals late in the season, but who would make a spectacular return to the International League. Buffalo outfielder Ollie Carnegie turned in his first big season (.333, 36 HR, 140 RBI) for the Bisons. But the IL's leading power hitter in 1932 was big (6'3", 225 pounds) Buzz Arlett.

A native of Oakland, Arlett spent his first pro seasons with the Oaks, beginning as a superb righthanded pitcher (he had season victory totals of 29, 25 and 22) but becoming a switch-hitting slugger and outfielder. After setting all-time home run (251) and RBI marks for the Pacific Coast League, he moved up to Philadelphia as a 32-year-old big league rookie in 1931. Although Arlett hit .313 he was peddled to the Orioles for 1932. En route to leading the IL in homers, RBIs and runs (.339, 54 HR, 114 RBI, 141 R), Arlett *twice* blasted four home runs in a single game (on June 1 and July 4). Sparked by this remarkable slugger, the Orioles walloped a league record 232 home runs.

Buzz Arlett returned in 1933 to lead the IL in homers and runs (.343, 39 HR, 146 RBI, 135 R). But the pennant race was all Newark. Despite the promotion of several stars, George Weiss acquired considerable new talent for manager Al Mamaux. Victory and strikeout leader Jim Weaver (25-11, 175 Ks) and starter-reliever Harry Smythe (21-9 in 54 games) provided excellent pitching, while the offense was led by MVP shortstop Red Rolfe (.326), first-sacker Johnny Neun (.309), and infielder Jack Saltzgaver (.305). The defending champs won 102 contests and another pennant by a margin of 14 ½ games.

But the Bears would not enjoy another trip to the Junior World Series. Frank "Shag" Shaughnessy, general manager of the Montreal Royals, had proposed a post-season playoff scheme similar to that used by pro hockey. According to the Shaughnessy Plan, at the end of the regular season the top four teams would square off in a series beginning with the first- and second-place clubs, and the third- and fourth-place teams, playing a best-of-five semifinals. The two winners then would be pitted in a best-four-of-seven finals match to determine the IL representative to the Junior World Series. The first-place team would be designated as pennant-winner, but the playoff titlist would advance to the series and would possess a handsome Governors' Cup for a year.

Inspired by the Newark runaway of 1932, the Shaughnessy Plan was designed to sustain fan interest throughout the season. Even late in the year, a second-division team might surge into fourth place, then win the semi-finals and finals, and perhaps the Junior World Series. The Shaughnessy Plan would prove to be almost as effective an antidote to Depression attendance woes as night games, and in time almost all minor leagues adapted some form of the playoff system. (It seemed fair to the pennant winner, for example, to pit the first vs. fourth and second vs. third teams, and the series would range from best-two-of-three to best-four-of-seven.)

Of course, if a pennant-winner was defeated in a short-series playoff, the full-season champs could be expected to howl—which is precisely what happened in the first Shaughnessy playoff. In 1933 Newark once again made a shambles of the IL pennant race, which meant that the inauguration of the Shaughnessy Plan was timely for other clubs around the league. The Bears downed second-place Rochester in the first playoff games, but the Red Wings stormed back to win the semifinal series with three straight victories. Buffalo, which finished fourth with a losing record (83-85) swept third-place

Baltimore in the semifinals, then downed Rochester, four games to two, in the finals. Buffalo righthander John Wilson (15-6, including iron-man doubleheader victories over Toronto) and outfielders Ollie Carnegie (.317, 29 HR, 123 RBI), Ollie Tucker (.323, 27 HR, 115 RBI) and Len Koenecke (.334 with 100 RBIs) were quality players, but the Bisons were overmatched in the Junior World Series by Columbus. Nevertheless, a fourth-place team with a sub-.500 record had participated in the postseason playoffs series, including the Junior World Series, and the players enjoyed playoff bonuses which totaled a significant percentage of their salaries. Playoff executives throughout the minor leagues immediately recognized the financial possibilities.

But Newark officials bitterly denounced a playoff system that had deprived their fine team of an appearance in the Junior World Series and Bears players of their much-needed playoff bonuses. Newark attempted to abolish the Shaughnessy Plan, but had to settle for a first-vs.-third and second-vs.-fourth semifinals, which was expanded to a best-four-of-seven format. Because of the ex-

tended season, the playoffs and Junior World Series had been played in frigid, rainy weather, and it was determined to reduce the 168-game schedule, in use since 1921, to the major league standard of 154 games.

Although he had built teams which had dominated the IL for two consecutive seasons, Al Mamaux lost his job over the traumatic 1933 playoff loss. The new manager was the former Yankee pitching great Bob Shawkey, who piloted the Bears to a third consecutive pennant behind outfielders George Selkirk (.357) and Jesse Hill (.349), newly acquired first baseman Dale Alexander (.336 with 123 RBIs), and pitchers Floyd Newkirk (11-4) and Walter "Jumbo" Brown (20-6), who led the IL in victories, ERA, complete games, shutouts, and winning percentage. But once again the Bears met frustration in the playoffs, falling in seven games to third-place Toronto. "It is eminently unfair to the players," fumed George Weiss, to no one in particular.

In 1935 Baltimore outfielder George Puccinelli led the International League in batting average, homers, RBIs, hits, runs and doubles (.359, 53 HR, 172 RBI, 204 H, 135 R, 49 2B). It was Puccinelli's second hitting

The Bisons of 1933 stormed to the first Shaughnessy playoff title behind longtime slugger Ollie Carnegie (front row, far right—.317, 29 HR, 123 RBI), right fielder Ollie Tucker (front, third from right beside his son—.323, 27 HR, 115 RBI), second baseman Fresco Thompson (front, fifth from right—.301), manager Ray Schalk (front, sixth from right), center fielder Leon Koenecke (top row, second from right—.334), and pitcher John Wilson (top, fourth from right—15-6).

title in four years, and only the second Triple Crown in league history (Dale Alexander recorded the first in 1928, and there would not be another until 1955). Puccinelli's career season brought him a richly deserved Most Valuable Player Award.

Montreal won the 1935 pennant, while Buffalo took the IL flag the next season. But in 1937 Yankee quality again kicked in at Newark. The returning manager was Oscar Vitt, a big league veteran who guided Hollywood to three Pacific Coast League pennants. A tough disciplinarian who stressed physical conditioning and precise execution of fundamentals, Vitt would manage perhaps the best team in the long history of the International League.

While George Weiss actively acquired new players and brought in athletes from the Yankees, the '37 Bears finished the exhibition schedule with eight consecutive victories and a 15-6 record. Early in the regular season the Bears dismantled the Maple Leafs, 23-1, then proceeded to overwhelm the rest of the league. Newark led the league in team hitting (.299), fielding, and double plays. Rookie right fielder Charlie Keller (.353) became he youngest player, at the age of 20, to win an IL batting title. The talented club roared to the pennant by a 25½-game margin. Although the Bears had been defeated in the opening round of the first four playoffs, 1937 would be a different story. The '37 Bears swept the Syracuse Chiefs in four straight, then took four in a row from the Baltimore Orioles to convincingly bring an overdue title to Newark.

The 1937 Junior World Series showcased the top teams of baseball's top two farm systems. The Columbus Red Birds of Branch Rickey's Cardinal organization defeated Newark in all three games at Ruppert Stadium. The Red Birds needed only a single victory in four home games to win the series.

TIME OUT

Suitcase Bob

Bob Seeds was a Texan who began his professional career at the age of 19 in 1926 with Enid of the Southwestern League. A right-handed outfielder who performed with speed and power, Seeds made the big leagues with Cleveland in 1930 (.285 in 85 games). During nine seasons, from 1930 though 1940, he played with the Indians, White Sox, Red Sox, Yankees and Giants, but only in 1932 did he appear in more than 85 games. He bounced so often from team to team, from the majors to the minors, that he became known as "Suitcase Bob."

Seeds spent 1935 (.315) and most of 1936 (.317) with Montreal, but he was acquired as insurance late in 1936 by the Yankees. He played in 13 games, but rode the bench as the Yankees won the World Series. The Yankees then sent him back to the International League, where he played center field for the magnificent 1937 Newark Bears (.305, 20 HR, 114 RBI).

Back with the Bears in 1938, Seeds ripped opponent pitching (.335) for an incredible 28 homers and 95 RBIs in merely 59 games! His greatest explosion came on Friday and Saturday, May 6 and 7, at Buffalo. Following a single in the second inning, he blasted four consecutive home runs over the left field fence at Offermann Stadium. In the eighth inning he came up for a sixth at-bat with the bases loaded, and he knocked in two runs with a single to center. The next day Seeds homered in the first inning, then again in the third. He walked in the fifth, then walloped his third home run of the day in the seventh. In the ninth inning he was retired for the only time in two days, on a three-two pitch that was called strike three but that Seeds always insisted was inside. In 10 at-bats he pounded out 9 hits, 7 home runs, and 17 RBIs.

On June 24 Seeds was sold to the New York Giants. He finished his big league career with a .277 lifetime average, but returned to the IL with the 1941 Orioles (.265), then was released early the next season. Bob Seeds finally unpacked his battered suitcase.

Toronto's 1935 Maple Leafs were managed by Ike Boone (front row, fourth from left), who hit .350 at the age of thirty-eight.

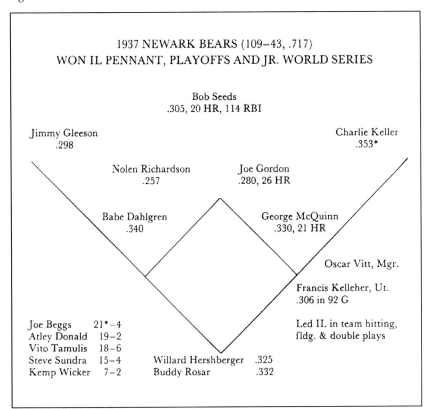

1937 NEWARK BEARS (109–43, .717)
WON IL PENNANT, PLAYOFFS AND JR. WORLD SERIES

Bob Seeds
.305, 20 HR, 114 RBI

Jimmy Gleeson .298

Charlie Keller .353*

Nolen Richardson .257

Joe Gordon .280, 26 HR

Babe Dahlgren .340

George McQuinn .330, 21 HR

Oscar Vitt, Mgr.

Francis Kelleher, Ut. .306 in 92 G

Led IL in team hitting, fldg. & double plays

Joe Beggs	21*–4
Atley Donald	19–2
Vito Tamulis	18–6
Steve Sundra	15–4
Kemp Wicker	7–2

Willard Hershberger .325
Buddy Rosar .332

Famed slugger Smead Jolley (.366 lifetime minor league average and .305 in four big league seasons) played for Albany in 1936, leading the IL with a .373 batting average, 52 doubles, and 221 hits. Jolley won a total of seven minor league batting titles.

But the Bears staged an incredible comeback, outscoring the Red Birds 29-6 in a four-game sweep. Colonel Ruppert happily brought the Bears into New York City for a first-class victory celebration.

Newark continued to win big in 1938, as George Weiss provided quality replacements for players promoted or traded. Young Charlie Keller was retained for more seasoning, and "King Kong" responded with another batting title and an even more impressive performance (.365, 22 HR, 129 RBI, and a league-leading 149 runs) than his spectacular rookie season.

Buffalo outfielder Ollie Carnegie, who turned 39 at midseason, won the home run

The 1937 Newark Bears, one of the greatest clubs in minor league history. Seated, L. to R.: George McQuinn, Jimmy Gleeson, Frank Kelleher, Joe Beggs, manager Oscar Vitt, Willard Hershberger, Vito Tomulis, Joe Gordon, Buddy Rosar. Standing, L. to R.: Jimmy Mack, Marius Russo, Steve Sundra, Phil Page, Jack Fallon, Nolen Richardson, Bob Seeds, Babe Dahlgren, Charles Keller, Atley Donald, Joe Fixster.

The 1939 Jersey City Giants won the pennant behind batting champ Johnny Dickshot (top row, fifth from left — .355), lefty Roy Joiner (middle row, far right—21-8), IL veteran Bill Harris (top row, fourth from left—18-10), and manager Bert Niehoff (middle, fifth from left).

and RBI titles (.330, 45 HR, 136 RBI), and was voted MVP. Toronto lefty Joe Sullivan (18-10) became the first victory leader in IL history to win fewer than 20 games.

For the second year in a row Newark easily outdistanced the rest of the league, winning the pennant by 18 games. The 1939 Bears also won the playoffs, before dropping the Junior World Series in seven games to Kansas City. But more championships soon would be claimed by the Bears. Just as Jack Dunn's Baltimore Orioles had produced the most sustained success of independent minor league baseball, the Newark Bears exhibited repeated success as the best club of the Yankee farm organization.

During the 1930s the International League had weathered the Great Depression with remarkable stability and had developed a postseason playoff system that would become a permanent part of the minor league scene. Also during this period it became obvious that success on the minor league level—both on the field and in the business office—increasingly depended upon major league connections. Despite resentment by local fans and owners, teams in the IL and throughout the minors became vassals of big league teams, with the good of an often faraway parent club the primary consideration. Year after year, however, the Newark Bears demonstrated the degree of sustained success that could be attained by a key member of an efficiently run farm system, and Montreal would prove this axiom during the coming decade.

Newark slugger Charley Keller won back-to-back batting crowns in 1937 (.353) and 1938 (.365), then took his hitting skills to the New York Yankees.

1940–1949

By the end of the 1939 season, the Second World War had erupted in Europe. Within another year a military and industrial buildup was under way in the United States, but there was little effect upon professional baseball until American entry in the conflict. Indeed, the 1939 pennant-winners, Jersey City's Little Giants, set a minor league record in 1940 with opening day ticket *sales* totaling 50,000—stadium seating capacity was only half that number. Rain delayed the opener three days, which cut actual attendance, but the Jersey City civic promotion indicated robust support of IL baseball. A similar promotion for the 1941 opener produced an eye-popping total of 56,391 ticket sales.

The playoff finalists of 1939 staged a fierce race for the 1940 pennant. Rochester (96-61) outlasted Newark (95-65), with Red Wing ace Mike Ryba (24-8) winning the MVP award. Righthanders Henry Girnicki (19-10), Herschel Lyons (19-12), and Bill Brumbeloe (18-11) also pitched well for the Red Wings.

Rochester had little offensive punch, though, ranking sixth in team hitting, while Newark—managed since 1938 by Johnny Neun—was strong in every category. Newark swept Jersey City in the 1940 playoff opener, beat Baltimore in a seven-game finals series, then won the Junior World Series over Louisville.

Newark followed the 1940 playoff and Junior World Series triumphs with back-to-back pennants. The 1941 Bears won the team hitting title and took the pennant by 10 games. Manager Johnny Neun's stable included ERA and percentage leader Johnny Lindell (23-4, 2.05, and a .298 batting average in 51 games), home run and RBI champ Frank Kelleher (.274, 37 HR, 125 RBI), and key returnees Hank Majeski (.303) and Tommy Holmes (.302).

The 1941 MVP was Buffalo righthander Fred Hutchinson, who pitched superbly (26-7) and who, like Lindell, was frequently used as a pinch-hitter (.392 in 72 games). Hutchinson had been the 1938 MVP in a Pacific Coast League (25-7 with a .313 batting average) as a 20-year-old rookie. Hutchinson's teammate, Virgil "Fire" Trucks, became the first IL hurler since 1925 to record 200 strikeouts (12-12 with a no-hitter and 204 Ks in 204 IP).

Less than two months after the 1941 Junior World Series, the Japanese attacked Pearl Harbor. The distractions of gathering war clouds already had begun to reduce attendance throughout the minor leagues. There were 43 minor circuits in 1940, with a total paid attendance of almost 20,000,000, but in 1941 attendance dropped to 16,000,000. Play resumed in the spring of 1942, although only 31 minor leagues opened operations. Players began to join the military, but personnel shortages would not become severe until the 1943, 1944, and 1945 seasons.

For Newark, 1942 seemed to bring business as usual, as George Weiss continued to find solid players for the Yankees' top farm club. The Bears led the IL in team hitting, fielding, and home runs. Third baseman Hank Majeski (.345 with 115 RBIs) paced the league in batting, RBIs, and hits. Second-sacker George Stirnweiss (.270 with 73 steals) collected the most stolen bases since 1919. Southpaw Tommy Byrne (17-4) was the league's percentage leader and the team's best hitter besides Majeski (.328 in 64 games). For the second year in a row, the Bears won the pennant by a 10-game margin, although the champs were upset in the playoff opener. Third-place Syracuse, which boasted MVP

victory leader Red Barrett (20-12, 2.05 ERA), and sidearmer Ewell "The Whip" Blackwell (15-10, 2.02 ERA), won the playoffs, but lost the Junior World Series to Columbus.

A few months later, on January 15, 1942, President Franklin D, Roosevelt wrote a letter to the commissioner of baseball, Judge Kenesaw Mountain Landis, expressing the hope that professional baseball would continue operations during the war as a boost to public morale. The major leagues and 31 minor circuits opened the 1942 season, but travel restrictions caused numerous problems. And as healthy young men joined the military by the millions, the manpower pool for baseball teams steadily declined. Soon rosters bulged with players past their prime, raw youngsters, and 4-Fs (the most famous 4-F, one-armed outfielder Pete Gray, was the Southern Association stolen base champ in 1944, and played 77 games for the St. Louis Browns in 1945). By 1943, only 10 minor leagues were in operation; there were 10 minor circuits again in 1944, and 12 in 1945.

The International League, the only minor league to finish the World War I season of

Rochester's 1940 champs featured a crack pitching staff which included MVP Mike Ryba (24-8, middle row, fourth from left), Henry Gornicki (19-10, middle, far right), Herschel Lyons (19-12, top row, far right), Bill Brumbeloe (18-11, middle, second from right), and future Brooklyn star Preacher Roe (bottom, fourth from right).

1918, continued to play throughout World War II without schedule interruptions or franchise changes. Although the quality of IL athletes remained surprisingly good in 1943, the quality of baseballs declined as manufacturers took shortcuts. It was thought that the yarn was not wound as tightly around the core, and for a time balata (a substance used in golf balls) was substituted for rubber, which was in short supply during the war.

With balata at the core, baseballs had little carry, and while the "balata ball" was in use, home run and RBI totals declined accordingly. Buffalo outfielder Ed "Shovels" Kobesky led the league with just 18 home runs, and only 9 players hit more than 9 homers. Newark collected the highest team total, with 76 roundtrippers, while Jersey City stroked merely 22 homers all season. Baltimore outfielder George Staller (.304, 16 HR, 98 RBI) became the first RBI champ in league history to knock in fewer than 100 runs. Team batting averages ranged from only .255 for Montreal to Jersey City's .232.

The pitchers, of course, were delighted with the less lively balls. Buffalo righthander Rufe Gentry (20-16) managed to win 20 games with a seventh-place club, and on April 25 he hurled an 11-inning no-hitter to defeat Newark, 1-0. The only other IL pitcher to have twirled 11 innings of no-hit baseball was Toronto's Urban Shocker; in 1960 Al Cicotte, also pitching for Toronto, fired an 11-inning no-hitter. On August 17, 1943, Rochester righthander Blix Donnelly (17-8) pitched a 9-inning no-hitter.

Jersey City righthander Lou Polli won the ERA title with a sparkling 1.85 rate in 220 innings, while the percentage leader was fireballing southpaw Joe Page of Newark (14-5). Although Buffalo righty Jack Tising was a 20-game *loser* (13-20), he could claim the patriotic distraction of working shifts at an airplane plant between starts.

Rochester's 20-year-old batting champ, switch-hitter—and future Hall of Famer—Red Schoendienst (.337), also led the IL in hits as well as putouts and assists by a shortstop. Toronto cruised to the pennant by a 10½-game margin but lost out to third-place Syracuse in the playoff finals. In the 1943 Junior World Series, however, Columbus racked up its third consecutive postseason triumph.

By 1944, rosters were loaded with teenage, 4-F, and over-the-hill players. In Baltimore, for example, 18-year-old Eddie Braum played 36 games at shortstop (.176), while 44-year-old manager Tommy Thomas had to

Syracuse outfielder Dutch Mele was one of the leading sluggers of 1945, the last war year (.299, 19 HR, 108 RBI).

take a couple of turns on the mound. The Orioles also lost their ballpark to flames, following a defeat on the night of July 3. But the Orioles took to the road while Municipal Stadium, the football facility, was being readied for baseball. Thomas also had his uniform adorned with the Diamond B arm patches sported by the champions of 1919-25, and the old magic worked again. The Orioles did not dominate the league, but outfielder "Howitzer Howie" Moss led the IL in homers, RBIs, doubles, and hits (.306, 27 HR, 141 RBI, 178 R), righthander Red Embree was the victory and strikeout king (19-10, 225 Ks), and second baseman Blas Monaco (.294) was the run leader and set an IL record with 167 walks.

By the last day of the season, however, Newark had slipped past Baltimore into first place, and the Orioles lost their final game. But Newark choked, losing a double-header finale to last-place Syracuse, which put Baltimore back into first place by a miniscule percentage margin of .0007. Baltimore and Newark faced off in the playoff finals, with the Orioles finally winning in the seventh game. Baltimore then traveled to Louisville for their first Junior World Series since 1925. The Orioles took two of three on the road, then retuned to Memorial Stadium—and a record crowd of 52,833 (on the same date in St. Louis only 31,630 turned out for a World Series game). The Colonels disappointed local fans with a 5-4 victory, which evened the series. But the Orioles won the next two games and the series.

Young catcher Sherm Lollar (he was 19 until August 23) was the hero of the Junior World Series, battering Louisville pitching for a .423 average and a grand slam home run. In 1945 Lollar hit his way to the batting crown (.364, 34 HR, 111 RBI) and the big leagues. The rise in home runs over 1943, in the IL and throughout professional baseball, re-flected the improvement in the quality of balls.

A decline in the quality of catchers probably was instrumental in an increase in base stealing. During the batting barrage of the 1930s, managers rarely gave base runners a steal sign, hoping that a power hit would bring in the run with less risk. From 1931 through 1937, the stolen base leaders rang up modest totals of just 25 to 33, and in 1939, 1940, and 1941 the theft champs stole just 22, 21, and 24. During the dead-ball era, team totals frequently exceeded 200 per year, but in the 1930s few teams stole as many as 100 bases. In 1937, for example, Montreal led the league with just 74 stolen bases, while Jersey

Slugging outfielder-third baseman "Howitzer Howie" Moss won four IL home run titles during the 1940s. (Courtesy IL)

City stole merely 38 bases all season. But in 1942 George Stirnweiss stole 73 bases; in 1944 and 1945 six teams totaled more than 100 steals each season; and in 1945 Newark stole 204 bases while Syracuse outfielder Walt Cazen led the league with 74 thefts. A primary reason for the upsurge was the lack of effective catchers. Because of the wartime player shortage, promising catchers were rapidly promoted to the major leagues. In 1945 only young Sherm Lollar (136 games for Baltimore) and big league veteran Al Todd (104 games for Montreal) remained in the IL long enough to catch 100 games. After the war, catching quality improved and teams returned to station-to-station baseball; the 1948 stolen base co-titlists managed just 18 thefts each; Montreal infielder Junior Gilliam led the IL in 1952 with only 18 steals; and in 1960 Buffalo center fielder Solly Drake won the crown with a record low of merely 16 stolen bases.

Montreal catcher Al Todd (.273) was 43 years old during the 1945 season. Buffalo hero Ollie Carnegie (.301 in 39 games) was brought back to the Bisons at the age of 46, and on September 3, 42-year-old Jersey City righthander Lou Polli twirled the year's only no-hitter, an 11-0 victory over Newark. (It was Polli's second IL no-hitter, the first coming over Jersey City in 1937 when he pitched for Montreal.) At the other end of the chronological scale, Buffalo pitchers Art Houtteman (3-3) and Billy Pierce (5-7) both began the season as 17-year-olds, and saw action with Detroit before the year ended. There were numerous other teenagers and veterans in their late thirties or forties around the IL during the final wartime season, but club executives somehow lined up replacements for men who were promoted to the major leagues or who exchanged flannel uniforms for khaki ones, and the game went on.

Montreal led the league in hitting and fielding, and boasted the IL's best pitching staff: victory and strikeout leader Jean Roy (25-11, with 27 complete games in 37 starts), ERA and percentage titlist Les Webber (11-3, 1.88 before going up to Brooklyn), and righthander John Gabbard (20-6). Two righthanded workhorses were Baltimore's John Podgajny (20-11 in 66 games, including 15 starts and 51 relief appearances) and Syracuse's Bob Katz (20-20, with 28 CG in 37 starts).

Bruno Betzel managed Montreal to the pennant over second-place Newark, but the Bears won the playoff finals from the Royals. Newark then lost the Junior World Series to Louisville, making the second of three consecutive appearances in the series.

Before the end of the season, Japan surrendered and World War II ended. Americans exuberantly embraced every available recreational opportunity, and for the next few years minor league baseball enjoyed an enormous boom. In 1946 the number of minor leagues jumped from 12 the previous year to 45, and by 1949 there were 59 minor circuits with an all-time record attendance of nearly 42,000,000. The proliferation of leagues caused the addition of Triple-A classification, comprising the International League, American Association, and Pacific Coast League. Attendance in the IL in 1946 soared (big league attendance increased 71 percent), remaining above 2,000,000 for four seasons.

Another big development of the 1946 season placed the International League in the van of events which would exert the most profound influence upon baseball, as well as upon American society. After the 1942 season, Branch Rickey moved from the St. Louis Cardinals to the Brooklyn Dodgers, and immediately the innovative executive secretly requested permission to "come up with a Negro player or two." Rickey felt that black athletes would offer the edge the Dodgers would need to overcome the vast stockpile of talent he had left with the Cardinals, and he also held the firm conviction that baseball should be integrated.

Not since the nineteenth century had black players appeared in predominantly white leagues; there had been no blacks in the IL since the late 1880s. The autocratic commissioner of baseball, Kenesaw Mountain Landis, opposed integration, but he died in 1945, just when black participation in World War II triggered widespread demand for the integration of baseball. For decades black players had been confined to the Negro leagues, which in many cities often rented the local professional stadium (including many IL ballparks through the years) and scheduled their games when the white teams were on the road. Even the Boston Red Sox, which would become the last big league team to integrate (in 1959) allowed Jackie Robinson and two other players to try out in the spring of 1945. Such tryouts were superficial affairs with no real intention of signing black players.

But Branch Rickey had developed a careful plan to introduce black players to the big leagues, and it would begin with the assignment of just the right man to just the right franchise in the high minors. Rickey thoroughly investigated a number of black athletes, finally settling on former UCLA football star Jackie Robinson. Robinson had played pro football, had honed his baseball skills in the Negro leagues, and had held an army commission during the war. Rickey met with Robinson in August 1945, and on October 23, 1945, it was announced that in 1946 Jackie Robinson would play for the Montreal Royals.

Montreal was the top club in the farm system that Rickey was building for the Brooklyn Dodgers. The large French-speaking population held a far more liberal view of blacks than the attitudes which prevailed in the United States, especially the South. There was little Southern influence in the Northeastern and Canadian cities of the International League, but harsh feelings and incidents still could be expected to swirl around the men who would break baseball's color line.

Robinson was 27 when he reported with his bride to the Dodgers' spring training camp in rigidly segregated Florida. Rickey had impressed upon the mature Robinson that on behalf of his race he must not fight back against prejudice, and he somehow en-

Montreal second baseman Jackie Robinson was sensational in 1946, leading the IL in hitting, runs and fielding, while reintroducing African-Americans to professional baseball. (Courtesy IL).

dured tremendous hostility without retaliating—except for his play.

Montreal was in Jersey City on April 18, 1946, for the IL opener, and 25,000-seat Roosevelt Stadium overflowed with fans and reporters. No minor league game had ever generated such attention. The large contingent of black spectators cheered wildly as Robinson went four-for-five, cracked a home run, stole two bases, scored four runs and knocked in four more during a 14-1 rout of the Giants. The new Montreal manager, Clay Hopper, overcame his Mississippi background and avidly supported his star second baseman.

When several Baltimore players expressed their refusal to play against Montreal, IL President Frank Shaughnessy telegraphed that he would arrange to have them suspended from baseball for life. Attendance at the Montreal Stadium broke all records as charter trains brought fans from the United States. Robinson silently endured harassment on the field and more media attention off the field than had ever been faced by a minor league player. He played superbly (.349, 113 R, 40 SB), leading the IL in batting and runs, and fielding by a second baseman.

Black pitchers John Wright and Roy Partlow also appeared on the Montreal roster (Wright actually was signed before Robinson), but both men crumbled under pressure and were sent down to Class C. In 1947 Rickey took the Dodgers and Montreal to Havana for spring training, to avoid racial conditions in Florida. Robinson remained on the Montreal roster and was joined by Partlow, catcher Roy Campanella, and towering pitcher Don Newcombe. Jackie Robinson went up to Brooklyn,

while Campanella, Newcombe and other talented black athletes played in the IL and other minor leagues before joining Robinson in the big leagues.

Baltimore slugger Howitzer Howie Moss collected his second IL home run title (.278, 38 HR, 112 RBI), while Oriole first baseman Eddie Robinson (.318, 34 HR, 123 RBI) won the RBI crown and the MVP award that many observers felt should have gone to Jackie Robinson. Syracuse righthander Earl Harrist (15-10) pitched two 5-0 9-inning no-hitters, on April 30 and July 29.

The 1946 Royals led the IL in team hitting, fielding, doubles, triples and stolen bases, racing to their second straight pennant by an 18½-game margin. Montreal easily won the Shaughnessy Playoffs, then dumped Louisville in the Junior World Series. Branch Rickey had begun signing legions of young ballplayers for Brooklyn in 1943, and within two years the best talent was beginning to pass through Montreal en route to the Dodgers. Rickey's Brooklyn farm system would produce a series of Dodger pennants,

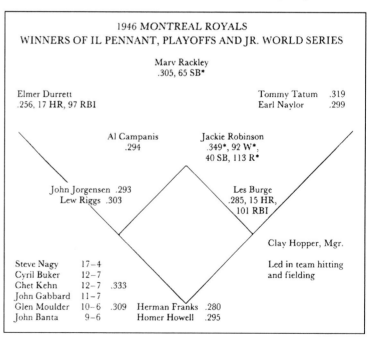

1946 MONTREAL ROYALS
WINNERS OF IL PENNANT, PLAYOFFS AND JR. WORLD SERIES

Marv Rackley
.305, 65 SB*

Elmer Durrett
.256, 17 HR, 97 RBI

Tommy Tatum   .319
Earl Naylor   .299

Al Campanis
.294

Jackie Robinson
.349*, 92 W*,
40 SB, 113 R*

John Jorgensen .293
Lew Riggs   .303

Les Burge
.285, 15 HR,
101 RBI

Clay Hopper, Mgr.

Led in team hitting
and fielding

Steve Nagy   17–4
Cyril Buker   12–7
Chet Kehn   12–7   .333
John Gabbard   11–7
Glen Moulder   10–6   .309   Herman Franks .280
John Banta   9–6   Homer Howell   .295

with concurrent success for their top farm club. Just as Rickey's Cardinal farm system had produced an IL dynasty in Rochester, and just as George Weiss' Yankee farm system had produced an even greater IL dynasty in Newark, so would Rickey's Dodger organization generate a string of IL championships for Montreal. The Royals finished first in 1945, 1946, 1948, 1951, 1952, 1955 and 1958, missed the playoffs only one time (1957) from 1943 through 1958, won the Governors' Cup in 1946, 1948, 1949, 1951, 1953 and 1958, and won the Junior World Series in 1946, 1948 and 1953.

The Montreal string was interrupted in 1947, when Jersey City (94-60) edged the Royals (93-60) by half a game. Stunned, the Royals were swept by third-place Syracuse in the playoff opener, and the Chiefs went on to win the finals in seven games over Buffalo.

"Howitzer Howie" Moss of Baltimore clamed his third home run crown with 53 roundtrippers, while Oriole righthander John Podgajny turned in another ironman performance (13-18, with 25 starts and 34 relief appearances). MVP outfielder Hank Sauer (.336, 50 HR, 141 RBI, 130 R) of Syracuse paced the league in RBIs and runs and finished second in hitting and homers— and became the only slugger in IL history to wallop 50 roundtrippers and not win the home run crown. Bruno Betzel guided Jersey City to the flag over Montreal; he had managed the Royals to the 1945 pennant, and would win again with Toronto in 1956.

Royals manager Clay Hopper brought Montreal back with a vengeance in 1948, winning the pennant by 13½ games over Newark, then reclaiming the Governors' Cup and beating St. Paul in the Junior World Series, four games to one. Montreal led the league in team hitting behind a dangerous lineup of batters that included future Dodger star Duke Snider (.327, 17 HR, 77 RBI in just

In 1947 MVP Syracuse outfielder Hank Sauer won the RBA title and finished second in hitting and homers (.336, 50 HR, 141 RBI). He lost the batting crown by a single point, while a late-season surge gave "Howitzer Howie" Moss 53 home runs. (Courtesy Syracuse Chiefs)

77 games) and lanky first baseman Chuck Connors (.307, 17 HR—including three grand slams), who later would turn to acting and achieve fame as Western TV hero *The Rifleman*. Big Don Newcombe (17-6) pitched a seven-inning no-hitter and became a Dodger starter the next year.

There was a remarkable display of offense by Buffalo during a Sunday doubleheader at Offermann Stadium on June 20, 1948. The Bisons dismantled the Syracuse Chiefs 28-11 and 16-12. Buffalo totaled 41 hits, including a league record 10 home runs in the first game. Outfielder Anse Moore was seven-for-nine with two homers in the first game.

Baltimore's right-handed slugger, Howitzer Howie Moss, won the 1948 home run crown (.301, 33 HR, 94 RBI), his third in a row. In

1944, his first season as an Oriole, Moss won the title with 27, then entered military service. He returned in 1946 with a league-leading 38, blasted 53 in 1947, and took his fourth title in 1948. Howitzer Howie's four home crowns stand alone, despite three-time efforts by Rocky Nelson (1954, 1955, 1958) and Frank Herrera (1959, 1962, 1965).

In 1949 Buffalo led the league in homers and team fielding and won a tight pennant race. But Montreal triumphed in the Shaughnessy Playoffs for the third time in four seasons. The Royals boasted MVP batting champ Bob Morgan (.327, 19 HR, 112 RBI), strikeout leader Dan Bankhead (20-6 with a .323 average in 58 games), first baseman Chuck Connors (.319, 20 HR, 108 RBI), and explosive outfielder Sam Jethroe (.326 with a league-high 154 runs and 17 triples). Jethroe's 89 stolen bases eclipsed Ed Miller's 1919 record of 87, although his new twentieth-century mark had been exceeded in 1888 (107), 1889 (97), and 1891 (106). The fleet Jethroe literally ran away

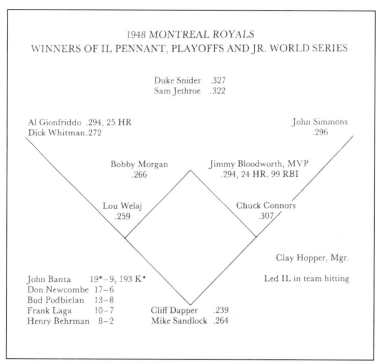

1948 MONTREAL ROYALS
WINNERS OF IL PENNANT, PLAYOFFS AND JR. WORLD SERIES

Duke Snider .327
Sam Jethroe .322

Al Gionfriddo .294, 25 HR
Dick Whitman .272

John Simmons
.296

Bobby Morgan
.266

Jimmy Bloodworth, MVP
.294, 24 HR, 99 RBI

Lou Welaj
.259

Chuck Connors
.307

Clay Hopper, Mgr.
Led IL in team hitting

John Banta   19*–9, 193 K*
Don Newcombe   17–6
Bud Podbielan   13–8
Frank Laga   10–7
Henry Behrman   8–2

Cliff Dapper   .239
Mike Sandlock   .264

The International League Hall of Fame was created in 1947. Standing in front of the plaque honoring the inaugural class of nine members, left to right: IL President Frank Shaughnessy; Ben Sankey, former Montreal shortstop; John L. McGowan, president of the IL Baseball Writers' Association; and William Manley, IL secretary-treasurer. Shaughnessy and Sankey were members of the Class of '47, and Manley would be voted into the Class of '53. (Courtesy IL)

with the title—his closest competitor, teammate Al Gionfriddo, stole just 29 bases.

Attendance for 1949 was 2,322,801, and another 141,740 fans attended the playoffs.

TIME OUT

Grand Slam King

Jersey City catcher Wes Westrum played 51 IL games in 1949 (.308 with 15 homers) before being called up to the New York Giants. On April 21 he walloped a bases-loaded home run, and on May 15 he blasted another grand-slam. The next night Westrum hit a third grand-slam, tying a league record set by Bob Seeds in 1938 and matched by Bert Haas in 1940, Blas Monaco in 1944, Sherm Lollar and Bobby Thomson in 1946, and Chuck Connors in 1948. Westrum established a new record with his fourth grand-slam on June 6, then cracked a fifth two days later. Westrum was promoted to New York on June 13, before he could add to his record of five grand-slams, and creating the question of how many more he might have slammed in the remaining two-thirds of the IL sea-

Admissions had stayed above two million in each of the postwar seasons. There had not been a franchise shift in the IL since 1937, when Jersey City replaced Albany. But in 1948, despite a second-place finish and the postwar boom, perennial power Newark drew only 170,000 fans. The Bears plunged to last place the next year, and attendance nose-dived to 88,170. After the 1949 season the Yankees unloaded their once-proud franchise to the Chicago Cubs, who moved the club to Springfield for the 1950 season. In 1950 Jersey City made the playoffs, but attendance was a paltry 63,191, and the franchise moved to Ottawa. The loss of the New Jersey cities with their keen rivalry was only the beginning of franchise movement for the IL. During the 1940s the International League had managed to continue operations throughout World War II, then had enjoyed unprecedented prosperity during the postwar baseball boom. But the next decade would bring a sudden reversal of fortunes and a new set of challenges for the International League.

1950–1959

By the middle of the twentieth century baseball's oldest minor league had survived the Spanish-American War, the Great Depression and two world wars, and during the last four seasons of the 1940s the IL had totaled more than two million fans per season. But in 1950 there was a plunge of more than 25 percent, to 1,729,126, although attendance at the playoffs increased slightly, to 143,413. In 1951 season attendance sagged to 1,612,780, and playoff admissions dropped to 106,398. The next year IL attendance stabilized at 1.7 million, but other minor leagues suffered staggering losses.

There were 59 minor circuits in 1949, with an all-time record attendance of 41,872,762. But the minor league decline started abruptly the next year, when a major league Game of the Day began to be broadcast over the Mutual Radio Network. By this time television was spreading nationwide, and on hot summer nights potential baseball fans could stay at home and watch their favorite TV shows in air-conditioned comfort. Little League baseball also exploded in popularity, and with two or three games per week and frequent practices, families stayed away from minor league parks in droves. Leagues

folded by the dozen, and circuits that remained in operation had to scramble for franchise cities. By 1963 there were only 18 minor leagues, with a total paid attendance of just 9,963,174.

In 1950 Rochester won the pennant for the first time in 10 years. Managed by Johnny Keane, the Red Wings led the IL in team batting, triples and home runs. Third baseman Don Richmond scored the most runs and won the first of two consecutive batting titles (.333, and .350 in 1951). MVP righthander Tom Poholsky was the victory, ERA and complete game leader (18-6, 2.17, and 21 CG in 25 starts), while starter-reliever Ken Wild was almost unbeatable (12-1).

On Sunday, August 13, 1950, Tom Poholsky and Andy Tomasic of Jersey City locked horns in a pitching duel unprecedented in IL history. The Red Wings scored a run off Tomasic in the first and in the second innings, while Poholsky yielded two unearned runs in the second. As a Red Wing Stadium crowd looked on, Poholsky then hurled 20 consecutive scoreless innings, while Tomasic matched him until the bottom of the twenty-second, when Dick Cole led off with a single. Tomasic balked and moved Cole to second base, and

56

pulled a line drive down the right field to win the game, 3-2.

In 22 innings the 20-year-old Poholsky yielded only 10 hits and 5 walks, and struck out 11. The two hurlers toiled for 5 hours and 15 minutes, while the 22-inning marathon broke a league record of 21 innings, set by Baltimore and Toronto on April 21, 1943.

During the 1951 season George "Specs" Toporcer, manager of Buffalo and the first non-pitcher to wear eyeglasses in the big leagues, suffered such a rapid deterioration of his eyesight that he was forced to resign (he was replaced by Coaker Triplett). Despite three eye operations, Toporcer was blind by November 1952. He had captained Rochester to four consecutive IL pennants, and he managed the Red Wings from mid-1932 through 1936. Toporcer wrote an autobiography, *Baseball from Backlots to Big League*, and became a popular inspirational speaker. He died in 1989 at the age of 90.

Walt Alston managed the Montreal Royals from 1950 through 1953, winning bask-to-back pennants in 1951 and 1952 and claiming the Governors' Cup in 1950, 1951 and 1953. In 1953 Alston downed Kansas City in the Junior World Series, then moved up to a Hall of Fame managerial career with the Dodgers. In 1976 Alston retired and was replaced as Dodger manager by Tommy Lasorda—who had been a mainstay of Alston's Montreal pitching

In 1950 fastballer Carl Erskine had a final tune-up with Montreal (10-6 in 18 games) before becoming a Brooklyn regular.

TIME OUT

Double Hat Trick

During the 1950 season, Toronto outfielder Bud Heslet (.256 with 21 homers) twice hit homers in one game. On May 21, during the seven-inning opener of a doubleheader at Maple Leaf Stadium, Heslet singled in his first turn at bat, then homered in the second, fourth, and sixth innings of a 13-2 rout. During the nine-inning nightcap of a doubleheader at Baltimore on August 14, Heslet went five-for-five with eight RBIs. He doubled, singled, and sent three balls out of Memorial Stadium, although the Orioles won, 10-9.

Only the Triple Crown winner, George Puccinelli, had ever hit three homers twice in a season, although Buzz Arlett, of course, twice blasted *four* homers in 1932.

staff in 1950 (9-4), 1951 (12-8), 1952 (14-5), and 1953 (17-8).

The 1953 Royals featured RBI champ Glenn "Rocky" Nelson, who would perform spectacularly before IL fans during the 1950s. A left-handed first baseman, Nelson had a sturdy physique at 5'11", 190 pounds. Nelson began his professional career in the Appalachian League at the age of 17 in 1942.

He spent the next three years in the military, then returned to baseball with a fine season in the Western Association.

He opened the 1948 season at Rochester, but after a miserable start (.056 in 11 games) the Cardinals moved him from the IL to Lynchburg in the Piedmont League, where he won the batting title (.371 and 105 RBIs in 117 games). Nelson spent 1948 with

Player-manager Harry "The Hat" Walker (.303, front row, center) led the Rochester Red Wings to the 1953 pennant. A potent offense was sparked by outfielders Tommy Burgess (.346, far right, middle row), Allie Clark (.328), Wally Moon (.307, front row, second from left), and Ed Mierkowiez (.303, middle, third from left), along with first baseman Charlie Kress (.317, 25 HR, 121 RBI, middle far left), and third sacker Don Richmond (.312, middle, third from left). Reliever Jack Crimian (13-5 in 62 games, middle row, fourth from left). (Courtesy Rochester Red Wings)

Rochester (.303), then was promoted to the Cardinals. During the next three seasons he played with the Cards, the Pittsburgh Pirates, Columbus of the American Association, and the Chicago White Sox.

Acquired by Brooklyn for 1952, he went one-for-three in Montreal and moved up to the Dodgers for the rest of the season. But Nelson enjoyed little success in the big leagues (.249 in 620 games), and he played in Montreal the next four years. In 1953 he played in every game and won the RBI title (.308, 34 HR, 136 RBI) as the Royals charged to the playoff championship and victory in the /Junior World Series over the Kansas City Blues.

The next season Nelson was the home run champ (.311, 31 HR, 94 RBI). In 1954 he sparked Montreal to the IL pennant, playing in every game while leading the league in batting average, homers, RBIs, and runs (.364, 37 HR, 130 RBI, 118 R). A splendid start in 1955 (.394 in 49 games) sent him back to the Dodgers, but before the season ended he was dealt to the Cardinals (.217 in 69 games with both teams).

He returned to the IL the next year with Toronto, making a strong contribution to the 1957 pennant-winners (.294, 28 HR, 102 RBI). Back with the Maple Leafs in 1958, he captured another Triple Crown (.326, 43 HR, 120 RBI). Nelson played the following three years with Pittsburgh, then went down to Denver of the American Association in 1962. He spent the last 57 games of the season with Toronto (.217) before retiring at the age of 37.

From 1947 through 1962, Rocky Nelson appeared with three IL teams during 10 seasons. Although Nelson played only five full seasons in the IL, he recorded two batting championships, three home run crowns, and three RBI titles. Rocky Nelson became the only man in league history to win *two* Triple

During an 18-year career, left-handed first baseman Rocky Nelson appeared with three IL teams during 10 seasons. Although he played only five full seasons in the IL, Nelson became the only man in league history to win two Triple Crowns, and to be named Most Valuable Player three times (in 1953, 1955, and 1958). (Courtesy IL)

Crowns, and to be named Most Valuable Player three times (in 1953, 1955, and 1958).

During the 1950s Havana was a tourist mecca, where fun-loving travelers cavorted on the beaches, sailed out on fishing excursions, and at night swayed to Latin dances, gambled in glamorous casinos, and sampled more exotic entertainments. But native Cubans flocked to ballparks in such numbers, according to Michael and Mary Oleksak in *Beisbol*, that nightclub owners unsuccessfully petitioned the government to reduce the number of weekly winter league night games from five to three.

The Cuban love affair with baseball began

in the 1870s, and soon there was a professional league as well as scores of amateur clubs throughout the island. During the twentieth century, major leaguers barnstormed in Cuba, talented Cubans played in the big leagues, and Cuba became a hotbed of winter league baseball. In 1946 the Havana Cubans and five Florida teams organized the Class C Florida International League. Playing in new, 35,000-seat Gran Stadium, the Cubans annually led the league in attendance while winning four pennants and two playoff titles through the 1953 season. Volatile fans enjoyed gambling and drinking rum and Coca Cola at the ballpark.

By this time promoter Roberto Maduro, who had worked with Clark Griffith of the Washington Senators to organize the Cubans, was convinced that a Havana team could operate successfully at the Triple-A level. Maduro approached the International League, promising to purge gambling at Gran Stadium and to reimburse the IL clubs $60,000 apiece to offset travel costs to Havana. IL owners agreed, and the 1954 schedule would bring each team to Havana for a 5-game series. Players' wives who rarely went to the expense and trouble of accompanying the team on road trips, eagerly planned excursions to exciting Havana. The Havana Sugar Kings replaced Springfield, which had suffered three consecutive last-place finishes and which had attracted only 85,000 fans in 1953.

Another major change for the IL occurred when Baltimore joined the American League after half a century as a bellwether of the IL. Late in the 1953 season, AL owners voted to move the moribund St. Louis Browns to Baltimore. The International League would receive a territorial indemnity of almost $49,000, and Richmond was readmitted to the circuit as a replacement franchise.

The 1954 International League, therefore, was composed of Montreal, Toronto and Ottawa in Canada, the Havana Sugar Kings, and Buffalo, Rochester, Syracuse and newcomer Richmond in the United States. Toronto was guided to the pennant by Luke Sewell, a noted American League catcher and a veteran big league manager. The Maple Leafs took the team batting title behind MVP Elston Howard (.330, 22 HR, 109 RBI, and a league-leading 16 triples). Toronto brought in 409,000 fans (almost one-fourth of the total IL attendance) and Havana attracted nearly 300,000 rooters, but overall league attendance slipped to 1,655,602. The playoffs drew merely 73,613, and last-place Ottawa pulled in fewer than 94,000 fans. But attendance also was weak in Columbus of the American Association, and when the parent Cardinals moved their AA franchise to

TIME OUT

Two Grand-slams Per Game

On Sunday, August 4, 1957, Buffalo shortstop Mike Baxes became only the fourth player in IL history to wallop two grand-slam home runs in one game. In the first game of a doubleheader against Havana, the Bisons buried the Sugar Kings, 20-1. Baxes led the onslaught with a four-for-six explosion, including a double, single, the two homers, and 10 RBIs. His first grand-slam cleared the tall screen at Offermann Stadium in the opening inning, and he cleaned the bases again in the third. Baxes hit only 11 more homers during the season, but he led the league in runs, doubles, and base hits (.303) and was voted Most Valuable Player.

Curiously, the other players who hit two grand-slams in a single IL game otherwise performed poorly during their season of record. Catcher Dan Howley of Montreal was the first to perform the feat, in 1915 (.247, with seven homers in 88 games). Tom Adams of Jersey City did not play in enough games to be listed in the 1927 *Guide*, while outfielder Joe Cicero appeared in just nine games for Newark in 1944 (.242).

Omaha, a group of Columbus baseball enthusiasts paid $50,000 for the Ottawa club. The Columbus Red Birds of the AA became the Columbus Jets of the IL.

Montreal won the 1955 pennant behind MVP Triple Crown winner Rocky Nelson and victory leader Ken Lehman (22-9), who pitched the first seven-inning perfect game since 1936. But despite a scintillating pennant race, attendance in 1955 drooped to 1,554,311. Syracuse finished fifth and drew only 85,000 fans, and the club was sold to owners who installed the team in Miami. With the South Florida economy at boom levels, the Miami Marlins would offer another exotic locale for the IL, as well as a handy rivalry for former Florida International League foe Havana. The Miami transfer was the fourth IL franchise move in three years.

Baseball's major showman-promoter, Bill Veeck, was in between big league jobs, and he agreed to help Miami's owners run the club. Veeck's master stroke was to place a Marlin uniform on the legendary Satchel Paige, bringing him into Miami Stadium in a helicopter. Veeck signed Paige to a contract on the spot, and Satchel, who was over 50, was taken to a rocking chair in the bullpen. Veeck booked the Marlins into the Orange Bowl on August 7, 1956, and 51,713 fans watched Paige outfox the Columbus Jets. Paige was effective all year (11-4 with a 1.86 ERA in 37 games), and he was a popular game attraction in Miami for two more seasons.

Montreal returned to the throne room in 1956. Buffalo finished in the cellar, but the Bisons boasted the IL's leading slugger. "Big Luke" Easter (6'4½", 240 pounds) was the league's home run and RBI champ (.306, 35 HR, 126 RBI) at the age of 41, and in 1957 he repeated the feat with even better numbers (.279, 40 HR, 128 RBI). In 1956 Richmond outfielder Len Johnston (.294 with 40 steals) won the first of an unprecedented three consecutive stolen base

In 1956 venerable hurler Satchel Paige—already in his 50s—made a spectacular IL debut as a Miami Marlin. Almost 52,000 fans came to Miami Stadium, and Satchel was a popular IL gate attraction for three seasons. (Courtesy IL)

titles (in 1978-1979-1980 Ed Miller, also playing for Richmond, tied Johnston's record, and so did Esix Snead in 2004-2005-2006).

In 1957 Toronto's Maple Leafs won their third pennant in four years. Toronto led the league in fielding and again boasted the IL's best pitching staff: victory leader Humberto Robinson (18-7), Don Johnson (17-7), Jim Pearce (15-8), and reliever Roberto Tiefenaur (2.14 ERA in a league-leading 68 games).

Buffalo manager Phil Cavaretta guided the Bisons from the 1956 cellar to a season-long challenge of Toronto, which fell just half a game short of the 1957 flag. The Buffalo charge was sparked by home run and RBI king Luke Easter, batting champ Joe Caffie (.330), co-victory leader Walt Craddock (18-8), Glenn Cox (12-5, with seven homers as a batter), and MVP shortstop Mike Baxes (.303), who led the IL in hits, runs, and doubles. Although Buffalo lost the pennant on the last day of the season, the Bisons perse-

vered and won the Governors' Cup. Buffalo posted the league's best attendance with over 386,000 admissions. The All-Star Game, played in Montreal, attracted an enthusiastic crowd of 16,000.

Montreal marched to the pennant in 1958, edging Toronto by 2½ games, then defeating the Maple Leafs in the playoff finals. The Royals were paced by victory leader Tommy Lasorda (18-6), while Toronto boasted ERA champ Bob Tiefenauer (17-5, 1.89) and stellar first baseman Rocky Nelson, who won his second Triple Crown and third MVP Award.

In 1959 Buffalo, managed by Kerby Farrell, won the pennant and drew over 413,000 fans, almost one-fourth of total league attendance. Star of the Bisons was new first baseman Frank Herrera, who replaced aging Luke Easter (the 44-year-old slugger caught on with Rochester and played for six more years). Herrera pounded his way to a

Slugging first baseman Luke Easter at Buffalo's Offermann Stadium, where he claimed back-to-back home run and RBI titles in 1956 and 1957 (.306, 35 HR, 126 RBI, and .279, 48 HR, 128 RBI— at the age of 42!).

Lefthander Tommy Lasorda was a solid starter for Montreal throughout the 1950s, and was the IL victory leader (18-6) in 1958. (Courtesy IL)

Triple Crown (.329, 37 HR, 108 RBI) and was named Most Valuable Player.

In 1959 Fidel Castro, who once had been scouted as a professional pitching prospect, had mounted a successful revolution against the regime of Fulgencio Batista. American players became so worried about traveling to Havana that IL president Frank Shaughnessy had to employ his considerable powers of persuasion to maintain the schedule. On June 24 Castro happily revived his curve ball during a two-inning exhibition preceding an IL contest between Havana and Rochester on July 24. Over 200,000 fans flocked into Gran Stadium in 1959, but their enthusiasm sometimes was excessive: two days after the exhibition game, jubilant fans fired guns into the air, and two men in Rochester uniforms supposedly were grazed. Rochester promptly headed back to the States, and Shaughnessy again had to exert pressure to keep teams playing in Cuba. Nevertheless, armed soldiers always were on duty at Gran Stadium, and players frequently—and nervously—heard gunfire from skirmishing in the suburbs.

The Sugar Kings finished third and

TIME OUT

"Time Out!"

The Havana Sugar Kings had no greater fan than Fidel Castro, the former pitcher turned revolutionary. After he rose to power in Cuba, Castro had a special seat constructed at Gran Stadium just behind the Sugar Kings' first base dugout.

Visiting players often were unsettled by the sound of gunfire from the outskirts of Havana, and by the youthful *soldados* armed with submachine guns who always were stationed in large numbers at Gran Stadium during ballgames. Native Cubans on the Havana roster were inducted into Castro's army.

During a trip to Cuba by Buffalo, the Bisons walloped a pitcher who had been awarded an officer's commission. Castro's patience quickly wore thin, and he shouted an order for a time out. The umpire sensibly called play to a halt.

Castro bounded out of his seat and stalked to the pitcher's mound. He shouted at the faltering hurler, slapped him on the cheek, then added a hard backhand. The Bisons flattened onto the floor of their third-base dugout, thinking an outburst of gunfire might be next. But Castro marched back to his seat, and when play resumed the pitcher-officer bore down with greatly improved intensity.

fought their way to the 1959 playoff title. The first three contests of the Junior World Series were scheduled to be held in Minneapolis, but after two games a severe weather front prompted the JWS Commission to play the remainder of the classic in Havana. More than 100,000 Cubans crowded into Gran Stadium, making 1959 the attendance champion of all Junior World Series. Fidel Castro came to each game protected by a large contingent of heavily armed soldiers, while Minneapolis players apprehensively listened to gunfire outside the stadium. Trailing three games to one, Minneapolis rallied to win the fifth and sixth contests and tie the series. In the seventh game the Millers nursed a 2-0 lead into the eighth inning, but the Sugar Kings evened the score, then delighted the crowd by pushing across the winning run in

the bottom of the ninth. It was the IL's first triumph in the Junior World Series in six years, and an exciting end to the 1950s.

Buffalo first baseman Frank Herrera won a Triple Crown (.329, 37 HR, 128 RBI) in 1959, and repeated as home run and RBI champ in 1962.

Buffalo's 1959 pennant-winners. (Courtesy Jacke Davis)

1960–1969

Change was in the air as the International League entered the 1960s. Frank Shaughnessy, now 75, retired in 1960 after serving expertly as league president since 1937. Thomas H. Richardson of Montreal was elected to replace the popular "Shag." Another change in the IL came in July 1960, after Fidel Castro declared himself a Communist and commenced seizure of all U.S.-owned property, including oil refineries, utilities, ranches, sugar mills, and banks. Visiting players found U.S. currency in great demand on the streets of Havana, although dollars were confined to the black market. The last IL team to visit Cuba was Buffalo, and when the Bisons flew out of Havana they saw clouds of black smoke billowing from American-owned oil tanks that had just been blown up. On July 13 the Havana franchise was transferred to Jersey City, which had not been in the IL since 1950.

Toronto dominated the league in 1960, winning the pennant by 17 games and taking the Governors' Cup with eight playoff victories against only one loss. The Maple Leafs, guided by Mel McGaha, then dumped Louisville in the Junior World Series.

Toronto righthander Al Cicotte won a pitcher's Triple Crown (16-7, 158 K, 1.87 ERA), leading a mound corps which set a new IL record with 32 shutouts (the old mark of 29 was established by Rochester's 1910 champs). Cicotte was responsible for eight of the shutouts, his last coming on September 3 against Montreal. In the first inning he walked the bases full, then struck out the side. He then retired 29 Royals in a row before an error produced a baserunner. Cicotte walked one more batter, but he struck out 11 and fired an 11-inning no-hitter to win, 1-0. (Cicotte's classic was the third and, to date, last 11-inning no-hitter in IL history). Cicotte's final regular season start came five days later. He missed another shutout by an unearned run, but beat Rochester on four hits, 4-1, to end the schedule with 56 consecutive innings without an earned run. Cicotte won 10 of his last 12 decisions, with the defeats by 1-0 and 2-1 margins. He then won three games in the playoffs, including a shutout, to record 15 straight complete games.

League attendance in 1960 dropped to a postwar low of 1,369,011, with only 52,408 at the playoffs, and in 1961 total admissions

65

sagged to 1,244,631. When Walter O'Malley moved the Dodgers from Brooklyn to Los Angeles in 1958, he opened a Triple A club in he Pacific Coast League at Spokane. Spokane, much closer to Los Angeles than Montreal, became the Dodgers' top affiliate. Although Montreal won the IL pennant in 1958, the next season brought a rare losing record, and in 1960 the Royals finished last. Long the IL attendance leader, Montreal suffered an unaccustomed decline at the gate, and the club moved to Syracuse for 1961.

Another franchise transfer sent the Marlins from Miami to San Juan. Attendance had dropped sharply after Miami's initial season, while Puerto Rico was a hotbed of winter baseball and a source of talented players. But the move to San Juan quickly proved to be a mistake, and on May 19 the Marlins shifted to Charleston, West Virginia. Charleston cheerfully continued the nickname (which saved money on uniforms), explaining that while no marlin fish could be found in West Virginia, plenty of mountaineers carried Marlin hunting rifles!

A different type of change occurred in Buffalo, where the Bisons were forced to abandon Offermann Stadium and move into War Memorial Stadium, a concrete football facility which was dubbed "The Old Rockpile." The converted football stadium, which later served as the home field for Robert Redford in *The Natural*, had a short right field fence that caused left-handed sluggers to drool. But the 1961 All-Star Game was held at The Old Rockpile, and an attendance record was set with 21,885 fans.

The Bisons inaugurated War Memorial Stadium into baseball with a championship performance. Managed by Kerby Farrell, the Bisons finished third, then breezed through the playoffs with a sweep of Charleston and a finals victory over Rochester, four games to one. Momentum carried the Bisons to a four-game sweep over Louisville in the Junior World Series. Center fielder Ted Savage (.325, 24 HR, 111 R, 31 SB) was named Most Valuable Player after leading the league in batting average, runs, hits, walks, and stolen bases.

The Columbus Jets won their first IL pennant in 1961. But franchise movement escalated. Jersey City finished last with an attendance of just 47,900 in 1960, then finished next-to-last in 1961 with only 61,940. Mercifully, the club was moved to Atlanta. Charleston replaced San Juan early in the 1961 season and finished second, but attendance was merely 78,801, prompting a transfer to Jacksonville, Florida.

The Jacksonville Suns promptly won the 1962 pennant behind batting champ Vic Davalillo (.346), who also led the IL in hits,

In 1961 the Buffalo Bisons moved into War Memorial Stadium, a concrete football facility which was dubbed "The Old Rockpile." The converted football stadium later served as home field for Robert Redford in the classic baseball movie, The Natural. *(Author photo)*

Outfielder Jacke Davis hit .303 for Buffalo's 1961 playoff champs. Davis also wore a Bisons uniform in 1960, 1962, and 1963. As a college coach, Davis was instrumental in sending several players to the IL. (Courtesy Jacke Davis)

triples, total bases, and steals; MVP shortstop Tony Martinez (.287); victory leader Joe Schaffernoth (18-11); and fellow righthander Ron Taylor (12-4). But third-place Atlanta rolled through the playoffs, then outlasted Louisville, four games to three, in the Junior World Series, for the fourth consecutive JWS triumph by an IL champ. Atlanta's most exciting player was strikeout champ Harry Fanok (12-10 with 192 Ks in 184 IP). During the 1950s and early 1960s, dozens of minor leagues were forced to disband because of plummeting attendance, but the most significant casualty was announced on November 29, 1962. The American Association had been especially damaged by the loss of key cities to major league expansion, and had operated in 1962 with only six teams. But when Omaha lost its major league affiliate, the AA was reduced to five clubs. National Association president George Trautman met with officials of all three Triple-A leagues for two days, but on November 29 he announced that after 61 years of operation the AA would be dissolved. The two remaining Triple-A circuits would expand to ten teams: the International League absorbed Little Rock and Indianapolis, while

TIME OUT

All-time IL Strikeout Record

On September 30, 1930, Buffalo lefthander "Dauntless Dave" Danforth fanned 20 Rochester batters to establish an IL record for strikeouts in a single game. The mark stood for 32 seasons, until another fireballing southpaw, 6'6" Bob Veale of Columbus, took on Buffalo at War Memorial Stadium on August 10, 1962. The Bisons came from behind in the ninth to win the opening game of a two-night doubleheader, 5-4.

In the second game, Veale took the mound for the Jets and struck out the side in the first inning, a feat that he repeated in the third, fourth, fifth, sixth, and ninth. In the other innings he whiffed four more Bisons, for a record-breaking total of 22. Only four Bisons were called out on strikes—18 went down swinging!

Ironically, Veale did not win the decision in his record-setting performance. With two out and two strikes on Bison Dan Cater in the ninth, Veale gave up a home run which tied the game, 5-5. Veale then whiffed John Hernstein for victim number 22, but he was removed for a pinch-hitter in the tenth. Bob Priddy then pitched three innings of one-hit relief before Columbus finally won in the twelfth, 6-5.

Veale was brought up to Pittsburgh and enjoyed a 13-year big league career. In 22 games for Columbus he went 8-5 and struck out 179 batters in just 134 innings.

the Pacific Coast League temporarily dropped Vancouver and added Denver, Oklahoma City, and Dallas-Fort Worth.

Extra travel would add to the problems of the surviving Triple-A leagues. The major leagues, quite properly concerned about the troubles assailing the top level of their farm systems, agreed to absorb additional travel expenses, which the IL estimated at $7,000 per club. A joint major league-minor league panel formulated a Player Development Plan which would pump substantial financial assistance into each farm system, and which would restructure organized baseball. In 1963 the remaining D, C and B leagues were abolished, although "rookie leagues" were created. Big league clubs each assumed responsibility for five minor league teams, including one in Triple-A and one in Double-A.

In 1963, for the first time since 1887, the International League opened play with ten teams. The circuit divided into a Northern Division, which included Buffalo, Richmond, Rochester, Syracuse and Toronto, and a Southern Division, with Atlanta, Columbus, Indianapolis, Jacksonville and Little Rock (the Arkansas Travelers). Playoffs would involve the top two teams from each division, but, of course, there would be no Junior World Series. The All-Star Game, played on August 19 in Buffalo, pitted the IL Stars against the New York Yankees. A record crowd of 28,524 gathered at The Old Rockpile to watch the Stars blank the Yankees, 5-0.

Both divisions featured tight races, and Indianapolis emerged atop the playoffs. In their first season in the IL the Indians claimed the best record of 10 teams, the pennant, and the Governors' Cup.

During the season the IL requested almost $94,000 in travel reimbursement from the major leagues, nearly double the preseason estimate. When the big leaguers refused to continue these payments for 1964, IL owners voted to drop Indianapolis and Little Rock and resume the familiar eight-team alignment. The big leagues then promised to provide travel reimbursement to Indianapolis and Little Rock if these clubs would join the Pacific Coast League, which became a 12-team league.

Average attendance for 1963 again declined in the IL, while the loss of a troubled franchise and the search for a new city continued to occur almost every year. Big league control of the minors, following the Player Development Plan and reorganization of 1963, became complete. The career minor leaguer became extinct and roster continuity disappeared as productive Triple-A players were moved up to the parent club with little consideration for the situation of the minor league team. Local fans angrily watched players come and go, and fan loyalty declined accordingly. But baseball's oldest minor league sharpened its spikes and proved as resilient and resourceful as ever.

Victory Park in Indianapolis, home base for the pennant-winning Indians of 1963. (Author photo)

The IL returned to its customary eight teams with no divisions in 1964 and attempted to repeat the All-Star success of 1963 by bringing another big league team into Buffalo to play the Stars. But the Cleveland Indians were not as appealing as Mickey Mantle, Yogi Berra, and other New York Yankees, and only 6,512 fans showed up.

The Jacksonville Suns survived a close race to claim the pennant, while fourth-place Rochester won the Governors' Cup. Rangy righthander Mel Stottlemyre starred for Richmond (13-3 with a 1.42 ERA).

Following the season, George H. Sisler, Jr., who had served as Rochester GM for 11 years, was elected to succeed league president Thomas Richardson. Richmond's franchise was moved to Toledo, a charter member of the American Association which had dropped out of the league in 1955. But a new stadium had been built in 1963, and in 1965 the Mud Hens reentered the IL (Toledo had played in the league in 1889).

After another tight race, Larry Shepherd again guided Columbus to the IL throne room. Third-place Toronto, managed by Dick Williams, raced through the playoffs to the 1965 Governors' Cup. The Maple Leaf lineup included MVP batting champion Joe Foy (.302), the only IL regular to hit over .300.

The All-Star Game was held in Atlanta, as the parent Milwaukee Braves took on the Stars in new Atlanta Stadium and drew a crowd of 16,626. The Braves moved to Atlanta for 1966, which brought Richmond back into the IL as a replacement for Atlanta.

Hard-driving manager Earl Weaver led Rochester to

the 1966 pennant, while Dick Williams brought the Governors' Cup to Toronto for the second year in a row. The Maple Leafs led the IL in team hitting and home runs behind batting champ Reggie Smith (.320), while the pitching staff featured victory leader Gary Waslewski (18-11). Ominously, this fine Toronto club attracted only 96,918 admissions. The All-Star Game was held in Toronto, but drew an all-time low of 2,484.

Talented righthander Tom Seaver showed enough promise in his rookie season for Jacksonville (12-12 with 188 Ks) to win promotion to the New York Mets for 1967. Two Jacksonville southpaws who later would star together for the Mets were 1967 ERA titlist Tug McGraw (10-9, 1.99) and strikeout champ Jerry Koosman (11-10 with 183 Ks in 176 IP).

Also in 1967 Richmond righty Ed Rakow (10-6) struck out 18 Maple Leaf batters in a June 14 contest. Syracuse righthander Stan Bahnsen, who pitched a seven-inning no-hitter for Toledo in 1966, fired a seven-inning perfect game against Buffalo on July 9.

Earl Weaver's Rochester Red Wings and

The high-powered Syracuse outfield of 1964. From left: Willie Horton (.288, 28 HR, 99 RBI), Jim Northrup (.312, 18 HR, 92 RBI), and Mack "The Knife" Jones (.317, 39 HR, 102 RBI) who led the IL in homers, RBIs, runs, triples, and total bases. (Courtesy Syracuse Chiefs)

At the age of 18, catcher Johnny Bench appeared in a 1966 game for Buffalo. The next year he slammed 23 homers in 98 games as a Bison, then moved up to a Hall of Fame career with Cincinnati..

the Richmond Braves, managed by Luman Harris, tied for first place. In a single-game playoff, Braves righthander Jim Britton hurled a three-hit shutout to bring Richmond its first IL crown. But the third-place Toledo Mud Hens led the IL in offense and battled their way to the playoff championship.

Toronto finished sixth and attendance dwindled to 67,216, with only 802 faithful rooters on hand for the final game. After 78 years as a mainstay of the International League, Toronto's historic franchise was sold to Walter Dilbeck. Dilbeck moved the club to Louisville, a storied baseball city which long had been a key member of the defunct American Association.

Jack Tighe, who had managed Toledo to the 1967 Governors' Cup, led the Mud Hens to the '68 pennant. The Mud Hens featured the

league's best pitching staff: righthanders Dick Drago (15-8) and Mike Marshall (15-9), and fastballing southpaw Jim Rooker (14-8 with 206 Ks in just 190 IP), who is the last IL strikeout champ to fan 200 or more batters.

But Toledo was downed in the playoff opener by fourth-place Jacksonville, which then swept Columbus in four games to win the Governors' Cup. Playoff attendance tumbled to a record low of 19,964. Jacksonville recorded the league's poorest attendance (83,950), and the New York Mets decided to move the club to Virginia's Tidewater area. The Tidewater Tides, centered in Norfolk and neighboring Portsmouth, promptly marched to the 1969 pennant. The Tides led the league in team hitting, while the pitching staff was anchored by percentage titlist Larry Bearnath (11-4 in 47 games). The following season the Tides moved into Norfolk's new Met Park, the first minor league stadium to feature a restaurant overlooking the playing field.

Despite a tight flag chase in which only seven and a half games separated the top five teams, season attendance dipped to a new low (1,035,957). Last-place Richmond provided the batting and stolen base champ, outfielder Ralph Garr (.329 with 63 steals). The next-to-last team was Buffalo, which employed Hector Lopez, the first black manager in the history of the IL. Third-place Syracuse won the playoffs behind manager Frank Verdi, who would lead the Chiefs to the pennant the next year.

The International League had struggled for two decades with the problems that had come to plague all of minor league baseball. Although a majority of minor circuits disbanded during this difficult era, the International League struggled on with strong leadership from determined owners and a resourceful IL front office, along with the high quality of baseball that fans always had enjoyed on IL playing fields. A new decade brought hope that the IL would enjoy renewed vigor.

1970–1979

The 1970s began with spectacular performances across the International League, although there were more of the painful franchise failures that had become all too familiar during the previous decade. Syracuse, under manager Frank Verdi, had won the 1969 pennant. In 1970 Verdi led the Chiefs to the pennant—the first in 78 years—then repeated as playoff winner. The pitching staff led the IL in team ERA and shutouts, as lefty Rob Gardner won the most games and the ERA title (16-5, 2.53).

Richmond outfielder Ralph Garr (.386 with 39 steals) repeated as batting champ and stolen base king, despite appearing in only 98 games. Garr was two official at-bats short of qualifying for the hitting title, but under rule 10.23a two at-bats were added to his total and he still easily won the crown.

Rochester outfielder Roger Freed was the second leading hitter, but he was more than 50 points below Garr. Freed was consoled with the RBI title (.334, 24 HR, 130 RBI); his 130 RBI was the highest total since 1955, and the greatest number since that date (it is unlikely that any modern hitter will ever approach his total before being brought up a big league club). Freed's teammate, Don Baylor, led the IL in doubles, triples, total bases, runs, and times hit by a pitch (.327, 34 2B, 15 3B, 22 HR, 107 RBI, 127 R).

The 1970 All-Star Game was held in Norfolk's new 6,000-seat Met Stadium. An overflow crowd watched the All-Stars beat the Baltimore Orioles, 4-3. In postseason play the Junior World Series was staged for the first time since 1962. When the big leagues added two more teams apiece in 1968, a total of four more Triple-A clubs was needed. The IL did not wish to expand again, and the Pacific Coast League already had 12 teams. The American Association reopened play in 1969 with six teams, as the PCL cut back to 10 clubs. The AA returned to eight teams in 1970, and the IL agreed to resume the Junior World Series. The IL had won the last four series that had been played, and Syracuse made it five in a row by downing Omaha, four games to one.

During the 1970 season, Buffalo fell victim to the problems that had plagued so many other minor leagues cities. The neighborhood around The Old Rockpile had deteriorated to the point that it was dangerous to attend games. Attendance in 1969 was just 77,808, and a weak club in 1970 (9-27) averaged only 708 diehard fans at home games. On June 4 league officials met in New York, and the decision was made to forfeit the franchise and place it at the disposition of the big league affiliate Montreal. A week later the Expos transferred the club to Winnipeg, which reestablished the International League in Canada.

Despite a second-place finish, Columbus also suffered from rising costs and declining attendance. Jets owners sold out to interests which returned Charleston, West Virginia, to the IL.

The 1971 season belonged to Rochester. The Red Wings, managed by Joe Altobelli, won the pennant by seven games, defeated fourth-place Syracuse and second-place Tidewater to cop the playoffs, then beat Denver in the Junior World Series, four games to three. Rochester led the league in

hitting and fielding, and the pitching staff featured strikeout and co-victory leader Roric Harrison (15-5 with 182 Ks in 170 IP), who struck out 18 Mud Hens in a July 21 game. Don Baylor (.313, 20 HR, 95 RBI) returned to the Red Wings and again led the league in doubles and times hit by a pitch. Baylor was joined on the All-Star Team by Harrison, catcher Johnny Oates, and MVP shortstop Bobby Grich (.336, 32 HR, 124 R, who paced the IL in hitting, homers, and runs.

Winnipeg finished next-to-last after taking over the Buffalo club during the 1970 season, and a last-place finish in 1971 produced only 95,954 admissions. For 1972 the Expos moved the franchise to Newport News and neighboring Hampton, the "Peninsula" area of Chesapeake Bay, where the Whips finished last and drew 48,681 fans. At least there was economy of travel as well as a natural rivalry between a trio of Virginia teams: Richmond, Tidewater, and, just across the bay, Peninsula.

In 1971 Rochester won the IL pennant, Governors' Cup, and Little World Series. For the second consecutive season, future big league star Don Baylor (top row, second from left, and .313, 28 HR, 95 RBI) led the IL in doubles and times hit by a pitch. The league MVP was shortstop Bobby Grich (front row, second from left, and .336, 32 HR, 124 R), who paced the IL in hitting, homers, and runs. The pitching staff featured strikeout and co-victory leader Roric Harrison (top row, fourth from right, and 15-5), who struck out 18 Mud Hens in a July 21 game. (Courtesy Rochester Red Wings)

The 1972 season produced one of the best pennant races in IL history. Only six games separated the top five teams, and the championship was not decided until the last day of the schedule. Louisville won the flag, with Charleston just one game behind and Tidewater only two and a half back.

Former Yankee star Hank Bauer guided Tidewater to the Governors' Cup. During the past few seasons the number of playoff games had been reduced: the Tides beat Charleston in the opener, two games to one, then took the finals from Louisville, three games to two. Late in the year Tidewater righthander Tommie More (11-5) pitched a seven-inning no-hitter, a feat matched by Syracuse southpaw Rich Hinton, while promising Toledo righty Joe Niekro (2-0 with an 0.64 ERA in two games) fired a seven-inning perfect game against the Tides en route back to Detroit.

The Junior World Series was not played in 1972 to accommodate the Kodak World Baseball Classic. The Eastman Company of Rochester, along with the Caribbean winter leagues and the three Triple-A leagues, sponsored the event, to be held in Hawaii. The Kodak Classic was a single elimination tournament made up of the host team (the Hawaiian Islanders of the PCL), of an all-star squad of Latin American players from the winter leagues, and of the post-season playoff winner from the IL (Tidewater), the PCL (Albuquerque), and the American Association (Evansville). Ominously, just 1,877 fans turned out for the opening game, which pitted the Islanders against the All-Stars. When the Islanders were eliminated early, local interest disappeared. Tidewater finished third, and just 992 spectators were on hand to watch the All-Stars defeat Albuquerque for the championship. Talk of playing another Classic between All-Stars from Japan and the Caribbean and the Triple-A leagues did not materialize, and it was decided to resume the Junior World series for 1973.

Another change came about in the IL franchise lineup for 1973, but this one would ultimately strengthen the venerable league. Although Louisville brought the 1972 pennant to Fairgrounds Stadium, the Kentucky State Fair Board decided to expand and redesign the facility, and the pennant-winning Colonels were evicted. The Boston Red Sox moved their Triple-A affiliate to Pawtucket, adjacent to one-time IL member Providence. Pawtucket was closer (40-odd miles) to its parent club than any other Triple-A city, and the franchise would become one of the strongest and most unique in minor league baseball.

Ticket booths at War Memorial Stadium in Hampton, home of the Peninsula Whips in 1972 and 1973. (Author photo)

For 1973 the IL organized into the American Division and National Division. Pawtucket, of course, was in the American Division, along with Rochester, Syracuse and Toledo. The tightly knit National Division included the Virginia franchises—Richmond, Tidewater, and Peninsula—and the capital city of West Virginia, Charleston.

Charleston, sparked by hulking outfielder—and future big league star—Dave Parker (.317 in 83 games), led the league in team hitting and homers and won the National Division by 10 games. Rochester won a tight American Division race, squeezing past Pawtucket by one game and Syracuse by three. Rochester was led by first baseman-outfielder Jim Fuller, who won the home run and RBI crowns (.247, 39 HR, 108 RBI) and was named Most Valuable Player. But Rochester fell to Charleston, three games to one, in the faceoff of division leaders to decide the IL pennant.

Pawtucket, in a brilliant inaugural season, won the battle of second-place teams against Tidewater, then defeated Charleston, three games to two, for the Governors' Cup. In the Junior World Series the PawSox downed Tulsa, four games to one. The Pawtucket lineup featured the league's top three hitters: outfielder Mike Cummings (.288), first baseman Cecil Cooper (.293), and batting champ Juan Beniquez (.298), who played second, short, third, and outfield as needed. (Only one other batting champ—Toronto's Jack Thoney, with a .294 average in 1906—had hit below .300.) Righthander Dick Pole paced the IL in strikeouts and ERA (12-9, 2.03, 158 K), and he fanned 19 Red Wings in a July 25 game. Two seven-inning no-hitters were pitched in 1973: one by Pole, and the other by Bill Kouns (8-6).

In 1969 and 1972, IL attendance had barely passed the one million mark, but in 1973 admissions dropped to 978,811, with an all-time low of 19,609 at the playoffs. Peninsula drew only 45,356, and the franchise was moved to Memphis for 1974. The attendance problems that had troubled the IL and other minor leagues for more than two decades had never seemed worse, while the search for franchise cities continued like a risky game of musical chairs.

During the mid-1970s, IL attendance continued barely to reach the one million mark each season, and two cities found it impossible to maintain their franchises. But in the late 1970s admissions around the league suddenly rose by 50 percent, and by the early 1980s attendance totals began to push the two million mark as franchise cities stabilized. After three decades of struggle, minor league baseball unexpectedly achieved new kevels of fan appeal and profitability.

Memphis was a new member of the IL for 1974, replacing Peninsula, which had attracted merely 45,356 fans in 1973. Again the league was organized into divisions—Northern and Southern—instead of National

Blues' Stadium, home of IL baseball in Memphis from 1974-1976. When the team name reverted to Chicks in 1978, the ballpark was rechristened Tim McCarver Stadium, after a favorite native son. McCarver, a noted big league catcher and broadcaster, observed: "I'm just glad they didn't want to name it Tim McCarver Memorial Stadium!" (Courtesy Memphis Public Library)

and American, as in 1973. But neither division enjoyed the excitement of a race: Memphis won the South by 11 games, while Rochester took the North by a 14-game margin. The Red Wings then downed Memphis, four games to two, to claim the IL pennant. In a battle of second-place teams, Syracuse defeated Richmond for the right to play Rochester for the Governors' Cup. The Red Wings would outlast Richmond, four games to three, to add the playoff title to their banner season.

The best player in the league did not star for any of these winning teams. But Pawtucket, with the worst record in the IL, boasted Jim Rice. The 21-year-old outfielder played in only 117 games before going up to the Red Sox for the rest of the season. Rice won the Triple Crown (.337, 25 HR, 93 RBI), then was voted MVP with a last-place club! Elsewhere around the IL, other future big league stars honed their skills, including Fred Lynn for Pawtucket (.282 with 21 homers), Gary Carter for Memphis (.268 with 23 homers), and Joe Niekro for Atlanta (8-1 in 30 relief appearances with a 2.09 ERA).

In 1975 the IL scrapped the division format and returned to an eight-team pennant race. Tidewater and Rochester ran off from the rest of the league, with the Tides nosing out the Red Wings by one game. The Tides then won the Governors' Cup, before falling to the Evansville Triplets, four games to one, in what has been the final Junior World Series to date.

Since the American Association resumed play in 1969, the Junior World Series had been staged only in 1970, 1971, 1973, and 1975. The major leagues wanted their most promising minor league players available by September, when big league rosters could be expanded from 25 to 40. To accommodate their parent clubs, minor leagues had reduced their schedules from 154 games to 140-146 games. The IL had scheduled 168 games per year from 1921 through 1933, then reduced to 154 games from 1934 through 1964. Beginning in 1965 the International League has scheduled from 140 to 148 games per season. By 1975 the IL Governors' Cup postseason playoffs were reduced from best-four-of-seven series to best-three of-five, and the Junior World Series was eliminated.

Tidewater outfielder Mike Vail won the 1975 batting title (.342) and was named MVP.

TIME OUT

The DH Experiment

The International League was one of the first professional circuits to experiment with the designated hitter rule. The DH was tried in the IL during the 1969 season. League president George Sisler, Jr., promoted the experiment as a means of accelerating offense by eliminating weak-hitting pitchers from the lineup, and as a way of speeding up games with fewer substitutions of pinch hitters for pitchers.

In 1968 team batting averages ranged from .240 to .273, but in 1969 the range increased from .256 to .283, with four clubs accumulating a higher average than the 1968 leader. The time span of 1969 games declined by about six minutes per contest.

But attendance decreased from 1,274, 388 in 1968 to 1,035,457 during the DH year, and the experiment was dropped. When the American League adopted the rule for 1973, however, the IL again tried out the DH. Curiously, the range of batting averages decreased, from .242 to .279 in 1972 to a low of .231 in 1973 and a high of just .263 with the DH. Attendance also declined again, and once more the DH rule was discontinued after just one season. The DH was resumed for good in the IL during the 1976 season, this time with a significant jump in team batting averages. National League affiliates were not allowed to use designated hitters—to the delight of the American League opponents!

Willie Randolph starred for Charleston (.339 in 91 games) and moved up to a standout career as a big league second baseman. Charleston righthander Odell Jones (14-9, 157 Ks, 2.68 ERA) led the league in victories and strikeouts, while Richmond reliever Pablo Torrealba (12-9 with a 1.45 ERA in 64 appearances) won the ERA crown with the stingiest average of any ERA champ since Buffalo's Ray Jordan in 1919 (1.43).

Toledo catcher Bill Nhorodny (.255 with 19 homers) was the home run champ with the lowest total since Buffalo's Ed Kobesky (18) during the wartime dead-ball season of 1943. Individual home run numbers had been relatively low because Triple-A stars were being called up to their parent club after enjoying good starts. But there was little rabbit in the ball in 1975: team home run totals ranged from 90 for Rochester to a paltry 46 for Syracuse, while team batting averages went from Charleston's .264 to Toledo's .229. The DH rule was adopted in the IL in 1976, and all offensive statistics increased significantly.

In 1976 Red Wing manager Joe Altobelli, who had produced IL pennants for Rochester in 1971 and 1973, brought another flag to the league's senior city. Syracuse finished second, 6 ½ games back, but no other team posted a winning record. In the playoffs, however, Rochester was upset by fourth-place Richmond, which finished 20 games behind the Red Wings. Syracuse swept Memphis in three games, then downed Richmond, three games to one, to claim the Governors' Cup.

The batting race was airtight, with Rochester second baseman Richard Dauer edging Charleston outfielder Miguel Dilone, .3358 to .3357. The speedy Dilone hit only .217 for Charleston in 1975, but he stole a league-leading 48 bases. He spent part of 1976 with Pittsburgh and played in just 100 IL games, but he repeated as stolen base champ with 61 thefts.

Rochester's pennant-winning mound corps featured Dennis Martinez, who rang up a rare pitcher's Triple Crown (14-8, 140 Ks, 2.50 ERA). Charleston righthander Rick Langford (9-5 in 16 games) twirled a nine-inning no-hitter, while Syracuse lefty Ron Guidry—soon to become the New York Yankees' best starter—was used as a reliever (5-1 with a sparkling 0.68 ERA in 22 appearances).

Although Memphis finished third in 1976, attendance was only 92,973, and the financially troubled franchise folded. Columbus rejoined the IL, with George Sisler, Jr., resigning after 11 years as league president to become the GM of the Jets. Harold M.

Bob Lemon managed Richmond in 1975, the year before he was named to the Hall of Fame. But in 1942, when he was 21, Lemon played third base for Baltimore, leading the IL in putouts, assists and errors. After service in World War II he converted to mound duty, and was a seven-time 20-game winner for Cleveland.

Cooper, a leading figure in Columbus baseball for decades, soon agreed to succeed Sisler as IL president. Cooper had become the clubhouse boy for the Columbus Red Birds of the American Association in 1935, worked in the front office until his entry into the military in 1942, then was instrumental in bringing Columbus into the IL in 1955, serving as GM until 1968. Personable, well-organized, and widely respected, President Cooper would continue the stable leadership that had been provided by Sisler.

Columbus finished next-to-last in 1977, but Sisler produced an eye-popping attendance of 457,251. There was a tight pennant race, only two teams had losing records, and the league jumped from a five-year attendance average of one million to more than a million and a half. Oddly enough, although Pawtucket won its first IL pennant, PawSox attendance was the poorest in the league (70,344). Pawtucket was led to the pennant by IL veteran Joe Morgan, who later would be promoted to manage the parent Red Sox. Although Pawtucket made it to the playoff finals, second-place Charleston executed a four-game sweep to win the Governors' Cup.

On July 7, 1977, Syracuse DH-outfielder Gene Locklear (.290 with 20 homers) blasted four home runs against Columbus. On June 1 against Toledo, Richmond southpaw Mickey Mahler (13-10) hurled a nine-inning no-hitter. The Braves' talented young slugger, Dale Murphy, led the league in RBIs, doubles, and total bases (.305, 22 HR, 90 RBI), and was voted All-Star catcher.

In 1978 Charleston charged to its second IL pennant behind the league's best offense. But fourth-place Richmond knocked off Charleston in the playoff opener, then beat Pawtucket, four games to three, to collect the Governors' Cup. Braves second baseman Glenn Hubbard (.336) was voted to the All-Star team, even though he played in only 80

games before a promotion to Atlanta. Despite anemic batting averages, Braves outfielder Ed Miller won the first of three consecutive stolen base titles, with theft totals of 36, 76 and 60.

During the next three seasons, Columbus fielded a championship dynasty unmatched in IL history. In the early decades of the International League it was possible for independent owners to build dominant clubs, most notably in Rochester from 1909 through 1911 and in Baltimore by Jack Dunn from 1919 through 1925. The St. Louis Cardinals' pioneer farm system produced four consecutive pennants in Rochester from 1928

George Sisler, Jr., served as GM of Rochester for 11 seasons, was IL president from 1966 through 1976, then was GM of Columbus until his retirement in 1989. He was crowned King of Baseball in 1989, and voted into the IL Hall of Fame in 2007. (Courtesy IL)

through 1931, followed immediately by three consecutive flags in Newark.

But the introduction of the Shaughnessy playoffs meant that there were two championship categories each season. In 1937 and 1938 Newark, as the top farm club of the New York Yankees, won both the pennant and the playoffs, while Montreal, jewel of Brooklyn's farm system, won both categories in 1946, 1948, 1951, and 1958. Other teams were victorious in both categories from time to time, but more frequently the pennant-winner was frustrated in the playoffs. Columbus, however, with a Yankee affiliation and veteran GM George Sisler at the controls, won three consecutive pennants in 1979,

1980 and 1981, then added the Governors' Cup each season.

Each Columbus club was guided by a different manager, beginning with Gene Michael in 1979. The Clippers led the league in team hitting and fielding, and cruised to the pennant by an eight-and-a-half game margin over second-place Syracuse. Columbus beat Tidewater in the playoff opener, then outlasted Syracuse in the finals, four games to three.

Columbus attendance soared past half a million, while league attendance was 1.9 million. Both of these excellent figures would be repeated during the next two seasons as the Columbus dynasty continued into the 1980s.

1980–1989

As attendance figures soared, the International League entered the 1980s with far more confidence and optimism than in recent decades. For 1980 Columbus, the defending champion, was managed by Joe Altobelli, who had won pennants for Rochester in 1971, 1974 and 1976, adding the Governors' Cup in 1971 and 1974. He worked the double triumph again with the '80 Clippers, outdistancing second-place Toledo by six games in the flag race. Fourth-place Richmond made the playoff opener close for the Clippers before bowing, three games to two; then Columbus beat the Mud Hens, four games to one, to keep the Governors' Cup.

Righthander Bob Kammeyer (16-8 for Columbus in 1979) repeated as victory leader in 1980 (15-7). Ken Clay (9-4 with a 1.96 ERA in 20 games) won the 1980 ERA title. Marshall Brant took over at first base and was named MVP after leading the league in homers and RBIs (.289, 23 HR, 92 RBI).

As a modern farm club, Columbus enjoyed little continuity from productive players during the dynasty years. Bob Kammeyer put in two good seasons, and second baseman Roger Holt also was present in 1979 (.280)

and 1980 (.213). Roy Staiger was the fielding leader at third in 1979 and returned for 90 games in 1980, but like most of the two-year players he was not productive offensively. Catcher Brad Gulden played part of each championship season, leading all IL backstops in fielding in 1979 and hitting well in 1981 (.295). Righthanders Greg Cochran (12-7 in 1980) and Dave Wehrmeister (11-3 in 1981) pitched for all three Clipper champs.

Marshall Brant returned for 1981 (.261, 25 HR, 95 RBI), alternating at first and as DH with Stave Balboni (.247, 33 HR, 98 RBI), who won the home run and RBI titles. The two righthanded sluggers gave Columbus the best one-two punch in the league. New manager Frank Verdi guided the Clippers to the 1981 pennant with a five-game margin over second-place Toledo. Columbus prevailed over fourth-place Rochester in the playoff opener, three games to two. In the best four-of-seven series with Richmond, Columbus won two of the first three games. Rain then delayed the series, the remainder of the playoffs was canceled, and the Clippers once more held onto the Governors' Cup.

Despite the overall rise in league admissions, attendance at All-Star games had been weak for years. With increasing pressure from the big leagues to complete the schedule as early as possible, it was decided to cancel the midseason break, and the IL All-Star Game—like the Junior World Series—was eliminated.

Columbus tried to win a fourth straight pennant in 1982 behind third baseman Tom Ashford (.331, a league-leading 35 doubles, and 101 RBIs), future Yankee superstar Don Mattingly (.315), and returning sluggers Marshall Brant (.282, 31 HR, 96 RBI) and Steve Balboni. Baboni repeated as home run champ (.284 with 32 homers) despite playing in only 83 games before a callup by the Yankees. On June 28 Balboni clubbed two

Wade Boggs of Pawtucket missed the 1980 batting title by one point, then edged Richmond outfielder Brett Butler for the 1981 crown by a fraction of a point. The future Hall of Famer also led the IL in hits and doubles (.335 with 41 2B).

home runs in one inning, a fact he also had performed on July 6, 1981.

But Richmond broke the Clipper stranglehold on the throne room. The Braves led the IL in team hitting and home runs, while fleet outfielder Albert Hall was the league leader in stolen bases (62) and triples (15). The Braves also featured the league's two winningest pitchers, righthanders Craig McMurtry (17-9) and Anthony Brizzolara (15-11), and ERA titlist James Lewis (12-6, 2.60).

All three playoff series in 1982 were sweeps. Fourth-place Rochester upset the Braves in three games, while Columbus met the same fate at the hands of Tidewater. The Tides, led by outfielder Kerry Tillman (.322), won three straight from Rochester and claimed the Governors' Cup.

In 1983 Columbus returned to the IL throne room, following three straight pennants (1979-1980-1981) and a second-place finish in 1982. The 1983 Clippers were led by home run and RBI champ Bryan Dayett (.288, 35 HR, 108 RBI), strikeout king and co-victory leader Dennis Rasmussen (13-10 with 187 Ks in 181 IP), and stolen base and run leader Otis Nixon (.291, 94 SB, 129 R), whose theft total is the highest of the twentieth century. In the typical fashion of the modern era, the most spectacular players only put in part of a season before being promoted to The Show: first baseman Don Mattingly (.340 with 37 RBIs in 43 games), DH-first baseman Steve Balboni (.274 with 27 homers and 81 RBIs in only 84 games), and, from Tidewater to the Mets, talented young outfielder Darryl Strawberry (.333 in 16 games) and right-hander Walt Terrell (10-1 in 12 games).

Fourth-place Tidewater upset Columbus in the playoff opener, while Richmond swept Charleston. The Tides then downed the Braves, three games to one, to win the Governors' Cup. The three Triple-A leagues had devised a round-robin AAA World Series for the 1983 postseason. Denver represented the American Association and Portland came from the PCL, but the IL's fourth-place team, Tidewater, won the first—and last—AAA World Series.

The first franchise movement since 1977 followed the 1983 season. A Maine attorney, Jordan Kobritz, intended to bring Triple-A baseball to his home state. Kobritz bought the Charleston Charlies, operated the team in

TIME OUT

The Longest Game—Ever!

It is altogether fitting that baseball's oldest minor league staged baseball's longest game. On a cold, windy Saturday night—April 18, 1981—Pawtucket hosted Rochester before 1,740 hardy fans. About 20 minutes before the scheduled 7:30 start, the outfield lights failed. A postponement was discussed, but the lights were restored in time to open play at 8:00 P.M.

The game was scoreless until the top of the seventh, when the Red Wings pushed across a run. Trailing 1-0 in the bottom of the ninth, the PawSox tied the game. As temperatures dipped well below the freezing mark and a chill wind blew in from center field, the two teams battled for 11 more scoreless innings. In the top of the twenty-first inning a routine out- field fly was tossed by the wind into a run-scoring double for the Red Wings. But in the bottom of the twenty-first the PawSox tied the score on another windblown double.

The Longest Game in Baseball History

"After a while," commented Dave Huppert, who caught 31 innings for Rochester, "to tell you the truth, I didn't feel anything, it was so cold. Around one o'clock or so, we all started to lose our concentration."

After the twenty-fifth inning, Pawtucket owner Bob Mondor announced to the few remaining spectators that all concessions would be on the house. Mondor attempted to have the umpires suspend the game, and when they re- fused he placed a call to IL president Harold Cooper. About 3:45 A.M. Cooper directed that play be suspended at the completion of the next inning. At 4:07 A.M., with only 27 diehard fans remaining at McCoy Stadium, the thirty-second inning ended with a score of 2-2. Mondor gave mini-season passes to the faithful 27, Dave Huppert caught nine innings in the next game, and when PawSox reliever Luis Aponte at last returned home, his wife angrily accused him of carousing all night.

Professional baseball's previous longest game was a 29-inning, 6-hour and 59-minute Class A contest played on June 14, 1966, between Miami and St. Petersburg of the Florida State League. It was decided that the IL marathon deadlock would be played off during Rochester's next road trip to Pawtucket, on June 23. But 11 days prior to the playoff, big league players went on strike, which focused the attention of the baseball world upon the minor leagues. The PawSox were besieged with requests of memorabilia, and the national media was present on June 23, along with 5,756 fans.

The top of the thirty-third was scoreless, but in the bottom of the inning Pawtucket finally won, 3-2, when Dave Koza knocked in Marty Barrett. Bob Ojeda was the winning pitcher, Steve Grilli suffered the loss, and Chris Speck gave up Koza's hit (ironically, neither Grilli nor Speck was on the Red Wing roster 67 days earlier, when the first 32 innings were played). Staged on April 18-19 (Easter Sunday) and June 23, the longest game lasted 33 innings, 8 hours and 25 minutes.

West Virginia in 1983, then transferred his club to Old Orchard Beach, Maine. Although Old Orchard Beach had a population of only 8,000, the brief summer season brings a million tourists to the seaside resort. Disregarding Harold Cooper's warning that the population was inadequate to support Triple-A baseball, Kobritz installed the Maine Guides in a new stadium christened "The Ballpark."

The Cleveland Indians' farm club had finished third in its last season in Charleston, but as the 1984 Maine Guides the team rose to second place, three and a half games behind Columbus. The Clippers repeated as champions, bringing Columbus to its fifth IL pennant in six years and accumulating more than 520,000 admissions. Clipper catcher-outfielder Scott Bradley (.335 with 84 RBIs) led the league in batting, RBIs, hits and games played, and was voted Most Valuable Player.

The 1984 playoffs were won by fourth-place Pawtucket, a no-name team which battled past Columbus and Maine to capture the Governors' Cup. The All-Star Game had been revived in 1983, but fewer than 2,400 fans turned out to see the 1984 contest in Rochester. The midseason talent show-case again was shelved.

In May 1984 Tidewater fireballer Sid Fernandez (123 Ks in 105 IP) fanned 17 hitters in a game against the Maine Guides. A year later the big lefthander again whiffed 17 batters, this time against Pawtucket. Fernandez went 4-1 in his first five games and was promoted to the Mets. Another repeat power-pitching performance was turned in by lefty Brad Havens. Moving over to Rochester from Toledo, he recorded his second consecutive strikeout title in 1985.

The Syracuse pitching staff featured percentage and victory leader Stan Clarke (14-4), All-Star reliever Tom Henke (0.88 ERA in 39 appearances), and ERA champ Don Gordon (8-5 with a 2.07 ERA in 51 relief appearances). The Chiefs' offense was triggered by DH-first baseman Willie Aikens (.311) and second-sacker Mike Sharperson (.289), the league leader in hits, runs, and triples. Although the Chiefs lost a 27-inning game to Pawtucket and a 21-inning contest to Columbus, manager Doug Ault guided Syracuse to its first pennant since 1970. But the Governors' Cup was won by third-place Tidewater.

The 1985 pennant race was one of the best in IL history, with only four games separating the top five teams. Six clubs enjoyed winning records, and total attendance exceeded two million for the first time since the postwar boom. Columbus again led the league in admissions (568,733), but excellent

The Diamond opened in Richmond in 1985. Following the 1984 season, Richmond's Parker Field was razed and during the next seven months The Diamond, seating more than 12,000, was erected at a cost of $8 million. (Author photo)

support also was recorded in Richmond (379,019), Syracuse (222,813), and Rochester (208,955).

Although Columbus dropped to seventh place the next year, the Clippers maintained impressive attendance (548,417). First-place Richmond (318,364) and second-place Rochester (308,807) helped the IL stay above two million in 1986. The pennant-winning Braves were sparked by first baseman Gerald Perry (.326) and stolen base champ Albert Hall (.270 with 72 steals). Richmond swept Tidewater in the playoff opener, then outfought Rochester, three games to two, to add the Governors' Cup to the year's honors.

Tidewater marched to the 1987 pennant with the league's best offense and the stingiest pitching staff. The most formidable moundsmen were percentage leader Don Schultze (11-1 in 15 starts) and reliever DeWayne Vaughn, who won the ERA title (2.66 in 50 games). Opposing pitchers had to face five of the IL's top seven hitters, includ-

ing MVP first baseman Randy Milligan (.326, 29 HR, 103 RBI), who led the league in hitting, RBIs, runs and total bases.

Columbus manager Bucky Dent led the Clippers to second place, then to three-game sweeps over Rochester and Tidewater in the playoffs. Once more Columbus posted the league's best attendance (507,599).

Veteran righthander Odell Jones, now pitching for Syracuse (12-7), won his third strikeout title. At the age of 22 in 1975, Jones posted his first crown while wearing a Charleston uniform. He was the league's best power pitcher again three years later with Columbus. Lefty Grove, who won four consecutive titles with Baltimore in the 1920s, is the only other pitcher to have recorded more the two IL strikeout crowns. On July 6, Pawtucket righthander Steve Curry hurled a no-hit victory over Richmond, the first nine-inning no-hitter since 1977.

Shortly after the close of the 1987 season, owners and executives of all three Triple-A

The 1986 Red Wings were playoff finalists. Ken Gerhart (top row, far right) led the league with 28 homers, while Odell Jones (middle row, fifth from left) won IL strikeout crowns in 1975, 1978, and 1987. (Courtesy Rochester Red Wings)

leagues met at Hollywood, Florida. For more than a decade IL president Harold Cooper and Joe Ryan, longtime president of the American Association (and a former IL club executive) had discussed the possibilities of interleague play. The IL and the AA had set up a schedule for 1917 which would include 48 interleague games per club, but the United States entered World War I a week before the season opened, and the experimental format was abandoned—until 1988.

Joe Ryan had retired in 1987 following a stroke, and Ken Grandquist, owner-president of the Iowa Cubs, had accepted official designation as AA president. But AA directors persuaded Harold Cooper to run the AA simultaneously with the IL from his offices in Grove City. Cooper and his assistant, Randy Mobley, felt that the time was ripe for interleague play, an idea that was being proposed in the major leagues. Once again, as so often in the past, the IL was on the cutting edge of baseball innovation.

Interleague play and an alliance were discussed late into the night by owners and GMs at an informal meeting in Harold Cooper's Hollywood hotel room. The next morning Cooper had breakfast with Randy Mobley while the owners conducted separate league meetings. Although Cooper and Mobley shared the impression that the new measures would not find approval, late in the day they were surprised to learn that the Triple-A Alliance had been established by directors of the International League and the American Association. The Pacific Coast League felt that the travel involved would be too difficult and expensive. But the IL and the AA were geographically closer; indeed, Buffalo of the AA had been a mainstay of the IL for decades, while Columbus and Toledo long had been members of the AA. Harold Cooper agreed to serve as commissioner of the Alliance, with Randy Mobley as his administrative assistant.

Each Triple-A Alliance club would play 42 interleague games, six against each of the eight members of the other league—three at home and three away. Fans would be able to see Triple-A players from 16 organizations instead of eight, a plan which was being counted on to boost attendance. A postseason Alliance Classic, a continuation of the Junior World Series, would be staged between the IL and the AA champions. Umpiring crews would be used during the seasons in both leagues, which would reduce resentment in certain cities and by certain teams against specific officials. The most entertaining innovation, however, was the Triple-A All-Star Game.

The two 23-man rosters were made up of stars from all 26 Triple-A teams. The best players in the IL, AA, and PCL were divided into American and National League squads, and the game was scheduled for July 13, 1988, at Buffalo's superb new Pilot Field. A capacity crowd of 19,500 thronged to Pilot Field as ESPN telecast the first Triple-A All-Star Game to a national audience. The American League squad pushed across an unearned run in the top of the ninth to win, 2-1.

The IL returned to a division format for 1988. Tidewater and Rochester won the East and West respectively with identical records (77-64), and were the only two IL clubs to enjoy winning seasons. The American Association teams prevailed over their IL opponents 187-131, although Rochester righthander John Mitchell fired a seven-inning no-hitter against Indianapolis, the eventual AA champion.

Tidewater's Eastern Division champs led the league in team hitting and staff ERA, while lefthander Dave West was the ERA and percentage champ (12-4, 1.80). Rochester boasted MVP third baseman Craig Worthington and batting champ Steve Finley (.314), who was the only full-season IL player to hit

In 1988 Toledo southpaw Steve Searcy (13-7 with 176 Ks in 170 IP) was the IL strikeout champ and co-victory leader, and was named the Most Valuable Pitcher in Triple-A Baseball. (courtesy Toledo Mud Hens)

over .300. Toledo southpaw Steve Searcy (13-7 with 176 Ks in 170 IP) was the strikeout champ and co-victory leader, along with Columbus righty Scott Nelson (13-6), who fired a nine-inning no-hitter against Maine.

Rochester defeated Tidewater, three games to one, to win the league championship. The handsome IL Governors' Cup was retired to a niche at Cooperstown (a new Cup would go to future playoff winners). In the first Alliance Classic, Rochester fell to Indianapolis, four games to two. Everyone was pleased with the Alliance experiment, and during the winter meetings it was agreed to continue the Alliance for three more years.

The Maine Guides finished last in 1986 and drew only 105,000 fans. Owner Jordan Kobritz realized that IL president Harold Cooper had been correct in predicting that Old Orchard Beach could not support a Triple-A team, but he hoped that a lower-level club could be maintained at The Ballpark. Kobritz negotiated a deal with NBI, a group working to bring Triple-A baseball to Scranton/Wilkes Barre. Lackawanna County Stadium was under construction, and NBI already owned Waterbury of the Double-A Eastern League. NBI offered Kobritz $2 million and Waterbury in exchange for the Maine franchise.

Rochester's 1988 Red Wings flourishing the Governors' Cup. (Courtesy Rochester Red Wings)

But when a question of territorial rights prohibited the transfer of the Eastern League club, Kobritz took legal action to keep the Guides in Old Orchard Beach. While a hotly contested court battle went on, the Guides stumbled to a seventh-place finish in 1987. Kobritz was unable to keep up payments on The Ballpark, and the courts decided in favor of NBI. But Lackawanna County Stadium still was unfinished, forcing NBI to conduct another losing, lame-duck season at Old Orchard Beach, before moving into their $22 million, 10,600-seat, state-of-the-art facility.

Although Scranton/Wilkes-Barre finished next-to-last in 1989, the Red Barons pulled 444,400 admissions into their magnificent new ballpark. Columbus again led the league with over 518,000, Richmond was second with 455,686, and only Toledo attracted fewer than 200,000. Total IL attendance soared to 2,613,247, establishing a new record (the old mark was 2,358,279, set in 1946).

For 1989 the IL and AA expanded their schedules from 142 to 146 games; there would be 102 league games and 44 interleague contests. This time the International League turned the tables on the American Association, winning the interleague competition 178-170. The Triple-A All-Star Game moved to the International League, and over 14,000 fans crowded into Harold M. Cooper Stadium in Columbus.

The 1989 batting champ was Columbus first baseman Hal Morris (.326). Syracuse took the title in the East, posting the divi-

In 1989 Rochester righthander Curt Schilling was the IL victory leader (13-11), and the next year the 23-year-old spent another half-season in the IL before moving up to major league stardom. (Courtesy Rochester Red Wings)

sion's only winning record. The Chiefs were led by home run champ Glen Hill (.321 with 21 homers), ERA titlist Jose Nunez (2.21 and 11-11 as a starter-reliever), and co-victory leader Alex Sanchez (13-7).

Richmond won a tight race in the West, then beat Syracuse, three games to one, to claim the new Governors' Cup. In the second Alliance Classic the Braves would face Indianapolis. The Indians had won four consecutive American Association championships, and Richmond fell in a four-game sweep. (Parent club Atlanta had announced the callup of 10 Richmond players, who would lose daily portions of the $68,000 big league minimum salary during postseason play, and who therefore entered the Alliance Classic demoralized over the pay they were about to lose.) But if the decade ended with disappointment on the field for the IL, attendance and overall prosperity showed every promise of continued growth.

Since 1977 Harold Cooper had presided over the International League with genial expertise, but after 13 years he retired from the IL offices at Grove City, outside Columbus. Cooper was succeeded by his longtime assistant, Randy A. Mobley. During baseball's Winter Meetings in December 1990, Mobley was confirmed as the twentieth president of the International League, as well as president of the American Association and commissioner of the Triple-A Alliance. During the 1990s Mobley provided sound leadership as streamlined new ballparks were opened across the league and as IL attendance soared to unprecedented levels.

In 1990 Columbus won the Western Division by eight games over Tidewater, while Rochester roared to the title in the East by a 21½-game margin over Scranton/Wilkes-Barre. Rochester and Columbus conducted a final playoff series, with the Red Wings prevailing, three games to two. But the IL again was frustrated in the Alliance Classic, as the Red Wings won just one game of five from Omaha.

Although Pawtucket had a losing record, PawSox fans cheered 21-year-old home run champ Phil Plantier (.259 with 33 homers), slugging first-sacker Mo Vaughn (.295 with 22 homers), who was out of the lineup for several weeks with a broken hand, and 34-year-old Rich Lancellotti (.223 with 20 homers), the active leader in minor league home runs.

For 1990 Columbus attendance increased to 591,340, Scranton/Wilkes-Barre jumped to 545,844, and the IL set another record with 2,832,518 admissions. But the very success enjoyed by the IL and other minor leagues brought trouble from an unexpected direction.

During the 1990 season, major and minor league owners locked horns over the Professional Baseball Agreement, which would expire January 12, 1991. The big leaguers were fully aware of recent minor league prosperity (upper-level franchises now were valued at $4 to $6 million), which was partially due to large subsidies by parent clubs for equipment, travel expenses, direct payments of estimated television revenue (up to $25,000 in Triple-A cities), and salaries. Triple-A teams have become taxi squads: an increasing number of talented players jump from Double-A to "The Show," but Triple-A rosters are stocked with veterans who might be called up several times per season to fill a temporary role for the parent club. Triple-A salaries often range as high as $30,000 per season, but only $200 monthly had to be provided by minor league clubs.

By 1990 major league teams were awarding million-dollar contracts to mediocre players, and multi-year, multi-million-dollar deals to more accomplished athletes. As major league economics escalated crazily, owners jealously contemplated the profit levels and growing independence of their minor league counterparts.

Major and minor league bargaining teams first met in July 1990. The big leaguers demanded almost total control over the minors, including league schedules, approval of franchise sales, transfers and expansion, an end to TV revenue payments, and authority of the major league commissioner over minor league affairs. Minor league owners were aghast, and finally walked away from the bargaining tables on October 24, 1990. The major leaguers announced a contingency plan which would organize all farm systems at spring training complexes in Florida and Arizona.

Faced with the dissolution of their leagues in favor of sterile complex baseball, many minor league owners complained of collusion and breach of contract, and threatened to bring anti-trust action against Major League Baseball. If complex baseball were adopted, it was contended that minor league players would become free agents, perhaps making it possible for the minors to return to the independently owned clubs of an earlier era. There was talk of organizing a third major league among the best minor league cities, with the rest of the minors providing farm systems.

The joint Winter Meetings were scheduled to be held the first week in December in

In 1991 Randy Mobley, administrative assistant to long-time IL president Harold Cooper (1978-1990), was elevated to league president. As of this writing Randy has served as president of the International League for 16 years, second only to the 23-year tenure of Frank Shaughnessy (1937-60). (Courtesy IL)

TIME OUT

But Will It Work?

Baseball players have always been notoriously superstitious, with little change as the game approached the twenty-first century. During 1990, for example, Pawtucket arrived in Oklahoma City on the heels of a five-game losing streak. Hoping for change of luck, the PawSox kept their batting practice jerseys on during the game, but the 89ers inflicted a sixth straight loss.

Syracuse enjoyed batter baseball magic. After losing 10 of 11 games at home, the Chiefs substituted "God Bless America" during pregame ceremonies for "The Star-Spangled Banner." The Chiefs won four straight, then after suffering a loss, Syracuse patriotically reinstated the National Anthem.

Los Angeles, but the major leaguers pulled out and conducted a separate meeting in Chicago. Negotiations were resumed, however, and there were long-distance talks during the simultaneous Winter Meetings. Major league owners unanimously approved a new Professional Baseball Agreement (PBA) that retained most of the original demands, and that required minor league clubs to send five percent of their revenues to their big league affiliates, beginning in 1992. Harold Cooper protested such "cheap" requirements, and many minor league owners were bitter over the seven-year PBA. But in the end there seemed to be no practical alternative, and reluctantly the minor leagues accepted. Ironically, the new PBA would increase costs to *both* major and minor league clubs, but at least the 1991 season could proceed as usual.

Columbus bolted to a 17-3 start and won the Western Division with the best record in the league, while Pawtucket outlasted a tight field in the East. Righthander Darrin Chapin provided Columbus starters with excellent relief (10-3 and a 1.95 ERA in 55 appearances), Clipper catcher John Ramos was a steady

The historic IL Governors' Cup, on display in the Richmond club offices during the summer of 1990. (Author photo)

hand at the plate (.308), and shortstop Jim Walewander led the league with 54 stolen bases. For the second year in a row, power in Pawtucket came from the bats of hot prospects Phil Plantier (.305 with 16 homers) and Mo Vaughn (.274 with 14 homers), and veteran slugger Rich Lancellotti (.209 with 21 homers), who hit 10 roundtrippers in the final month to win the home run crown.

Syracuse outfielder Derek Bell was voted MVP after leading the IL in batting, runs, RBIs, hits, and total bases (.346 with 93 RBIs). During the season, baseball fans enjoyed the play of two speedy outfielders who also were pro footballers: Deion Sanders (Richmond Braves/Atlanta Falcons) and D.J. Dozier (Tidewater Tides/Minnesota Vikings). On the last day of the season Tidewater shortstop Tim Bogar played all nine positions, and in Rochester infielder Shane Turner and Tommy Shields both played every position during the final game!

Attendance for 1991 exceeded three million, a new league record, led by another spectacular total from Columbus (606,371). In the playoffs Columbus executed a three-game sweep over Pawtucket to claim another Governors' Cup. But the Clippers could manage only one victory in five games against Denver in the Alliance Classic.

It was the fourth and final Alliance Classic. The Triple-A Alliance contract ran out after the 1991 season, and the increased travel expenses caused by the Professional Baseball Agreement rendered interleague play unprofitable. Furthermore, IL owners had determined to adapt as successfully as possible to the new conditions imposed by the PBA, while the American Association adamantly resisted the measure. The Triple-A Alliance was discontinued, and the American Association elected a president (Branch Rickey III) and moved their offices to Louisville.

In 1992 the Columbus Clippers stormed to their seemingly perennial place in the throne room, recording 95 victories in winning the Western Division, then executing a three-game sweep over Richmond in the opening round of playoffs. In the Eastern Division Scranton/Wilkes-Barre finished first and beat Pawtucket to face Columbus in the finals. The series went to the fifth and final game in Columbus. Trailing 3-1 in the bottom of the ninth, the Clippers staged a three-run rally to win a second consecutive pennant. The sixth playoff victory brought the Columbus win total for the year to 101.

Clipper first baseman J.T. Snow (.313) was the Most Valuable Player, while the 1990 MVP, Columbus slugger Hensley Meulens, was the 1992 home run and RBI leader. Outstanding pitching performances included a seven-inning, 1-0 perfect game by Richmond righthander Pete Smith; a nine-inning, 1-0 no-hitter by Tidewater righty Dave Telgheder; and a seven-inning, 2-0 no-hitter by Ben Rivera, a righthander who came down from the National League and started two games for Scranton/Wilkes-Barre (2-0 with a 0.00 ERA).

For 1993 the International League acquired expansion franchises in Ottawa and Charlotte, while Norfolk moved from old Metropolitan Park to a beautiful palace beside the sea, Harbor Park. Harbor Park averaged almost 8,000 fans per night, more than the capacity of their previous stadium, while six cities established all-time season attendance marks. Canada's capital city enthusiastically embraced the return of professional baseball, as the Ottawa Lynx played before home crowds totaling 693,043—a record-breaking number that erased the IL single-season

IL executives at the 1991 Winter Meetings. Standing L. to R.: Elliott Curwin, Rochester president; Gene Cooke, Toledo GM; Mike Tamburro, Pawtucket president; Dave Rosenfield, Tidewater GM and executive vice-president. Seated, L. to R.: Bill Terlecky, Scranton/Wilkes-Barre GM; Ken Schacke, Columbus GM; Randy Mobley, Il president; Bruce Baldwin, Richmond GM; Anthony "Tex" Simone, Syracuse GM and executive vice president. Not pictured: Joe Altobelli, Rochester GM, and Lou Schwechheimer, Pawtucket GM. (Courtesy IL)

mark set by Baltimore in the postwar boom year of 1946. International League admissions established an eye-popping new season total of more than 4.7 million.

In 1993 youthful prospect Chipper Jones hit .325 as Richmond's shortstop and was named Rookie of the Year. (Courtesy IL)

New to the IL, Charlotte battled to the pennant behind MVP third baseman Jim Thome (.372, 25 HR, 102 RBI), a future big league star who led the league in batting average and RBIs. Another Charlotte Knight slugger, Sam Horn, led the IL with 38 homers. For Syracuse Tim Brown twirled a seven-inning, 2-0 perfect game; Ottawa hurlers Chris Nabholz and Bruce Walton combined for a 4-0, nine-inning no-hitter; and in the opening game of a July 4 doubleheader, Scranton/Wilkes-Barre righthander Tyler Green pitched a 3-1, seven-inning no-hitter. Talented Richmond shortstop Chipper Jones fulfilled his enormous promise (.325) before moving up to stardom with the Atlanta Braves.

Future big league stars continued to dominate IL diamonds in 1994. MVP Syracuse outfielder Shawn Green led the league in hitting (.344) before a callup to Toronto. Green was joined on the IL All-Star Team by slick-fielding shortstop and Syracuse teammate Alex Gonzalez (.284) and by Charlotte outfielder Brian Giles (.313). Righthander Julian

In 1994 Pawtucket won the Western Division. (Courtesy IL)

Tavarez of Charlotte and Brad Woodall of Richmond were co-victory leaders with identical records (15-6), while Woodall also claimed the ERA title (2.42). Gifted righthander Jose Lima fired a 4-0, nine-inning no-hitter for Toledo, while Syracuse pitcher Felipe Lira tossed a 4-0, seven-inning no-hitter.

Pawtucket charged to a 23-7 start in 1994, then held on to win the Eastern Division. In the West Richmond trailed by several games through early August, then rallied for a 19-9 surge that brought a division title.

Late in the season, on August 12, the Major League Players Association called a strike which halted big league play and directed media attention to the IL and other quality minor league operations. ESPN and TBS gave national TV coverage to IL regular season games, and ESPN telecast the playoff finals—a three-game sweep of Syracuse by Richmond.

The MLPA strike was not settled during the off-season, and in the spring of 1995 there was constant turnover in IL rosters as big league clubs considered opening the year with replacement players. When a labor agreement finally was reached, an abbreviated 144-game schedule was launched in the big leagues. IL teams still bristled, therefore, with talented players on the cusp of major league careers.

For example, Columbus shortstop Derek Jeter starred in 123 Clipper games (.317 with a league-leading 96 runs) before finishing 1995 with the Yankees. Columbus righthander Mariano Rivera twirled a 3-0, five-inning no-hitter, then also went up to the Yankees. Big righthander Jason Schmidt secured the ERA title (8-6, 2.25) before leaving Richmond for Atlanta, while righty Jason Isringhausen had a brilliant half season with Norfolk (9-1 in 12 starts, 1.55 ERA) before pitching almost as well in the second half (9-2, 2.81 ERA) for the Mets. Robert Perez, a

hard-hitting outfielder for Syracuse in 1993 (.294) and 1994 (.304), won the 1995 batting title (.343), then finished the year with Toronto.

Ottawa won their first Governors' Cup in 1995, but the next year Columbus returned to the throne room, finishing the schedule 42-19, rolling through the playoffs under the skillful guidance of manager Stump Merrill. Batting champ Billy McMillon of Charlotte won the 1996 title with the highest average (.392) since Wade Boggs in 1981 (.353) and until the present—the best average in more than a quarter of a century. The 42 home runs slugged by Toledo MVP Phil Hiatt was the greatest total in half a century, since Rocky Nelson's 43 roundtrippers in 1958. And Pawtucket's 209 home runs were the highest team total since Baltimore's 232 homers in 1932.

Late in the 1994 season, during his third year as a pro, 23-year-old shortstop Derek Jeter played 35 games and hit.349. The next year he batted .317 in 123 games for Columbus, winning promotion to the New York Yankees. (Courtesy IL)

The 17 victories posted by Pawtucket righthander Brian Rose (17-5) in 1997 was the most since Craig McMurtry in 1982 (although in 1998 Shannon Withem won 17 games for Syracuse). Rose also won the 1997 ERA title, and he was named Rookie of the Year and Most Valuable Player. The most spectacular hitting feat of the '97 season was turned in by Toledo outfielder Bubba Trammell, who blasted four home runs in a 13-inning game on August 9 against Richmond. Rochester reeled off a 23-6 record in July and soared to their nineteenth IL pennant, then won their tenth Governors' Cup.

For 1998 the International League added four teams: Buffalo, Durham, Indianapolis, and Louisville. With the dissolution of the American Association, the eight AA franchises were split between the two remaining Triple-A leagues, the IL and the Pacific Coast League. Buffalo had spent 83 years in the International League until leaving professional baseball during the 1970 season. Long a mainstay of the American Association, Indianapolis had won the IL pennant in 1963, its only previous season in the International League. Durham and Louisville each were storied baseball cities, bringing rich traditions to the IL. With 14 teams the International League now boasted its largest membership in IL history, arranged in three divisions: North (six teams), South (four), and West (four). The revamped look of the IL in 1997 also included two splendid new ballparks, Frontier Field in Rochester and Alliance Bank Stadium in Syracuse.

On the field Norfolk infielder Todd Haney (.345) won the batting title, Charlotte slugger Brian Daubach was the home run (35) and RBI (124) king, Louisville second baseman Ron Belliard (.321, 114 R) scored the most runs, and Buffalo pitcher Jason Jacome (14-2) was the percentage leader. Indianapolis first baseman Roberto Petagine

was voted Most Valuable Player after belting 24 homers with 109 RBIs in only 102 games. Petagine had won the award in 1997 while playing for Norfolk, and became the only IL player to be voted MVP in consecutive seasons.

The 1998 playoffs would feature the three division winners and the team with the next-best record as a wild card. Buffalo, which had won the American Association playoffs in 1997, took the IL crown in the fifth game of the finals behind ace hurler Jason Jerome. The Bisons then advanced to the inaugural Triple-A World Series in Las Vegas, but Buffalo lost to the PCL champion New Orleans, three games to one. During their first season back in the International League, the Bisons played before 768,748 fans—a new IL record.

Versatile infielder-outfielder Roberto Petagine won back-to-back MVP awards in 1997 and 1998. With Norfolk in 1997 he hit .317 with a team record 31 homers and 100 RBIs. Despite playing only 102 games with Indianapolis in 1998, he hit .331 with 24 homers and 109 RBIs. (Courtesy IL)

The 1990s closed with an explosive offensive performance by Durham's MVP first baseman Steve Cox (.341, 49 2B, 125 RBI), who led the IL in batting, hits, runs, doubles, and RBIs. Buffalo third sacker Russell Branyan stroked one-fifth of his 30 home runs in just two games: on April 17 he blasted three homers in a game at Ottawa, and on July 22 he clubbed three more in a game at Indianapolis. The playoff finals were held in North Carolina, with Charlotte outlasting the Durham Bulls, but the Knights lost to PCL champion Vancouver in the Las Vegas Triple-A World Series. Overall, however, the International League had posted another fine season to cap an enormously successful decade.

In 1998 infielder Todd Haney, a veteran big leaguer, won the IL batting title (.345) while playing for Tidewater. (Courtesy Don Clinton)

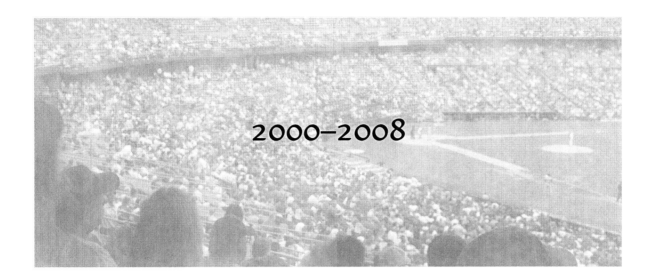

2000–2008

The opening of a new ballpark symbolized the successful beginning of the International League's third century of play. From the small wooden parks of the nineteenth century to the streamlined, modernistic stadiums of the contemporary IL, games that still would be recognizable to kranks of the 1880s now may be enjoyed by twenty-first century fans in palatial surroundings that would inspire awe among nineteenth century kranks.

Magnificent Louisville Slugger Field welcomed legions of RiverBats fans in 2000. With a seating capacity of 13,200, Louisville Slugger Field attracted a league-leading attendance total of 685,863.

On June 1, 2000, Pawtucket right-hander Tomo Ohka (9-6 before a call up to Boston) fired a nine-inning perfect game to defeat Charlotte, 2-0. The Japanese pitcher's classic was only the third nine-inning perfecto in IL history, and the first in nearly half a century. (Chester Carmichael hurled one for Buffalo in 1910, and Dick Marlowe pitched another one for Buffalo in 1992.)

Within a couple of weeks, on June 17, Leo Estrella of Syracuse tossed a seven-inning perfect game against Indianapolis. Two seven-inning no-hitters also were recorded in 2000; by Larry Luebbers of Louisville on May 14, and by Paxton Crawford of Pawtucket on July 18. Not since 1974 had four no-hitters been pitched—an impressive accomplishment in any season, but a special achievement in an age when starting pitchers rarely work complete games.

The Indianapolis Indians emerged atop the 2000 playoffs to claim their second IL pennant. The Indians beat Memphis, the PCL champs, to register the first IL victory in the Las Vegas Triple-A World Series. After the season, however, IL owners voted not to travel to Las Vegas in 2001, and the Series was indefinitely suspended.

In 2001 slugger Izzy Alcantara won the first of two consecutive home run crowns (36 for Pawtucket, then 27 for Indianapolis in 2002). Meanwhile, Colorado pitcher Brandon Knight recorded the second of two consecutive strikeout titles (138 in 2000 and 173 in 2001). Brandon Duckworth of Scranton/Wilkes-Barre was the pitching star of 2001 (13-2, 2.63 ERA), collecting the victory, ERA, and percentage crowns, along with designa-

Izzy Alcantara won back-to-back home run titles in 2001 (with Pawtucket) and 2002 (with Indianapolis). (Courtesy IL)

September 10, with the RiverBats winning by the margin of a bases-loaded walk, 2-1.

The following morning, September 11, the nation was staggered by a series of murderous terrorist attacks with passenger planes. IL President Randy Mobley cancelled the rest of the playoff series and declared Louisville, victors in the opening game of the finals, as winner of the 2001 Governors' Cup. With 6,757,150 admissions during 2001, the IL reached another attendance record.

Outfielder Raul Gonzalez starred for Louisville's 2001 championship club (.299), then elevated his game the next season (.335) and was voted 2002 MVP. The 2002 Rookie of the Year was 20-year-old outfielder Carl Crawford, a standout for Durham (.297) be-

Hard-hitting outfielder Raul Gonzalez (.299 in 2001 and .333 in 2002) led Louisville to the 2001 Governors' Cup, then was voted MVP in 2002. (Courtesy IL)

tion as Most Valuable Pitcher and Rookie of the Year.

During a three-game tune-up in the IL with Norfolk, major league veteran Steve Trachsel (2-0) twirled a seven-inning no-hitter, defeating Ottawa 3-0 on May 27 before returning to the Mets. MVP catcher Toby Hall played 93 games with Durham, enough to earn the 2001 batting championship (.335), before catching 47 games for Tampa Bay (.298).

Buffalo, Louisville, and Norfolk dominated their respective divisions, while Scranton/Wilkes-Barre earned the wild card slot for the 2001 playoffs. Each opening round went all five games, with the RiverBats shutting out the Tides in their deciding contest, while the Red Barons outlasted the Bulls in a 19-inning finale. Scranton/Wilkes-Barre and Louisville began play for the Governors' Cup on

The Most Valuable Pitcher of 2002 was Joe Roa of Scranton/Wilkes-Barre. Sensational in 17 starts (14-0, 1.86 ERA), Roa was promoted to the Phillies after midseason. (Courtesy IL)

fore winning promotion to Tampa Bay. Ottawa outfielder Endy Chavez won the batting title (.343), while RBI champ Kevin Witt drove in 107 runs for Louisville.

Righthander Joe Roa was brilliant in 17 starts for Scranton/Wilkes-Barre (14-0, 1.86 ERA) before being called up to Philadelphia. Roa and Alan Newman (10-0 with Durham in 1999) are the only two pitchers in IL history to post a perfect record in at least 10 decisions.

The Mud Hens opened a new stadium, Fifth Third Field, in downtown Toledo in 2002. Celebrating with their first winning record in more than a decade, the Mud Hens won a West Division title and presented their loyal fans with Toledo's first playoff appearance in 19 seasons.

But Toledo's year was ended by the Durham Bulls. Winners of the South Division, the Bulls made memorable their 100th anniversary in pro baseball. A three-game sweep

The 2003 IL All-Stars defeated the PCL All-Stars, 13-9, in the Triple-A All-Star Game at AutoZone Park in Memphis. (Courtesy IL)

over Toledo in the playoff opener led to another sweep over Buffalo in the finals, with a 2-0 shutout in the third game giving Durham its first Governors' Cup since joining the IL in 1998.

The Bulls made it two in a row the next year. Durham repeated as South Division champs, lost their opening playoff game to Louisville, then won three straight from the RiverBats. Now on another playoff roll, the Bulls swept Pawtucket in the finals to keep the Governors' Cup for another year.

The 2003 MVP was Fernando Seguignol, a first baseman and DH for Columbus who win the hitting and home run titles (.341 with 28 HR). Second baseman Chase Utley (.323) had an All-Star season for Scranton/Wilkes-Barre, and so did Richmond catcher Johnny Estrada (.328). Norfolk's Esix Snead won the first of three consecutive stolen base crowns (61 in 2003, 40 in 2004, and 46 for Richmond in 2005). Two other Richmond players, Len Johnston (1856-1957-1958) and Ed Miller (1978-1979-1980) have won back-to-back-to-back stolen base titles in the IL.

On August 10, 2003, 6'5" righthander Bronson Arroyo became the fourth IL pitcher to hurl a nine-inning no-hitter, beating Buffalo 7-0. A fine season for Pawtucket (12-6) brought Arroyo the IL's Most Valuable Player Award and a promotion to Boston where he became a fixture in the Red Sox rotation.

Excellent pitching performances continued the next season. On August 1, 2004, Charlotte hurler Tetsu Yofu worked a nine-inning no-hitter, defeating Durham 5-0. Robert "Bull" Ellis, a 6'5" righthander who was in the Diamondback rotation in 2001 during Arizona's world championship season, threw a seven-inning no-hitter on June 6, 2004, as Scranton/Wilkes-Barre edged Louisville, 1-0, with Mike Smith's home run the only hit of a classic pitcher's duel. Although Indianapolis suffered a losing season in 2004, righthander

Ben Hendrickson pitched superbly (11-3, 2.02 ERA) earning the ERA crown, Pitcher of the Year honors, the IL starting assignment in the Triple-A All-Star Game, and a mid-year callup to the parent Milwaukee Brewers. Richmond reliever Matt Whiteside set an IL record with 38 saves.

Toledo slugger Marcus Thames blasted three home runs in a game on April 25; Jet Borchard clubbed three homers for Charlotte on May 23; and on August 17 Buffalo outfielder Ryan Kudwick ripped three roundtrippers, including two in one inning. Rookie of the Year Jason Kubel led the IL in batting (.343) while roaming Rochester's outfield, and Buffalo shortstop Jhonny Peralta (.326) was named Most Valuable Player.

Tall righthander Robert "Bull" Ellis, pitching for Scranton/Wilkes-Barre on June 6, 2004, twirled a seven-inning, 1-0, no-hitter—the last IL no-hitter as of this writing. (Courtesy Robert Ellis)

MVP Peralta and slugger Ryan Ludwick led a potent Buffalo lineup that included infielder Brandon Phillips (.303), outfielders Grady Sizemore (.287) and Franklin Gutierrez (.287), Chris Clapinski (.312), and All-Star DH Ernie Young (27 HR, 100 RBI). The Bisons posted a team average of .297—the highest since Newark in 1938—and led the IL in hits, runs, doubles, runs, and RBIs. Steady righthander Kyle Denney (10-5) led the pitching staff. After a slow start, Manager of the Year Marty Brown guided the Bisons to a 59-29 finish (.670) and a 10-game margin over the North Division. Buffalo then came from behind in both playoff series, defeating Durham and Columbus to win the Governors' Cup.

Three times in 2004 IL sluggers blasted three home runs in a single game, but in 2005 the feat was accomplished four times. On May 1 Mud Hen Jack Hannahan ripped three homers; on June 2 Bison Dusty Wathan hit three; on July 5 Austin Kearns clubbed three for Louisville; and 10 days later Chase Lambin sent three out for Tidewater. Pawtucket's All-

Star catcher, Kelly Shoppach, hit two of his 26 homers in a single inning on April 23.

On April 15 Mitch Jones of Columbus hit a homer, then a triple, double and single to complete a cycle in reverse. On May 14 Toledo's Dewayne Wise blasted a grand slam in the first inning, then collected the other hits for a cycle. Toledo's Ramon Martinez banged out six singles in an April 26 game, while Richmond's Bill McCarthy went six-for-six with two doubles and a homer on May 14. In a season with explosive offense, All-Star pitcher Zach Duke (12-3) was impressive with Indianapolis, and another Indian hurler, Ian Snell, fired a nine-inning no-hitter on May 15 against Norfolk.

Toledo, a perennial loser throughout most of its history, struggled to the IL's worst record in 2004. But in 2005 Manager of the Year Larry Parrish led the Mud Hens to the West Division title with the best season record (89-55) in Triple-A. The Mud Hens prevailed in a five-game opening series against powerful Norfolk, then won the Governors' Cup

IL President Randy Mobley and Administrative Assistant Chris Sprague with the Governors' Cup at the league offices in Dublin, Ohio. Randy and Chris provided the author invaluable assistance with the creation of this book. (Photo by Karon O'Neal)

with a three-game sweep over Indianapolis. Toledo had not won a league championship in 38 years, and the worst-to-first leap was the IL's first in 41 seasons, and only the seventh in the long history of the International League.

Toledo's taste of success propelled the Mud Hens to another championship season in 2006 behind first sacker Josh Phelps (.308, 24 HR, 90 RBI). Trailing Rochester two games to one in the finals, Toledo won a 6-0 shutout in Game Four, then exploded for four home runs to crush the Red Wings, 4-1, in Game Five. The once-hapless Mud Hens had won their second consecutive Governors' Cup.

The 2006 batting champ was Louisville outfielder Norris Hopper (.347), and the MVP and home run leader was Durham first baseman Kevin Witt (.291, 36 HR, 99 RBI). Charlotte boasted the league's most formidable pitching duo, Charlie Haeger (14-6) and Heath Phillips (13-5). The ERA titlist was Scranton/Wilkes-Barre ace Brian Mazone (13-3, 2.03 ERA).

The International League and Pacific Coast League had not engaged in a post season playoff since 2000, when Indianapolis defeated Memphis in the third—and final—Las Vegas Triple-A World Series. But for 2006 the IL and PCL agreed to a "Winner-Takes-All Championship Game" at Oklahoma City's AT&T Bricktown Ballpark. The "Bricktown Showdown" featured a near-sellout crowd of 12,572 and a national TV audience. The Tucson Sidewinders of the PCL surged to a last-inning, 5-2 victory over Toledo. The Bricktown Showdown was on exciting success, and soon the league presidents, Randy Mobley and Branch Rickey, announced that the championship game would be repeated in 2007 and 2008.

The opening of the 2007 season was plagued by miserable weather. Drenching rain and heavy snowfalls devastated the schedule, forcing a succession of postpone-

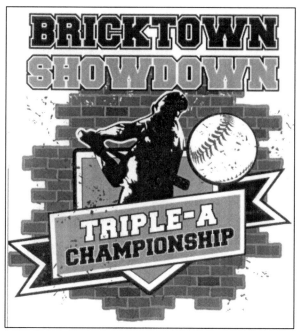

Bricktown Showdown logo. (Courtesy IL)

ments, while other games were played in marginal weather with marginal crowds. Following this turbulent start, however, the rest of the season—including makeup games—fell into place. Although Ottawa pulled a total attendance of only 125,894, Indianapolis increased attendance ten percent, and Louisville led the league with 635,915—an average of 9,210 fans per game.

A few weeks into the season, on May 1, Columbus outfielder Brandon Watson singled in the fifth inning of a game against Rochester. From this innocent beginning, Watson hit safely in 43 straight games, breaking the IL record of 42 consecutive games set by Jack Lelivelt of Rochester in 1912.

Buffalo outfielder Ben Francisco (.318 in 95 games) won the batting title, while Toledo third sacker Mike Hessman (.254, 31 HR, 101 RBI) led the league in homers and RBIs.

Hessman, outfielder Timo Perez (.309), and hurlers Virgil Vasquez (12-5 with two shutouts) and Ron Chiavecci (12-6) led

TIME OUT

King of Baseball

Beginning in 1951, an annual award has been given for lengthy service and dedication to an executive who is crowned "King of Baseball." Two years later the distinguished president of the International League, Frank "Shag" Shaughnessy, was proclaimed King of Baseball. Shag began a four-decade association with the International League in 1921 when he was 38. With a background as a pennant-winning player—manager in the minor league, Shag spent four seasons managing Syracuse, then took over the reins at Providence and at Reading. He became GM at Montreal in 1932, soon implementing the post-season playoff plan that would be adopted throughout the minor leagues. As field manager Shag led Montreal to the IL pennant in 1935, but a year later he was elected league president, serving with distinction until 1960.

George Sisler, Jr., served as GM of Rochester for 11 seasons, was president of the IL from 1966 through 1976, and was general manager of Columbus until retiring in 1989. Three times Sisler was voted Triple-A Executive of the Year, and in 1989 he was coroneted King of Baseball.

Max Schumacher, president of the Indianapolis Indians, has devoted his talents to the Indians for more than half a century, and *Baseball America* named Indianapolis the Triple-A Team of the 1990s. Fittingly, in 1997, at the end of his 41st year of service to the Indians, Schumacher was presented the crown and robes of the King of Baseball.

Dave Rosenfield's career as a baseball executive spans half a century, including 45 with the Norfolk Tides. As GM Rosenfield engineered Norfolk's elevation to Triple-A and membership in the IL in 1969, and he supervised the construction of two stadiums. It was very much in the tradition of International League super-executives that Rosenfield was crowned King of Baseball in 2004.

Toledo to another division championship in the West. Scranton/Wilkes-Barre was sparked to the North title by Brandon Watson and outfielder Shelley Duncan (.295 with 25 homers). In the South, Durham and Richmond battled throughout the season for first place. Led by batting champ Ben Francisco and pitchers Mitch Talbot (13-9) and Jeff Niemann (12-6), Durham won the division, while Richmond took the Wild Card slot behind second baseman Martin Prado (.316), shortstop Yunel Escobar (.333), outfielder Brandon Jones (.300), and relief pitchers Manny Acosta (9-3, 2.26 ERA) and Buddy Hernandez (9-3, 3.13).

Durham and Richmond defeated Toledo and Scranton-Wilkes-Barre, respectively, in the opening round of playoffs, then prepared

In May and June of 2007, Columbus outfielder Brandon Watson hit safely in 43 consecutive games, breaking the old record of 42, set by Jack Lelivelt of Rochester in 1912. (Courtesy IL)

to resume their season-long competition. The best-of-five Governors' Cup Series was scheduled for Tuesday through Saturday, September 11-15. On Tuesday and Wednesday the two teams won a game apiece in Durham. The first game in Richmond, on Thursday, was won by Durham, but Friday's contest was rained out, setting up a Saturday doubleheader. With their backs to the wall, the Richmond Braves rallied in front of their home fans, winning the afternoon game, 6-2, then claiming the Governors' Cup with a 7-1 triumph on Saturday night.

While the Braves headed to Oklahoma City for the second Bricktown Showdown on Tuesday, Brandon Jones—who had starred in the playoffs—was whisked to the parent club, starting for the Atlanta Braves on Sunday and Monday. Jones then was flown to Oklahoma City to rejoin Richmond for the Showdown, which was nationally televised over ESPN. Perhaps Jones and his teammates were spent by their all-out efforts in the playoffs, because Sacramento dominated the game, scoring five runs on a pair of homers in the third and marching to a 7-1 victory. But IL President Randy Mobley and PCL President Branch Rickey, Jr., were interviewed over nationwide

TV, and the evening proved to be an opportune showcase for the highest level of minor league baseball.

The 2008 season would feature a celebration of the 125th anniversary of International League baseball. A significant facet of the commemoration was the revival of the IL Hall

Baseball fans long have enjoyed staging weddings in minor league parks. Baseball weddings have been held in many IL parks, including this ceremony in front of Ottawa's pitching mound. (Courtesy IL)

A popular feature of baseball weddings calls for the newlyweds to pass beneath a line of crossed bats. (Courtesy IL)

of Fame, with an induction ceremony to be held at each stadium in the League. A traveling exhibit was organized to bring to each ballpark the original and current Governors' Cup trophies, the IL Hall of Fame plaques, and various other artifacts. A media series titled "This Day in International League History" was distributed to be run on radio and TV broadcasts, in IL ballparks, and on websites. Auctions for autographed commemorative items were scheduled, while fans were given the opportunity to engage in on-line contests related to the IL history. And this book was commissioned for distribution during the 125th season.

A major change for 2008 was the transfer of Ottawa's franchise to Allentown, Pennsylvania. Ottawa fielded a team in the IL for a total of twenty seasons, but declining attendance could not sustain AAA baseball. Allentown was a charter member of the IL in 1884, but the last professional baseball franchise left town following the 1960 season.

After nearly half a century without pro baseball, state funding for stadiums made it possible to build a new ballpark. The Ottawa Lynx were affiliated with the Philadelphia Phillies, and Allentown—a short drive to the north—was a natural site for the Phils' AAA club.

With the loss of Ottawa—the sixth Canadian city to hold an IL franchise—all fourteen "International" League cities were in the United States. But it is fitting in the 125th year of the IL that a charter city, Allentown, has returned to the league. Richmond also is a charter member, and the other twelve cities boast rich histories in professional baseball. Rochester missed the inaugural season of the IL, joined the league in 1885, then missed three seasons during the 1890s—and none since, participating in 121 of the 125 years. Buffalo and Syracuse each have fielded teams in 94 IL seasons. The International League enters its 125th season with a unique past in baseball and enormous promise for the future.

International League executives at IL meeting on September 18, 2007. Top row, L. to R.: Dan Mason, Rochester GM; Dan Rajkowski, Charlotte VP/GM; Mike Buczkowski, Buffalo VP/GM; Lou Schwechheimer, Pawtucket Executive VP/GM; John Simone, Syracuse GM; Jeremy Ruby, Scranton/Wilkes-Barre Executive VP/COO. Middle row: Bruce Baldwin, Richmond GM; Ken Young, Norfolk President; Gary Ulmer, Louisville President; Joe Napoli, Toledo VP/GM; Joe Finley, Lehigh Valley Co-owner; Craig Stein, Lehigh Co-owner. Bottom row: Cal Burleson, Indianapolis VP/GM; Max Schumacher, Indianapolis President; Randy Mobley, IL President; Dave Rosenfield Norfolk GM; Ken Schnacke, Columbus President/GM; Mike Birling, Durham GM. Not pictured: Mike Tamburro, Pawtucket President; Tex Simone, Syracuse Executive VP/COO. (Courtesy IL)

Nicknames

When 19-year-old George Herman Ruth was signed out of a Baltimore reform school by Jack Dunn, the raw youth was called "Dunnie's Babe," giving birth to baseball's most famous nickname. Also regarded as mere boys by older veterans were "Babe" Dahlgren, "Kid" Foster, and "Kid" Keenan. A more mature demeanor was suggested by "Pop" Foster, "Pop" Joiner, "Pop" Prim, "Dad" Lytle, and "Uncle Bill" Alvord.

For more than a century the most common nickname among IL players has been derived from striking hair color. The roster of carrot-topped International Leaguers has included "Red" Schoendienst, "Red" Howell, "Red" Killefer, "Red" Hardy, "Red" Oldham, "Red" McKee, "Red" Smythe, "Red" Stallcup, "Red" Embree, "Red" Shea, "Red" Lynn, "Red" Adams, "Red" Wingo, "Red" Davis and "Red" Worthington. Variations included "Brick" Eldred, "Rosy" Ryan, and "Reddie" Grey, the older brother of western novelist Zane Grey. "Sandy" Griffin also was labeled because of the color of his hair, and so were "Whitey" Kurowski, "Whitey" Moore and "Whitey" Konikowsky.

Other physical characteristics branded "Curly" Ogden, "Fat Bob" Fothergill, "Heavy" Blair, "Baldy" Rudolph, John "Ugly" Dickshot, and Nick "Tomato Face" Cullop. "Wee Willie" Keeler stood only 5'4½", and his contemporary, "Wee Willie" Clarke, also had a diminutive physique. Bigger, stronger players included Walter "Jumbo" Brown, "Big Boy" Kraft, "Big Ed" Klepfer, "Big Ed" Stevens, "Big Bill" Dinneen, "Big Bill" Massey, and "Bull" Ellis. Carmen "Specs" Hill was the first professional pitcher to wear glasses, and "Specs" Toporcer and "Specs" Kliemann also used spectacles before the practice became commonplace. Notable items of dress also led to descriptive nicknames, as exemplified by "Socks" Perry, "Socks" Siebold, "Boots" Day, George "High Pockets" Kelly, Bill "High Pockets" Lawrence, and Harry "The Hat" Walker.

Playing styles resulted in numerous nicknames. Frank "Beauty" McGowan often made beautiful plays while roaming center field. Already famous for pitching doubleheaders and for leading the National League in games and innings, "Iron Man" Joe McGinnity more than lived up to his sobriquet in the IL, pacing the circuit in victories, games, and innings two years in a row (422 and 408), when he was 38 and 39. Allen "Rubberarm" Russell was the 1915 strikeout champ, while other fastball pitchers included the 1928 strikeout leader, "Gunner" Antrell, the 1941 leader, Virgil "Fire" Trucks, and "Mercury" Myatt, "Cannonball" Crane, and "Cannonball" Titcomb. On the other hand, Walter "Boom Boom" Beck was notorious for giving up home runs. Control problems plagued "Wild Bill" Hallahan, "Wild Bill" Donovan, and "Wild Bill" Piercy, and John "Duster" Mails frequently sent batters sprawling in the dirt with inside pitches. Frank "Herky-Jerky" Horton had a disjointed delivery, Ewell "The Whip" Blackwell had a devastating sidearm motion, "Ace" Elliott had his moments as a stopper, and scores of southpaw hurlers included "Lefty" Grove, "Lefty" Davis, and "Lefty" Marr.

"Rip" Jordan could bust a fastball past opposing hitters, but "Rip" Russell regularly ripped opposing pitchers for extra-base hits and "Rip" Collins ripped the first home run out if Rochester's Red Wing Stadium. "Wagon Tongue" Keister wielded a heavy bat, and other sluggers were "Boomer" Wells, H. H. "Hard-hitting" Smith, "Wildfire" Schultz, "Rocky" Nelson, "Bam Bam" Hensley Meulens, and "Hammerin' Hank" Sauer. "Deerfoot" Barclay was a fleet runner, but "Turkeyfoot" Brower rarely tested a good throwing arm.

Veteran barnstormers in the off-season included "Globetrotter" Earle and Clarence "Choo Choo" Coleman, while Harry "Suitcase" Simpson and "Suitcase" Bob Seeds went from team to team with transient regularity. Less exotic transportation was suggested by Fay "Scow" Thomas, who was decidedly overmatched by "Battleship" Greminger.

Personality traits often led to descriptive appellations, as in the case of firebrand players "Sparky" Anderson, "Pepper" Martin, and "Pep" Young. A happy demeanor identified "Sunny" Jim Bottomley, "Sunny" Jim Dygert, "Hap" Myers, "Happy" Finneran, and "Happy" Harnett. Other identifiable traits singled out Lew "Noisy" Flick, George "Showboat" Fisher, "Stuffy" Stewart, catcher "Rough" Carrigan, feisty "Bad Bill" Egan, and "Whisperin' Bill" Barrett. Free Spirits included "Dizzy" Carlyle, "Cuckoo" Jamieson, and Willie "Puddinhead" Jones. The insensitive humor of the 1890s permanently branded deaf-mute Luther Taylor "Dummy," while gullible rookies included "Green" Osborne, "Rube" Kisinger, and "Rube" Sutor.

Becoming one of America's most famous evangelists, Billy "Parson" Sunday spent years as a professional outfielder. "Deacon" Jones, "Parson" Nicholson, "Preacher" Hebert, and "Preacher" Fasholz also held strong religious beliefs. But like many other players, the intensely competitive pitcher, "Preacher" Roe, received a tongue-in-cheek nickname which suggested opposite traits.

During the early decades of professional baseball, players who had acquired a smattering of education or who preferred reading as a pastime were called "Doc": "Doc" Carney, "Doc" Casey, "Doc" Adler, "Doc" Crandall, "Doc" Farrell, "Doc" Hoblitzel, "Doc" Kennedy, "Doc" Leggett, and "Doc" Smoot. But Baltimore pitcher Merle Theron "Doc" Adkins had a genuine interest in medicine and studied at Johns Hopkins University during the off-seasons. He received an M.D. in 1907—and continued to pitch for years!

Culinary preferences labeled "Pretzels" Pezullo, "Rawmeat" Bill Rodgers, "Buttermilk" Tommy Dowd, and "Sugar" Kane. Geographical origins determined the nicknames of Massachusetts native "Harvard" Eddie Grant, Californian "Death Valley" Scott, "Tex" Erwin, and Southerners "Dixie" Walker, "Rebel" McTigue, and Travis "Stonewall" Jackson.

Forrest "Woody" Jensen and "Woody" Williams were leery of "Matches" Kilroy and Steve "Smokey" Sundra. In the IL forest was an impressive menagerie: "Moose" McCormick, "Foxy" Bannon, "Mule" Shirley, "Rabbitt" Whitman, "Bunny" Fabrique, "Bunny" Hearne, "Kitty" Bransfield, Fred "Bear" Hutchinson, George "Mouse" Earnshaw, "Sparrow" McCaffrey, "Grasshopper" Mains, curveballer "Snake" Wiltse, "Chick" Hafey, "Piggy" Ward, "Chicken" Wolf, Emmit "The Great Dane" Nelson, and Cliff "Mickey Mouse" Melton.

IL officialdom included "Sheriff" Blake, "Sheriff" Robinson, "General" Stafford, "Chief" Koy, "Count" Charles Campau, "Duke" Snider, "Duke" Carmel, Paul "Duke" Derringer, and "King" Bader. Ethnic backgrounds identified "Dutch" Henry, "Dutch" Lieber, "Heinie" Batch, "Heinie" Smith, Lou "The Mad Russian" Novikoff, and Pete "The Polish Wizard" Jablonowski.

During the early years of World War I, Wallace Schultz pitched for the Providence Grays. Like many other Americans of German heritage, he avidly supported the Fatherland, at least until American entry into the war in 1917. Schultz boasted that Germany could beat all other European countries combined, but when newspapers reported that 75,000 Germans had been killed in France, his teammates smothered him with dozens of copies of the story. Although other players normally called him "Toots," Schultz was immediately rechristened "Kaiser."

Double nicknames were not uncommon among players of the International League: "Dandy" Dave Danforth, for example, also became known as "Dauntless" Dave, and speedy outfielder Maurice Archdeacon was called "Flash" as often as "Mercury." And almost everyone, it sometimes seemed, was assigned at least one sobriquet: "Derby Day" Bill Clymer, "Oil Can" Boyd, Joe "Poison" Brown, Leon "Caddy" Cadore, "Oyster" Burns, "Snuffy" Stirnweiss, "Dasher" Troy, "Slicker" Parks, "Wiggles" Porter, "Buttercup" Dickerson, Luke "Hot Potato" Hamlin, "Cowboy" Ed Tomlin, "Shovels" Kobesky, "Buttons" Briggs, "Farmer" Brown, "Ward Six" Bannon, Weiser "Wheezer" Dell, "Ziggy" Sears, "Cozy" Dolan, "Snooks" Dowd, "Sport" McAlister, John "Black Jack" Wilson, "Jocko" Conlan, "Jocko" Halligan, "Cupid" Childs, and "Bunions" Zeider.

Throughout baseball history countless bench jockeys and leather-lunged fans, as well as sportswriters and broadcasters in search of a touch of color, have produced a wealth of cleverly descriptive or insulting nicknames. There is no richer collection of these personal labels than that accumulated during the 125 years of IL play.

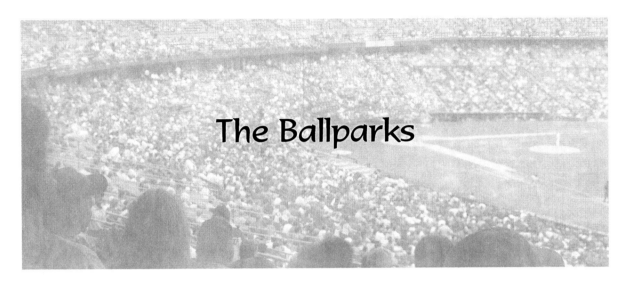

The Ballparks

"When I think of Pilot Field, I think of a baseball place in the heart of Buffalo. It's like what they talk about in baseball as a mystical kind of experience; a patch of green in the middle of a city where you can withdraw and your cares go away."

BOB RICH, JR.
Buffalo Bisons President

Baseball stadiums are the only athletic facilities called "parks." The national pastime is still that, a pastime, which intersperses moments of brilliant individual plays with time to relax and contemplate player shifts on the field, anticipated developments such as a tiring pitcher or a sacrifice bunt, and similar nuances of the game. The leisurely pace of baseball is in direct contrast to the fanatical violence of football and the frenetic pace of basketball. A major part of the seductive attraction of baseball is following the home team through a long season, becoming familiar with each player, enjoying the camaraderie of fellow fans—all at a friendly park which becomes a home away from home during six months of scheduled play.

During the early years of the IL, baseball was played at "grounds." These grounds featured wooden, roofed grandstands, with plank bleachers down the foul lines and plank fences around the outfield. Outfield distances were vast: Rochester's Bay Street Park boasted such an expansive outfield that horse-drawn carriages and automobiles could park inside the fences; and Springfield's Hampden Park had no fences until 1908, and then the center field distance was 500 feet with power alleys of 450 feet. Of course, this was the era of dead balls and thick bats, when home runs were rare and usually inside-the-park shots. Since it was difficult to hit the ball over even a close fence, a big outfield was desirable in order to attract overflow crows for weekend games and holiday double-headers.

Seating capacities were small, but no one was turned away. Extra fans stood down the foul lines and were packed in behind roped-off areas in front of the outfield fences. There was little room to catch foul flies, and long hits that bounded into the outfield crowds were ground-rule doubles.

107

Rochester's Culver Field burned in 1892. Although the ballpark was rebuilt five years later, in 1906 the right field stands collapsed during a game, triggering numerous lawsuits from injured patrons. Olympic Park in Buffalo burned in 1898, the Toronto park at Hanlon's Point was consumed by flames in 1909, and Baltimore's Oriole Park was leveled in a 1944 blaze. MacArthur Stadium in Syracuse suffered

The IL's most venerable ballpark opened in 1932 as Red Bird Stadium. But in 1984 the 15,000-seat facility underwent a multi-million dollar renovation and was renamed Harold M. Cooper Stadium. In 2009 the historic ballpark will be replaced by Huntington Park.

a fire in 1969 which destroyed the stands directly behind home plate. This gap remained for several years, until the grandstand was completely rebuilt. Harrisburg's Island Park in the Susquehanna River and Richmond's Mayo Island Park in the James River suffered damage on several occasions because of flooding. After Mayo Island Park burned in 1941, owner Eddie Mooers purchased a more favorable site and built Mooers Field.

Richmond fans first went through turnstiles in 1915 at the Broad Street Park. An earlier innovation was the first Ladies' Day, on June 10, 1885, at the Hop Bitters Grounds in Rochester. Lights were in-

Built in 1928, Montreal Stadium (also known as Delorimier Downs and Hector Racine Stadium, seated nearly 18,000. The right field line was just 295 feet from home plate. (Courtesy Bibliotheque Centrale de Montreal)

Buffalo's splendid Pilot Field opened in 1988 and attracted a record minor league attendance totaling 1,147,651. (Courtesy Buffalo Bisons)

Grandstand at Buffalo's renamed Dunn Tire Park. (Photo by Karon O'Neal)

stalled at Buffalo's Bison Stadium in 1930. The first International League night game was played on July 3 in Buffalo, but before the end of the season four more teams were playing under the lights, and soon every IL city would stage night games.

Most ballparks built during the first few decades of IL play were located alongside a trolley line to facilitate mass transit. Then as now, outfield fences were decorated with advertising, and at virtually every professional ballpark during the early 1900s the American Tobacco Company—manufacturers of Bull Durham Tobacco—erected a sign promising that any player who hit a ball against the sign would receive $25. At Royals Stadium in Montreal, Pal Razor Blades cut a hole in their sign and offered a two-year supply of razor blades to any hitter who knocked a ball through the hole. The most unusual outfield feature at any IL ballpark was the four-foot Plexiglass addition atop the fence at Havana's Gran Stadium. Because of the volatility of Latin fans and players, the Plexiglass was added to keep angry outfielders from climbing into the stands!

Numerous football stadiums have been used, at least briefly, for IL games. The all-time attendance record (57,313) was set in Miami on August 7, 1950, when Bill Veeck rented the Orange Bowl and staged one of his most colorful promotional efforts. Baltimore's Memorial Stadium was renovated from a football facility for baseball after Oriole Park burned in 1944. War Memorial Stadium was built for football in Buffalo by the WPA during the Depression, but in 1961 "The Old Rockpile" became the home of Bison baseball. Left-handed sluggers salivated over the short right field, but a tall screen soon eliminated cheap homers. (War Memorial Stadium was the cinematic home of the New York Knights in Robert Redford's 1983 movie, *The Natural*.) From 1951 through 1954, the Ottawa Athletics of the International League played in Landsdowne Stadium, home of Canadian football. When used for baseball, Landsdowne Stadium had a short right field (and during the 1930s a ball hit over the left fielder's head would roll indefinitely, generating numerous inside-the-park homers until a fence was erected across the field).

Most early ballparks were built by owners with a background in business. These men, involved in manufacturing and construction, built baseball facilities with the no-nonsense features of their warehouses: sturdy, no frills, and with steel girders for roof supports.

"I Got It" statuary at left field at Toledo's Fifth Third Field. (Author photo)

Miami Stadium, constructed in 1949 and the home of IL baseball from 1956 through 1960, was notable for its high, cantilevered grandstand roof which required no support beams and therefore offered unobstructed vision for every fan.

Such improvements began to be incorporated into new International League ballparks, and by the 1980s the IL boasted a growing number of streamlined facilities that appealed to fans as family entertainment centers. In 1989 the Scranton/Wilkes-Barre Red Barons began playing in "The Lack"—Lackawanna County's $22 million, 10,600-seat Multi-Purpose Stadium located in a breath-taking mountain setting. The Tides moved into splendid Harbor Park in 1993, and fans could watch ships come and go just beyond the outfield fence. That same year Charlotte joined the International League, hosting IL games in handsome Knights Stadium, built in 1990 outside of the city and across the state line in South Carolina. In 1997 two longtime IL neighbors, Rochester and Syracuse, moved into excellent new ballparks, Frontier Field and P&C Stadium (now Alliance Bank Stadium).

With the dissolution of the American Association in 1998, Buffalo rejoined the International League, playing in state-of-the-art, 19,500-seat Pilot Field, which had been erected in 1989 with the hope of being expanded into a major league stadium. Also moving over from the American Association for 1998 were Indianapolis and Louisville: the Indians played in a superb stadium, two-year-old Victory Field; in 2000 Louisville built palatial Louisville Slugger Field. Durham moved up in classification to the IL in 1998, playing downtown in magnificent, three-year-old Durham Bulls Athletic Park.

The newest stadium in the International League is a grand palace, Fifth Third Field, which has rejuvenated downtown Toledo. In

2008 Allentown will open IL play in Coca Cola Park, under construction as of this writing, and the first stadium in the United States to be sponsored by the world-famous corporation. Other new stadiums are being planned for Richmond, even though the Diamond is only a little more than twenty years old, and for Charlotte, which intends to move downtown, even though Knights Stadium was built in 1990. The league's oldest ballpark is Cooper Stadium in Columbus, built in 1932. Although handsomely renovated, Cooper Stadium will be replaced by a downtown facility, Huntington Park, in 2009.

Every International League stadium boasts luxury boxes, giant electronic scoreboards, food courts and restaurants, and an imaginative variety of other fan-friendly features. International League games are staged in a collection of ballparks unsurpassed in the world of minor league baseball.

Alliance Bank Stadium, home of the Syracuse Chiefs, is the only IL ballpark with artificial turf. (Author photo)

Seating outside luxury box at Durham Bulls Athletic Park. (Author photo)

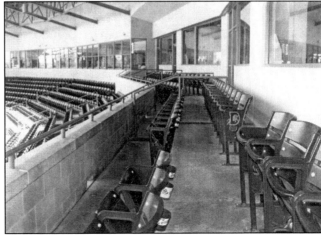

International League
Hall of Fame

With minor league baseball at a peak of popularity in 1947, the International League Baseball Writers Association decided to establish a Hall of Fame for players, managers, or umpires who had excelled in the storied IL. Impressive lifetime records had been set in the IL by solid players who spent most of their careers in the minor leagues. Outfielder Ollie Carnegie never played a major league game, but in thirteen seasons with Buffalo he blasted 258 home runs and collected 1,044 RBIs, both all-time IL records. In seventeen seasons with five IL teams, first baseman Ed Onslow became the all-time league leader in games played, hits, and triples, while righthander Johnny Ogden won 213 games during twelve seasons with three IL teams. Such players were mainstays of their teams year after year, adding significantly to the continuity relished by baseball fans.

On June 12, 1947, the IL Baseball Writers Association announced the first nine inductees of the International League Hall of Fame. For the next thirteen years—1948 through 1960—three new inductees were selected annually. In 1961, 1962, and 1963, with interest in minor league baseball in the

doldrums, only one inductee per year was added. Following 1963 the IL Hall of Fame became inactive. Although there were fifty-one inductees, only two—Herb Pennock and Jackie Robinson—were also voted into the National Baseball Hall of Fame in Cooperstown. Most of the players who starred for several seasons in the International League did not become big league standouts. A notable exception was Lefty Grove, who pitched brilliantly for Baltimore for five seasons (109-36 and four consecutive strikeout titles), then went on to win 300 games in the American League. Although voted into the National Baseball Hall of Fame, Grove is a curious omission from the IL Hall of Fame.

Dormant for more than four decades, the International League Hall of Fame has been revived as part of the celebration for the 125th anniversary of the IL. On August 20, 2007, at Cooper Stadium, former league presidents Harold Cooper and George Sisler, Jr., became the first men inducted into the IL Hall of Fame in forty-four years. In 2008 twenty-eight more men will be inducted, with a ceremony for at least one new Hall of Famer in each of the fourteen IL cities. Fourteen more inductees will be added in 2009, seven in the Class of 2010, and three more in each subsequent year. Considering the vast success of the International League, the resurrection of the IL Hall of Fame is suitable and timely.

– – –

CLASS OF 1947

Ollie Carnegie, OF (Buffalo, 1931-41, 1945)

Charles Keller, OF (Newark, 1937-38, 1949)

Ernest Lanigan, IL Secretary (1911-29); IL Information Director (1935-42)

Frank McGowan, OF (Newark, 1921; Baltimore, 1930-34, 1938-39; Buffalo, 1934-37; Mgr. (Baltimore, 1933)

Steve O'Neill, C (Reading, 1925; Toronto, 1926, 1929-31; Mgr. Toronto, 1929-31; Buffalo (1938-40)

Ben Sankey IF (Montreal, 1934-39; Syracuse, 1939; Baltimore, 1939-41)

Frank Shaughnessy, 1B/Mgr. (Syracuse, 1921-25); Mgr. (Providence, 1925); Reading, 1926; Montreal, 1934-36); IL President (1937-60)

Billy Southworth, OF ((Rochester, 1928-32; Toronto, 1940); Mgr. (Rochester, 1928-32, 1939-40)

Fred "Dixie" Walker, OF (Jersey City, 1930-31; Toronto, 1931; Newark, 1932, 1935); Mgr. (Rochester, 1955-56; Toronto, 1957-59)

CLASS OF 1948

Herb Pennock, P (Providence, 1915, 1916)

Dick Rudolph, P (Toronto, 1907-12)

Alphonse "Tommy" Thomas, P (Buffalo, 1918-20; Baltimore, 1921-25, 1935, 1941, 1943-44); Mgr. (Baltimore, 1940-49)

CLASS OF 1949

Ed Holly, SS (Rochester, 1908-10; Montreal, 1910-11; Toronto, 1912-13; Newark, 1918); Mgr. (Montreal, 1928-32)

Bill Meyer, Mgr. (Newark, 1942-45)

George "Specs" Torporcer, 2B (Syracuse, 1921, 1925; Rochester, 1928-34; Jersey City, 1931); Mgr. (Jersey City, 1931)

CLASS OF 1950

Jack Dunn, 2B (Toronto, 1896; Providence, 1905-06; Baltimore, 1907-11); Mgr. (Providence, 1905-06; Baltimore, 1907-28)

Jewel Ens, IF (Providence, 1913-14; Syracuse, 1921); Mgr. (Syracuse, 1942-49)

Dan Howley, C (Montreal, 1914-17; Toronto, 1918); Mgr. (Montreal, 1914-17; Toronto, 1918, 1923-26, 1933, 1937-38)

CLASS OF 1951

James "Rip" Collins, 1B (Rochester, 1926-30)

Al Mamaux, P (Reading, 1923-24; Newark, 1926-33; Albany, 1935); Mgr. (Newark, 1930-33; Albany, 1935-36)

Ed Onslow, 1B (Providence, 1913-17, 1925; Toronto, 1918-24; Rochester, 1925-27; Baltimore, 1928-29; Newark, 1929); Mgr. (Toronto, 1922; Providence, 1925)

CLASS OF 1952

Billy Murray, OF (Buffalo, 1886; Providence, 1894-99); Mgr. (Providence, 1894-1902; Jersey City, 1903-06)

Jack Ogden, P (Newark, 1918; Rochester, 1919, 1933; Baltimore, 1920-27, 1933-34)

George "Hooks" Wiltse, P/1B (Jersey City,

1915; Buffalo, 1918-19; Reading, 1926); Mgr. (Jersey City, 1915; Buffalo, 1918-24; Reading, 1926)

CLASS OF 1953

Estel Crabtree, OF/IF (Rochester, 1933-40, 1942); Mgr. Rochester, 1940)

William Manley, IL Secretary-Treasurer (1929-52); IL Employee (1911-52)

Fred Merkle, 1B (Rochester, 1921-25; Reading, 1927); Mgr. (Reading, 1927)

CLASS OF 1954

Joe Boley, SS (Baltimore, 1919-26)

Fred Hutchinson, P (Buffalo, 1940-41)

Bill Kelly, 1B (Buffalo, 1922-26, 1928, 1930; Newark, 1927); Mgr. (Springfield, 1951-52); IL Umpire (1934, 1937-39)

CLASS OF 1955

Jack Berly, P (Rochester, 1928-30, 1934-35, 1940-41; Baltimore, 1935-36; Toronto, 1936-40)

Luke Hamlin, P (Toronto, 1933, 1943, 1945-48)

Merwin Jacobson, OF (Rochester, 1916; Toronto, 1917, 1927-28; Baltimore, 1919-24, 1933; Jersey City, 1925; Newark, 1928-29)

CLASS OF 1956

George Earnshaw, P (Baltimore, 1924-28)

Joe McCarthy, 2B (Buffalo, 1914-15)

Jimmy Ripple, OF (Montreal, 1929-35, 1940; Rochester, 1941-42; Toronto, 1942-43)

CLASS OF 1957

Christian "Bruno" Betzel, Mgr. (Montreal, 1944-45; Jersey City, 1946-48; Syracuse, 1950-53; Toronto, 1956)

Ike Boone, OF (Newark, 1931; Jersey City, 1932; Toronto, 1933-36); Mgr. (Toronto, 1933-36)

James "Rube" Parnham, P (Baltimore, 1917-20, 1922-24, 1926; Reading, 1927; Newark, 1927)

CLASS OF 1958

Jack Bentley, 1B/P (Baltimore, 1916-17; 1919-22; Newark, 1927-28; Rochester, 1931)

George Selkirk, OF (Rochester, 1927, 1933; Jersey City, 1928-31; Newark, 1932-34, 1946; Toronto, 1932); Mgr. (Newark, 1946-47)

Jimmy Walsh, OF (Baltimore, OF (Baltimore, 1910-12, 1922-23; Akron, 1920; Newark, 1921; Jersey City, 1924, 1928-29; Buffalo, 1925-26; Toronto, 1927); Mgr. (Newark, 1921)

CLASS OF 1959

Frederick "Fritz" Maisel, IF (Baltimore, 1911-13, 1919-28); Mgr. (Baltimore, 1929-32)

William "Harry" Smythe, P (Baltimore, 1930-33; Montreal, 1934-38)

George Stallings, C (Toronto, 1887; Toledo, 1889); Mgr. (Buffalo, 1902-06, 1911-12; Newark, 1908; Rochester, 1920-27; Montreal, 1928)

CLASS OF 1960

"Howitzer" Howie Moss, OF/3B (Jersey City,

1943; Baltimore, 1944, 1946-48, 1951; Springfield, 1951)

Glenn "Rocky" Nelson, 1B (Rochester, 1947-48; Montreal, 1952-56; Toronto, 1957-58, 1962)

Jackie Robinson, 2B (Montreal, 1946)

CLASS OF 1961

Pat Powers, Mgr. (Trenton, 1884; Jersey City, 1887; Rochester, 1889; Buffalo, 1891); IL President (1893-1905, 1907-10)

CLASS OF 1962

Joe Brown, 3B (Reading, 1924-25; Newark, 1926; Syracuse, 1927; Rochester, 1928-30, 1932-33; Jersey City, 1931-33; Buffalo, 1933; Toronto, 1934)

CLASS OF 1963

Dick "Twitchy" Porter, IF/OF (Baltimore, 1921-28; Newark, 1935-36; Syracuse, 1937-40); Mgr. (Syracuse, 1938-40; Toronto, 1948)

CLASS OF 2007

Harold Cooper, IL President (1978-90); GM (Columbus, 1955-68); IL Vice-President (1990-Present)

George Sisler, Jr., IL President (1966-76); GM (Rochester, 1955-65; Columbus (1977-89); IL Vice-President (1989-2006)

International League
Cities Today

Allentown
(LEHIGH VALLEY IRONPIGS)

The first franchise change in fifteen years—Ottawa to Allentown in 2008—has brought a charter city back into the IL. Allentown was one of only three cities to open and complete the inaugural season of the Eastern League. Only five teams were still playing at the end of the summer of 1884, and although Allentown finished next-to-last, the Pennsylvania city had provided a stability that was badly needed by the fledgling league. Allentown did not again field a team in the Eastern League until 1894, once more finishing next-to-last, this time in a seven-team circuit.

Allentown was active in other leagues during the late 1800s. The "Lumber City" played in the Pennsylvania State League in 1887. The next year Allentown placed a team in the Central League, and in 1889 held a franchise in the Eastern Inter-State League. At mid-season of 1890 Allentown fielded a replacement team in the Pennsylvania State League, then spent 1892 and 1893 in this circuit as the Allentown Colts. In 1895 the Allentown Goobers stepped into the Pennsylvania State League at mid-season. From 1898 through 1900 the Allentown Peanuts were part of the Atlantic League.

Although there were no twentieth-century appearances in the IL, Allentown sporadically supported professional baseball in several other circuits. The city had a club in the Class B Tri-State League from 1912 through 1914. A decade and a half passed before the Allentown Dukes joined the Class A Eastern League in 1929, winning the pennant and the playoffs. But after 1932 three Depression seasons passed without pro baseball. In 1936 the Allentown Brooks played in the Class A New York-Penn League for a season.

Two years later the Allentown Dukes entered the Class B Inter-State League, storming to the pennant and winning the playoffs. For the next four seasons Allentown played as the Fleetwings, then in 1944 the team became the Cardinals. The 1944 Cardinals won the Inter-State League pennant, and won again in 1949. During the 1940s Allentown boasted three batting champs: Ed Lavigne in 1942 (.319, with a league-leading 95 RBIs); William Marks in 1946 (.372); and Larry Ciaffone in 1948 (.373).

The Inter-State League disbanded after the 1952 season, but in 1954 the Allentown Cardinals resurfaced in the Class A Eastern League, winning the playoffs in 1955. A change of affiliation in 1958 brought a change of name, and the Allentown Red Sox played in the Eastern League for three more seasons.

For years Allentown played in a ballpark built adjacent to the Allentown trolley barn, with a short left field fence and a high wall—like Fenway Park. The seating capacity was just 3,500, and after the club moved to a larger park, the old facility was razed—only to be rebuilt in 1976 as a Bicentennial project. Breadon Field on Seventh Street could accommodate 5,500 fans, and was renamed Max Hess Stadium after being purchased by a local busi-

nessman. But after Allentown dropped out of pro baseball following the 1960 season, the stadium site was sold to developers of the Lehigh Valley Mall.

Following an absence of nearly half a century, professional baseball returned to Allentown. A group of backers decided to cap-

Future home of the Lehigh Valley Iron Pigs in Allentown. When this photo was taken by the author in May 2007, construction was ahead of schedule.

Drawing of Allentown's future Coca-Cola Park.

italize on the availability of state funding for stadiums and erect a $34 million ballpark to attract a Class A franchise. While these plans were materializing, it was learned that Ottawa's IL franchise would become available for the 2008 season. Allentown's investment group secured funding to upgrade their stadium to a $48 million AAA facility. Naming rights were sold to Coca-Cola, and Coca-Cola Park would become the only stadium in the United States to bear the name of the famous corporation.

The Lehigh Valley IronPigs—an historical reference to the area's economy—was the colorful nickname selected for the team. The IronPigs will be the AAA affiliate of the nearby Philadelphia Phillies, and it will be possible to whisk a minor league prospect from Allentown to the parent club within an hour.

Year	Record	Pcg.	Finish
1884	30-41	.422	Fourth
1894	43-32	.573	Seventh

Buffalo
(BISONS, PAN-AMS)

A primitive form of baseball was played in Buffalo as early as the 1830s, and the Niagaras of 1857 became the city's first uniformed nine. In anticipation of the International League, the Niagaras hosted—and beat—a club from Hamilton, Ontario, on August 16, 1860. This contest probably was the first international baseball game, and shortly afterward the Niagaras traveled to Hamilton and trounced another Canadian team. During the extraordinary explosion of baseball after the Civil War, at least 100 nines played each other in Buffalo. But the Niagaras remained the premier amateur team.

The first professionals formed an independent club, which played late in the 1877 season. The following year the Buffalo Bisons joined baseball's first minor league, the International Association. Future Hall of Famer Jim Galvin turned in an incredible iron man performance, pitching in almost every game, working about 900 innings, and going 72-25 with 17 shutouts and 96 complete games. Joseph M. Overfield, the best baseball historian a city could hope to have, also calculated that Galvin was 10-5 in exhibitions against National League teams.

The next season the Bisons joined the National League, playing big league ball for seven years. Jim Galvin continued to be the mainstay of the pitching staff during most of this period, but the Bisons could not finish higher than third. Following a seventh-place finish in 1885, the Bisons shifted to the two-year-old International League.

During its first three IL seasons, Buffalo featured a black player, Frank Grant, who played second, outfield, and pitcher. Grant was an excellent hitter each year (.344, .366, and .331), but because of racial problems around the league an IL color line was drawn by 1889. Mike Walsh was Buffalo's pitching star of 1886 (27-21) and 1887 (27-9).

When Buffalo joined the IL in 1886, the Bisons continued to lease Olympic Park, a wooden facility at Summer Street and Richmond Avenue which was also rented out for

The pennant-winning 1906 Buffalo Bisons. Manager George Stallings (center) also brought an IL flag to Buffalo in 1904. Mound ace Rube Kisinger (top left—he spelled his name with one "S") won 117 games for Buffalo and set a league record with 31 career shutouts. Jake Gettman (lower left) spent 12 seasons with five IL clubs, and fellow outfielder Jimmy Murray (lower right) played in the IL for nine years.

football, lacrosse, cricket, bicycling, and other events. The lease ran out after the 1888 season, but Buffalo owners dismantled the facility and used the lumber to erect a new Olympic Park on Michigan Avenue at Ferry Street. This location would serve as the site of pro ball in Buffalo until the end of the 1960 season.

In 1890 baseball enthusiasts in Buffalo backed a franchise in the Players' League, a major league composed of rebellious big leaguers dissatisfied with the autocratic ownership of the era. Buffalo's IL club, attempting to compete against major leaguers, compiled a 6-12 record and almost no attendance, and the franchise was moved to Montreal on June 3.

The Bisons returned resoundingly in 1891, recording Buffalo's first IL pennant after the Players' League folded. The manager was future IL president Pat Powers, whose best weapon was a fine pitching staff: Les German (34-11, and the team's highest batting average, .314), Robert Barr (24-9), and Bill Calihan (15-7). Buffalo tore the league apart; several teams folded, and when the survivors desperately devised a split schedule, the Bisons also won the second half.

There were no more pennants during the 1890s, but a local player, Jimmy Collins, became a Bison in 1893 (.286) and 1894 (.352), before moving up to a Hall of Fame career in the big leagues. Versatile Jake Drauby (he played infield, outfield or pitcher, as needed) won the batting title in 1893 (.379), and was almost as dangerous the next season (.350).

Largely because of the distractions of the Spanish-American War, the 1898 season was financially precarious in Buffalo and throughout the IL. Bisons' owner Jim Franklin therefore decided to join Ban Johnson's ambitious new Western League in 1899. Two years later, when the circuit elevated itself to major league status, Ban Johnson dropped Buffalo in order to place a franchise in Boston.

The Bisons returned to the IL in 1901 but finished last. Jim Franklin tried to change the name to "Pan-Ams," because of the Pan-American Exposition held in Buffalo in 1901, but fans stuck with "Bisons." Franklin pulled out after the season, and an expert, hard-driving baseball man, George Stallings, took over as president and manager. Stallings immediately thrust the Bisons into contention, finishing second in 1902 and 1903. Outfielder Jake Gettman (.343) and third-sacker Dave Brian (.335) led the offense in 1902, while the pitching staff centered around Cy Ferry (22-4) and Cy Hooker (22-9). Gettman (.334) and Ferry (20-8) were almost as good the next year, while fans cheered another local player, Billy Milligan (21-6). The Memorial Day doubleheader drew more than 30,000 fans, as Buffalo set a new league attendance record of 305,119.

In 1904 Stallings brought Buffalo its first pennant since 1891, behind first-sacker Myron Grimshaw (.325) and newly acquired Rube Kisinger (24-11). Although Kisinger (20-15) and Billy Milligan (19-16) again pitched well the next year, player sales dropped the Bisons into the second division. But Stallings quickly rebuilt another championship team, winning the 1906 flag behind Kisinger (23-12), Jake Gettman (.291), Lew Brockett (23-13), and Bill Tozer (16-6). In 1904 and 1906 Buffalo won the first two Little World Series, defeating American Association champs St. Paul and Columbus.

Because of personal problems, George Stallings left baseball after his second title in three years. But the 1907 Bisons came in second behind the pitching staff of Kisinger (15-10), Milligan (17-12), and Tozer (21-10). Kisinger continued to pitch for the Bisons for three more seasons, hurling ten shutouts for the second division club of 1909. Kisinger's 31 career shutouts for Buffalo constitute an IL record, and he won 117 games as a Bison.

Buffalo won the 1915 pennant on the last day of the season. Key players were King Bader (top row, No. 4, and 20-18), right fielder Les Channell (5, and .304), Fred Beebe (7, and 27-7), manager Patsy Donovan (11), first baseman Joe Judge (12, and .320), second baseman Joe McCarthy (13), George Gaw (14, and 16-9), left fielder Charley Jamieson (17, and .307), center fielder Flash Gilhooley (19, and .322), and Phifer Fullenwieder (20, and 17-12).

From 1910-1929, outfielder Jimmy Walsh played 13 seasons for six IL teams. In 1926, at the age of 40, he won his second consecutive IL batting crown (.388) as a Buffalo Bison.

On August 9, 1910, Bison right-hander Chet Carmichael fired the league's first perfect game at Jersey City. The next year southpaw Ad Brennan (14-8) pitched two no-hitters against Jersey City, although the Skeeters won the second classic 1-0 in the tenth. George Stallings returned to the Bisons for 1911 and 1912, but could not finish above fourth. In 1912 Fred Beebe dueled Dick Rudolph of Toronto 19 innings before losing 4-3, but Beebe was the Bisons' leading pitcher in 1912 (16-10), 1913 (20-12), 1914 (22-10), and 1915 (27-7).

During the 1914 and 1915 seasons, the Bisons again had to face major league competition, this time against a Federal League franchise. A second-place finish in 1914 was not good enough to keep the team from being sold to Joseph Lannin, wealthy owner of the Boston Red Sox and the Providence Grays. Lannin's connections and the field leadership of Patsy Donovan promptly produced back-to-back pennants. Starring for the 1915 champs were Beebe in his best year, two-time stolen base champ Frank "Flash" Gilhooley (.322 with 53 SB, along with 62 SB in 1914), first baseman Joe Judge (.320), and left fielder Charley Jamieson (.307). Standouts for both teams were pitchers King Bader (20-18 and 23-8) and George Gaw (16-9 and 16-13), and right fielder Les Channell (.304 and .329). Stepping forward in 1916 were Al Tyson (19-9), utility man Bob Gill (.309 in 109 games), and outfielders George Jackson (.320) and Merlin Kopp (.290). The two-time champs were honored by a trio of banquets, and another dinner plus a parade before they left for spring training in 1917.

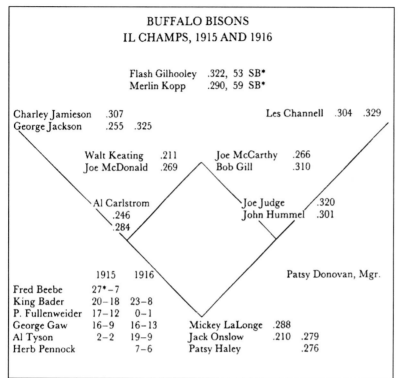

BUFFALO BISONS
IL CHAMPS, 1915 AND 1916

Flash Gilhooley   .322, 53 SB*
Merlin Kopp   .290, 59 SB*

Charley Jamieson .307   Les Channell   .304   .329
George Jackson   .255   .325

Walt Keating   .211   Joe McCarthy   .266
Joe McDonald   .269   Bob Gill   .310

Al Carlstrom   Joe Judge   .320
       .246   John Hummel   .301
       .284

           1915   1916   Patsy Donovan, Mgr.
Fred Beebe   27*–7
King Bader   20–18   23–8
P. Fullenweider   17–12   0–1
George Gaw   16–9   16–13   Mickey LaLonge .288
Al Tyson   2–2   19–9   Jack Onslow   .210   .279
Herb Pennock   7–6   Patsy Haley   .276

But 1917 brought sixth place and the distractions of another war—and bankruptcy. Lannin, however, deftly conducted a series of behind-the-scenes negotiations, somehow acquiring outright title to the Olympic Park property and to the Bisons. George Wiltse was appointed manager in 1918 and held the post until 1924, bringing the Bisons into third place five times. In 1920 the Bisons pulled off two triple plays, including the second unassisted triple in league history, by second baseman Walter Keating. Also in 1920 Flash Gilhooley returned to Buffalo (.343 with 45 SB), and he turned in another fine season in 1921 (.314 with 55 SB).

In 1920 Joe Lannin sold the Bisons to a Buffalo group headed by popular, enthusiastic Frank Offermann. Under his leadership Olympic Park was gradually dismantled late in the 1923 season, and by the next year 13,000-seat Bison Stadium was ready at a cost of $265,000. A gifted promoter, Offer-

mann became club president in 1928, made the Bisons one of the first minor league teams to have radio broadcasts, introduced night baseball to the International League in 1930, and poured his personal funds into the team. When he died at the age of 59 in 1935, the ballpark was renamed Offermann Stadium.

"Big Billy" Kelly took over first base in 1922 (.305), and sparked the offense in 1923 (.350 with 128 RBI), 1924 (.324, 28 HR, 155 RBI), 1925 (.318, 26 HR, 125 RBI), and 1926 (.330, 44 HR, 151 RBI). Kelly was the RBI champ the last two years, and the home run king in 1926. Venerable outfielder Jimmy Walsh won back-to-back batting titles in 1925 (.356, 22 HR, 122 RBI) and 1926 (.388, 17 HR, 131 RBI)—at the ages of 39 and 40. Billy Webb held down third base in 1922 (.313), 1924 (.309), 1925 (.330), and 1926 (.318). In 1925, while serving as player-manager, he blasted three home runs in one game—including two in one inning. Two months into the next season, however, he was severely beaned (the ball caromed almost to the press box), cutting short his playing career.

"Derby Day Bill" Clymer, a former Bison player and manager, returned to Buffalo as field general in 1926. The next year he led the Bisons to a club record of 112 victories and a pennant, behind the hitting heroics of center fielder Al Tyson (.375), shortstop Andy Cohen (.353), and first baseman Del Bissonette (.365, 31 HR, 167 RBI, 168 R), who led the IL in RBIs, hits, runs, doubles, triples, and total bases. Clymer almost repeated in 1928, losing by a percentage point to Rochester on the final day of the season.

A fan favorite of this period was George "Showboat" Fisher, who held down right field and hit impressively in 1927 (.320), 1928 (.335), and 1929 (.336, 36 HR, 124 RBI). Another heavy hitter was Al Moore, who played left field in 1929 (.327), 1930 (.342), and 1931 (.346). On July 13, 1929, Showboat, Moore, and other Bisons banged out 11 hits in a row against Baltimore. The next year, on August 18, "Cowboy Ed" Tomlin played all nine positions during a 24-2 rout of Reading, and on August 27 and 28 first baseman Russ Wrightstone (.386) hit safely in nine consecutive at-bats.

In 1931 the Bisons purchased 32-year-old outfielder Ollie Carnegie, who was in his first full season of professional baseball (he turned to baseball only after becoming jobless during the Depression). The 5'7" righthander was a powerful slugger whose best seasons were 1932 (.333, 36 HR, 140 RBI), 1934 (.335, 31 HR, 136 RBI), 1935 (.293, 37 HR, 153 RBI), 1938 (.330, 45 HR, 136 RBI), and 1939 (.294, 29 HR, 112 RBI). During the latter two seasons Carnegie led the league in homers and RBIs, and his 45 roundtrippers in 1938 set an all-time Buffalo record. After his release in 1941, he continued to hit over .300 in the PONY League, and in 1945 he returned to the short-handed Bisons at the age of 46 (.301 in 39 games).

Hall of Fame catcher Ray Schalk began a six-year managerial tenure in 1932, and the following season drove a sub-.500 (83-85) fourth-place club to the IL's first Shaughnessy Playoff championship. Outfielders Ollie Tucker (.323, 27 HR, 115 RBI), Ollie Carnegie (.317, 29 HR, 123 RBI) and Len Koenecke (.334), as well as shortstop Greg Mulleavy (.337), led a fine offense, but the Bisons barely made the playoffs with a last-day victory over Rochester. Buffalo then breezed through playoff series with Baltimore and Rochester, although the Cinderella story ended with a Junior World Series loss to Columbus.

Schalk guided the Bisons into the playoffs again in 1935, then the following season produced a first-place finish and another playoff title. Once more, however, Buffalo was defeated in the Junior World Series. Although Ollie Carnegie missed most of the year with an ankle injury, he was ably replaced in left by John Dickshot (.359, 17 HR, 112 RBI). Other offensive leaders included MVP center fielder Frank McGowan (.356, 20 HR, 111 RBI), first baseman Eddie Fletcher (.344), and right fielder Ed Boland (.301, 20 HR, 102 RBI). Southpaw Carl Fischer was hard to beat in 20 appearances (13-2), and 36-year-old righty Bill Harris (15-10) pitched a seven-inning perfect game in June, then the next month twirled a nine-inning no-hitter, en route to the IL strikeout title.

At the age of 39, Ollie Carnegie led the Bisons to the 1938 playoffs finals and was voted Most Valuable Player. The 1939 playoff club was sparked by Carnegie, shortstop Lou Boudreau (.331 before being promoted to Cleveland for the last third of the season), and southpaw Al Smith (16-2, including 15 consecutive victories). Hal White (16-4 with a 2.43 ERA) was the 1940 ERA and percentage champ, while Earl Cook (15-12) hurled a doubleheader shutout against Jersey City, blanking the Skeeters 2-0 and 2-0 on Thursday, August 15, then shutting out Syracuse four days later. Fastballer Virgil "Fire" Trucks won the strikeout title of 1941 (12-12 with 204 Ks), but he was overshadowed by the MVP performance of victory leader Fred Hutchinson (27-6), who also was the team's best hitter (.392 in 72 games).

In 1943 Rufus Gentry pitched well for a seventh-place club (20-16, including an 11-inning no-hitter). Center fielder Mayo Smith, a fifth-year Bison whose batting average had never been higher than .281, won the hitting title in 1944 (.340) against wartime pitching. Hall of Fame second baseman Bucky Harris, who had played for Buffalo on the way up in 1918 and 1919, returned as manager in 1944 and 1945 and general manager in 1945 and 1946, before going back to the big leagues as a manager, executive, and scout.

A fine right-handed hitter, Coaker Triplett, moved into left field in 1946, and he was an important offensive figure for six years (.303, .315, a league-leading .353 in 1948, .322 for the 1949 champs, .337, and .347 as player-manager in 1951). Manager-GM Paul Richards led Buffalo to the 1949 pennant, although the first-place Bisons lost in the playoff finals. Richards was a master teacher of young pitchers, and the 1949 champs boasted Bob Hooper (19-3), Saul Rogovin (16-6), and Clem Hausmann (15-7). Richards, Hooper and Rogovin left the next year, and the Bisons nosedived from first place to last.

On August 15, 1952, righthander Dick Marlowe (10-10) pitched a perfect game in Baltimore; the only other nine-inning perfecto in IL history was turned in by another Bison, Chet Carmichael, in 1910. On August 27, 1954, another righthander, Frank Lary (15-11), retired 26 Toronto hitters in a row, only to see the twenty-seventh lace a single up the middle to spoil a perfect game bid.

In 1956 Buffalo acquired a 41-year-old slugger named Luke Easter, the first black Bison since the 1880s. Despite his age, the 6'4½" 240-pound first-sacker led the league in homers and RBIs in 1956 (.306, 35 HR, 106 RBI) and 1957 (.279, 40 HR, 128 RBI), including the first two home runs ever launched over the tall center field scoreboard at Offermann Stadium. After another productive season in 1958 (.307, 38 HR, 109 RBI), he was released but continued to play with Rochester until the age of 49.

Manager Phil Cavaretta guided the Bisons to a close second-place finish in 1957, followed by a playoff championship (and another loss in the Little World Series). Easter led the offense, with help from outfielders Joe Caffie (.330) and Russ Sullivan (.314), and shortstop Mike Baxes (.303). The best pitchers were lefty Walt Craddock (18-8) and slugging righthander Glenn Cox (12-5, with 7 homers). Although the team dropped to seventh place in 1958, Cox had an even better season (16-9, with 7 more homers).

The next year new manager Kerby Farrell guided a surge to first place, although the Bisons dropped the playoff opener. The championship lineup starred first-sacker Frank Herrera, who won the Triple Crown (.329, 37 HR, 128 RBI) and was voted Most Valuable Player. The Bisons outdrew every other team in minor league ball, with a paid attendance exceeding 413,000.

After the 1960 season, Offermann Stadium was razed so that a junior high school could be constructed. Replacing the site of Bisons' baseball since 1889 was War Memorial Stadium, which had been built as a football facility by the WPA in 1936-37. "The Old Rockpile" was converted for baseball with a short right field, and in 1983 it was used in filming Robert Redford's classic baseball movie, *The Natural*.

Kerby Farrell immediately brought a title to War Memorial Stadium. Behind the hitting of MVP batting champ Ted Savage (.325 with 24 homers), first baseman Don Mincher and third-sacker Felix Torres (both with 24 homers), and outfielder Jacke Davis (.303), the Bisons made the playoffs with a third-place finish, then lost just one postseason game. There was a four-game sweep of Charleston in the playoff opener, Rochester fell in the finals, four games to one, then there was another sweep of Louisville in the Junior World Series.

Frank Herrera returned from the Phillies in 1962 to lead the IL in homers and RBIs (.295, 32 HR, 108 RBI). In the latter half of 1966, 18-year-old catcher Johnny Bench came up from Peninsula of the Carolina League, but he broke his finger in his first game as a Bison and missed the rest of the season. The next year, however, he slammed 23 homers in 98 games and was permanently promoted to Cincinnati.

By 1967 neighborhood conditions around War Memorial Stadium had deteriorated to the point that most games were played at Hyde Park in Niagara Falls, and at the end of the year the Reds pulled out of Buffalo. A working agreement was arranged with the Washington Senators for 1968, and outfielder Bryant Alyea slammed 31 homers in 87 games, while first baseman Bob Chance hit 29. The next year Hector Lopez became the first black manager in IL history. War Memorial Stadium became virtually untenable, with attendance sinking to 77,808, and the Senators canceled their agreement with Buffalo.

The 1970 Bisons immediately became mired in

Buffalo's War Memorial Stadium, built as a football facility, was converted for baseball for the Bisons in 1961.

last place, and when the record dropped to 9-29 the club was barely averaging a home attendance of 700. The Montreal Expos had arranged a working agreement with the Bisons, but on June 4 IL officials decided to forfeit the franchise to Montreal, which transferred it to Winnipeg.

Eight years passed without professional baseball, until a Double-A franchise was obtained in the Eastern League in 1979. The Eastern League Bisons were purchased in 1983 by Rich Products Corporation. Robert E. Rich, Jr., president of the immense frozen food company, determined to bring big league baseball back to Buffalo. Rich achieved attendance miracles at The Old Rockpile, and in 1985 Buffalo moved up to the American Association after Rich bought Wichita's Triple-A franchise.

Relentlessly pursuing a big league team, Rich assembled a large, long-range staff. In 1988 the Bisons moved into splendid Pilot Field. Built at a cost of $42 million adjacent to Buffalo's revitalized downtown area, Pilot Field was a 19,500-seat stadium which could be expanded to 40,000 within a matter of months.

"We're going to put numbers on the board baseball just can't ignore," promised Rich, and in 1988 Buffalo established a new minor league attendance record (1,186,651). Buffalo attracted more than one million fans for six consecutive years, including 1,240,951 in 1991. Buffalo outdrew weak major league clubs during these seasons, but no big league franchise was forthcoming.

During the 1990s Buffalo appeared regularly in the American Association playoffs, and in 1997 the Bisons won the AA pennant. But 1997 was the last year of the American Association, and Buffalo moved to the expended International League.

The 1998 Bisons drove toward a second consecutive pennant behind percentage leader Jason Jacome (14-2) and sluggers Tony Lovullo (.326) and Alex Ramirez, who pounded 34 homers and drove in 103 runs. In the first playoff game, against Syracuse, Ramirez hit for the cycle, and the Bisons went on to a three-game sweep. In the finals Buffalo outlasted Durham, three games to two, then advanced to the AAA World Series in Las Vegas. Bison infielder Jeff Manto was at his best during the playoffs, belting three doubles and a homer, and leading all hitters in the AAA World Series with a spectacular .533 average. Despite Manto's efforts, Buffalo lost the series to New Orleans, three games to one.

Buffalo's Pilot Field opened in 1988, a streamlined, state-of-the-art downtown stadium. (Author photo)

After winning the 1998 pennant, the Bisons missed the International League playoffs the next year, although slugger Russell Branyon twice blasted three home runs in a single game on his way to a total of 30 roundtrippers on the season. In 2000 the Bisons and Scranton/Wilkes-Barre tied for the Northern Division title. Buffalo beat SWB in a one-game playoff to win the division crown, but lost the opening series to SWB, one game to three.

In 2001 the Bisons, lead by Karim Garcia (a team-leading 31 home

Buffalo's handsome downtown stadium was renamed Dunn Tire Park. (Photo by Karon O'Neal)

"Bisons Championship Corner" in left field at Dunn Tire Park. (Photo by Karon O'Neal)

All-Star catcher-infielder Ryan Garko (.303, 19 HR, 77 RBI) led the Bisons to the 2005 playoffs. Buffalo battled Indianapolis in the opening series, but lost in the fifth game. Outfielder Jason Dubois (.275, 22 HR, 87 RBI) made the 2006 All-Star Team, and outfielder Ben Francisco (.318) won the 2007 batting title. For 150 years, beginning with the uniformed Niagara Nine of 1857, baseball fans have been able to enjoy quality play in Buffalo.

runs and 85 RBIs), again met SWB in the playoff opener—and again lost, two games to three. The 2002 Bisons boasted a powerful offense, including outfielders Karim Garcia (.396 before a callup) and Jody Gerut (.322, also in part of a season); catcher Josh Bard (.297); and infielders Brandon Phillips (.283) and Chris Coste (.328). For the third year in a row Buffalo and SWB faced each other in the playoff opener, and this time Buffalo roared to a three-game sweep. But in the finals the Bisons were the victims of a sweep by Durham.

The 2003 Bisons did not make the playoffs, but in 2004 Buffalo fielded a pennant-winner. Jack Cressend (10-1) and Kyle Denney (10-5) led the pitching staff, while a strong offense was triggered by Most Valuable Player Jhonny Peralta (.326, 15 HR, 86 RBI), infielder Brandon Philips (.303), outfielder Grady Sizemore (.287), and slugger Ernie Young, who led the team with 27 home runs and 100 RBIs. The Bisons defeated Durham, three games to two, in the playoff opener, and beat Richmond in four games to claim another Governors' Cup.

Year	Record	Pcg.	Finish
1886	50-45	.526	Fifth
1887	65-40	.619	Second
1888	47-59	.443	Sixth
1889	41-66	.383	Seventh
1890	6-12	.333	Sixth
1891	89-35	.718	First
1892	53-58	.477	Sixth
1893	61-53	.535	Fourth
1894	64-62	.508	Fifth
1895	63-61	.508	Fifth
1896	70-53	.569	Second
1897	74-58	.561	Third
1898	63-59	.516	Fourth
1901	45-88	.338	Eighth
1902	88-45	.662	Second
1903	79-43	.648	Second
1904	89-46	.659	First (won LWS)
1905	63-74	.460	Fifth
1906	85-55	.607	First (won LWS)
1907	73-59	.553	Second
1908	75-65	.536	Fourth

1909	72-79	.477	Fifth		1948	71-80	.470	Sixth
					1949	90-64	.584	First (won opener, lost finals)
1910	69-81	.460	Sixth					
1911	74-75	.497	Fourth					
1912	71-78	.478	Fifth		1950	56-97	.366	Eighth
1913	78-75	.510	Fourth		1951	79-75	.513	Fourth (lost opener)
1914	89-61	.593	Second		1952	71-83	.461	Fifth
1915	86-50	.632	First		1953	86-65	.572	Third (lost opener)
1916	82-58	.586	First		1954	71-83	.461	Sixth
1917	67-84	.444	Sixth		1955	65-89	.422	Sixth
1918	53-68	.438	Sixth		1956	64-87	.424	Eighth
1919	81-67	.548	Third		1957	88-66	.571	Second (won opener and finals, lost JWS
1920	96-57	.627	Third		1958	69-84	.454	Seventh
1921	99-69	.589	Third		1959	89-64	.582	First (lost opener)
1922	95-72	.569	Third					
1923	83-81	.506	Fifth		1960	78-75	.510	Fourth (lost opener)
1924	84-83	.503	Third		1961	85-67	.559	Third (won opener, finals, and JWS)
1925	78-84	.481	Fourth					
1926	92-72	.561	Fourth		1962	73-80	.477	Sixth
1927	112-56	.667	First (lost LWS)		1963	74-77	.490	Eighth
1928	92-76	.548	Second		1964	80-69	.537	Third (lost opener)
1929	83-84	.497	Fifth		1965	51-96	.347	Eighth
					1966	72-74	.493	Fifth
1930	74-91	.448	Sixth		1967	63-76	.453	Seventh
1931	61-105	.367	Eighth		1968	66-81	.449	Seventh
1932	91-75	.548	Third		1969	58-78	.426	Seventh
1933	83-85	.494	Fourth (won opener and finals, lost JWS)		1970	9-29	.237	Eighth
1934	76-77	.497	Fifth		1998	81-62	.566	First (won North, opener and finals, lost Triple-A World Series)
1935	86-67	.562	Third (lost opener)					
1936	94-60	.610	First (won opener and finals, lost JWS)		1999	72-72	.500	Ninth
1937	74-79	.484	Fifth		2000	86-59	.593	First (won North, lost opener)
1938	79-74	.516	Fourth (won opener, lost finals)		2001	91-51	.641	First (won North, lost opener)
1939	82-72	.532	Third (lost opener)		2002	87-57	.564	Second (won opener, lost finals)
1940	76-83	.478	Sixth		2003	73-70	.510	Sixth
1941	88-65	.575	Third (lost opener		2004	83-61	.576	First (won North, opener and finals)
1942	73-80	.477	Seventh					
1943	66-87	.431	Seventh		2005	82-62	.569	Second (won North, lost opener)
1944	78-76	.506	Fourth (lost opener)					
1945	64-89	.418	Sixth		2006	73-68	.578	Seventh
1946	78-75	.510	Fifth		2007	75-67	.528	Sixth
1947	77-75	.507	Fourth (won opener, lost finals)					

Charlotte
(KNIGHTS)

Charlotte's first season in Organized Baseball was a mixture of success and failure. One of six charter members of the Class C North Carolina League, Charlotte roared to a 39-8 record behind batting champ Buck Weaver (not the Buck Weaver of Black Sox notoriety). But attendance and financing were inadequate, and Charlotte withdrew from the league on July 9, 1902. The next day Wilmington also withdrew, then the league disbanded two days later, declaring Charlotte champion of the abbreviated season.

In 1905 Charlotte helped organize the Virginia-North Carolina League, a four-team Class D Circuit which operated only one season. Three years later Charlotte helped form another Class D loop, the Carolina Association, which became the North Carolina State League in 1913. Charlotte played in this circuit from 1908 until 1917, when play halted in May because of wartime conditions. The club won the 1916 pennant and produced three batting champs: Al Humphrey in 1909 (.296), F. P. Wofford in 1911 (.392), and Harry Weiser in 1914 (.333).

Charlotte joined the Class C SALLY in 1919, winning the championship in 1923, the year the league was elevated to Class B status. Clarence Mitchell won the 1920 hitting title (.320), and Ernest Padgett was the 1922 batting champ (.333).

The Depression caused the SALLY to suspend operations after the 1930 season, but Charlotte moved to the Class C Piedmont League and won pennants in 1931 and 1932. The 1931 club (100-37) dominated the Piedmont behind Frank Packard, who led the league in batting, runs, hits, homers and RBIs (.366, 21 HR, 123 RBI, 145 R); Charlotte finished with a 13½-game lead over second-place Raleigh, then beat Raleigh in the playoffs. But Charlotte sagged to the cellar in 1935, and did not play in 1936. Charlotte rejoined the Piedmont League in 1937, however, and played through the 1942 season. Robert Estalella was the 1937 batting and home run champ (.349 with 33 homers), then sparked Charlotte to the 1938 playoff title by leading the Piedmont in batting, homers, runs, and RBIs (.378, 38 HR, 123 RBI, 134 R).

During these years Charlotte played at old Hayman Park, a cozy wooden ballpark with left field just 286 feet down the line, right field 309 feet away, and center 410 feet from the plate. Charlotte had become part of the Washington farm system, and by 1940 Senators' owner Clark Griffith decided to build a new ballpark at a site he had acquired at 400 Magnolia Avenue. In 1941 the Hornets moved into their new home, $40,000 Clark Griffith Park. There was a good lighting system, the wooden grandstand seated 4,000, including 600 reserved seats, and bleachers accommodated another 1,500. But after two seasons, Clark Griffith Park stood empty, because the Hornets did not play during the last three years of World War II.

In 1946 Charlotte helped form the Class B Tri-State League, then won the new circuit's first pennant and playoff. Charlotte repeated as playoff champs the next year, then in 1951 finished first (100-40), 15 games ahead of second-place Asheville, as Francisco Campos won the batting crown (.368). The next year Bruce Barnes was the hitting champ (.370), sparking Charlotte to the 1952 playoff title. Charlotte won another playoff championship the following season, then moved up to the Class A SALLY for 1954. Charlotte won the SALLY playoffs in 1957, and rose to Double-A with the league in 1963.

The Charlotte Hornets thus became part of the Southern League, finishing fourth during the inaugural season of 1964. The Hornets were fifth in 1965, then sixth in 1966. By this time a favorite of Charlotte fans was righthander Garland Shifflett, who spent six seasons, 1963-68, in a Hornet uniform. Another fan favorite of even longer tenure in Charlotte was Minnie Mendoza, who played 10 seasons for the Hornets: 1960-61, 1963-68, and 1971-72. Through the years Mendoza played second, third, short and outfield, leading the SL in various offensive categories, including batting titles in 1967 (.297) and 1971 (.316).

In 1969 Charlotte won the SL pennant, and the next year outfielder Steve Brye was the batting champ (.307). In 1971, because of a shortage of franchises in the Southern League and the Texas League, a "Dixie Association" merger was tried. Charlotte won the Eastern Division and the playoffs—and the only Dixie Association pennant, as the two leagues regrouped separately for 1972.

The big baseball news of 1972 in Charlotte was the decision of the parent Minnesota Twins to place a Class A club alongside the Double-A Hornets in Clark Griffith Park. When the SL Hornets were on the road, the Charlotte Twins would host a Western Carolinas League opponent. But the strategy of daily games at Griffith Park did not work. In 1972 the Hornets drew nearly 70,000 fans, but in 1972 the Hornets attracted fewer then 31,000, while the Twins pulled in a miniscule attendance of 12,835. Minnesota moved their Class A club to Geneva of the New York-Pennsylvania League and transferred their SL franchise to Orlando.

Charlotte was without pro baseball for three seasons. Clark Griffith tried unsuccessfully to sell his old ballpark to various businesses, and in 1974 he announced his intentions to demolish Griffith Park. But the next year Jim Crockett, a prominent Charlotte businessman and sportsman, purchased the facility for $87,000, renaming it Crockett Park. Baltimore moved its SL franchise from Asheville to Charlotte, and Crockett's sister, Frances, an experienced businesswoman, became GM of the Charlotte Orioles.

The 1976 O's made the SL playoffs behind future Baltimore star Eddie Murray

Frances Crockett, GM of the Charlotte Orioles, standing on the pitcher's mound at Crockett Park in 1976, the year the Crockett family brought professional baseball back to Charlotte. (Courtesy Charlotte Knights)

(.298), All-Star infielders Blake Doyle (.299) and Martin Parrill (.274), and righthander Dave Ford (17-7), who led the SL in victories, strikeouts, innings, complete games and shutouts. The next year the O's finished at the bottom of the Eastern Division, despite the efforts of batting champ Mark Corey (.310), home run leader Tom Chism (.298 with 17 homers), ERA titlist Sammy Stewart (9-6, 2.08), and victory leader Bryn Smith (15-11). Following another season in the Eastern cellar, the O's made the 1979 playoffs, although, as in 1976, Charlotte was defeated in the opening round.

In 1980 manager Jimmy Williams again led the O's to the playoffs, executing a three-game sweep over Savannah for the Eastern Division crown, then defeating Memphis to claim the SL championship. The offense was led by future Baltimore standout Cal Ripken, Jr. (.276 with 25 homers).

Charlotte won another SL championship in 1984, even though the O's barely made the playoffs. The O's finished the first half at the bottom of the Eastern Division, but rallied to tie Orlando for the second-half lead. In a one-game playoff, Charlotte beat Orlando, 4-3, for the right to play Greenville for the division title. The O's downed Greenville, three games to one, then swept Knoxville in three games for the pennant.

A few weeks before the start of the 1985 season, Crockett Park was ravaged by fire following a high school game. But makeshift seating was put together, and the O's continued to play in the shell of their old ballpark. Charlotte repeated as Eastern Division champs, defeating Columbus in the playoff opener before dropping the finals to Huntsville, three games to two. In 1987 Charlotte beat

Jacksonville for another Eastern Division crown, but lost the finals to Birmingham.

By this time momentous changes were occurring within Charlotte's professional franchise. After the 1987 season Frances Crockett sold the club to Charlotte businessman George Shinn, who announced his intention to pursue a Triple-A franchise. Shinn signed Roman Gabriel, the former NFL quarterback who had been a high school baseball star in

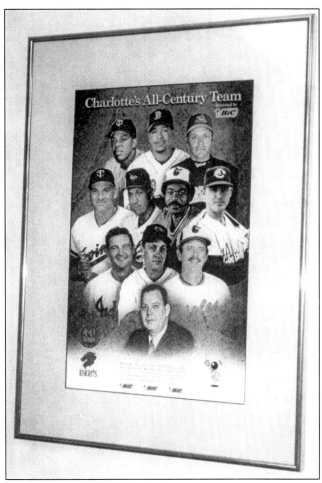

Charlotte's All-Twentieth Century Team occupies a prominent spot in the club offices. Outfielders are on the top row: Tony Oliva, Manny Ramirez, Brian Daubach. Infielders are on the middle row: Harmon Killebrew, Cal Ripkin, Eddie Murray, Jim Thome. On the bottom row are pitchers Early Wynn and Curt Schilling, and catcher Rick Dempsey. At bottom is manager Calvin Griffith. (Courtesy Charlotte Knights)

North Carolina, to take charge of baseball operations. The team nickname was changed to "Knights," and the long-time affiliation with Baltimore was ended in 1989 as the Knights became a Cubs' farm club.

A new stadium was essential, and Shinn acquired a building site on the outskirts of the city, at Rock Hill in York County, *South* Carolina. Knights Castle was planned to be a 10,000-seat, $12 million, state-of-the-art facility that could be expanded into a 70,000-seat stadium for NFL football. While Knights Castle was under construction during the 1989 season, the Knights played in a temporary park in the future parking lot, with an attendance of 157,720. Knights Castle opened in 1990, and attendance for a losing team jumped to 271,502, the most of any SL team. In 1991 attendance rose to 313,791, the largest of any Double-A club, and at mid-season Charlotte was awarded a Triple-A expansion franchise for the 1993 season. Knights Castle was the site of the 1992 Double-A All-Star Game, and the season attendance was 338,047—again the largest of any Double-A club and a fitting send-off for the 1993 International League.

The Knights marched into the IL with a championship team. Guided by future big league manager Charlie Manuel, the Knights boasted a powerful offense led by MVP third baseman Jim Thome (.332, 25 HR, 102 RBI), who topped the IL in batting and RBIS, and slugger Sam Horn who clubbed a league-leading 38 home runs— still the most of any Charlotte hitter in Triple-A. Righthander Chad Ogea (13-8)

Knights Stadium, home of the Charlotte Knights, is located a few miles below the state line in Fort Mill, South Carolina. (Photo by Karon O'Neal)

Charlotte's mascot, Homer, embracing two young fans at Knights Stadium. (Courtesy Charlotte Knights)

tied for the league lead in victories. The Knights beat Richmond, three games to one, in the playoff opener. Meeting Rochester in a finals series that went to the fifth game, the

Knight in armor standing guard in Charlotte's executive offices. (Photo by Karon O'Neal)

The residence of Knights' Head Groundskeeper Eddie Busque stands on a hill above the center field fence. (Author photo)

Knights won the Governors' Cup in their inaugural season in Triple-A.

Charlotte returned to the playoffs the next year, behind aggressive righthander Julian Tavarez (15-6, who tied for most wins in the IL). Again facing Richmond in the opener, the Knights fell in four games. In 1996 Charlotte became the first IL club in more than two decades to hit over .300 as a team, and Rookie of the Year Billy McMillon (.352) won the batting crown.

McMillon returned the next year long enough to blast three home runs in a May 14 game against Ottawa. Russ Morman led the IL with 38 home runs as the 1997 Knights used a late-season charge to make the playoffs. But Charlotte dropped the playoff opener to Columbus, three games to one.

The following season Brian Daubach led the league with 35 homers and 124 RBIs. In 1999 Luis Raven blasted 33 roundtrippers— the third consecutive year that a Charlotte slugger was the IL home run champ. Raven also drove in 125 runs, the highest RBI total posted to date by a Charlotte batter in Triple-A. Directed by IL Manager of the Year Tim Spencer, the Knights seized the 1999 Wild Card. Charlotte battled Scranton/Wilkes-Barre in the playoff opener before winning the fifth and deciding game, 10-5. Facing Durham in the finals, Charlotte won the Governors' Cup in four games. Going on to the Triple-A World Series in Las Vegas, the Knights jumped out to a two-games-to-one lead before PCL champ Vancouver won the final two games.

During Charlotte's first seven seasons in the International League the Knights had made the playoffs four times, won two pennants, fielded four home run champs, a batting titlist, and a Most Valuable Player. Although the Knights now entered a playoff slump, Charlotte fans continued to enjoy superb individual performances. The most valuable pitcher of 2000, for example, was righthander Jon Garland (9-2), who led the IL in winning percentage. In 2002 Joe Crede (.312 with 24 homers before promotion to the White Sox) was named All-Star third baseman, and the 2003 Rookie of the Year was infielder Aaron Miles (.304), who led the IL in hits. Miles' teammate, Brian Cooper, led the league with 15 victories. In 2004 righthander Felix Diaz (10-2) secured the winning percentage title before a callup to the White Sox, and on August 1 Tetsu Yofu pitched a nine-inning no-hitter over Durham.

The 2006 Knights won the Southern Division behind third baseman Josh Fields (.305 with 19 homers), pitching aces Charlie Haegen (14-6) and Heath Phillips (13-5), veteran first sacker Ernie Young (.300), and outfielder Ryan Sweeney (.296). Charlotte's return to the playoffs was brief, as Toledo won the opening series in four games. Charlotte's all-time attendance for a single game was set on July 4, 2006, as nearly 15,000 fans overflowed Knight Stadium—seating capacity 10,002. Although Knight Stadium is less than two decades old, in 2007 plans were set in motion to leave the South Carolina facility for a new ballpark in bustling downtown Charlotte.

Year	Record	Pcg.	Finish
1993	86-55	.610	First (won Southern Division, opener and finals)
1994	77-65	.542	Third (lost opener)
1995	59-81	.421	Ninth
1996	62-7	.440	Eighth
1997	76-65	.539	Fourth (lost opener)
1998	70-73	.490	Eighth
1999	82-62	.569	Third (won opener and finals, lost Triple-A World Series)
2000	78-65	.545	Sixth
2001	67-77	.465	Tenth
2002	55-88	.385	Thirteenth
2003	74-70	.514	Sixth
2004	68-74	.479	Ninth
2005	57-87	.396	Thirteenth
2006	79-62	.560	Second (won South, lost opener)
2007	63-80	.441	Thirteenth

2007 Charlotte Knights. (Courtesy Charlotte Knights)

Columbus
(JETS, CLIPPERS, YANKEES)

Columbus boasts a tradition of baseball that traces back to 1876, when a club of pros called the Columbus Buckeyes took on all comers. The following season the Columbus Buckeyes became charter members of the first minor league, the International Association. In 1888 the Buckeyes brought major league ball to Columbus by joining the expansion of the old American Association. Buckeye pitcher "Dummy" Herndon, a deaf-mute, could not hear umpires' calls, and the arbiters developed a set of hand signals which proved so popular with fans that they solidified as the ball-strike and out-safe signals that are used today.

Columbus played in the American Association for two seasons, joined the Ohio State League in 1887, then became the Columbus Senators of the Tri-State League the next year. In 1889 Columbus rejoined the American Association, dropping out after the 1891 season when the AA and the National League merged as a 12-team circuit. The

Columbus Reds joined the Western League for its inaugural season of 1892, while the Columbus Statesmen entered the Inter-State League in 1895. Through 1901, reassuming the Senators' nickname, Columbus alternated between the Western and the Inter-State leagues. In 1902 Columbus became a charter member of the new American Association, and would remain in the AA for the next 53 seasons.

Early in their tenure in the AA, the Columbus Senators moved into baseball's first concrete-and-steel stadium. The original Columbus Buckeyes had played at a diamond laid out on a grassy lot located between the old Union Depot and North High Street. In 1883 wooden Recreation Park opened at a site bounded by Meadow Lane (later Monroe Street), Parsons Avenue, and Mound Street (roughly where Interstates 70 and 71 intersect today). The outfield fences were so deep that no ball ever was hit out of the park, and a small structure in far center field housed the team *horse*. A second Recreation Park went up in 1887 at a location closer to the heart of town, between Kossuth, Jaeger (later Fifth), East Schiller (later East Whittier), and Ebner streets. At the new Recreation Park outfield distances again were vast—400 feet down the foul lines.

After the Western League disbanded in 1892, the ballpark site was sold to land developers, and the grandstand and fences were dismantled and peddled for lumber. When Columbus returned to professional baseball in 1895, games were played on a crude field at Spruce and High streets. By the next season Central Athletic Park had been erected at Jenkins and Moler avenues. The wooden stadium featured a center field clubhouse with a shower (visiting teams, of course, had no facilities and had to return to the hotel for bathing). In 1900 the Senators leased from Robert Neil a location nearer to town, and

2,000-seat Neil Park quickly went up on Cleveland Avenue just west of Columbus Barracks and south of the Franklin Brewery. After a profitable season in 1904, club owners purchased the site from Robert Neil, then spent $23,000 on baseball's first concrete-and-steel stadium (Pittsburgh's Forbes Field would become the first concrete structure in the big leagues in 1909). The concrete grandstand at Neil Stadium was double-decked and seated 6,000, and lumber from the old grandstand went into bleachers which could accommodate another 5,000 fans.

Perhaps inspired in their splendid new stadium, the Senators reeled off three consecutive championships in 1905, 1906, and 1907. The second and third Little World Series were played in 1906 and 1907, but Columbus lost to IL champs Buffalo and Toronto. A long pennant drought ensued, lasting until the St. Louis Cardinals made Columbus a key member of their vast and successful farm system in 1931. The team nickname was changed to Red Birds, and it was decided to construct a new stadium on West Mound Street. Red Bird Stadium was equipped with lights, and the brick outfield fence was far from home plate: left field was 457 feet away, although eventually a chain-link fence reduced the incredible distances.

Red Bird Stadium opened in 1932, and the club responded with a playoff title and victory over Buffalo in the Junior World Series. The next year the Red Birds won the pennant, repeated as playoff champs, then downed Toronto in the JWS. In 1937 there was another flag and playoff crown, but Columbus lost the JWS to Newark. In 1941 the Red Birds won the pennant, and in 1941, 1942, and 1943 there were three consecutive playoff victories followed by three straight triumphs in the Junior World Series. In 1950 the Red Birds finished third, then recorded

another playoff title and their sixth Junior World Series victory, this time over Montreal.

During the next three years, however, the Red Birds finished eighth, seventh, and seventh. By 1954 attendance had become so consistently poor that the Cardinals decided to move their American Association franchise to Omaha. However, eleven baseball enthusiasts put up $10,000 each to reestablish pro ball in Columbus. The Ottawa franchise of the International League was purchased for $50,000, while the stadium was bought from the Cardinals for $450,000. Nick Cullop was brought in as field manager, and Harold Cooper (who had been clubhouse boy for the

Harold Cooper became clubhouse boy for the Columbus Red Birds in 1936, later won promotion to general manager, and eventually served as president of the International League. President Cooper was instrumental in the formation of the Triple-A Alliance in 1988 and served as first commissioner of the Alliance. (Courtesy Harold M. Cooper)

Red Birds in 1935 and worked in various capacities for the team until he entered the military in 1942) agreed to serve as general manager, a position he held until 1968. He became president of the International League in 1977, and in 1988 the "Czar" took charge of the new Triple-A Alliance. Following a multi-million-dollar renovation, in 1984 the splendid Columbus facility was reamed Harold Cooper Stadium.

The Columbus Jets finished seventh in their first three IL seasons. In 1955 Columbus fans enjoyed the slugging of outfielder Russ Sullivan (.319 with 29 homers and 94 RBIs in 119 games), who twice blasted three home runs in a single game. The next year Curt Roberts (.320 in 87 games) walloped four homers in a seven-inning game against Havana, while Bob Spicer was the league's percentage leader (12-4 in 56 appearances).

In 1959 percentage leader Al Jackson (15-4) and strikeout champ Joe Gibbon (16-9 with 152 Ks) led Columbus to second place, and two years later, the Jets recorded their first IL pennant behind lefthanders Jackson (12-7) and fireballing strikeout king Bob Veale (14-11 with 208 Ks in 201 IP). The next flag came in 1965, as the Jets made the first of six consecutive playoff appearances. The Jets reached the finals in five of those years, but could not win the Governors' Cup. The 1965 pennant-winners featured home run champ Frank Herrera (.287 with 21 homers) and stolen base titlist George Spriggs, who repeated in 1966. Big southpaw Wilbur Wood was the 1966 ERA champ (14-8, 2.41), while slick-fielding outfielder Elvio Jimenez won the 1967 batting title (.340). Jimenez hit well again the next year (.315), and so did Al Oliver (.315). George Spriggs won his third stolen base crown for the 1968 playoff titlists, and lefty Dave Roberts led the IL in victories and winning percentage (18-5).First baseman Bob Robertson played only 105 games but blasted a league-leading 34 homers for the 1969 finalists. The 1970 finalists featured percentage leader Dick Colpaert (12-3 in 46 relief appearances) and MVP first-sacker George Kopacz (.310, 29 HR, 115 RBI).

Although Columbus fielded consistent winners, attendance was disappointing, and spiraling costs triggered a franchise transfer to Charleston

Built in 1932 as Red Bird Stadium, the Columbus ballpark was renamed Jet Stadium in 1955, Franklin County Stadium in 1977, and Cooper Stadium in 1985. The IL's oldest ballpark will be replaced in 2009 by Huntington Park in downtown Columbus. (Cooper Stadium poster photographed by Karon O'Neal)

after the 1970 season. Six years later, though, Harold Cooper was instrumental in returning IL baseball to his hometown, as the Memphis franchise was brought to Columbus. Franklin County purchased and refurbished the stadium, and George H. Sisler, Jr., stepped down as IL president to become GM of the Columbus Clippers (Harold Cooper was elected league president at the Winter Meetings).

Sisler put together an exemplary organization in Columbus, and an affiliation with the Yankees in 1979 produced immediate success. The Clippers attained unprecedented domination of the IL in 1979-80-81, winning three consecutive pennants and three consecutive playoff titles. In 1982 the Clippers finished second, then won back-to-back pennants in 1983 and 1984. From 1979 through 1985 the Clippers recorded seven straight playoff appearances and five IL flags. In 1987 the second-place Clippers won another playoff title. George Sisler retired following the 1989 season, but the Clippers won the Western Division the next two years and posted the best record in the IL in 1991.

The 1991 Clippers swept Pawtucket in three games to claim another Governors' Cup, although Columbus then lost the fourth—and final—Alliance Classic to Denver. In 1992 the Clippers roared to 95 victories and the best record in the IL. The playoffs expanded to two rounds, with the two division champs facing the second-place teams in the opening series. The powerful Clippers disposed of Richmond with a three-game sweep, then met Scranton/Wilkes-Barre in a memorable finals series. Opening at The Lack, Columbus lost a 4-3 decision, then evened the series with a victory in the 13th inning of Game Two. Returning to Columbus, the Clippers squandered a lead and lost Game Three. In Game Four Columbus blew an eight-run lead, but won in the 11th inning.

In the bottom of the ninth in Game Five the Red Barons led 3-1. But the Clippers rallied for three runs and won their second consecutive Governors' Cup behind manager Rick Down. The six playoff victories gave Columbus a total of 101 wins for 1992.

During the previous 14 seasons Columbus had finished first seven times, made 11 playoff appearances, won five playoff titles, and showcased award-winning athletes. Batting titles were claimed by Mike Easler in 1978 (.330), MVP Scott Bradley in 1984 (.335), Juan Bonilla in 1985 (.330), and Hal Morris in 1989 (.326). First baseman Marshall Brant was named MVP after leading the 1980 IL in homers and RBIs (.289, 23 HR, 92 RBI). "Big Steve" Balboni won the same two titles the next season (.247, 33 HR, 98 RBI), then re-

Columbus first baseman Hal Morris, the 1989 batting champ (.326). (Courtesy Columbus Clippers)

peated as home run champ despite appearing in just 83 games in 1982 (.284, 32 HR, 86 RBI). Third sacker Tucker Ashford was the 1982 MVP (.331), while Dan Pasqua won the award in 1985 (.321, 18 HR, 69 RBI) in only 78 games).

In 1983 Brian Dayett led the IL in homers and RBIs (.288, 35 HR, 108 RBI), Steve Balboni was not far behind (.274, 27 HR, 81 RBI in just 84 games). Otis Nixon was the stolen base champ (.291 with 94 thefts), and Dennis Rasmussen paced the league in victories and strikeouts (13-10 with 187 Ks in 181 IP). Righthander Bob Kammeyer was the victory leader in 1979 (16-8) and 1980 (15-7). ERA champs included Ken Clay in 1980 (9-4, 1.96), James Lewis in 1982 (12-6, 2.60), and Jim Deshaies in 1984 (10-5, 2.39) Jay Buhner was the home rub champ for the 1987 playoff kings (.279 with 21 homers), while the 1990 Western Division champs produced victory leader Dave Eiland (16-5) and MVP Hensley Meulens (.285, 26 HR, 96 RBI).

The 1992 pennant-winners featured MVP batting champ J.T, Snow (.313), hit leader Gerald Williams (.285), stolen base titlist Mike Humphreys (37 steals), and ERA champ Sam Militello (2.29). Hensley Muelens returned in 1992 to lead the league in home runs (26), RBIs (100), and runs scored (96). Meulens and Tony Lovullo each hit three home runs in a single game.

Future pitching star Andy Petitte spent part of 1994 (7-2) with Columbus, and so did shortstop Derek Jeter (.349 in 35 games) and righthander Mariano Rivera (4-2 in six games). Rivera, a future Yankee relief ace, was still being used as a starter, and on June 26, 1995, he pitched a five-inning no-hitter against Rochester. Also returning to the 1995 Clippers was Jeter, who led the IL in runs scored (.317, 96 R).

Following a three-year absence from the playoffs, the 1996 Clippers swept Norfolk in three games, then launched a sweep against Rochester to win the Governors' Cup for the seventh time. The Clippers also had won all six playoff games in 1987, and became the only club to win two playoff series without a defeat *twice*. The only other IL teams to sweep two playoff series were Newark (eight games in 1937), Tidewater (six games in 1982), and Durham (six games in 2002).

Stump Merrill, manager of the 1996 champs, led the Clippers back to the playoffs the

Game action at Cooper Stadium in Columbus, the Clippers vs. the Louisville Sluggers, May 20, 2007. (Author photo)

next year. Columbus beat Charlotte, three games to one, in the opener, then dueled Rochester in the finals until losing the fifth game. The 1999 Clippers reached the playoffs behind ERA leader Ed Yarnell (3.47) and strikeout champ Jeff Juden (151 Ks), but suffered a sweep by the Durham Bulls. Fireballer Brandon Knight kept the strikeout title in Columbus in 2000 (138 Ks) and 2001 (173 Ks).

The 2003 MVP was switch-hitting DH-first baseman Fernando Seguignol (.341 with 28 homers), who led the IL in batting and home runs. Infielders Andy Phillips (.318, 26 HR, 85 RBI) and Felix Escalona (.308), along with tall southpaw Alex Graman (11-6 and a league-leading 129 Ks), led the Clippers to the 2004 playoffs, where Richmond prevailed in a five-game opening series.

On May 1, 2007, center fielder Brandon Watson cracked a fifth-inning single in a game against Rochester. The 25-year-old outfielder continued hitting, day after day, week after week. On June 9 Watson batted safely in his 42nd consecutive game, matching the IL record set by Jack Lelivelt with Rochester in 1912. Watson singled against Ottawa the next day to make the record his own. The streak ended at 43 consecutive games, and during the record-breaking streak Watson batted .360 with 25 multi-hit games. Watson played 103 games with Columbus before being called up to Washington, hitting .313 in IL play.

After three-quarters of a century in the IL's most venerable ballpark, Columbus is preparing to move to a new downtown facility. The 2008 season will conclude 76 years in the historic park that has been called Red Bird Stadium (1932-54), Jet Stadium (1955-70), Franklin County Stadium (1977-84), and Cooper Stadium (1985-2008). When the International League begins its 126th season in 2009, Columbus will welcome fans to beautiful new Huntington Park.

In 2009 Columbus fans will approach new Huntington Park through the Home Plate Entrance. (Courtesy Columbus Clippers)

Looking down the right field line at Huntington Park—in 2009. (Courtesy Columbus Clippers)

Year	Record	Pcg.	Finish
1955	64-89	.418	Seventh
1956	69-84	.451	Seventh
1957	69-85	.448	Seventh
1958	77-77	.500	Fourth
1959	84-70	.545	Second (lost opener)
1960	69-84	.451	Sixth
1961	92-62	.597	First (lost opener)
1962	80-74	.519	Fifth
1963	75-73	.507	Fifth
1964	68-85	.444	Sixth
1965	85-61	.582	First (won opener, lost finals)
1966	82-65	.558	Second (lost opener)
1967	69-71	.493	Fourth (won opener, lost finals)
1968	82-64	.562	Second (won opener, lost finals)
1969	74-66	.529	Fourth (won opener, lost finals)
1970	81-59	.579	Second (won opener, lost finals)
1977	65-75	.464	Seventh
1978	61-78	.439	Seventh
1979	85-54	.612	First (won opener and finals)
1980	83-57	.593	First (won opener and finals)
1981	88-51	.633	First (won opener and finals)
1982	79-61	.564	Second (lost opener)
1983	83-57	.593	First (lost opener)
1984	82-57	.590	First (lost opener)
1985	75-64	.540	Fourth (won opener, lost finals)
1986	62-77	.446	Seventh
1987	77-63	.550	Second (won opener and finals)
1988	65-77	.458	Fifth
1989	77-69	.527	Third
1990	87-59	.596	Second (won Western Division, lost finals)
1991	85-59	.590	First (won Western Division, won finals, lost AllianceClassic)
1992	95-49	.660	First (won Division, opener and finals)
1993	78-62	.557	Third
1994	76-68	.521	Fourth
1995	71-68	.511	Fourth
1996	85-67	.599	First (won Western Division, opener and finals)
1997	79-63	.556	Third (won Western Division and opener, lost finals)
1998	67-77	.465	Twelfth
1999	83-58	.589	First (won West, lost opener)
2000	75-69	.521	Eighth
2001	67-76	.469	Ninth
2002	59-83	.415	Twelfth
2003	76-68	.528	Fourth
2004	80-64	.556	Third (won West, lost opener)
2005	77-67	.535	Fifth
2006	69-73	.486	Ninth
2007	64-80	.444	Twelfth

Durham
(BULLS)

Bull Durham, the delightful 1988 baseball movie starring Kevin Costner, Tim Robbins and Susan Sarandon, was filmed at Durham's classic minor league ballpark. The filmmakers could have found no better location to represent minor league baseball for their atmospheric motion picture.

Professional baseball in Durham dates back more than a century, to the newly-organized Class D North Carolina League. The club was owned by Judge W.G. Branham, a baseball enthusiast who, 30 years later, would be elected president of the National Association of Baseball. The North Carolina League folded after a couple of months, but Judge Branham had another club ready when the circuit reorganized for 1913. The Bulls played at Hanes Field on the campus of Trinity College. Five winning seasons followed, and Durham was in first place when the league disbanded because of World War I during the 1917 season.

Durham was a charter member of the Piedmont League, a Class D circuit organized in 1920 (and soon elevated to Class C status, then to Class B). Twice during the 1920s the Bulls went from last to first, 1923-24 and 1928-29. Hobe Brumitt was the batting champ (.356) for the 1924 champs, and Harry Smith won the title (.385) the next year. In July 1926 the Bulls began playing at wooden El Toro Park. When El Toro Park was dedicated, on July 26, baseball commissioner Judge Kenesaw Mountain Landis rode Durham's mascot—a live bull—around the new stadium.

In 1930 the Bulls won the playoff title, and in 1932 Tom Wolfe was the batting champ (.366 with 39 homers) and set the all-time Durham home run record. Depression

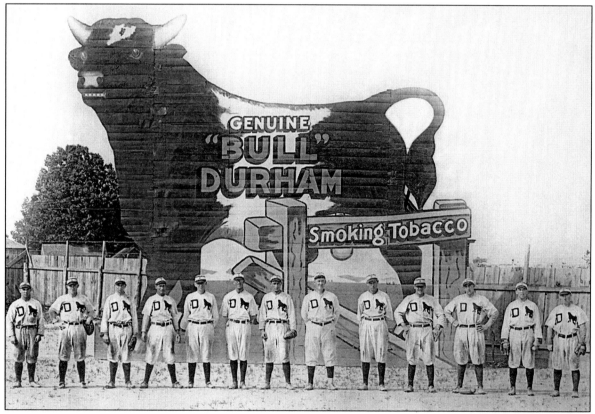

The 1913 Durham Bulls of the Class D North Carolina State League, posing for their team photo in front of giant outfield sign. (Courtesy Durham Bulls)

conditions caused the Bulls to disband in 1934 and 1935, but Durham rebounded strongly in 1936. Southpaw Johnny Vander Meer (19-6, 295 Ks) set the all-time league record for strikeouts (and two years later became the only pitcher in major league history to throw back-to-back no-hitters). The fireballer whiffed 20 batters in one game, and he was voted *The Sporting News* Minor League Player of the Year. Vander Meer's teammate, first baseman Frank McCormick, was the batting champ and RBI king and set a team record for hits (.381, 211 H, 138 RBI).

In 1933 El Toro Park was purchased by the city and renamed Durham Athletic Park. On the night of June 17, 1939, just hours after a league victory, a devastating fire erupted. Within two weeks a Herculean construction effort produced a concrete and steel grandstand, and rebuilding would be completed after the season.

The Bulls won back-to-back playoff titles in 1940 and 1941, and John Burman was the 1941 batting champ (.327). The Piedmont

League did not operate during the war season of 1944, but the next year Durham joined the new Class C Carolina League. Eddie Neville set all-time Durham records with 25 wins in 1949 and a 1.72 ERA in 1952, as well as 21 victories in 1953. Emil Karlick was the 1952 batting champ (.347) and Bill Radulovich (.349) kept the crown in Durham the next year. The Bulls fashioned the most victories in the Carolina League in 1951 and 1957, and won the 1957 playoffs.

On June 8, 1963, a 19-year-old rookie made his debut with Durham, after starting the season with Modesto. Joe Morgan pinch hit with a man on base and ripped a two-run homer. The young second baseman hit .332 in 95 games as a Bull, then was promoted to Houston and a 22-year, Hall of Fame career. To date Morgan is the only Hall of Famer to play with Durham.

In 1965 and 1967 the Bulls won the Western Division, along with the 1967 playoffs. The next season Durham and Raleigh merged to form the Raleigh-Durham Mets. A year later Raleigh-Durham affiliated with Philadelphia, and Phillies' prospect Greg Luzinski (.289, 31 HR, 92 RBI) led the club to another playoff championship. The 18-year-old first baseman won the home run title, and the next year began a 14-year big league career.

After the 1972 season the Raleigh-Durham club disbanded, and not until 1980 would Durham resume play. Rejoining the Class A Carolina

Fans lined up in 1989 at the gate of El Toro Stadium, longtime home of the Durham Bulls and site of the 1988 movie Bull Durham. *(Courtesy Durham Bulls)*

League, the Durham Bulls won their division as speedy Albert Hall stole 100 bases to lead the league and establish an all-time club record. Durham posted the highest attendance in the Carolina League, then led the league virtually every year into the 1990s. In 1990 the Bulls became the first Class A club to pass 300,000 (300,499).

Owner Miles Wolff already had begun negotiating with local officials to build a new stadium that would seat 10,000 to 12,000 fans, with the aim of moving Durham into Triple-A ranks. In 1990 Wolff sold the Bulls to Jim Goodman, who shared his goals, although it would take years to achieve both a new ballpark and a Triple-A franchise.

Affiliation with the Braves brought a number of future Atlanta Stars to Durham in the 1990s. In 1990 19-year-old slugger Ryan Klesko was promoted to Durham for the last 77 games of the season (.274 with 47 RBIs). The next year promising young catcher Javy Lopez made the Carolina League All-Star Team. In 1992 hot prospect Chipper Jones played 70 games for Durham (.277) before moving up to Greenville for the last half of the season. Another brilliant young player, 19-year-old center fielder Andruw Jones, started 1996 with Durham (.313 with 17 homers, 43 RBIs, and 65 runs in 66 games) before promotions to Greenville, Richmond and Atlanta.

On April 6, 1995, Durham Bulls Athletic Park opened with an overflow crowd of 10,886. When expansion and realignment brought four new franchises—including Durham—into the International League, the stadium was renovated and enlarged. The most notable feature was Durham's traditional "Blue Monster" in left, which was raised eight feet to a new height of 32 feet.

Elevation to Class Triple-A meant the end of 45 seasons in the Carolina League, but the historic Durham Bulls flourished in the

International League under affiliation with Tampa Bay and the managerial skills of Bill Evers. With 14 teams, the IL created three divisions. Durham seized the lead in the South Division on the last Day of April and cruised to the division title with a nine-game lead over Norfolk. In the opening round of playoffs the Bulls swept Louisville in three games,

Entrance to the downtown ballpark of the Durham Bulls. (Author photo)

The famous Durham Bulls outfield sign. "HIT BULL WIN STEAK" and, below, "HIT GRASS WIN SALAD." (Photo by Karon O'Neal)

then narrowly lost the finals to Buffalo, three games to two.

Handsome "Diamond View" office building overlooking right field at Durham Bulls' Athletic Park. (Photo by Karon O'Neal)

The Durham Bull. (Photo by Karon O'Neal)

Outfield prospect Randy Winn started the 1998 season with Durham, but after 29 games as leadoff hitter (.285 with 29 runs) he was promoted to Tampa Bay. Winn was back in Durham for 46 games the next year (.353) and for 79 games in 2000 (.330).

The 1999 Bulls paced the league with an eye-popping .295 team average. Randy Winn came down from Tampa Bay to make a late-season contribution (.353), while MVP first baseman Steve Cox (.341, 49 2B, 107 R, 125 RBI) led the IL in average, hits, doubles, runs and RBIs. The Bulls repeated as South Division champs and again swept the opening playoff series, this year over Columbus. But as in 1998 the Bulls dropped the finals, with Charlotte winning, three games to one.

In 2000 Randy Winn was leadoff man for the first

half of the season (.330), shortstop Alex Sanchez won the stolen base title (.291 with 52 steals), slugger Ozzie Timmons clubbed 29 homers while leading the IL with 104 RBIs and 100 runs scored, and third baseman Aubrey Huff (.316 with 20 homers in 108 games) was named Rookie of the Year before a callup by Tampa Bay. For the third year in a row Durham won the South Division, but lost the opening series to the eventual playoff champ, Indianapolis, three games to two.

Following three straight division titles, Durham missed the 2001 play-offs despite the efforts of batting champ and All-Star catcher Toby Hall (.335). But in 2002—Durham's 100th anniversary in professional baseball—the Bulls roared to their first IL pennant behind Rookie of the Year Carl Crawford (.296). After recapturing the South Division crown by a four-game margin, the Bulls won six playoff games in a row, sweeping Toledo in the opener and Buffalo in the finals. The IL Governors' Cup represented Durham's first league championship in 33 years.

The next championship came the following season. In 2003 Bill Evers directed the Bulls to their fifth division title in six IL seasons. Opening the playoffs at home, Durham lost the first game to Louisville, then reeled off three straight victories to advance to the finals against Pawtucket. Durham's momentum resulted in a sweep of the PawSox and back-to-back Governors' Cup triumphs.

Although the Bulls failed to make the playoffs in 2004, a 10-1 victory at Syracuse on June 8 gave Bill Evers his 500th win as Durham manager. The Bulls missed postseason play again in 2005, but attracted 520,371 fans to set an all-time season attendance record. The 2006 Bulls also missed the playoffs but produced the IL's Most Valuable

Player and home run champ in first sacker Kevin Witt (.291, 36 HR, 99 RBI).

In 2007 The Bulls stormed to the division

Birthday section featuring Durham's famous "Wool. E. Bull." (Photo by Karon O'Neal)

Wool E. Bull at a Durham game. (Courtesy Durham Bulls)

title behind the pitching of victory leader Mitch Talbot (13-9) and Jeff Niemann (12-6), as well as the steady offensive production of outfielder Justin Ruggiano (.309 with 20 homers). After fighting off Richmond in the South, Durham swept three games from Toledo in the playoff opener. In the finals Durham resumed a season-long duel with Richmond, winner of the Wild Card and of an opening series with Scranton/Wilkes-Barre. Durham and Richmond battled to the fifth game before the Braves prevailed, but it was the fourth time in ten IL seasons that the Bulls had reached the finals.

Year	Record	Pcg.	Finish
1998	80-64	.556	Third (won South and opener, lost finals)
1999	85-60	.580	Second (won South and opener, lost finals)
2000	81-62	.566	Fourth (won South, lost opener)
2001	74-70	.514	Fifth
2002	80-64	.556	Fifth
2003	73-67	.521	Fifth (won South, opener and finals)
2004	77-67	.535	Fourth (lost opener)
2005	65-79	.453	Twelfth
2006	64-78	.451	Eleventh
2007	80-63	.559	Third (won South and opener, lost finals)

First baseman Kevin Witt (.291, 36 HR, 99 RBI), who led the IL in homers and RBIs and was voted Most Valuable Player of 2006. (Courtesy Durham Bulls)

Indianapolis
(INDIANS)

In 1876, after at least a decade of amateur play, professional baseball was brought to Indianapolis by the Blues, who played on a diamond at the fairgrounds racetrack before moving to a wooden ballpark on South Street between Alabama and Delaware streets. The

Indianapolis Blues played in a circuit called the International League in 1877, then joined the National League the following season.

There was not another professional club in Indianapolis until 1883, when a new park was built at Seventh Street and Tennessee Avenue. Because of blue laws, Sunday games were played outside the city limits at Bruce Grounds. The Indianapolis Hoosiers played in the American Association in 1884, shifted to the Western League for 1885, then returned to the National League from 1887 through 1889. Indianapolis reentered the Western League in 1892 and moved into a vast new park on East Ohio Street—the nearest fence was 469 feet from home plate. After winning pennants in 1895, 1897, and 1899, the team moved into yet another new ballpark on Washington Street.

Indianapolis became a charter member of the new American Association in 1901, and remains the only club to play in every AA season. The Indians of 1930 were the first American Association team to perform under lights. The next season the club moved into a 14,500-seat stadium on 16th Street (nostalgic Victory Park became the cinematic home of the 1919 Black Sox in the motion picture *Eight Men Out*). Indianapolis won the first American

Max Schumacher has been the heart of Indianapolis baseball for more than half a century, and in 1997 he was named King of Baseball. (Courtesy IL)

Association pennant on the last day of the 1902 season, and other championships were added in 1908, 1917, 1928, 1949, 1954, 1956, 1961, and 1962.

During six decades of American Association baseball, Indianapolis fans had been treated to performances of numerous gifted players. At the age of 18 in 1908, future

Built in 1928, Victory Park in Indianapolis long hosted American Association baseball. But in 1963, when the Indians spent a lone season in the IL, Indianapolis carved out the league's best record and won the playoffs. Nostalgic Victory Perk became the cinematic home of the 1919 Black Sox in the 1988 motion picture Eight Men Out. *(Author photo)*

Hall of Fame southpaw Rube Marquard led the AA in victories, innings and strikeouts (28-19, 367 IP, 250 Ks), and in six consecutive games pitched a no-hitter and four shutouts. In 1954 another brilliant lefthander, 20-year-old Herb Score, was named AA Rookie of the Year and MVP after leading the league in almost every pitching category (22-5, 21 CG in 32 GS, 2.62 ERA, 250 IP, 330 K, 140 W). Score established the all-time American Association strikeout record, fanned 17 in one game, and won the pitcher's Triple Crown.

Indianapolis won the first American Association pennant in 1902, behind a superb pitching staff: right-handers Tom Williams (24-12) and Jack Sutthoff (24-13), and southpaws Win Kellum (25-10) and Frank Killen (16-6). Lefthander Teller Caveat pitched for Indianapolis for six seasons, 1918 through 1923, enjoying his best years in 1919 (28-16) and 1921 (23-16). Former big leaguer Bill Burnwell, who suffered a finger mutilation during World War I but found his curve to be more effective, hurled for the Indians from 1923 through 1934. The right-hander enjoyed back-to-back 20-win seasons in 1925

(24-9) and 1926 (21-14), overall he was 175-143 with the Tribe, and he returned to Indianapolis as manager in 1945 and 1946.

Following the Tribe's back-to-back pennants in 1961 and 1962 the American Association disbanded. But Indianapolis was added to the International League for 1963—and finished in first place for the third year in a row.

The Arkansas Travelers of Little Rock also became part of the IL in 1963, and the major leagues agreed to pay the league a travel subsidy of almost $94,000 for taking in Indianapolis and Little Rock. Longtime big league catcher Rollie Hemsley was named manager. The Indians continued an affiliation with the Chicago White Sox, and seven returnees from the 1962 champs were in Hemsley's opening day lineup. During the season a number of ex-big leaguers wore Indian uniforms, including outfielders Gene Stephens (.305, 17 HR) and Harry "Suitcase" Simpson (.382 in 11 games), and pitchers Warren Hacker (9-4 in 47 games) and Herb Score (0-6, the injured southpaw's final attempt at a comeback).

Righthanders Fritz Ackley (18-5, 2.76 ERA) and Joe Shipley (15-7) were the team's best starters. Ackley led the IL in victories and was named Pitcher of the Year. The infield was outstanding: Deacon Jones at first (.343 and 19 homers in 97 games), Ramon Conde at second (.299), Charles Smith at short (.231 with a team-leading 25 homers), and Don Buford at third (.336, 42 SB). Buford was the batting champ, led the league in hits, runs and stolen bases, and was an easy choice for MVP.

Center field entrance to Victory Field in Indianapolis. (Author photo)

Indianapolis ended the schedule in a tie for the Southern Division title with Atlanta. The Tribe won a coin toss to stage the one-game playoff at Victory Field. Ackley twirled a two-hit shutout as the Tribe out-dueled the Crackers, 1-0.

Syracuse, champions of the Northern Division, came to Indianapolis for the first three games of a best-of-seven title series. The Indians won all three home contests, 11-2, 2-1, and 5-1. In Syracuse they battled 11 innings before losing 4-3, but came back with a 6-5 victory, again in 11 innings, to clinch the IL pennant in their first season in the league.

In a showdown between second-place clubs, Atlanta swept Toronto in four games for the right to play Indianapolis for the Governors' Cup. The Tribe won the first two games at home, but dropped the third decision in a contest marred by fights. Indianapolis would win the first two games in Atlanta and claim the Cup.

Indianapolis had no chance to defend its International League crown, because IL owners were determined to return to eight teams. Indianapolis caught on with the Pacific Coast League and traveled the vast distances of the PCL for five seasons, although there were no playoff appearances.

By this time Max Schumacher was exerting a strong impact on the franchise. Young Schumacher joined the club in 1956 as ticket manager, but his industry and executive talents resulted in a steady rise to general manager and team president. In more than half a century of service Schumacher has provided vision and continuity of leadership to the Tribe.

When the American Association reorganized in 1969, Indianapolis eagerly assumed

Indianapolis greats Herb Score, Ken Griffey, Al Lopez, and Randy Johnson, displayed proudly outside the center field entrance to Victory Field. On the other side are Larry Walker, Joe Sparks, Dave Concepcion, and Roger Maris. (Author photo)

The Indianapolis Indians tribal tipi overlooks the ballpark from center field. (Author photo)

its familiar place in the league. The Tribe produced the 1969 batting champ and MVP in outfielder Bernie Carbo (.359). The Indians won the Eastern Division in 1971, 1974 and 1978, but lost the finals each year. One year later an Indian institution departed the Tribe after half a century. Norm Beplay, who became a part-time public address announcer for the Indians at old Washington Park in 1929 and who had been the regular PA man since 1942, retired at the end of the 1979 season.

In 1982 the Indians won the Eastern Division and the finals. Although the Tribe dropped to last place in 1985, the next year Indianapolis roared to the best record in the AA, then won the playoffs and the first of four consecutive pennants: 1986, 1987, 1988 and 1989. The 1987 and 1989 titlists were led by battling champs Dallas Williams (.357 in his fifth year with the Indians) and Junior Noboa (.340).

The American Association and the International League formed the Triple-A Alliance in 1988, including a postseason "Alliance Classic" between the champions of the two leagues. Indianapolis won the 1988 Classic, four games to two, over Rochester, then swept Richmond in four games in 1989.

In 1994, although the Alliance Classic had been discontinued, Indianapolis returned to the American Association throne room. Even though the Indians made the playoffs the next three years, there were no further AA pennants. As a result of major league expansion and realignment, the American Association disbanded after the 1997 season, and Indianapolis, Buffalo and Louisville of the AA rejoined the International League.

Indianapolis began IL play in a new stadium, a longtime dream of Max Schumacher. Victory Field opened on July 11, 1996, on a prominent corner in downtown Indianapolis. Named "the Best Minor League Ballpark in America" by various national publications, Victory Field was built for $20 million and can accommodate at least 15,500 fans. The grandstand seats 12,500 and 3,000 more enjoy games from 28 luxury suites, as well as suite lounges, party terraces, a party deck, bleachers, and a lawn area. On July 11, 2001—the fifth anniversary of the stadium's opening—Victory Field hosted the Triple-A All-Star game. A sellout crowd of 15,868 and a national TV audience watched the PCL Stars out slug the IL stars, 9-5.

In 2000, the first year of an affiliation with Milwaukee, Steve Smith managed the Indians to a West Division title. Horacio Estrada led the IL with 14 victories, while outfielder Chris Jones sparked the offense (.315). In the playoff opener Indianapolis had to win the last two games in Durham to advance to the finals. Again the series went five games, as the Tribe outlasted Scranton/Wilkes-Barre to win the IL pennant. The Indians next met Memphis in the third Triple-A World Series. The first two Series had been won by the PCL champs, but Indianapolis defeated Memphis in four games to bring the title to the International League (the Series thereafter was discontinued).

The next year Indian slugger Micah Franklin blasted three home runs during a September 1 game against Toledo. The 2004 ERA title was won by Indian hurler Ben Hendrickson (2.02). Fireballing right-hander Ian Snell (11-4) pitched a nine-inning no-hitter on May 15, 2005, striking out nine and beating Norfolk 4-0 behind a three-run homer by leftfielder Jon Nunnally. Southpaw Zach Duke roared to a 12-3 start before the end of June. Although promoted to Pittsburgh (8-2 with a 1.81 ERA), Duke's sizzling first half earned him the IL's Most Valuable Player Award for 2005.

The 2005 offense featured catchers Ronny Paulino (.306 with 19 homers) and Ryan

Doumit (.345 with 12 homers), and outfielders Chris Duffy (.308) and Nate McLouth (.297). Manager Trent Jewett guided the Tribe to the Wild Card slot in the playoffs. In the opener Buffalo won both games at Victory Field. The series shifted to Buffalo with the Bisons needing only one more win, but the Indians charged to three straight road victories to advance to the finals. The come-from-behind effort had spent the Tribe, however, and Toledo swept the Indians to take the Governors' Cup.

The 2006 Indians posted a winning record behind the IL's best defense, including 74 errorless games. Catcher Carlos Maldonado (.283) led all catchers in fielding percentage (.996), while flashy shortstop J.J. Furmaniak won the Tribe's Defensive Award. Indianapolis and Toledo tied for the title in the West, but the Mud Hens won a single-game playoff, then advanced to their second consecutive Governors' Cup. For the third consecutive year the Indians led the league in stolen bases: 163 in 2005; 180 in 2006; and 163 again in 2007. The 2007 Indians jumped ten percent in attendance, from an average of 7,608 fans per game in 2006 to 8,303. Total attendance for 2007 was 586,785, the highest at Victory Field since 2001.

Zach Duke Most Valuable Pitcher

Southpaw Zach Duke was named Most Valuable Pitcher for 2005. Duke started 16 games for Indianapolis (12-3, 2.92 ERA), then was just as effective in 14 appearances for Pittsburgh (8-2, 1.81 ERA). (Courtesy IL)

Year	Record	Pcg.	Finish
1963	88-67	.562	First (won opener and finals)
1998	76-67	.531	Sixth
1999	75-69	.521	Seventh
2000	81-63	.563	Fifth (won West, opener and finals, lost Triple-A World Series)
2001	66-78	.458	Eleventh
2002	67-76	.469	Ninth
2003	64-78	.451	Twelfth
2004	66-78	.458	Eleventh
2005	78-66	.542	Fourth (won opener, lost finals)
2006	76-66	.535	Fifth
2007	70-73	.490	Eighth

Louisville
(COLONELS, REDBIRDS, RIVER BATS, BATS)

Few cities can claim as rich a baseball heritage as Louisville. On April 19, 1865, the Louisville Club played the Nashville Cumberlands in an open field that is today 19th and Duncan. Although Louisville triumphed, 22-5, it was the city's first game and the spectators had to ask the official scorer who won. The scorer was Mrs. John Dickens, wife of the Nashville captain and shortstop and the first woman ever identified officially with the new sport. The Louisville catcher was Theodore F. Tracy, who courageously became the first backstop ever known to play "under the bat"—catchers had no protective equipment and always positioned themselves 30 or 40 feet behind the plate.

Members of the Louisville Club had to pay $2 per month in dues, and were fined 10 to 25 cents for swearing on the field—$3.30 was collected in 1865! By the next year the team played at a diamond bounded by Third, Fifth, Oak and Park streets, although the ballpark soon was moved to a site now occupied by St. James Court.

This park would be the home of Louisville's first professional team. Late in 1875 a series of meetings was held in Larry Gatto's Saloon on Green Street to organize the National League, and when play began in 1876 Louisville fielded one of the original eight NL teams. After it was learned that four Louisville players accepted $100 each to throw a crucial series with Hartford, the players were banned from professional baseball and Louisville dropped out of the National League.

But in 1882 the American Association was organized as a major league to challenge the National League, and Louisville provided one of six charter clubs. Eclipse Park was located at 28th and Elliott streets, and the team was called the Louisville "Eclipse," an awkward nickname which gave way to several sobriquets during succeeding seasons (after a disastrous storm killed 75 Louisville residents in 1890, the players were dubbed "Cyclones"). Throughout the 1880s the team's best hitter was Pete Browning, who won AA batting crowns in 1882 (.382) and 1885 (.367). In 1884 Browning broke his favorite bat—one he had made himself (shades of Roy Hobbs and "Wonder Boy")—and he went to the shop of wood-turner J. F. Hillerich at First Street near Market. Hillerich and Browning worked into the night to craft a bat that the slugger praised throughout the league. Within a short time the little woodturning shop became Hillerich & Bradsby, the bat-making giant which turned out Louisville Sluggers.

The best pitcher of the 1880s was left-hander Toad Ramsey (37-27 in 1886 and 39-27 the next year). Once offered $100 to pitch a game, Toad suggested that instead he be paid $5 per strikeout. He whiffed 24, and earned $120! In 1888 Louisville players conducted baseball's first player strike when new owner M. H. Davidson decided to levy a fine for every fielding error. For two days the team boycotted games in Baltimore, causing Louisville to forfeit, but on the third day resistance crumbled. The players returned to

Pete Browning, Louisville batting champ of the 1880s, was responsible for the creation of the famed Louisville Slugger bats. (Courtesy of the Louisville Redbirds)

the field, continued to make errors—and paid Davidson's fines!

During the calamitous Johnstown Flood of 1889, the team was on a train which was marooned by high waters, and the Colonels were missing and presumed lost for two days. The 1889 Colonels were hapless, losing 26 games in a row, changing managers seven times during the season, and finishing 27-111 (.195). But the next year the club rocketed from last to first, winning Louisville's only major league pennant. The American Association folded after the 1891 season, but Louisville was absorbed into the National League.

During the 1890s, future Hall of Famers Rube Waddell, Hughey Jennings, Fred Clarke, Jimmy Collins, Dan Brouthers, and the legendary Honus Wagner played for the Colonels, and Wagner became the first player to have his autograph inscribed on a Louisville Slugger bat. In his first game as Louisville's third baseman, Jimmy Collins became the first third sacker to leave his base, playing toward shortstop or into left field, as

Louisville Colonels of 1909 in their dugout at Eclipse Park. (Courtesy Louisville Redbirds)

the situation dictated (and in an 1885 game at Eclipse Park, St. Louis first baseman Charles Comiskey became the first man at his position to play off the bag). Late in the 1899 season the grandstand at Eclipse Park burned, forcing all remaining games to be played on the road. The Louisville "Wanderers" won what proved to be Louisville's final major league game, 25-4 over Washington. After the season the National League reduced its size from twelve to eight teams, and Louisville was one of the clubs eliminated.

In 1901 Louisville formed its first minor league team, the Colonels of the Western Association. By June, however, the club folded and was sold to Grand Rapids, and the league shut down before the month ended. But when the minor league American Association was organized in 1902, a new team of Colonels became charter members (replacing Omaha, which was to be one of the eight original cities—until it was decided that Omaha was too far away from the other seven cities). Owner George "White Wings" Tabeau hastily built a new Eclipse Park at 7th and Kentucky, which was not quite finished for the season

opener. The grandstand was soaked with paint and roofed with tar paper; Eclipse Park was a fire trap, and would eventually succumb to flames, but it hosted American Association baseball for 21 seasons. After the ballpark burned in 1922, it was replaced by Parkway Field, a steel-and-concrete facility costing $100,000 and seating 14,500. The outfield was vast, with dead enter located 507 feet from home plate, although left field was near enough to cause construction of a tall, Fenway Park-style fence. Parkway Field served as home of the Colonels for 33 years.

Louisville won its first AA pennant in 1909, followed by flags in 1916 and 1921, when the Colonels whipped Jack Dunn's great Baltimore team in the Little World Series. There were back-to-back pennants in 1925 and 1926, but the Colonels were defeated by Baltimore and Toronto in the Little World Series. The 1930 champs lost to Rochester in the post-season classic. But the 1939 Colonels inched into the AA playoffs with a losing record, then won the playoffs and the Junior World Series over IL titlist Rochester. The next year Louisville repeated as playoff winner but fell to Newark in the Junior World Series.

A third-place Colonels club won the 1944 playoffs before dropping the Junior World Series to Baltimore. The following season, however, another third-place team made it to the Junior World Series, then beat Newark. In 1946 the Colonels finished first and won

Opening day at Louisville's Eclipse Park, 1913. Paying customers were never turned away. Any hit that went into the overflow crowd behind the rope was a ground-rule double. (Courtesy Louisville Redbirds)

the playoffs, but lost the Junior World Series to Montreal. The second-place Colonels of 1954 took the playoff and the Junior World Series over Syracuse.

In 1957 the Louisville team moved from Parkway Field to Fairgrounds Stadium. Beginning in 1960, the Colonels fought their way to the Junior World Series for three consecutive years, defeating Toronto, then losing to Buffalo and Atlanta. But the 1962 loss to Atlanta in seven games proved to be a minor disappointment when the American Association disbanded after the season. Efforts to join the International League were fruitless, and Louisville found itself without profes-

sional baseball for the first time in the twentieth century.

Early in 1964, Charles O. Finley, the colorful but controversial owner of the Kansas City Athletics, signed a two-year contract for his team to play in Fairgrounds Stadium. However, American League owners blocked his attempt to move the A's to Louisville. Finally, in 1968, Walter Dilbeck, an Evansville real estate man, bought Toronto's International League franchise and took the club to Louisville. The Boston Red Sox, longtime affiliate of the American Association Colonels, again established a working agreement with Louisville.

The manager was Eddie Kasko, and righthander Galen Cisco (11-12, 2.21 ERA) was the ERA titlist. Still, the Colonels finished seventh in their first International League

During a long career spent primarily in the minor leagues, heavy-hitting first baseman Jay Kirke played seven seasons for Louisville. While with the Colonels he won the 1921 American Association batting title (.386) and set the AA season record for hits (282). Although Kirke never appeared in the International League, he played for seven IL cities while they were in different leagues. (Courtesy Louisville Redbirds)

Lefthanded outfielder Earle Combs entered pro ball with Louisville in 1922 (.344) and 1923 (.380), then spent 12 seasons with the New York Yankees and was voted into the Hall of Fame in 1970. (Courtesy Louisville Redbirds)

Veteran second baseman Joe McCarthy played for Buffalo in 1914 and 1915, leading the International League in assists both seasons. In 1916 he moved to Louisville of the American Association for the final six years of his playing career. McCarthy assumed the managerial reins in 1919, finally leaving the Colonels on 1926 for a Hall of Fame career as a big league manager.

season. In 1969 Kasko guided the Colonels to second place, just 1½ games behind Tidewater. Catchers Harold King (.322 in 106 games) and Bob Montgomery (.292 in 134 games) both were named to the All-Star Team, along with shortstop Luis Alvarado (.292), who led the IL in runs, hits, and doubles. Outfielder Al Yates also was productive at the plate (.294), while the best pitchers were Gerald Janeski (15-10) and Billy Farmer (12-10). The Colonels paced the league in staff ERA and team fielding, but lost to Syracuse in the opening round of playoffs.

Bob Montgomery again was the All-Star

catcher (.324) in 1970, and outfielder Al Yates improved at the plate (.304). Billy Farmer wore a Louisville uniform long enough (3-2) to fire a seven-inning no-hitter over Toledo. But overall the Colonels were weaker, and sank to sixth under manager Billy Gardner. Darrell Johnson took over the managerial reins the next season and outfielder Ben Ogilvie enjoyed a fine year (.304 with 17 homers), but Louisville could rise no higher than fifth.

In 1972 Johnson led the Colonels to the pennant in a race so tight that only six games separated the top five teams. Louisville led the IL in team hitting (.279) by a margin of 21 points behind RBI leader Dwight Evans (.300, 17 HR, 95 RBI), fellow outfielders Chris Colletta (.319) and Roger Nelson (.301), first baseman Cecil Cooper (.315), shortstops Juan Beniquez (.294 in 66 games), and Mario Guerrero (.292 in 69 games), and utility man John Mason (.307). Vic Correll (.271) was named All-Star catcher, southpaw Craig Skok (15-7) led the IL in victories, and second baseman Buddy Hunter was the best fielder at his position. The only letdown of the season occurred when the champions were defeated, three games to two, in the playoff finals.

The 1972 flag proved to be Louisville's swan song in the International League for the time being. The Kentucky State Fair Board decided to expend and redesign Fairgrounds Stadium primarily for football, and after the season the pennant-winning Colonels were evicted. Since there was no other suitable ballpark, Louisville was forced to give up professional baseball, and the Red Sox transferred their talented roster to nearby Pawtucket.

Nine years passed without pro ball in Louisville, but in 1981 Louisville banker Dan Ulmer headed a group dedicated to obtaining an American Association club. Ulmer persuasively sold A. Ray Smith on bringing his Cardinal affiliate to Louisville (since 1977 the

American Association team had move from Tulsa to New Orleans to Springfield). The Louisville Baseball Committee financed a $4.5 million remodeling of Fairgrounds Stadium, and the timing of Smith and Ulmer proved perfect. Louisville citizens were starved for baseball and anxious for a pleasant, wholesome, affordable center for family entertainment. The 1982 Redbirds provided a winning club, fans turned out in droves from opening night, and Smith became so popular that when he wandered through the stands each evening in his checkered sport coat, the crowd would chant, "A. Ray! "A. Ray!" By the end of the season Louisville had established a new minor league attendance record with more than 868,000 paid admissions.

The Redbirds put a championship team on the field for the next three years, and from 1982-1985 Louisville led all minor league clubs in attendance. The 1983 Redbirds became the first minor league club in history to break the one million mark—the latest in a long line of remarkable baseball achievements for Louisville.

In 1995 Louisville returned to the American Association throne room, defeating Indianapolis and Buffalo in the playoffs. Two years later, when the American Association disbanded, these three clubs moved into the International League for 1998.

Louisville's last season in the IL, 1972, had resulted in a playoff run that fell just one victory short of the Governors' Cup. The 1998 Redbirds won the West Division by half a game over Indianapolis. Speedy infielder Ron Belliard ignited the offense (.321), scoring a league-leading 114 runs—the most by any IL player in the previous 15 years, and the most in the 10 years since. In the playoff opener Louisville was swept by Durham.

Louisville's Fairgrounds Stadium was converted for baseball after the 1981 season and renamed Cardinal Stadium. In 1983 the American Association club attracted more than one million fans. (Courtesy Louisville Redbirds)

The next season brought a name change, from Redbirds to Riverbats, and a stolen base title by Greg Martinez, with 48 thefts. On May 14, 2000, Riverbat hurler Larry Luebbers beat Charlotte, 5-0, with a seven-inning no-

Outside Louisville Slugger Field is a statue of Hall of Famer Pee Wee Reese, Louisville's favorite former player. (Photo by Karon O'Neal)

hitter. A month earlier the Riverbats opened the schedule with magnificent new Louisville Slugger Field. The 13,200-seat stadium was full, and even though the Riverbats finished below .500, Louisville drew a league-leading 685,863 fans for the season.

In 2001 Dave Miley guided the Riverbats to another West Division title by a whopping 16½—game margin. Outfielder Raul Gonzalez (.299) led the IL in hits and sparked a fine offense. In the playoff opener the Riverbat pitching staff posted three shutouts in five games against Norfolk. Louisville won the first game of the finals over Scranton/Wilkes-Barre, 2-1, with another strong pitching performance. The next morning, September 11, 2001, the nation was stunned by a vicious terrorist attack. A day later IL President Mobley halted the playoffs and awarded the Governors' Cup to Louisville.

Outfielder Raul Gonzalez had an even better season in 2002 (.333) and was voted the league's Most Valuable Player, while All-Star DH Kevin Witt led the IL with 107 RBIs. The 2004 Riverbats won another West Division crown, but lost the playoff opener in four games to eventual Governors' Cup winner Durham.

Third baseman Edwin Encarnacion was

Spectacular sign proclaiming Louisville Slugger Field. (Photo by Karon O'Neal)

voted a 2005 All-Star, and on July 5, 2005, outfielder Austin Kearns (.342, 7 HR, 21 RBI in part of a season) blasted three home runs in a game over Indianapolis. The next year outfielder Chris Danorfia (.349 in 83 games) fell short of qualifying for the hitting title. But outfield teammate Norris Hopper (.347 in 98 games) had a longer stint with the Riverbats and brought Louisville its first IL batting championship.

The 2007 Bats performed a second consecutive winning season and led the IL in attendance, with a season total of 653,915 and an average of 9,210 per game. Club president Gary Ulmer was voted IL Executive of the Year, the first time the honor had been awarded to a Louisville official. Twenty-year-old Jay Bruce, a first-round pick by the Cincinnati Reds in 2005, was selected as Baseball America's Minor League Player of the Year. The hard-hitting outfielder started 2007 with Class A Sarasota (.325), moved up to Class AA Chattanooga (.333), then was promoted to Louisville, where he played 50 games (.305 with 11 homers). Over the season Bruce hit .305 with 46 doubles, 8 triples and 26 home runs, a total of 80 extra base hits and 300 total bases.

Year	Record	Pcg.	Finish
1968	72-75	.490	Sixth
1969	77-63	.550	Second (lost opener)
1970	69-71	.493	Sixth
1971	71-69	.507	Fifth
1972	81-63	.563	First (won opener, lost finals)
1998	77-67	.535	Fifth (won West, opener and finals, lost Triple-A World Series)
1999	63-81	.438	Tenth
2000	71-73	.493	Ninth
2001	84-60	.583	Third (won West, opener and finals)
2002	79-65	.549	Sixth
2003	79-64	.552	Second (won West, lost opener)
2004	67-77	.465	Tenth
2005	66-78	.458	Eleventh
2006	75-68	.524	Sixth
2007	74-70	.514	Seventh

Norfolk
(TIDES—TIDEWATER)

Before allying to form a Triple-A franchise in the International League, Norfolk and Portsmouth conducted one of the keenest rivalries in baseball history. The Tidewater cities entered pro ball in 1894 as charter members of the Virginia League. The circuit lasted just two years, but Norfolk moved into the Atlantic League, which disbanded in 1899. The next year Norfolk and Portsmouth joined a reorganized Virginia League, but the league folded before the schedule could be played out. Taking advantage of fan interest in their rivalry, however, the Norfolk Phenoms and the Portsmouth Band of Bears played 40 more games against each other— the longest series in professional baseball! Pitching for Norfolk in 1900 was 19-year-old Christy Mathewson (who was labeled

"Mathews" in Virginia League box scores); after compiling a brilliant record (20-2), the future Hall of Famer was sold to the New York Giants at mid-season.

In 1906 the Virginia League again was revived, and Norfolk and Portsmouth once more were enlisted. The Class C circuit operated until 1928; Norfolk participated in every season, while Portsmouth missed only 1911 and 1917. The Norfolk Tars won Virginia League flags in 1909 and 1914, and the Portsmouth Truckers won pennants in 1920, 1921, and 1927. The 1923 Truckers starred Hack Wilson, a stubby slugger who won the Triple Crown (.388, 19 HR, 101 RBI), then move to a Hall of Fame career. Another future Hall of Famer, shortstop Pie Traynor, broke in with the Truckers as a 20-year-old rookie in 1920.

After the Virginia League halted play in 1928, Norfolk joined the Class B Eastern League in 1931, but the circuit folded in July 1932. Two years later, the New York Yankees decided to establish a Norfolk club in their growing farm system. Under Yankee owner-

ship, the Norfolk Tars joined the Class B Piedmont League and immediately recorded a pennant. After the 1934 championship the Tars won again in 1936, 1938 and 1945, then won four straight flags from 1951 through 1954. Year after year, the Yankees paraded talented young ballplayers through Norfolk, including Yogi Berra, Phil Rizzuto, Whitey Ford, Gerry Priddy, and Tidewater native Bob Porterfield. The most appreciative and vocal fans were the Loyal Tar Rooters, who clustered in seats behind the home dugout.

Norfolk continued its profitable rivalry with Portsmouth, which entered the Piedmont League in 1935 and won pennants in 1943 and 1950. Portsmouth's longtime owner was Frank D. Lawrence, a dynamic and community-minded baseball man who built a fine concrete-and-steel stadium for his team. But in 1949 Lawrence astutely predicted, despite postwar prosperity, that television and other forces would wreck minor league baseball, unless the majors subsidized the minors. Soon minor leagues began to fold by the dozens, and despite four straight pennants the Yankees pulled out of Norfolk. Local owners tried to revive the Tars, but the team died in 1955, and so did Lawrence's club—and the Piedmont League soon would follow.

Norfolk's historic Myers Field became a farmers' market, as produce sellers set up stalls beneath the grandstand. The first professional ballpark, Lafayette Park, oc-

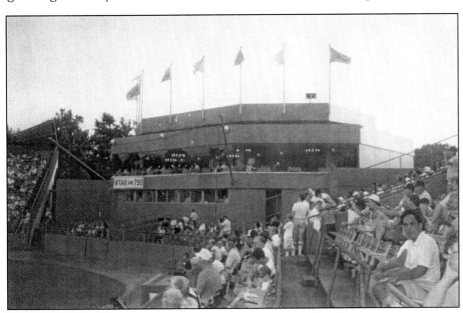

Tidewater fans at Met Park in 1990. (Author photo)

cupied part of the site until it was replaced early in the twentieth century by League Park, located where Virginia Transit Company garages now stand. League Park soon gave way to Bain Field, built just around the corner on 20th Street. In 1939 Dr. Edward Myers, a local dentist, began construction of a ballpark on a six-acre tract he owned, and Myers Field opened during the summer of 1958, but the following December fire gutted the grandstand.

As the adjacent Norfolk-Portsmouth-Virginia Beach area boomed with growth, there was interest among businessmen as well as baseball enthusiasts to create a Tidewater club. In 1958 Joe Ryan, general manager of the Miami Marlins, was sent to the Tidewater area to explore the possibilities of moving the International League team to Norfolk, but the lack of a stadium killed the deal for 1959. The 1960 All-Star Game of the Sally League was played in Portsmouth's Lawrence Stadium to an appreciative crowd of 6,000. The following year Bill MacDonald, millionaire owner of the Miami Marlins, organized the Tidewater Tides of the Sally League. The Tides played for two years before being squeezed out after the 1962 season, primarily because of the distances from other Sally League cities. MacDonald pulled out, but Tidewater Professional Sports was organized to take over the club. Dave Rosenfield was hired as GM, a position he still holds, and

the Tides joined the Class A Carolina League through the 1968 season, when the New York Mets decided to move their Triple-A IL affiliate from Jacksonville to Tidewater.

Just as ownership by the New York Yankees brought an immediate pennant and extended success to the Norfolk Tars, ownership of the Tides by the New York Mets produced a first-year pennant and one winner after another for more than two decades. The 1969 Tides, managed by Clyde McCullough, led the IL in hitting behind first baseman Mike Jorgensen (.290 with 21 homers), and outfielders Amos Otis (.327 in 71 games) and Jim Gosger (.341 in 58 games). The best pitchers were southpaw Jon Matlack (14-7) and right-handed reliever Larry Bearnath (11-4), who led the league in winning percentage.

In 1970 the defending champs were able to move out of Lawrence Stadium and into Metropolitan Park on Northampton Boulevard in Norfolk. Although the seating capac-

Entrance to beautiful Harbor Park, home of the Norfolk Tides since 1993. (Photo by Karon O'Neal)

ity was less than 6,000 (Triple-A crowds of the period averaged only 3,000), Met Park was the first minor league stadium to boast a restaurant overlooking the field of play. There was an immediate impact on attendance, with 142,000 fans coming to Met Park, in contrast to a meager 67,000 during the championship year of 1969.

The Tides followed the championship year of 1969 with three more playoff teams. The fireballing Matlack returned to lead the 1970 pitching staff (12-11), and a fine offense was paced by outfielders Rodney Gaspar (.318) and Ed Kranepool (.310 in 47 games), along with infielder Teddy Martinez (.306). The 1969 and 1970 teams were defeated in the opening round of playoffs, but the 1971 Tides battled to the finals before losing to Rochester, three games to two. Former Yankee great Hank Bauer managed the Tides to second place, relying upon a mound corps that posted the league's stingiest ERA. Buzz Capra (13-3, 2.19 ERA) was the ERA champ, and Jim Bibby (15-6) led the IL in victories, while

offense was provided by hit and RBI leader Leroy Staton (.324, 23 HR, 101 RBI) and a lineup which led the league in homers.

In 1972 Bauer guided the Tides to third place in a tight pennant race, then won the playoff title. The Tides were anchored around first baseman George Theodore (.296) and righthanders Harry Parker (14-9) and Tommy Moore (11-5). The 1973 cub posted a winning record and the league's best ERA, but finished fifth, and the seventh-place team of 1974 also missed the playoffs.

The Tides roared back, battling neck and neck with Rochester for the 1975 pennant. The two teams finished the schedule in a deadlock, but Tidewater won a single-game playoff, then downed Charleston and Syracuse in postseason play to cop all IL championship honors for the year. Outfielder Mike Vail (.342) became the first Tidewater player to win an IL batting title and to be named MVP. Other key hitters were RBI champ Roy Staiger (.281 with 81 RBIs) and first baseman Brock Pemberton (.297).

Tidewater led the league in team fielding and staff ERA; the best pitchers were righthander Craig Swan (13-7) and lefty Bill Laxton (11-4).

The next year Tidewater plunged to seventh place, despite the play of All-Star catcher John Stearns (.310). In 1977 the Tides bounced back into the playoffs behind reliever Mardie Cornejo (11-6 with 56 appearances)

Third-base-side grandstand at Harbor Park. (Photo by Karon O'Neal)

and starter Roy Jackson (13-7). It was back to second division in 1978, but the following season ERA champ Scott Holman (13-7, 1.99 ERA) and veteran righthander Roy Jackson (12-7) led a weak-hitting club (.239) to another playoff berth. Despite the presence of future big league standouts Mookie Wilson (.295) and Juan Berenguer (9-15 with a league-leading 178 Ks in only 157 IP), the 1980 Mets again slid into the second division.

From 1981 through 1988, Tidewater produced eight consecutive winning teams, missing postseason play only in 1984. By 1982 the last three Tidewater playoff teams (1977, 1979, and 1981) had not made it past the opening round, but the third-place Tides of '82 swept Columbus in the opener and Rochester in the finals to claim another championship. Tidewater's balanced offense was charged by outfielders Kerry Tillman (.322) and Gil Flores (.322 in 83 games).

The next year was even better. Davey Johnson took over the managerial reins from Jack Aker and welcomed back Kerry Tillman (.255), Gil Flores (.312 in 88 games), and pitchers Ron Darling (10-9) and Walt Terrell, who was brilliant in 12 games (10-1) before an inevitable callup to New York. Switch-hitting infielder Wally Backman (.316) turned in a performance that placed him with the Mets to stay, while young outfielder Darryl Strawberry demonstrated the promise of stardom in a late-season promotion (.333 in 16 games) from the Texas League. The fourth-place Tides knocked off first-place Columbus in the opener, three games to two, then retained the Governors' Cup

by defeating Richmond in three games out of four. A Triple-A World Series had been organized, and Tidewater won a round-robin playoff against Denver of the American Association and Portland of the Pacific Coast League.

Davey Johnson, Darryl Strawberry, Wally Backman, Ron Darling, and other stars of the '83 champs were promoted to the Mets, and Tidewater dropped out of the playoff picture. But outfielders LaSchelle Tarver (.326) and John Christensen (.316) were the league's number-two and number-three hitters, while left-hander Bill Latham (11-3) and reliever Wes Gardner (1.61 ERA in 40 games) were standout pitchers. In 1985 Tarver returned (.311) and so did Latham (13-8) and Gardner (7-6 with a 2.82 ERA in 53 games), who anchored a pitching staff that recorded the IL's best ERA. Manager Bob Schaefer also enjoyed the services of stocky infielder Kevin Mitchell (.290) and All-Star outfielder Billy Beane (.284 with 19 homers and a league-leading 34 doubles). The third-place Tides edged the Maine Guides in the opener, 3-2, then collected another Governors' Cup by

Part of Norfolk's busy harbor is in view just beyond the outfield of Harbor Park. (Photo by Karon O'Neal)

disposing of Columbus in four games. The 1986 Tides led the league in team hitting and ERA, featuring All-Star third-sacker Dave Magadan (.311), league-leading shortstop Alfredo Pedrique (.293), outfielders Stan Jefferson (.290) and Mark Carreon (.289), All-Star reliever Randy Myers (2.35 ERA in 45 games), and Most Valuable Pitcher John Mitchell (12-9). But this fine roster could only reach fourth place, and the Tides were swept by first-place Columbus in the playoff opener.

Sky box interior at Harbor Park. (Photo by Karon O'Neal)

Tidewater provided the first-place team for the next two years. The 1987 Tides again led the IL in team hitting and ERA with a stellar lineup; MVP first baseman Randy Milligan (.326, 29 HR, 103 RBI), who led the league in homers, RBIs, walks, runs, and total bases; Kevin Elster (.310), who was the IL leader in hits and doubles; outfielders Andre David (.300) and Mark Carreon (.312), the doubles leader; ERA champ DeWayne Vaughn (2.66 in 50 appearances); percentage leader Don Schultze (11-1); and Dwight Gooden in a highly successful rehab assignment (3-0). Manager Mike Cubbage repeated in 1988, winning the newly-created Eastern Division by an 11-game margin. Once more the Tides posted the league's best team ERA and batting average. Mark Carreon again was named an All-Star outfielder, southpaw Dave West (12-4 with a sparkling 1.80 ERA) was the ERA and percentage champ, and on June 27 John Mitchell beat Indianapolis, 1-0, with only the seventh seven-inning perfect game in more than a century of IL play.

The success of Tidewater in the International League had been a model of consistency. In 22 years the Tides had suffered only four losing seasons. There had been five first-place finishes, 14 playoff appearances, five playoff titles, and victory in the 1983 Triple-A World Series.

Another winning season followed in 1989, as Tom O'Malley won the RBI title and was voted MVP. The next year Manny Hernandez (12-11 with 157 Ks) was the strikeout king, while outfielder Keith Hughes (.309) missed the batting title

"Riptide," mascot of the Tides, sports a baseball nose. (Courtesy IL)

by one point. On May 15, 1992, Dave Telgheder fired a nine-inning no-hitter to defeat Pawtucket, 1-0.

In 1993 the Tides moved into a splendid new stadium, Harbor Park, which seated more than 12,000 fans. Tidewater enjoyed a record attendance which, along with the addition of expansion franchises in Charlotte and Ottawa, allowed the IL to post a record season attendance of more than 4.7 million and became the first minor league to break the four million mark in a single season.

Two years later Tidewater established all-time franchise attendance records through the combined lure of magnificent Harbor Park and another playoff team. Righthander Jason Isringhausen was brilliant (9-1 in 12 starts with a 1.55 ERA). He led the league in winning percentage and, despite a mid-sea-

son callup to the Mets (9-2 in 14 starts), he was voted Rookie-of-the-Year and Most Valuable Pitcher. Versatile Butch Huskey played third, first and outfield while leading the league in homers (.284, 28 HR, 87 RBI), including three during a May 29 game against Toledo. The Tides bolted to a dominating start, and expectant fans flocked to Harbor Park night after night. In the playoff opener against rival Richmond, a standing-room-only crowd of 13,727 set the single-game attendance record for Norfolk, while season attendance totaled a record 586,317. The Tides defeated Richmond, three games to two, but would win only one game against Ottawa in the Governors' Cup finals.

Quality pitching continued to be a Tidewater trademark in 1996 as Mike Fyhrie led the IL with 15 victories and a 3.04 ERA, while Mike Gardiner (13-3) was the percentage titlist. Beginning with Eric Hillman (10-1) in 1994, a Tidewater pitcher posted the IL's

Norfolk GM Dave Rosenfield has devoted 45 years to the Tides, and in 2004 he was crowned King of Baseball. (Courtesy IL)

U.S. Coast Guard color guard at a Norfolk Tides game. (Courtesy IL)

best winning percentage four years in a row: Isringhausen (9-4) in 1995, Gardiner (13-3) in 1996, and Jim Dougherty (10-1) in 1997.

In 1998 steady-hitting infielder Todd Haney won the batting crown with the highest average (.345) ever achieved by a Tidewater batter. The Tides had a winning season (77-63) the next year, then returned to the play-offs in 2001. Manager John Gibbons directed the Tides to a 12-game margin in the South Division, while Pete Walker led the IL with 13 victories. The playoff series with Louisville opened at Harbor Park, where the teams split the two games. In Louisville the Tides won another contest, but suffered a shutout in Game Five.

Another South Division title by an even larger margin—14 games—came in 2005 under Ken Oberkfell, who was named Minor League Manager of the Year by *Baseball America*. Jason Scobie (15-7) led the league in wins, and offense was provided by All-Star DH Brian Daubach (.325) and a trio of play-ers who spent only part of the season in Norfolk: infielders Jeff Keppinger (.337) and Andy Hernandez (.303), and outfielder Victor Diaz (.300). Tidewater faced Toledo, the eventual champions, in the playoff opener and battled to the fifth game before being eliminated.

Although Tidewater has not reached the playoffs during the last two seasons, there re-mains no finer setting for minor league base-ball than Norfolk's Harbor Park.

Year	Record	Pcg.	Finish
1969	76-59	.563	First (lost opener)
1970	74-66	.529	Fourth (lost opener)
1971	79-61	.561	Second (won opener, lost finals)
1972	78-65	.545	Third (won opener and finals)
1973	75-70	.517	Fifth
1974	57-82	.410	Seventh
1975	86-55	.610	First (won opener and finals, lost JWS)
1976	60-78	.435	Seventh
1977	73-67	.521	Third (lost opener)
1978	69-71	.493	Fifth
1979	73-67	.521	Fourth (lost opener)
1980	67-72	.482	Sixth
1981	70-68	.507	Third (lost opener)
1982	74-63	.540	Third (won opener and finals)
1983	71-68	.511	Fourth (won opener, finals, and AAA World Series)
1984	71-69	.507	Fifth
1985	75-64	.540	Third (won opener and finals)
1986	74-66	.529	Fourth (lost opener)
1987	81-59	.579	First (won opener, lost finals)
1988	77-64	.546	First (won Eastern Division, lost playoff)
1989	77-69	.527	Third
1990	79-67	.541	Third
1991	77-65	.542	Third
1992	56-86	.394	Eighth
1993	70-71	.496	Sixth
1994	67-75	.472	Eighth
1995	86-56	.606	First (won Eastern Division and opener, lost finals)
1996	82-59	.582	Second (lost opener)
1997	75-67	.528	Fifth
1998	70-72	.493	Seventh
1999	77-63	.550	Fifth
2000	65-79	.451	Tenth
2001	85-57	.599	Second (won South, lost opener)
2002	70-73	.490	Eighth
2003	67-76	.469	Tenth
2004	72-72	.500	Seventh
2005	79-65	.549	Third (won South, lost opener)
2006	57-84	.404	Thirteenth
2007	69-74	.483	Ninth

Pawtucket
(RED SOX, PAWSOX)

Pawtucket is located to the northeast of Providence, Rhode Island, and local baseball fans were able to enjoy IL ball with a short trip to the capital city from 1891 through 1917 and in 1925. Pawtucket itself had placed a team in the Class D Athletic Association in 1908 and the Class C Colonial League in 1914, but neither lasted more than one season. Amateur and semipro teams were highly popular, however, and the WPA erected McCoy Stadium in 1942. Built on a 40-acre swamp known as Hammond Pond, the 6,000-seat ballpark was named after Pawtucket manager Thomas P. McCoy, and it was completed at the astronomical—and locally controversial—cost of $1.5 million.

McCoy Stadium hosted its first professional team during the postwar baseball boom. The Pawtucket Slaters (named after historic Slater Mill), a Class B affiliate of the nearby Boston Braves, played in the New England League from 1946 until the circuit folded after the 1949 season. Although 17 years passed without pro ball, McCoy Stadium was repaired in 1966 to welcome the Paw-

tucket Indians of the Double-A Eastern League. Owner Jerry Waring had transferred his Cleveland affiliate from Reading, but after two seasons he moved the Indians to Waterbury, Connecticut. Although there was no pro ball in 1968, the next year enterprising minor league club owner Joe Buzas brought his Pittsfield Red Sox to town for two Eastern League games in McCoy Stadium. Attendance was so good that Buzas moved the franchise to Pawtucket for the 1970 season.

Red Sox officials appreciated the convenience of an affiliate located just 40 miles from Fenway Park, and after the 1972 season Buzas acquired Boston's IL franchise from a Louisville group. Buzas shifted his Eastern League club to Bristol, Connecticut, and Triple-A baseball arrived at Pawtucket. Players wore Red Sox uniforms and were known as "Red Sox" or "PawSox."

The Triple-A team was an immediate success, finishing third in the IL, then defeating Tidewater and Charleston to claim the Governors' Cup. The PawSox were victorious three games to two in both playoff rounds, whereupon Pawtucket dropped Tulsa, four games to one, to win the Junior World Series. Righthander Dick Pole took the ERA and strikeout titles (12-9, 2.03, 158 Ks) while whiffing 19 batters in one game and tossing a seven-inning no-hitter in another. The league's top three hitters were PawSox: versatile Juan Beniquez (.298), who played second, third, short and outfield; big first baseman Cecil Cooper (.293 with 15 homers); and outfielder Mike Cummings (.288), who led the IL in hits.

But attendance was a disappointing 78,592, and that total barely improved to 80,268 when the PawSox plunged to last place in 1974. The 1974 club did showcase two future Boston stars, outfielder Fred Lynn (.282 with 21 homers) and MVP Jim Rice, who blasted his way to a Triple Crown while playing in only 117 games before a callup (.337, 25

A PawSox fire plug outside the ballpark. (Author photo)

A Pawtucket tradition continues at the end of the 1989 season, with players tossing baseballs to fans at the final game. (Courtesy Pawtucket PawSox)

HR, 93 RBI). There was another last-place finish in 1975, but attendance improved to 118,289, the league's third-best total. First baseman Jake Baker won the 1976 home run crown (.254 with 36 homers) but could not lift the PawSox out of the second division.

Phil Anez had bought the PawSox from Joe Buzas after the 1974 season, and in 1976 the franchise was awarded to Marvin Adelson of Sudbury, Massachusetts, who announced plans to move the club to Worcester. Complications quickly arose, and on January 28, 1977, the franchise was placed in the hands of Ben Mondor.

The jovial Mondor, a retired mill owner, provided consistent, successful leadership for the club. Mondor began to fly his team on all road trips (at a cost $30,000 in 1978), and he placed the PawSox in good hotels and provided generous meal money. The PawSox conducted four youth clinics per year (in April, May, July, and August) at McCoy Stadium, attracting as many as 2,500-3,000 young players to be tutored by the pros. Mondor and his longtime team president, congenial Mike Tamburro, developed an approach at odds with most promotion-minded minor league operations, but one that is perfectly suited to conservative New England fans and to the parent Boston Red Sox. The PawSox focused on selling baseball, a traditional strategy accentuated by the nostalgic atmosphere of McCoy Stadium. Tamburro began in 1977 to sell the idea that the PawSox are a feeder club, allowing fans to witness the development of the stars of the future. McCoy Stadium is a theme park where spectators can "catch a rising star"—as the passage of Wade Boggs, Roger Clemens, "Oil Can" Boyd and a host of other future big leaguers would prove.

Ben Mondor and Mike Tamburro enjoyed instant success in Pawtucket as manager Joe Morgan led the PawSox to their first IL pennant. Outfielder-first baseman Wayne Harer won the batting title (.350), starter-reliever Allen Ripley was the percentage leader (15-4), third baseman Ted Cox was named MVP (.334), righthander James Wright finished second in the ERA race (12-8, 2.94), and outfielders Richard Berg (.312) and Luis Delgado (.281) contributed greatly at the plate and in the field. The PawSox finished first by two games, then beat Richmond in the playoff opener before falling to Charleston in the finals.

The next year Joe Morgan led the PawSox to second place, downed Toledo in the opener, three games to two, but again lost the finals, in seven games to Richmond. Wayne Harer fell off more than 100 points (.247), but offense was provided by MVP catcher Gary Allenson (.299 with 20 homers) and outfielders David Coleman (.270 with 24 homers) and Garry Hancock (.303). The best pitchers were Charles Rainey (13-7) and John Tudor (7-4).

Impressive returnees in 1979 were batting champ Garry Hancock (.325), MVP third baseman Dave Stapleton (.306), RBI and home run leader Sam Bowen (.235, 28 HR, 75 RBI), and lefty John Tudor, who finished second in the ERA chase (10-11, 2.93). Nevertheless, the PawSox suffered the first of five consecutive losing records. Wade Boggs (.306) was at McCoy Stadium by 1980, and the next year he led the league in batting, hits, and doubles (.335 with 41 2B), while teammate Bob Ojeda won the 1981

ERA title (12-9, 2.13). A McCoy Stadium spectacular of 1981 was baseball's longest game, a 33-inning marathon won by the PawSox, 3-2 (and described in the chapter on the 1980s).

In 1984 Pawtucket finished fourth, then charged to the Governors' Cup by defeating the Maine Guides, three games to two, in the finals. Key players were catcher-outfielder John Lickert (.294), All-Star third baseman Steve Lyons (.268 with 17 homers) and righthanded reliever Charles Mitchell (10-4). The next year Mitchell led the league in relief appearances (2.90 ERA in 63 games), but the PawSox dropped into the cellar.

The 1986 team finished third behind MVP first baseman Pat Dodson (.269, 27 HR, and a league-leading 102 RBI), and All-Star outfielders LaSchelle Tarver (.320) and Mike Greenwell (.300 with 18 homers in 89 games). But Pawtucket lost the playoff opener in 1986 and again in 1987. The fourth-place PawSox of l987 featured All-Star DH Sam Horn (.321 with 30 homers and 84 RBIs in just 94

In 1991, as in other seasons, PawSox players and coaches work with young fans on their baseball techniques. (Author photo)

games), as well as veteran Pat Dodson (.275 with 18 homers), shortstop Jody Reed (.296), and promising outfielder Todd Benzinger (.323 in 65 games). Righthander Steve Curry (11-12) hurled a no-hitter over Richmond, and other members of a deep pitching staff included Bob Woodward (12-8), John Leister (11-5), and Steve Ellsworth (11-8).

Three losing seasons followed, but the 1990 PawSox showcased home run champ Phil Plantier (.253 with 33 homers), popular first baseman Mo Vaughn (.295 with 22 homers), and Rich Lancellotti (.223 with 20 homers), the leading home run hitter among active minor leaguers. In 1991 Lancellotti led the team in homers (.209, 17 HR), while Phil Plantier (.305 with 16 homers), Mo Vaughn (.274 with 14 homers), catcher Todd Pratt (.292), outfielder Jeff Stone (.281), and third-sacker Scott Cooper (.277 with 15 homers) hit for average. Righthanders Paul Quantrill (10-7) and Eric Hetzel (9-5) led the pitching staff as the PawSox won the Eastern Division. Pawtucket faced Columbus, champions of the

Western Division, as the Triple-A affiliates of the arch-rival Red Sox and Yankees competed for the IL Governors' Cup. The PawSox could not get started, and Columbus rolled to a three-game sweep.

The 1992 PawSox made the playoffs despite a losing record (71-72), then lost the opener to Scranton/Wilkes-Barre. In 1993 righthanded curveballer Aaron Sele (8-2 with a 2.19 ERA in 14 starts) was named Most Valuable Pitcher, despite a successful mid-season promotion to the Red Sox (7-2 in 18 starts).

The 1994 PawSox featured a solid pitching staff, including righthanders Frank Rodriquez, the IL strikeout leader with 160 Ks, Tim Vanegmond (9-5) and, in a short stint Jeff Pierce (6-1). Catcher Eric Wedge (.286 with 19 homers) was a mainstay of the offense. Pawtucket won the Eastern Division, but lost the playoff opener to Syracuse in four games.

The PawSox won the East again in 1996. The offense was explosive, blasting 209 home runs, the greatest team total since Baltimore clubbed 232 homers in 1932—a 168-game season (as opposed to 144 games in 1996). On April 14 Brent Cookson ripped three roundtrippers in a game against Columbus, and on August 10 Dwayne Hosey hit three balls out of McCoy Stadium in a contest against Ottawa. But when the playoffs began Rochester defeated Pawtucket, three games to one.

The following season Pawtucket earned the wild card slot behind righthanded

McCoy Stadium in Pawtucket was built in 1942, and has been handsomely renovated and expanded. (Courtesy IL)

ace Brian Rose (17-5, 3.02 ERA), who led the IL in wins and ERA. Rose was voted Rookie-of-the-Year and Most Valuable Pitcher, but the PawSox again fell in the playoff opener to Rochester, three games to one.

Juan Perra was the 1998 strikeout leader with 146 Ks, and on July 22 he twirled a nine-inning no-hitter against Durham. In 1999, as in 1996, Pawtucket sluggers repeated the feat of twice blasting three home runs in a single game: Michael Coleman against Norfolk on June 4, and Izzy Alcantara against Columbus one month later, on July 4. Izzy hit 36 roundtrippers in 2001 to claim the IL home run title, and on June 23 he again pounded three in one game, this time against Durham.

During the 2000 season, Japanese righthander Tomo Ohko (9-6 before a callup to Boston) fired only the third nine-inning perfect game in 116 years of International League play. The first two came from Buffalo pitchers: Chester Carmichael in 1910 and Dick Marlowe in 1952. Nearly half a century later, on June 1, 2000, Ohko was flawless in a 2-0 masterpiece over Charlotte.

Just three seasons later, on August 10, 2003, the fourth nine-inning perfecto was twirled by 6'5" righthander Bronson Arroyo, who beat Buffalo 7-0. The 26 year old Arroyo had been claimed on waivers by the Red Sox in February 2003. In Pawtucket (12-6 with 155 Ks in 149 innings—and a perfect game) Arroyo earned the IL Most Valuable Pitcher Award.

Arroyo was joined on the 2004 All-Star Team by Paw Sox outfielders Lou Collier and Andy Abad, who led the IL with 93 RBIs. Buddy Bailey, who had been named Manager of the Year after leading Pawtucket to a 1996 division title, won the award again in 2004. Bailey and the PawSox took the North

Division crown with the best record in the 14-team league. Traveling to Ottawa for the play-off opener, the PawSox won both road games. Back in Pawtucket the Lynx took the next two games, but Lou Collier's home run in Game Five was the margin of a 3-1 victory. The dramatic series drained the PawSox, however, and Durham swept Pawtucket in the finals.

In 2004 PawSox fans enjoyed All-Star performances from outfielder Adam Hyzdu (.301, 29 HR, 79 RBI) and third baseman Earl Snyder, who was the IL's power king with 36 homers and 104 RBIs. Catcher Kelly Shoppach was the third PawSox named to the All-Star Team, and in 2005 he blasted 26 home runs and repeated as All-Star catcher.

Curt Schilling on the mound during a 2005 rehab assignment with Pawtucket. As a young fireballer with Rochester in 1989, Schilling led the IL in victories, then became a major league star. Rehab appearances by standout big leaguers provide season highlights for IL fans. (Courtesy IL)

The 2005 Paw Sox fielded another winning team, and Pawtucket's loyal fans responded with a record season attendance of 688,421.

Year	Record	Pcg.	Finish
1973	78-68	.534	Third (won opener, finals, and JWS)
1974	57-87	.396	Eighth
1975	53-87	.379	Eighth
1976	68-70	.493	Fifth
1977	80-60	.571	First (won opener, lost finals)
1978	81-59	.579	Second (won opener, lost finals)
1979	66-74	.471	Fifth
1980	62-77	.446	Seventh
1981	67-73	.479	Sixth
1982	67-81	.486	Fifth
1983	56-83	.403	Eighth
1984	75-65	.536	Fourth (won opener and finals)
1985	48-91	.345	Eighth
1986	74-65	.532	Third (lost opener)
1987	73-67	.521	Fourth (lost opener)
1988	63-79	.444	Sixth
1989	62-84	.425	Eighth
1990	62-84	.425	Seventh
1991	79-64	.552	Second (won Eastern Division, lost finals)
1992	71-72	.497	Fourth (lost opener)
1993	60-82	.423	Eighth
1994	78-64	.549	Second (won Eastern Division, lost opener)
1995	70-71	.496	Seventh
1996	78-64	.549	Third (won Eastern Division, lost opener)
1997	81-60	.574	Second (lost opener)
1998	77-64	.546	Fourth
1999	76-68	.528	Sixth
2000	82-61	.573	Third
2001	60-82	.423	Thirteenth
2002	60-84	.417	Eleventh
2003	83-61	.576	First (won North and opener, lost finals)
2004	73-71	.507	Fifth
2005	75-69	.521	Sixth
2006	69-75	.479	Tenth
2007	67-75	.472	Tenth

The Pawtucket mascots, Paws and Sox. (Courtesy IL)

Richmond
(BRAVES, VIRGINIAS, VIRGINIANS, CLIMBERS)

When a physician advised Richmond shoemaker Henry Boschen to take up some form of outdoor recreation, "Daddy" Boschen organized a professional baseball team. During the late 1870s, Boschen pitched for his club, served as manager, and set up a diamond at "Boschen Field" near the Richmond, Fredericksburg, and Potomac Railroad yards. But as professional leagues began to be organized, the Virginia Baseball Club was formed in June 1883 to secure a franchise in an established circuit.

Richmond was a charter member when the Eastern League opened play in 1884. The Richmond Virginias hosted opponents at Virginia Park at the west end of Franklin Street. But in August the 30-28 Richmond club was lured into the American Association. The Virginias went 12-30 in Richmond's only appearance in a major league.

The next season the Virginias played in another circuit dubbed the Eastern League, and in 1890 and 1892 a team called the Giants played all comers at a park on Mayo Island in the James River. In 1894 the Richmond Crows—clad in black, of course—

played in the Virginia League at West End Park, then changed the team name to Bluebirds for 1895 and 1896. Moving to Broad Street Park, the Richmond Johnnie Rebs were members of the Atlantic League from 1897 through 1899. The club participated in the Virginia-Carolina League the next year, then (as the Lawmakers or Colts) in the Virginia League from 1906 through 1912. Broad Street Park, which seated 4,800 and incorporated the wall of a house in the right field fence, bulged with an overflow crowd of 19,000 at the 1908 Labor Day doubleheader.

In 1913 the Colts moved to another facility named Broad Street Park, located on railroad property at Addison and Broad streets. But after the 1914 season the Virginia League franchise was moved to Rocky Mount, North Carolina, so that Richmond could return to the International League. Jack Dunn had put together a superb IL team in 1914 in order to go head-to-head with Federal League competition in Baltimore, but the major leaguers prevailed and Dunn had to sell off his best players. For 1915 Dunn transferred his depleted club to Richmond, after local sports enthusiasts raised $12,500, as territorial compensation for the Virginia League.

Righthander Allen "Rubberarm" Russell won the strikeout title (21-15, 239 Ks) and moved up to an 11-year American League career, but there was little other talent on the Climbers. Although the Climbers finished next-to-last, Richmond sportsmen bought out Dunn, who purchased the Jersey City franchise and moved back to Baltimore. The Climbers (also called the Virginians) moved up only to sixth place in 1916, and the next year finished in the cellar. The railroad reclaimed the Broad Street Park property in order to erect a new depot, and the 1917 Climbers played at 4,400-seat Lee Park, built in 1912 at North Boulevard and Moore Street.

Because of wartime conditions it seemed

unlikely that the International League would operate in 1918. Although there was a last-minute reorganization of the IL, Richmond was squeezed out and rejoined the Virginia League as the Colts. After three seasons the Colts moved back to the rebuilt ballpark at Mayo Island. There was a short fence in left at Island Park (also known as Tate Field), and an employee sometimes was stationed in a boat to retrieve baseballs from the river. Visiting teams and umpires had to dress and shower in their hotels, but lights were added in 1933. Although floods regularly damaged the ballpark, Tate Field was continuously used until fire destroyed the grandstand in 1941.

Colts owner-manager Eddie Mooers, who had bought the Colts in 1932 by assuming the club's debts, sold his Mayo Island property and built a $100,000 ballpark at Belleville, Carlton, Norfolk, and Roseneath streets. Mooers Field featured a 4,500-seat concrete grandstand, bleachers that seated 6,000, and a cinder block fence.

The Colts played in the Class B Piedmont League from 1933 through 1953, when Baltimore left the IL to join the American League. Local investors hoped to bring the International League franchise to Richmond, and IL president Frank Shaughnessy contacted Eddie Mooers. But Mooers insisted upon such difficult conditions for the sale or rental of his park that the IL owners turned elsewhere. Mooers sold the territorial rights to the new IL owners, then converted his ballpark for stock car races. In 1958 Mooers Field was purchased by real estate developers, who razed the old ballpark.

Parker Field, built in 1934 on North Boulevard as a fairgrounds facility, was selected as an IL playing site, and $200,000 was pledged by Richmond citizens within a two-hour period for the necessary renovations. The Richmond Virginians (often called the "Vees") were affiliated with the New York Yankees. Luke Appling, the longtime White Sox shortstop who would later be named to the Hall of Fame, was the first manager of the Virginians. But the Vees finished next-to-last in 1954, then dropped to the cellar in 1955, and former Yankee pitcher "Steady Eddie" Lopat was appointed manager for 1956. The 38-year-old lefthander started 21 games (11-6), and righthander Al Cicotte (15-12) helped lift the Vees to fifth place. Outfielder Len Johnston (.294 with 40 steals) won the first of three consecutive stolen base crowns.

Lopat did not pitch the next year, but Jim Coates won the strikeout title (14-11, 161 Ks), fellow righthander Bill

The 1916 Richmond Climbers were led by outfielder Wilbur Bankston (No. 3), who hit .325.

Having just concluded a long major league career, former Yankee lefty Eddie Lopat was player-manager at Richmond in 1956 (11-6).

Bethel was equally effective (15-7), and first-sacker John Jacluk posted the league's second-highest batting average (.322). The Vees made the playoffs with a third-place finish but dropped the opening round to Buffalo. The team sagged to sixth the next year, then bounced back into the playoffs in 1959 and 1960. Although Richmond finished last in team hitting (.236) in 1959, lefthander Bill Short (17-6) helped propel the Vees to the playoff finals, where they fell to the Havana Sugar Kings. In 1960 manager Steve Souchak guided a no-name club to second place.

Richmond dropped to sixth place in 1961, then finished seventh for three consecutive seasons. The Yankees moved their IL franchise to Toledo for 1965, but Richmond was without pro ball for only one year. In 1966 the Milwaukee Braves of the National League moved to Atlanta, and Atlanta placed their IL franchise in Richmond. The Richmond Braves finished fourth and battled to the playoff finals behind outfielder Bill Robinson (.310) and first baseman Jim Beauchamp (.319 with 35 homers), who missed the batting title by one point.

Manager Luman Harris brought Richmond its first IL pennant in 1967. Beauchamp won the home run title despite playing in only 96 games (.233 with 33 homers), and he was joined on the All-Star team by second baseman Felix Millan

Before being demolished late in 1984, Richmond's Parker Field hosted IL pennant-winners in 1967 and 1982, as well as the Governors' Cup champs of 1978. (Courtesy Richmond Braves)

(.310), MVP outfielder Tommie Aaron (.309), and righthander R. L. Reed (14-10). Righthander Jim Britton (12-7) fired a three-hit shutout over Rochester in a sudden-death playoff for the pennant, but Richmond lost the playoff opener to Toledo.

Richmond dropped into the cellar the next two seasons and did not reappear in the playoffs until 1974. But outfielder Dave Nicholson won the home run and RBI titles in 1968 (.226, 34 HR, 86 RBI), and first baseman Hal Breeden was the home run king of 1970 (.293, 37 HR, 116 RBI). Outfielder Ralph Garr became Richmond's only batting champ, winning back-to-back hitting *and* stolen base titles in 1969 (.329, 63 SB) and 1970 (.386, 39 SB in 98 games).

In 1974 manager Clint Courtney led the Braves to a playoff berth for the first time in seven seasons. Richmond slipped to sixth place the next year, despite the efforts of ERA champ Pablo Torrealba (12-9 and a sparkling 1.45 ERA in 64 games as a reliever). In 1976 the Braves began a string of eight consecutive playoff appearances. Jack McKeon managed the fourth-place Braves to the 1976 finals before falling to Syracuse. Tommie Aaron was the manager the following season, as future Atlanta superstar Dale Murphy led the IL in RBIs (.305, 22 HR, 90 RBI).

The 1978 Braves featured home run and RBI champ Henry Small (.289, 25 HR, 101 RBI), All-Star second baseman Glenn Hubbard (.336 in 80 games), righthander Rick Mahler (9-5), and stolen base leader Ed Miller. Tommie Aaron guided the fourth-place Braves to an upset over first-place Charleston in the playoff opener, then outlasted Pawtucket, four games to three, to bring Richmond its first Governors' Cup.

In 1979 and 1980 the Braves lost the playoff opener, but righthander Tom Boggs was the 1979 strikeout champ (15-10, 138 Ks), first baseman-catcher Charles Keller tied for the RBI title (.255, 21 HR, 75 RBI), and outfielder Ed Miller repeated as stolen base king (.234 with 76 steals). Miller won his third straight stolen base crown the following year (.209 with 60 steals), matching the three consecutive theft titles of Len Johnston in the 1950s.

The 1981 Braves finished second behind three key players: southpaw Ken Dayley (13-8 with 162 Ks), who led the IL in victories, strikeouts, innings, starts, and walks; co-victory leader Larry McWilliams (13-10); and MVP outfielder Brett Butler (.335, 93 R, 103 W), who paced the league in runs and walks, and lost the batting title to Pawtucket's Wade Boggs by a fraction of a percentage point. The Braves beat Tidewater, three games to two, in the playoff opener. In the finals with Columbus, the Braves were trailing, 2-1, when bad weather halted the playoffs. The Governors' Cup was awarded to the Clippers.

Not satisfied with second place, manager Eddie Haas led the Braves to the 1982 pennant, although Richmond suffered a disappointing loss to Rochester in the playoff opener. Outfielder Albert Hall was the stolen base champ (.263 with 62 steals), righthander Craig McMurtry (17-9) was the victory leader, and other strong performances were turned in by third baseman Brook Jacoby (.299 with 18 homers), first-sacker Gerald Perry (.297, 15 HR, 92 RBI), run leader Paul Runge (.280, 15 HR, 106 R), and righthander Anthony Brizzolara (15-11).

In 1983 Haas guided Richmond to second place behind Jacoby (.315, 25 HR, 100 RBI), Perry (.314), Runge (.273), Brizzolara (9-7), outfielder Lenny Vargas (.289 with 19 homers), and slick-fielding shortstop Paul Zuvella (.287). The Braves swept Charleston in the playoff opener, but lost the finals to Tidewater. Zuvella improved the next season (.303), but the Braves had a losing record and the eight-year playoff string was broken. Following the 1984 season, Parker Field was razed. During the next seven months an $8-million stadium was erected on the same site. The Diamond seats more than 12,000 and boasts 15 "Superboxes" and numerous other luxury features. Although the 1985 team also missed the playoffs, attendance jumped from 165,187 in 1984 to 379,019, and in 1986 admissions exceeded 403,000.

The 1986 team deserved record crowds. Gerald Perry missed the batting championship by two points (.326), right-hander Charlie Puleo (14-7 with 124 Ks) led the league in victories and shared the strikeout crown with teammate Steve Shields (9-8), and outfielder Albert Hall returned to win another stolen base title (.270, 72 SB). Manager Roy Majtyka guided the Braves to the pennant by a margin of four games, then beat Tidewater and Rochester in the playoffs to claim the Governors' Cup.

The next two clubs posted losing records, but in 1989 the Braves won the Western Division, then beat Eastern Division champ Syracuse and swept Indianapolis in four games to win the Alliance Classic. This championship club was anchored by victory and percentage leader Gary Eave (13-3), strikeout titlist Kent Mercker, All-Star second baseman

Mark Lemke (.276), righthanded reliever Mark Eichhorn (1-0 with a 1.32 ERA and 19 saves in 25 games), and outfielder Greg Tubbs (.301). The manager was former Richmond slugger Jim Beauchamp.

The parent Atlanta Braves increasingly emphasized pitching, as reflected by Richmond's 1989 mound corps, and by future

The Diamond opened in Richmond in 1985. (Courtesy Richmond Braves)

The symmetrical grandstand at the Diamond. (Photo by Karon O'Neal)

Richmond pitching staffs. In 1990, for example, Paul Marak won the ERA title (2.49) and Armando Reynoso kept it in Richmond in 1991 (2.61). On May 3, 1992, righthander Pete Smith (7-4, 2.14 ERA in 15 starts) hurled a seven-inning perfect game to defeat Rochester 1-0. Although Smith was called up at mid-season to Atlanta, where he was spectacular (7-0, 2.05 ERA in 12 games), fellow righty David Nied (14-9, 159 Ks, 2.84 ERA) led the IL in victories and strikeouts.

In 1992 Richmond began a four-year playoff run. The Braves were led by Smith and Nied, as well as by two hard-hitting future big leaguers, third baseman Vinny Castillo and Ryan Klesko. In the playoff opener Richmond was swept by Columbus, but the Braves would have even more talent in 1993.

Richmond's opening day lineup in 1993 featured Atlanta's hottest prospect, shortstop Chipper Jones (.325 with 89 RBIs and a league-leading 93 runs). First sacker Ryan Klesko hit cleanup (.274 with 22 homers), gifted Javy Lopez (.305 with 17 homers) was the catcher, and hard-hitting Tony Tarasco (.330) was in right. The opening-day pitcher was Mike Birkbeck, who won, 9-0, against Scranton/Wilkes-Barre, and went on to lead the IL in victories (13) and strikeouts (136). The Braves established the league's second-best record (80-62), but again suffered disappointment in the opening round of playoffs, losing to Charlotte in four games.

In 1994 southpaw Brad Woodall (15-6, 2.38 ERA) led the league in victories and ERA and was voted Most Valuable Pitcher. Future big leaguers Eddie Perez and Tyler Houston split the catching duties, while Mike Mordecai (.280) played shortstop. Manager of the Year Grady Little drove the Braves to a 19-9 run at the end of the season producing the IL's best record and the Western Division crown. Reversing the previous year's results, Richmond downed Charlotte in four games in the playoff opener, then swept Syracuse to claim the franchise's fourth Governors' Cup.

Future National League ace Jason Schmidt (8-6 in 19 starts with a 2.25 ERA) was the 1995 ERA champ in the IL. The 1995 Braves could not defend their championship, falling to Norfolk in an opening series that went to five games.

In 1997 right fielder Tommy Gregg won the batting title (.332), while first baseman Randall Simon led the IL with 102 RBIs. Both marks are all-time Brave records, along with the 11-run explosion in a single inning against Charlotte on May 1. The next year Simon set another all-time Braves' record by knocking in 10 runs against Charlotte on June 27, 1998.

Righthander Trey Hodges (15-9) led the IL in victories in 2002, while Doug Linton won the strikeout title (160 Ks). In 2003 Johnny Estrada (.328) was the All-Star catcher, and southpaw Andy Pratt claimed the strikeout crown (161 Ks). The

Braves' dugout at the Diamond. (Photo by Karon O'Neal)

2004 strikeout leader was Chuck Smith—the third year in a row a Braves' pitcher fanned the most IL hitters.

The 2004 Braves had a strong offense led by All-Star second baseman Pete Orr (.320), along with third baseman Wilson Betemit (.278) and center fielder Ryan Langerhans (.298, 20 HR, 79 RBIs). The speedy Langerhans was the leadoff man and scored 103 runs, the all-time Braves' record. Another all-time mark was posted by All-Star reliever Matt Whiteside, whose 38 saves was the most ever recorded in the IL. Behind manager Pat Kelly this fine team won the South Division and the playoff opener, downing Columbus in five games. Richmond hosted the first game of the finals, pounding Buffalo, 11-4. But heavy rain and poor playing conditions forced IL President Randy Mobley to move the rest of the series to Buffalo's Dunn Tire Park, where the Bisons won three games in a row.

In 2005 the Braves acquired fleet Esix Snead to play center field and lead off the batting order. Snead had won two consecutive stolen base titles with Norfolk, and he made it three in a row with 46 in 2005. Righthander Kyle Davies (5-2) moved up to the Braves at mid-season (7-6), along with catcher Brayan Pena (.326).

Following two consecutive cellar finishes, the 2007 Braves roared to another Governors' Cup. Anchored by second baseman Martin Prado (.316), fleet outfielder Brandon Jones (.300), slick-fielding shortstop Yunel

Escobar (.333 before a callup to Atlanta), and long relievers Buddy Hernandez (9-3 in 47 games) and Manny Acosta (9-3, 2.26 ERA in 40 games), the Braves battled Durham in the South throughout the season. Durham won the division, but Richmond claimed the Wild Card slot and beat Scranton/Wilkes-Barre, three games to one, in the playoff opener.

Richmond and Durham again squared off

The massive outfield scoreboard at The Diamond is typical of fan-pleasing scoreboards around the IL. (Photo by Karon O'Neal)

Richmond's biggest Brave overlooks the entrance to The Diamond. (Author photo)

in the finals. The Braves and Bulls split the two games in Durham. The Bulls won the first game in Richmond, and needed only one more victory. But the Friday game was rained out, setting up a Saturday double-header. The Braves took the afternoon contest, 6-2, to tie the series, then completed their comeback with a 7-1 triumph in the nightcap. After hitting a home run and playing 18 innings on Saturday, Brandon Jones flew to Atlanta to start Sunday's game in The Show. After starting Monday night for Atlanta, Jones flew to Oklahoma City to rejoin the Richmond Braves for the Bricktown Showdown. Sacramento won, 7-1, but the Braves still had the satisfaction of bringing the Governors' Cup back to Richmond.

Year	Record	Pcg.	Finish
1884	30-28	.517	Seventh
1915	59-81	.422	Seventh
1916	64-75	.460	Sixth
1917	53-94	.361	Eighth
1954	60-94	.390	Seventh
1955	58-95	.379	Eighth
1956	74-79	.484	Fifth
1957	81-73	.526	Third (lost opener)
1958	71-82	.464	Sixth
1959	76-78	.494	Fourth (won opener, lost finals)
1960	82-70	.539	Second (lost opener)
1961	71-83	.461	Sixth
1962	59-95	.383	Seventh
1963	66-81	.449	Seventh
1964	65-88	.425	Seventh
1966	75-72	.510	Fourth (won opener, lost finals)
1967	81-60	.574	First (lost opener)
1968	59-87	.404	Eighth
1969	56-83	.403	Eighth
1970	73-67	.521	Fifth
1971	69-71	.493	Sixth
1972	65-78	.455	Sixth
1973	53-93	.363	Eighth
1974	75-65	.536	Third (lost opener)
1975	62-75	.453	Sixth
1976	69-71	.493	Fourth (won opener, lost finals)
1977	71-69	.507	Fourth (lost opener)
1978	71-68	.511	Fourth (won opener and finals)
1979	76-64	.543	Third (lost opener)
1980	69-71	.493	Fourth (lost opener)
1981	83-56	.597	Second (won opener, lost finals)
1982	82-57	.590	Second (lost opener)
1983	80-59	.576	Second (won opener, lost finals)
1984	66-73	.475	Sixth
1985	75-65	.536	Fifth
1986	80-60	.571	First (won opener and finals)
1987	56-83	.403	Eighth
1988	66-75	.468	Fourth
1989	81-65	.555	Second (won Western Division and finals, lost Alliance Classic)
1990	71-74	.490	Fourth
1991	65-79	.451	Eighth
1992	73-71	.507	Third (lost opener)
1993	80-62	.563	Second (lost opener)
1994	80-61	.567	First (won Western Division, opener and finals)
1995	75-66	.532	Second (lost opener)
1996	62-79	.440	Seventh
1997	70-72	.493	Sixth
1998	64-80	.444	Thirteenth
1999	64-78	.451	Tenth
2000	51-92	.357	Fourteenth
2001	68-76	.472	Seventh
2002	75-67	.528	Seventh
2003	64-79	.448	Thirteenth
2004	79-62	.560	Third (won South and opener, lost finals)
2005	56-88	.389	Fourteenth
2006	57-86	.399	Fourteenth
2007	77-64	.546	Fourth (won opener and finals, lost Bricktown Showdown)

Rochester

(HOP BITTERS, FLORISTS, COLTS, CHAMPS, BRONCHOS, BEAU BRUMMELS, BROWNIES, BUSTLERS, RED WINGS)

Rochester has fielded a team in 122 of 125 years of IL operation. The senior member of the IL has made 42 playoff appearances, 17 more than the next closest club. There have been 19 pennants, including four in a row, 1928, 1929, 1930, and 1931. Ten Governors' Cups have been brought back to Rochester, the most of any team in the league. Rochester has played in the Little World Series, Junior World Series, or Alliance Classic 11 times, winning in 1930, 1931, 1952, and 1971. Rochester fans have enjoyed the performances of 20 Hall of Fame players and managers, and of 19 batting champs, beginning with Doc Kennedy in 1885 (.387) and, most recently, Jason Kubel in 2004 (.343).

Organized baseball in Rochester dates back to 1858, when the new sport swept across New York State. Nicknamed the "Flour City" because of the prominence of the milling industry, Rochester fielded the Flour City, Live Oak, and University clubs. The Live Oaks had a team song, "The Live Oak Polka," and games were played on Franklyn Square. After the Civil War, there was an Atlantic club east of the Genesee River and a Pacific club on the city's west side. These and other amateur nines began to play teams from Syracuse and Buffalo, and the Excelsiors became Rochester's best club.

In 1877 Rochester placed a team in the International Association, baseball's first minor league. Asa T. Soule, president of the Hop Bitters Manufacturing Company, operated the "Hop Bitters" for a few seasons, requiring his players to take a spoonful of his tonic before each game. The club went on long barnstorming tours, but in Rochester games were staged at the Hop Bitters Grounds north of Main Street on North Union and Weld streets.

During the 1880s Rochester experienced a 54 percent population growth to 134,000, and the manufacturing center—there were 64 shoe factories and George Eastman was beginning to produce Kodak cameras—became New York's third largest city. When the New York State League organized as a six-team circuit in

John Ganzel, an experienced big league player and manager, guided Rochester to three consecutive pennants in 1909, 1910, and 1911.

1885, a local stock company backed a Rochester club. This is considered the second season of the IL, and Rochester went on to play every other year except 1890 (there was a team in the big league American Association) and 1893, although the team dropped out before the end of the schedule in 1897 and 1898.

Among a parade of hitting titlists, outfielder George "Pooch" Puccinelli (.391) banged out the highest Rochester batting average in 1931 (.391). Other impressive performances by Rochester batting champs included those by Bob Fothergill in 1922 (.383) and Rip Collins in 1930 (.376, 40 HR, 180 RBI). Third baseman Don Richmond won back-to-back titles in 1950 (.333) and 1951 (.350), while MVP awards were voted to batting champs Red Schoendienst in 1943 (.337) and Merv Rettenmund in 1968 (.331). Rip Collins blasted his way to the home run and RBI crowns in 1929 (.315, 38 HR, 134 RBI), and so did MVP winners Mike Epstein in 1966 (.309, 29 HR, 102 RBI) and Jim Fuller in 1973 (.247, 39 HR, 108 RBI). Home run champ Bobby Grich was named MVP in 1971 (.336, 32 HR, 83 RBI), while Russ Derry won consecutive home run crowns in 1949 (.279, 42 HR, 122 RBI) and 1950 (.281, 30 HR, and a league-leading 102 RBIs). In 1899 outfielder Count Campau led not only the IL but all minor leagues in home runs—with a grand total of eight!

There have been only two pitchers' Triple Crowns in IL history, and one was turned in by Rochester righthander Dennis Martinez in

Rochester's 1910 Hustlers, IL champs. Club stalwarts included left fielder Herbie Moran (top left, No.1), infielder Joe Ward (3), utility man Heinie Batch (5), center fielder Green Osborne (6), catcher Henry Blair (8), pitcher Jim Holmes (12), pitcher Ed Lafitte (14), third baseman Hack Simmons (18), pitcher George McConnell (19), manager John Ganzel (21), pitcher Pat Ragan (22), and owner-president C.T. Chapin (23).

1976 (14-8, 140 K, 2.50 ERA). Victory and strikeout titles were won by Paul Derringer in 1930 (23-11, 164 K) and Bob Weiland in 1936 (23-13,171 K), while Dominic Ryba (24-8) and Tom Poholsky (18-6 with a league-leading 2.17 ERA) earned the MVP awards of 1940 and 1950. Robert Barr was the victory leader of 1889 (29-14), and George McConnell was superb for the championship club of 1911 (30-8).

Future Hall of Fame pitchers Dazzy Vance (1918), Bob Gibson (1958 and 1960), and Jim Palmer (1967 and 1968) wore Rochester uniforms while learning their trade. Hall of Fame sluggers Stan Musial (1941, .326) and Johnny Mize (1933, .352; 1934, .339; and 1935, .317) finished their minor league apprenticeships as Red Wings, and future Hall of Fame umpire Jocko Conlan was a Rochester outfielder in 1924 (.321), 1925 (.309), and 1926 (.286). Catcher Al Head was a heavy hitter for Rochester in 1924 (.306), 1925 (.360), 1926 (.351), and 1927 (.333). Slugging outfielder Russ Derry was a fan favorite from 1947 through 1952, and third baseman Steve Demeter hit over .300 in his five seasons as a Red Wing during the 1960s. In 1938 Sammy Baugh, the superstar NFL quarterback, played infield for Rochester, entertaining fans during pregame exhibitions by throwing footballs into distant peach baskets.

Rochester's first IL pennant came in 1899, when manager Al Buckenberger guided his club to first place by a margin of nine games. In 1901 Buckenberger produced another flag by a nine-game margin. A strong offense featured third-sacker "Battleship" Greminger (.343), outfielder George Barclay (.339, 46 SB, 112 R), and first baseman-stolen base champ Harold O'Hagan (.320, 51 SB, 113 R), who pulled off baseball's first recorded unassisted triple play the next year.

Rochester teams had been called "Hop Bitters," "Colts," "Champs," "Bronchos," "Brownies" and "Beau Brummels," but in 1909 the club was rechristened "Hustlers." Manager John Ganzel led the Hustlers to consecutive pennants in 1909-10-11, a three-year dynasty described in the third chapter. Seventeen seasons passed without another pennant, but in 1928 Rochester became the top farm club in the prototype St. Louis Cardinal system. The team was dubbed the "Red Wings," an appellation appropriate to the Cardinals' organization that became synonymous with Rochester baseball.

From 1928 through 1931 the Red Wings reeled off four consecutive pennants under

Rochester won its fourth consecutive pennant in 1931. The Red Wings featured Ray Pepper (No.3), Al Moore (4), Showboat Fisher (5), future IL Triple Crown-winner George Puccinelli (6), Herman Bell (13), Carmen Hill (14), Ray Starr (15), former Orioles star Jack Bentley (18), future Hall of Famer George Sisler (20), and Specs Torporcer (23).

the expert guidance of player-manager Billy Southworth, as well as the leadership of team captain "Specs" Torporcer, who played second base in all four seasons of Rochester's dynasty. The 1928 Red Wings (90-74) barely edged Buffalo (92-76) for the flag, but Rochester's next three teams won more than 100 games: 1929 (103-65); 1930 (105-62); and 1931 (101-67). In 1928 and 1929 the Red Wings lost the Little World Series to the American Association champs, but the next two years Rochester defeated Louisville and St. Paul.

In 1939 the Red Wings won a Governors' Cup behind outfielder Allen Cooke (.340) and Estel Crabtree (.337), and righthanders Silas Johnson (22-12) and Dominic Ryba (18-12, and .310 in 55 games). The next season Ryba became Rochester's last 20-game winner (24-8) while leading the Red Wings to the 1940 pennant. Billy Southworth managed this club, as he had the pennant winners of 1928-31, along with the playoff titlists of 1939. The Red Wings made nine consecutive playoff appearances from 1948 through 1956, and from 1948 through 1976 Rochester missed the playoffs merely five times.

Rochester won the 1950 pennant behind MVP Tom Poholsky, batting champ Don Richmond, and home run-RBI leader Russ Derry. In 1952 player-manager Harry "The Hat" Walker (.365) and Don Richmond (.329) led the Red Wings to the Governors' Cup. The next year Walker (.303), Richmond (.312), outfielder Tommy Burgess (.346 with 22 homers), and first baseman Charles Kress (.317, 25 HR, 121 RBI) spearheaded a deep offense which pounded out another pennant. The 1955 and 1956 clubs produced back-to-back playoff titles, and another Governors' Cup came in 1964.

Home run and RBI champ Mike Epstein was named Most Valuable Player after sparking Rochester to the 1966 pennant,

Rochester's All-Time Red Wings Team features several major league stars. (Courtesy IL)

during a season which showcased the managerial talent of Earl Weaver. The 1971 Red Wings won the flag then claimed the Governors' Cup before capping a banner season by downing Denver in a memorable Junior World Series (because of an NFL conflict in Denver, all games were played in Rochester, and the series went to the seventh game). This championship team featured MVP home run champ Bobby Grich (.336 with 32 homers), outfielder Don Baylor (.313, 20 HR, 95 RBI), and strikeout and victory leader Roric Harrison (15-5 with 182 Ks in 170 IP). In 1976 Triple Crown pitcher Dennis Martinez and batting champ Rich Dauer (.336) led the Red Wings to another pennant. All three championship teams of the 1970s were managed by Joe Altobelli.

A subsequent championship drought ended with pennants in 1988 and 1990. Outfielder Steve Finley was the only IL player of 1988 to hit above .300 (.314) for the season, while the 1990 champs featured RBI champ Len Gomez (.277, 26 HR, 97 RBI) and percentage leader Mike Weston (11-1 with a 1.98 ERA). In 1993 the Red Wings won the Eastern Division, then beat Ottawa, three games to two, in the playoff opener. The series for the Governors' Cup also went five games, but the Red Wings lost the deciding contest to Charlotte. The next year Jeff Manto (.310, 31 HR, 100 RBI) won the home run and RBI titles.

The 1995 Red Wings began a playoff run that climaxed with Rochester's tenth Governors' Cup. The Red Wings won the Eastern Division in 1995 but lost the

playoff opener to Ottawa in five games. Righthander Jimmy Haynes led the IL in victories (12) and strikeouts (140 Ks). The 1996 Red Wings were the wild card entry in the playoffs and beat Pawtucket in the opener, three games to one, only to be swept by Columbus in the finals. But there was no disappointment in 1997. Red Wings won the Eastern Division with the best record in the league. Rochester beat Pawtucket in four games in the playoff opener, then outlasted Columbus in the finals, three games to two.

Marv Foley, who piloted all three playoff clubs, was named Manager of the Year for 1997. The Red Wings played before an all-time Rochester record attendance of 540,842, and these fans enjoyed championship baseball in the handsome surroundings of new Frontier Field.

Rochester's first season in the IL was played at Hop Bitters Grounds. In 1886 the Rochester Bronchos moved into new Culver Field at the northwest corner of University and Culver. Culver Field burned in 1892, and

Rochester fans at Silver Stadium in 1990. (Author photo)

there was no professional park in Rochester for three years. Riverside Park opened in 1895 on the east bank of the Genesee River

A fierce Red Wing guards the entrance to Rochester's Frontier Field. (Photo by Karon O'Neal)

Mule made of old leather ball gloves on display at Rochester's Frontier Field. (Author photo)

north of Norton Street, and for three seasons it was the home of the Rochester Brownies—named for George Eastman's popular new camera! Culver Field was rebuilt for 1898, and the newly named Beau Brummels moved back for a decade. In 1906, however, the right field bleachers collapsed, causing numerous injuries and lawsuits, and after the next season Culver Field was acquired as a building site by the Gleason Works.

The Beau Brummels settled into Bay Street Park, located on the south side of Bay Street east of Webster Avenue. The outfield was so vast that automobiles and horse-drawn carriages parked inside the fence. In 1928 Red Wing Stadium was built at 500 Norton Street, and almost 15,000 fans watched the opening game in 1929. Lights were installed during the 1933 season, and there were numerous stadium renovations, including a $4.5-million project in 1986. The all-time record crowd was 19,006 on May 5, 1931, while the season attendance record of 443,533 was set in 1949. Renamed Silver Stadium in 1968 after Morrie Silver, who twice saved professional baseball in Rochester, the old ballpark hosted 14 million fans during seven decades of International League play. But in 1997—just in time for another championship season—the Red Wings moved into downtown Frontier Field, with a seating capacity of 10,800.

Although a long playoff absence ensued, Frontier Field continued to be the scene of stellar performances. Slugger Calvin Pickering was the RBI king of 2001, while lefty Carlos Pulido went 12-5 in 2003 on his way to Minnesota. The next year All-Star first baseman Justin Morneau hit .306 with 22 homers in only 72 games before going up to Minnesota. Another member of the 2004 All-Star team, outfielder Jason Kubel, was the batting champ (.343), while Dave Gassner (16-8) was the 2004 victory leader. In 2005 Travis

Bowyer (4-2, 2.78 ERA, 23 saves) was named All-Star reliever, and another member of the staff, Boof Bonser, led the IL with 168 strike-outs. Pat Neshek was the 2006 All-Star reliever (6-2, 14 saves, 1.95 ERA), and in 2007 Kevin Slowey (10-5, 1.89) was the ERA champ. From the Hop Bitters to the Beau Brummels, from the Hustlers to the Red Wings, Rochester has played an irreplaceable role in IL history.

Eye-catching grass design at Rochester's Frontier Field. (Photo by Karon O'Neal)

Year	Record	Pcg.	Finish
1885	40-36	.526	Second
1886	56-39	.589	Second
1887	49-52	.485	Seventh
1888	64-43	.598	Third
1889	60-50	.545	Third
1891	36-60	.375	Seventh
1892	68-57	.544	Fourth
1895	47-82	.364	Seventh
1896	68-58	.540	Third
1897			Dropped out
1898			Dropped out
1899	71-42	.628	First
1900	77-56	.579	Second
1901	88-49	.642	First
1902	56-76	.424	Sixth
1903	34-97	.260	Eighth
1904	28-105	.211	Eighth
1905	51-86	.372	Seventh
1906	77-62	.554	Fourth
1907	59-76	.437	Seventh
1908	55-82	.401	Eighth
1909	90-61	.596	First
1910	92-61	.601	First
1911	98-54	.645	First
1912	86-67	.562	Second
1913	92-62	.597	Second
1914	72-77	.483	Sixth
1915	69-69	.500	Fourth
1916	60-78	.435	Seventh
1917	72-82	.468	Fifth
1918	60-61	.496	Fifth
1919	67-83	.447	Sixth
1920	45-106	.298	Seventh
1921	100-68	.595	Second
1922	105-62	.624	Second
1923	101-65	.608	Second
1924	83-84	.497	Fourth
1925	83-77	.519	Third
1926	81-83	.494	Fifth
1927	81-86	.485	Sixth
1928	90-74	.549	First (lost LWS)
1929	103-65	.613	First (lost LWS)
1930	105-62	.624	First (won LWS)
1931	101-67	.601	First (won LWS)
1932	88-79	.527	Fifth
1933	88-77	.533	Second
1934	88-63	.583	Second (won opener, lost finals)

1935	61-91	.401	Seventh
1936	89-66	.574	Second (lost opener)
1937	74-80	.481	Sixth
1938	80-74	.519	Third (lost opener)
1939	84-67	.556	Second (won opener and finals, lost JWS)
1940	96-61	.611	First (lost opener)
1941	84-68	.553	Fourth (lost opener)
1942	59-93	.388	Eighth
1943	74-78	.487	Fifth
1944	71-82	.464	Seventh
1945	64-90	.416	Eighth
1946	65-87	.428	Seventh
1947	68-86	.442	Fifth
1948	78-75	.510	Fourth (lost opener)
1949	85-67	.559	Second (lost opener)
1950	92-59	.609	First (won opener, lost finals)
1951	83-69	.546	Second (lost opener)
1952	80-74	.519	Third (won opener, finals, and JWS)
1953	97-58	.630	First (won opener, lost finals)
1954	86-68	.558	Third (lost opener)
1955	76-77	.497	Fourth (won opener and finals, lost JWS)
1956	83-67	.553	Second (won opener and finals, lost JWS)
1957	74-80	.481	Fifth
1958	77-75	.507	Third (lost opener)
1959	74-80	.481	Fifth
1960	81-63	.526	Third (won opener, lost finals)
1961	77-78	.497	Fourth (won opener, lost finals)
1962	82-72	.532	Fourth (lost opener)
1963	75-76	.497	Third
1964	82-72	.532	Fourth (won opener and finals)
1965	73-74	.497	Fifth
1966	83-64	.565	First (lost opener)
1967	80-61	.567	Second (lost opener)
1968	77-68	.527	Third (lost opener)
1969	71-69	.507	Fifth
1970	76-64	.543	Third (lost opener)
1971	86-54	.614	First (won opener, finals and JWS)
1972	76-68	.528	Fourth (lost opener)
1973	79-67	.541	Second (lost opener)
1974	88-56	.611	Second (won opener and finals)
1975	85-56	.603	Second (lost opener)
1976	88-50	.638	First (lost opener)
1977	67-73	.479	Sixth
1978	68-72	.486	Sixth
1979	53-86	.381	Eighth
1980	74-65	.532	Third (lost opener)
1981	69-70	.496	Fourth (lost opener)
1982	72-68	.514	Fourth (won opener, lost finals)
1983	65-75	.464	Sixth
1984	52-88	.371	Eighth
1985	58-81	.417	Seventh
1986	75-63	.543	Second (won opener, lost finals)
1987	74-65	.532	Third (lost opener)
1988	77-64	.546	First (won finals, lost Alliance Classic)
1989	72-73	.497	Fifth
1990	89-56	.614	First (won opener, lost Alliance Classic)
1991	76-68	.528	Fourth
1992	70-74	.486	Fifth
1993	74-67	.525	Fourth (won Eastern Division and opener, lost finals)
1994	67-74	.475	Fifth
1995	73-69	.514	Third (won Eastern Division, lost opener)
1996	72-69	.511	Fourth (won opener, lost finals)
1997	83-58	.589	First (won Eastern Division, opener and finals)
1998	70-74	.486	Ninth
1999	61-83	.424	Twelfth
2000	65-79	.451	Tenth
2001	60-84	.417	Fourteenth
2002	55-89	.382	Fourteenth
2003	68-75	.476	Ninth
2004	73-71	.507	Fifth
2005	75-69	.521	Sixth
2006	79-64	.552	Third (won opener, lost finals)
2007	77-67	.535	Fifth

Scranton
(MINERS, RED BARONS, YANKEES)

Scranton made its first appearance in the International League when the circuit expanded to 10 teams in 1887. A prosperous coal-producing community, Scranton labeled its baseball team the "Miners." But there was little to cheer about in 1887, as Scranton could manage merely 19 victories in its first 74 games, then disbanded. Interest in baseball remained strong, however, and Athletic Park was built in 1894.

The following year Scranton rejoined the IL, by then called the Eastern League. William Barnie, a veteran big league player and manager, was named field general, but the club could finish no higher than sixth. Scranton kranks at least enjoyed the hitting of first baseman "Wee Willie" Clark (.391 in 34 games before being sold to New York), pitcher-outfielder "Matches" Kilroy (.373 in 55 games), second baseman "Piggy" Ward (.357), and a pitcher-outfielder named Meaney (.348).

In 1896 Scranton sank to the cellar, despite the efforts of Meaney (.336), now a full-time outfielder, and outfielder P. Eagan (.329). Eagan again hit well in 1897 (.302), along with second baseman Frank Bonner (.360), first sacker "Big Bill" Massey (.313), and outfielders Griffin (.352 in 43 games) and Walters (.341). But Scranton suffered a third consecutive losing season, and did not rejoin the league.

Scranton, along with archrival Wilkes-Barre, played in the Penn State League in 1902. Two years later, the Miners joined the Class B New York State League, followed in 1905 by the Wilkes-Barre Coal Barons. The neighboring cities played until the circuit disbanded in 1917, then became charter members of the Class B New York-Pennsylvania League in 1923. In 1937 the league, a Class A organization, changed is name to the Eastern League, and later became one of just ten minor leagues to operate throughout World War II.

Scranton and Wilkes-Barre were key members of this fine league, maintaining stable franchises and one of the keenest rivalries in organized baseball. Until the 1930s Sunday ball remained illegal, and for Sabbath games the Miners had to leave Athletic Park for the grounds in nearby Dickson City (the Dickson Park had a vast outfield; owners offered a deed to the facility to any player would could hit a homer over the center field fence—788 feet away!). Athletic Park finally gave way to showplace Dunmore Stadium in 1940, after a record 317,000 fans filed into the old ballpark to support the 1939 championship team. The name "Miners" was replaced by "Red Sox" when Boston acquired controlling interest in the club.

Pennants were recorded in 1926, 1935, 1939, 1940, 1942, 1946, and 1948, when the Red Sox also won the postseason playoffs. Beginning in 1933, fleet outfielder Joe Cicero recorded the first of five consecutive stolen base championships, while southpaw Joe

Shaute won three straight percentage titles in 1934 (16-3), 1935 (21-7), and 1936 (20-7). On May 23, 1943, lefty Chet Covington (21-7) pitched the only nine-inning perfect game in league history. In 1946 righthander Tommy Fine (23-2) won 17 consecutive games, while southpaw Mel Parnell (13-4) established an all-time league record with a 1.30 ERA. Mike Martineck won the batting championship in 1935 (.369), and Sam Mele was the 1946 titlist (.342).

Despite the artistic success of the franchise, however, unemployment wracked the area coal industry by the late 1950s, and in 1952 Boston sold its interest in the club. There was a final season under the St. Louis Browns in 1953, then Dunmore Stadium was vacated for good by the pros. A supermarket later was built after Dunmore was razed, while the main gate of Scranton Memorial Stadium now marks the location of home plate at old Athletic Park.

A quarter of a century after the loss of pro baseball in Scranton, attorney John McGee spearheaded a drive to build a stadium and acquire a Triple-A franchise. McGee formed the Multi-Purpose Stadium Research Organization in 1978, and businessman Bill Gilchrist eventually donated a 50-acre site adjacent to the Montage ski resort in Moosic, a suburb of Scranton located 10 miles from Wilkes-Barre. With the assistance of Lackawanna County commissioners, Northeastern Baseball, Inc. (NBI) was organized in 1984 with McGee as president. Financial support was lined up from Lackawanna County, Scranton, Luzerne County, Wilkes-Barre, and the State of Pennsylvania, and 2,151 season tickets were sold by January 1985. Bill Terlecky, general manager at Syracuse, was employed as GM by NBI, which purchased the Double-A Waterbury franchise of the Eastern League. A Triple-A club was the NBI goal, but none was available, and the stadium could not be built until a team was secured. Ground was broken for a two-year, $7.5-million construction project which expanded to four years and $22 million.

After the Maine Guides finished in the IL cellar in 1986, owner Jordan Kobritz agreed to sell his club to NBI for $2 million and the Waterbury franchise. But when the territorial rights problem blocked the transfer of Waterbury's club, Kobritz sued to keep his team in Maine. In the meantime, construction delays caused NBI to move their unprofitable Waterbury operation to Williamsport. When Maine beame the Triple-A affiliate of Philadelphia, NBI tailored Lackawanna County Multi-Purpose Stadium ("The Lack") to the same

Lackawanna County Stadium opened in 1989 as a $22 million baseball palace. (Author photo)

outfield dimensions and artificial surface as the Phillies' Vets Stadium. Court decisions finally upheld the sale of the Guides, but The Lack still was incomplete, and NBI and Terlecky were forced to operate the 1988 Maine Phillies in Old Orchard Beach, where a meager 80,000 fans turned out for a lame-duck seventh-place team.

At last The Lack was ready for IL baseball. Drawing upon area traditions, NBI christened its team the Scranton/Wilkes-Barre Red Barons, after the Scranton Red Sox and the W-B Barons. The 1989 Red Barons finished a disappointing seventh, but paid attendance was 445,000. Area sports fans were starved for professional baseball and took immense pride in The Lack. The 10,600-seat stadium sits in a superb mountain backdrop, and boasts luxury skyboxes, the Hardball Café, and a vast 70' x 30' message center—the first one in the minors that was separate from the scoreboard.

Despite another losing season in 1990, paid attendance increased to 546,000, second-highest in the league. Todd Frowirth, a 6'4" righthander, was the IL's best reliever, leading the league in appearances, saves, and games finished (9-6, 67 G, 21 S, 52 GF).

In 1992 Mike Williams pitched his way (9-1) to the first of two consecutive percentage titles (9-2 in 1993). The 1992 Red Barons won the Eastern Division, bringing SWB its first IL division crown. Led by Manager of the Year Lee Elia, the Red Barons downed Pawtucket, three games to one, to take the playoff opener. SWB and Columbus met for the Governors' Cup in a memorable series. At The Lack the Red Barons won, 4-3, then lost on a two-run homer in the 13th inning of the second game. When the series switched to Columbus, the Red Barons staged a late-inning rally to go up two games to one. In Game Four Columbus built a seven-run lead, but the Red Barons again stormed back to a 9-9 tie—only to lose in the 11th inning. In the fifth and deciding game the Red Barons had a 3-1 lead in the ninth inning, following a rain delay of nearly two hours, but Columbus rallied for three runs in the bottom of the ninth to claim the Governors' Cup.

On July 25, 1992, Ben Rivera fired a seven-inning no-hitter against Pawtucket. During this exciting season more than 598,000 fans were attracted to The Lack, establishing the all-time SWB attendance record.

Six seasons passed before the Red Barons returned to the playoffs—for four years in a row. In 1999 the Red Barons won the North Division after a three-way race, then battled Charlotte to the wire in the playoff opener before losing, three games to two. The following season featured another tight division race. At the end of the regular season SWB and Buffalo were tied in the North. In a one-game playoff—the IL's first in a quarter of a century—Buffalo beat the Red Barons, 7-3, for the division crown. SWB, now the Wild Card, again faced Buffalo in the playoff opener. The Red Barons defeated the Bisons in four games and advanced to the finals against Indianapolis. The Red Barons and the Indians split their first two games at The Lack. Moving the series to Indianapolis, the Red Barons and the Indians again split consecutive one-run decisions. The deciding fifth game was a pitcher's duel, but the Indians prevailed and won the Governors' Cup.

In 2001 the Red Barons won the North with a club which featured strong pitching, including Brandon Knight, who won his second straight strikeout title, and Most Valuable Pitcher Brandon Duckworth (13-2, 2.63 ERA), who led the IL in victories, ERA, and winning percentage. For the second year in a row the Red Barons faced Buffalo in the playoff opener. The Red Barons lost the first game at The Lack, but won two of the next three. In the fifth game SWB scored two early runs, but Buffalo evened the score in late innings. The 2-2 tie lasted until the 19th inning, when the Red Barons scored four runs to win the series. In the opening game of the

Shane Victorino, speedy center fielder for Scranton/Wilkes-Barre, hit .310 and led the IL with 16 triples from the Red Barons' leadoff spot. Victorino was selected as the IL's 2005 MVP, then finished the season with Philadelphia (.294 in 21 games). (Courtesy IL)

Entrance to PNC Field, still known to some fans as "The Lack." (Author photo)

Governors' Cup series, Louisville edged SWB, 2-1, on a bases-loaded walk. The next morning, September 11, 2001, the United States was jolted by murderous terrorist attacks. IL President Randy Mobley cancelled the remaining playoffs and awarded the Governors' Cup to Louisville.

The 2002 Red Barons posted the league's best record and repeated as division champs behind righthander Joe Roa (14-0, 1.86 ERA), who was selected Most Valuable Pitcher despite a midseason promotion to Philadelphia. Roa posted the most victories without a defeat in IL history. For the third year in a row the Red Barons faced Buffalo in the playoff opener, but the Bisons finally found revenge with a three-game sweep. SWB's Marc Bombard was voted Manager of the Year.

In 2004 big righthander Robert "Bull" Ellis twirled a seven-inning no-hitter to defeat Louisville, 1-0. The next year infielder Danny Sandoval (.331) won the batting championship, while outfielder Shane Victorino (.310 with 18 homers) was the Most Valuable Player.

The 2006 Red Barons rang up the best season record among the fourteen IL teams, although the North Division champs lost the playoff opener. The next-season Scranton/Wilkes-Barre became the Triple-A affiliate of the New York Yankees and again won more games than any club in the International League. Led by ERA champ Brian Mazone (13-3, 2.03 ERA), the SWB Yankees compiled the best team Earned Run Average (3.28) in the league. Catcher Carlos Ruiz (.307) and second baseman Joe Thurston (.282) were placed on the All-Star Team, while John Russell was named Manager of the Year. Although the team once more fell in the playoff opener, there is every expectation that the SWB Yankees will continue the winning ways of recent years.

Year	Record	Pcg.	Finish
1887	19-55	.256	Tenth
1895	44-72	.379	Sixth
1896	44-67	.396	Eighth
1897	52-63	.452	Sixth
1989	64-79	.448	Seventh
1990	68-78	.466	Fifth
1991	61-73	.455	Eighth
1992	84-58	.592	Third (won Northern Division and opener, lost finals)
1993	62-80	.437	Eighth
1994	62-80	.437	Eighth
1995	70-72	.493	Eighth
1996	70-72	.493	Fifth
1997	66-76	.465	Eighth
1998	67-75	.472	Eleventh
1999	78-66	.542	Fourth (won North, lost opener)
2000	85-60	.586	Second (lost opener)
2001	78-65	.545	Fourth (lost opener)
2002	91-53	.632	First (won North, lost opener)
2003	73-70	.510	Sixth
2004	69-73	.486	Eighth
2005	69-75	.479	Ninth
2006	84-58	.592	First (won North, lost opener)
2007	84-59	.587	First (won North, lost opener)

Impressive scenery for SWB Yankees' fans at PNC Field. (Photo by Karon O'Neal)

Syracuse
(STARS, STEERS, SKYCHIEFS, CHIEFS)

A primitive form of baseball was played in Syracuse as early as the 1830s, and the evolving game was so popular that in 1845 it was banned from Clinton and Hanover squares because of congestion. The Syracuse Baseball Club first played in 1858; the Central City Club was a crack nine of the 1860s; and the Syracuse Star Baseball Club was formed in 1866. In 1876 the Stars became the city's first professional team, compiling a 46-13 record behind curveballer Harry McCormick. The Stars played at Lakeside Park beside Onondaga Lake and between State Fair and Hiawatha boulevards. In 1878 the Stars moved to Newell Park, bounded by East Raynor, Gorton, Mulberry, and South Salina streets.

The 1878 Stars joined the International League for 1879. But the Stars dropped out after a disappointing 15-27 start with the big leaguers, and there was no more pro ball in Syracuse until the first affiliation with the IL. In 1885 the Stars helped form the New York State League, hosting visiting members of the new circuit in Star Park at South Salina, Oneida, Temple, and West Taylor streets. Syracuse won the 1885 pennant, finished

sixth and third the next two years, then captured another flag in 1888. Conny Murphy won 34 games and the 1888 ERA title (1.27), while offense was provided by shortstop Ollie Beard (.350) and outfielders Rasty Wright (.349) and Lefty Marr (.342). The champs also featured two black players, catcher Fleet Walker and pitcher Bob Higgins.

Conny Murphy was almost as effective the next year (28-18), and John Keefe (24-15) was another reliable starter. The offense was led by second baseman Cupid Childs (.341) and Rasty Wright (.309), and the 1889 Stars finished a strong second. Syracuse moved to the big league American Association in 1890, but after a poor season the Stars returned to the IL. Outfielder-first baseman Buck West was the 1891 batting champ (.336) as the Stars finished third. But after a weak start in 1892, the Syracuse Ball Club disbanded and the franchise moved to Utica on July 11.

In 1894 the Stars rejoined the IL, playing at Crescent Park. Three seasons later, Syracuse won the 1897 pennant behind outfielder Abel Lezotte (.323), third baseman Jud Smith (.313), second-sacker "Bad Bill" Eagan (.306), and a superb pitching staff: victory leader John Malarkey (27-14), Henry Lampe (22-13), and future big league star Vic Willis (21-16). The Stars dropped to fifth the next year, then became mired in the cellar for three consecutive seasons, 1899 through 1901. The team dropped out of the circuit, but played in the Class B New York State League from 1902 through 1917. A highlight of these years was future Hall of Fame pitcher Grover Cleveland Alexander, who had a splendid season in 1910 (29-14). In 1907 the Stars moved to Hallock Park on North Salina Street near Onondaga Lake.

The New York State League disbanded in 1917, and the next year Jersey City's IL franchise was shifted to Syracuse. But wartime conditions thwarted baseball success, and the franchise was shifted again in August, finishing the 1918 schedule in Hamilton. In 1920 the Newark club was moved to Syracuse, and a new Star Park was erected on West Genesee Street to accommodate IL play. The 1920 Stars lost 116 games, however, and from 1920 through 1926 Syracuse finished no higher than sixth. Future Hall of Famer "Sunny Jim" Bottomley played first base (.348) for the 1922 Stars, but Syracuse fans had little to cheer about, even though the club was part of the St. Louis Cardinals' prototype farm system. In 1927 Cardinal talent finally brought a second-place finish behind catcher Gus Mancuso (.372); outfielders Homer Peel (.328, 114 R, 107 RBI), Howard Williamson (.327, 114 R) and stolen base champ Harry Layne (.323, 50 SB, 138 R, 114 RBI); first baseman Frank Hurst (.323, 100 R, 127 RBI); and strikeout (and walk) leader "Wild Bill" Hallahan (19-11, 195 Ks).

The Cardinals decided that Star Park was inadequate, and when the city balked at financing a new stadium, the franchise was moved to Rochester—which promptly reeled off four consecutive pennants. Syracuse, in the meantime, played in the New York Pennsylvania League in 1928 and 1929, increasingly regretted the absence of high quality baseball, and after the 1933 season agreed to build a stadium if Jersey City owner

John Corbett would transfer his club. Municipal Stadium (renamed MacArthur Stadium in 1942) was built in 48 days at Second Street North and East Hiawatha Boulevard; the facility cost $300,000 and seated more than 12,000. John Corbett asked fans to submit team names, and "Chiefs" replaced the traditional "Stars" nickname.

The 1934 Chiefs finished seventh, but the next year Syracuse rose to second, then swept Newark in the playoff opener and downed first-place Montreal, four games to three, to claim the Governors' Cup. Key players were third-sacker John Kroner (.323, 15 HR, 112 RBI), outfielder Dom Dallesandro (.317), and ERA champ Joe Cascarella (11-7, 2.35). The Chiefs slipped to seventh the next year but made the playoffs in 1937 and 1938. Righthander Lloyd Moore won the 1937 strikeout title despite pitching in only 21 games (11-6, 149 Ks in 142 IP), and third-sacker James Outlaw hit well for both playoff teams (.306 and .339). A popular player of

The Syracuse Stars of 1886, defending champs of the IL. Manager Henry Ormsby (dark suit, center), guided the 1885 pennant-winners. (Courtesy Onondaga Public Library, Syracuse)

this era was 6'9" southpaw John Gee, a Syracuse native who pitched for the Chiefs in 1937 (4-3), 1938 (17-11), and 1939 (20-10). Gee was sold to Pittsburgh for $75,000 and became the tallest athlete ever to pitch in the big leagues, but arm troubles made him ineffective after 1939.

John Corbett sold the Chiefs to Syracuse businessman Clarence Schnidler in 1940, and two years later a working agreement with the Cincinnati Reds was arranged. Throughout the eight years of the affiliation, Jewel Ens was the Syracuse manager, leading the Chiefs to the playoff finals five times and capturing the Governors' Cup in 1942, 1943, and 1947.

The 1942 champs had the league's poorest team batting average (.235), but the pitching staff featured MVP victory leader Red Barrett (20-12), sidearmer Ewell "The Whip"

Blackwell (15-10), Nate Andrews (16-12), and Tommy de la Cruz (13-14). The next year de la Cruz became the ace (21-11 with a 1.99 ERA), second baseman Roland Harrington (.291 with 52 thefts) won the stolen base crown, and Hank Sauer (.275) took over first base. The only disappointments of these two seasons were consecutive losses to Columbus in the Junior World Series.

The Chiefs plummeted to the cellar in 1944 and finished next-to-last in 1945, but the next season began three straight playoff appearances. The second-place Chiefs of 1946 battled to the finals before losing to Montreal. In 1947 "Hammerin' Hank" Sauer returned to Syracuse and blasted his way to the MVP award (.336, 50 HR, 141 RBI, 130 R). Hitting cleanup behind Sauer was left-handed Dutch Mele (.315, 20 HR, 100 RBI), who played eight seasons for Syracuse during the 1940s. Quality pitching was provided by southpaw victory leader Jim Prendergast (20-15) and right-hander Jake Wade (19-9). The Chiefs swept Montreal in the opener and outlasted Buffalo, 4-3, in the finals but fell to Milwaukee in a seven-game Junior World Series. The next year veteran Syracuse hurler Dixie Howell (17-12), fellow righty Ed Erautt (15-7), and RBI champ Clyde Vollmer (.289, 32 HR, 104 RBI) led the Chiefs back to the playoff finals before losing to Montreal.

Although the productive relationship with the Reds was severed after the 1949 season, Bruno Betzel piloted the Chiefs to playoff berths in 1951 and 1952. Lefty Bill Miller (16-10, 131 Ks) was the 1951 strikeout

Second baseman Frank Drews played the first of six seasons for Syracuse in 1945. He is circling third base past coach Jewell Ens. Note the umpire in the dark suit and tie. (Courtesy Syracuse Chiefs)

champ, while righthander Bob Keegan (20-11) led the 1952 IL in victories. In 1954 the Hoffman family sold the Chiefs to local businessman Marty Haske, who arranged a working agreement with the Phillies. New manager Skeeter Newsome promptly led the Chiefs to another playoff trophy, downing Montreal in the finals, 4-3, before once again suffering disappointment in the Junior World Series. Young Jim Owens was the ERA champ (17-9, 2.87), fellow righthander John Meyer won the strikeout title (15-11, 173 Ks), and first baseman Marv Blaylock (.303 with 22 homers) sparked the offense.

Owens won the strikeout crown the next year (15-11, 161 Ks), but the Chiefs dropped out of the playoffs and attendance fell to 85,191. After the season Marty Haske sold the club to owners who shifted the franchise to Miami.

MacArthur Stadium stood empty for five seasons, until a community-owned group brought the Montreal franchise to Syracuse for 1961. The Chiefs finished last in 1961 and 1962, but an affiliation with Detroit in 1963 brought three consecutive playoff appearances. The 1963 club won the Western Division but lost the playoff opener, as southpaw Willie Smith (14-2) and righty Alan Koch (11-2) proved almost unbeatable. The next year the Chiefs battled to the playoff finals behind victory and ERA leader Bruce Brubaker (15-9, 2.63), fellow righthander Paul Foytack (11-1), lefty Jack Hamilton (7-4 in 13 games) and a superb outfield: Mack Jones (.317, 39 HR, 102 RBI, 109 R, 13 3B), who led the IL in homers, RBIs, runs, triples and total bases; Jim Northrup (.312, 18 HR, 92 RBI); and Willie Horton (.288, 28 HR, 99 RBI). Jack Hamilton won the 1965 ERA crown (12-10, 2.42) for the fourth-place Chiefs, who dropped the playoff opener to first-place Columbus.

The Chiefs spent the next two seasons in the cellar, suffered another losing season in 1968, then went on a championship tear. Manager Frank Verdi guided the 1969 Chiefs to third place, beat Louisville in the opener, three games to two, then raced past Columbus to capture another Governors' Cup. Righthander Ron Klimkowski led the league in ERA and victories (15-7, 2.18). The next year was even better, as Verdi drove the Chiefs to the pennant, repeated as playoff titlist, then produced Syracuse's first Junior World Series triumph by downing Omaha, four games to one. Southpaw Rob Gardner was the ERA and victory leader (16-5, 2.53), righthander Hal Reniff handled the relief chores (10-3 in 58 games), and offense was provided by first baseman Tolia Solaita (.308, 19 HR, 87 RBI), third-sacker Len Boehmer (.288) and DH Ron Blomberg (.275).

These two fine teams played in a fire-damaged ballpark. Early in the 1969 season the stands directly behind home plate were destroyed, and those seats were not replaced for years. (The grandstand at MacArthur Park was completely rebuilt after the 1987 season.) Veteran Chiefs' employee and Syracuse native Tex Simone began a successful tenure as GM with the 1970 champs, and the genial executive still operates the club.

Bobby Cox was appointed field manager in 1973, and for the next three years he guided the Chiefs to the playoff finals. The Chiefs lost to Rochester in 1974 and to Tidewater in 1975, before winning the Governors' Cup in 1976, three games to one over Richmond. ERA champ Larry Gura (2.14) and fellow lefthander Scott McGregor (13-10) were mainstays of the 1974 Chiefs, and righthander Dick Sawyer pitched well in 1974 (8-7, 2.80), 1975 (13-9, 2.47), and 1976 (9-4, 2.75). The star of the 1976 championship team was MVP shortstop Mickey Klutts (.319 with 24 homers).

The Chiefs failed to make the playoffs in

1977, despite the efforts of outfielder Darryl Jones (.330 in 93 games), victory leader Larry McCall (16-7), and All-Star shortstop Greg Pryor (.271). The next year Syracuse changed affiliation from the Yankees to the Blue Jays—and plunged into the IL cellar. But in 1979 the Chiefs finished second, beat Richmond in the opener, 3-2, then finally succumbed to Columbus in the seventh game of the finals. The best players were first-sacker Greg "Boomer" Wells (.274) and righthanded reliever Steve Grilli (9-7 with a 2.01 ERA in 49 appearances).

Five consecutive losing seasons followed, but in 1985 the Chiefs vaulted from seventh place to the pennant. Southpaw Stan Clarke led the league in victories and winning percentage (14-4), righthander Don Gordon was the ERA champ (8-5, 2.07), Tom Henke provided almost flawless relief (2-1 with 18 saves and an 0.88 ERA in 39 games), and the offense was triggered by DH Willie Aikens

(.311), second baseman Mike Sharperson (.289), and outfielder Rick Leach (.283). Sharperson repeated as All-Star second sacker the next year (.289 again), and he improved his performance in 1989 (.299 in 88 games). Righthander Odell Jones was the 1987 strikeout champ (12-7 with 147 Ks), while infielder Eric Yelding led the league in 1988 with 59 stolen bases.

In 1989 Syracuse won the Eastern Division with the best record in the IL. Starter-reliever Jose Nunez was the ERA champ (11-11, 2.21), fellow righthander Alex Sanchez led the league in victories (13-7), outfielder Glen Hill won the home run title (.321 with 21 homers), and Frank Cabrera was named All-Star catcher (.300). The next two years brought losing records, but in 1991 Syracuse fans enjoyed the heroics of Derek Bell (.346, 89 R, 93 RBI), who led the league in batting, hits, runs, RBIs and total bases, strikeout champ Pat Hentgen (8-9, 155 Ks), first base-

Alliance Bank Stadium in Syracuse, home of the Chiefs. (Photo by Karon O'Neal)

man Domingo Martinez (.313 with 17 homers), and outfielder Turner Ward (.330). On June 1, 1993, Tim Brown hurled a seven-inning perfect game to beat Toledo, 2-0.

The 1994 Chiefs showcased talented outfielder Shawn Green (.344) and shortstop Alex Gonzalez (.284). Green was the IL batting champ and Rookie of the Year. Both Green and Gonzalez were named to the All-Star Team, along with reliever Randy St.

Claire, who led the league with 33 saves. The Chiefs secured the wild card slot, then beat Pawtucket in the playoff opener before being swept by Richmond in the finals.

Robert Perez, an outfield stalwart in 1993 (.294) and 1994 (.304), won the batting crown in 1995 (.343) and led the league with 172 hits. The next year outfielder Shannon Stewart (.298 with 35 steals) was the stolen base king, and on September 1 slugger Ricky Cradle blasted three home runs in a game against Pawtucket. In 1997 outfielder Rich Butler (.300, 24 HR, 87 RBI, 93 R) led the league in hits and runs scored.

Chiefs third-base dugout at Alliance Bank Stadium. Note the double row of sky boxes. (Photo by Karon O'Neal)

The Chiefs moved into a fine new ballpark in 1997. Since 1934 Syracuse had played in MacArthur Stadium, which seated 10,500 (on July 17, 1993, a standing-room-only crowd of 13,124 established the all-time single-game attendance record). New Alliance Bank Stadium could seat 11,071 fans, and in 1999 Syracuse set a season attendance record with a total of 446,025 fans.

The first Alliance Park playoff team was fielded in 1998. The Most Valuable Pitcher was Shannon Withem, who led the IL with 17 victories. Two sluggers hit three home runs in a single game, Pat Lennon against Columbus on August 5, and Kevin Witt one month later against Ottawa. The Chiefs forged the second-best

Durham Bulls hitters taking batting practice at Alliance Bank Stadium in Syracuse on May 22, 2007. (Photo by Karon O'Neal)

Wendy Simone Shoen and her daughter, Ariel Shoen. Wendy, the daughter of Executive VP/Chief Operating Officer Tex Simone, has worked for the club since girlhood, and currently is Director of Marketing. Ariel is a Jill of All Trades who intends to become a baseball executive. (Photo by Karon O'Neal)

Scooch, mascot of the Syracuse Chiefs. (Photo by Karon O'Neal)

record in the league (80-62), but had to settle for the wild card slot and were swept by Buffalo in the playoff opener.

In 2000 Chad Mottola led the league with 33 home runs and was named Most Valuable Player. On June 17, 2000, Leo Estrella fired a seven-inning perfect game to beat Indianapolis, 5-0. Against Charlotte on June 25, 2003, Simon Pond clubbed three homers in a single game. In 2005 outfielder John Ford-Griffin (.254, 30 HR, 103 RBI) was the home run and RBI king, and was voted Most Valuable Player.

Since 1997, the year the Community Owned Baseball Club of Central New York moved into their new stadium, the team nickname had officially been changed to SkyChiefs. But fans continued to call their team "Chiefs," and for 2007 "SkyChiefs" was changed in favor of "Chiefs." Also for 2007 the Community Owned Baseball Club of Central New York acquired a new president, Ron Gersbacher, following the long and stable presidency of Don Waful (1969-2006).

Year	Record	Pcg.	Finish
1885	45-32	.584	First
1886	46-47	.491	Sixth
1887	61-40	.604	Third
1888	81-31	.723	First
1889	64-44	.593	Second
1891	56-42	.571	Third
1894	63-56	.529	Third
1895	62-53	.539	Fourth
1896	59-62	.488	Fifth
1897	86-50	.623	First
1898	52-63	.452	Sixth
1899	39-68	.364	Eighth
1900	43-84	.339	Eighth
1901	45-87	.341	Eighth
1918			Dropped out
1920	33-116	.221	Eighth

1921	71-96	.425	Sixth
1922	64-102	.386	Seventh
1923	73-92	.442	Sixth
1924	79-83	.488	Sixth
1925	74-87	.460	Sixth
1926	70-91	.435	Seventh
1927	102-66	.607	Second
1934	60-94	.390	Seventh
1935	87-67	.565	Second (won opener and finals)
1936	59-95	.383	Seventh
1937	78-84	.513	Third (lost opener)
1938	87-67	.567	Second (lost opener)
1939	81-74	.523	Fifth
1940	71-90	.441	Seventh
1941	70-83	.458	Sixth
1942	78-74	.513	Third (won opener and finals, lost JWS)
1943	82-71	.536	Third (won opener and finals, lost JWS)
1944	68-84	.447	Eighth
1945	64-89	.418	Seventh
1946	81-72	.529	Second (won opener, lost finals)
1947	88-65	.575	Third (won opener and finals, lost JWS)
1948	77-73	.513	Third (won opener, lost finals)
1949	73-80	.477	Sixth
1950	74-79	.484	Sixth
1951	82-71	.536	Third (won opener, lost finals)
1952	88-66	.571	Second (lost opener)
1953	58-95	.379	Seventh
1954	79-76	.510	Fourth (won opener and finals, lost JWS)
1955	74-79	.484	Fifth
1961	56-98	.364	Eighth
1962	53-101	.344	Eighth
1963	80-70	.533	Third (won Western Division, lost opener)
1964	88-66	.571	Second (won opener, lost finals)
1965	74-73	.503	Fourth (lost opener)
1966	54-93	.367	Eighth
1967	63-77	.450	Eighth
1968	72-75	.490	Fifth
1969	75-65	.536	Third (won opener and finals)
1970	84-56	.600	First (won opener, finals, and JWS)
1971	73-67	.521	Fourth (lost opener)
1972	64-80	.444	Seventh
1973	76-70	.521	Fourth
1974	74-70	.514	Fourth (won opener, lost finals)
1975	72-64	.529	Third (won opener, lost finals)
1976	82-57	.590	Second (won opener and finals)
1977	70-70	.500	Fifth
1978	50-90	.357	Eighth
1979	77-63	.550	Second (won opener, lost finals)
1980	58-81	.417	Eighth
1981	60-80	.429	Seventh
1982	64-76	.457	Sixth
1983	61-78	.438	Seventh
1984	58-81	.417	Seventh
1985	79-61	.564	First (lost opener)
1986	72-67	.518	Fifth
1987	68-72	.486	Sixth
1988	70-71	.496	Third
1989	83-62	.572	First (won Eastern Division, lost finals)
1990	62-83	.428	Sixth
1991	73-71	.507	Sixth
1992	60-83	.420	Seventh
1993	59-82	.418	Ninth
1994	71-71	.500	Fifth (won opener, lost finals)
1995	59-82	.418	Tenth
1996	67-75	.472	Seventh
1997	55-87	.387	Ninth
1998	80-82	.563	Second (lost opener)
1999	73-71	.507	Eighth
2000	74-66	.529	Seventh
2001	71-73	.493	Sixth
2002	64-80	.444	Tenth
2003	62-79	.440	Fourteenth
2004	66-78	.458	Tenth
2005	71-73	.493	Eighth
2006	64-79	.448	Twelfth
2007	64-80	.444	Eleventh

Toledo
(Mud Hens)

No team in minor league baseball is more readily identifiable than the Toledo Mud Hens. The eccentric character Klinger (Jamie Farr) on the classic television series M*A*S*H sported a Mud Hens jersey and cap, and the surge of baseball nostalgia in recent years has made the "Mud Hen" more popular than ever.

Toledo's first professional baseball team won the Northwestern League pennant in 1883, then shifted to the big league American Association the next year. In 1889 Toledo and neighboring Detroit joined the International Association as replacements for Troy and Albany. Detroit won the IL pennant, but Toledo first baseman Perry Werden won the batting title (.394). Hitting even better was an experienced big league outfielder, Billy Sunday (.398 in 31 games). Sunday had logged seven seasons in the National League, but a poor start with Pittsburgh (.239) sent him to Toledo, where he blasted minor league pitching. He went back to the National League in 1890, but soon "Parson" Sunday

turned to full-time religion, becoming America's foremost evangelist.

Another veteran big leaguer, third baseman Bill Alvord, also hit well for Toledo (.308), and so did shortstop Tom Nicholson (.302). Most of the pitching was handled by righthander Fred Smith (21-16) and lefthander Ed Cushman (18-14 with 194 Ks). Toledo finished fourth, then the team rejoined the American Association for 1890, taking Werden, Alvord, Nicholson, Smith, and Cushman back to the big leagues. But the American Association years of 1884 and 1890 would be Toledo's only two major league seasons. Returning to the minors, Toledo won back-to-back pennants in the Inter-State League of 1896 and 1897.

By this time Toledo games were played in Bay View Park, located in the northeast section of town near the confluence of the Maumee River and Lake Erie. Abounding in nearby marshlands was a species of gallinule or coot referred to as "mud hens," and since the playing field often was wet and muddy, Toledo fans began calling the players Mud Hens. Early pro teams had been Toledo Sox and other sobriquets, but the Toledo Mud Hens would provide baseball with one of the most memorable sports nicknames. In 1902 Toledo became a charter member of the new American Association, and the Mud Hens moved into double-tiered Swayne Field in 1909. Charley Somers owned both Toledo and Cleveland of the American League, and during the Federal League seasons of 1914 and 1915 the Mud Hens were moved to Cleveland to block a possible Federal League franchise. In 1914 Swayne Field hosted a team in the Class C Southern Michigan League, but the Federal League disbanded a year later, and the American Association returned to Toledo.

Veteran National League outfielder Casey Stengel made his managerial debut with

Former big league outfielder Casey Stengel spent five seasons, 1926-31, as player-manager of Toledo, leading the 1927 Mud Hens to the American Association pennant.

Toledo in 1926, and the next year he led the Mud Hens to a pennant and victory over Buffalo in the Little World Series. Toledo's other AA flag came in 1953, but the Mud Hens spent most seasons in the second division, and the franchise was moved to Wichita for 1956. The Kroeger Company purchased Swayne Field and razed the historic old stadium to erect a retail outlet.

Civic leader Ned Skeldon successfully pushed for the construction of a 10,000-seat stadium in 1963 and for the acquisition of Richmond's International League franchise two years later. Lucas County Recreation Center and the Ohio Baseball Hall of Fame were adjacent to the ballpark, which was renamed Ned Skeldon Stadium in June 1988, just three months before Toledo's "Mr. Baseball" died.

After a 76-year absence, Toledo returned to the IL as an affiliate of the New York Yankees. In 1965 righthander Pete Mikkelson pitched a no-hitter, and the next year righty Stan Bahnsen tossed a seven-inning no-hitter (he fired another one in 1967 for Columbus). But there were few other highlights as the Mud Hens finished seventh and sixth, and in 1967 Toledo changed affiliations to the Boston Red Sox.

The '67 Mud Hens posted the league's highest batting average behind outfielder Wayne Comer (.290), who led the IL in runs and total bases, and All-Star shortstop Tom Matchik (.289), who blasted three home runs in a game with Richmond. Manager Jack

Toledo's Interstate League champs of 1896 played in Bay View Park, which had a wet field and nearby "mud hens." (Courtesy Toledo Mud Hens)

Tighe guided the Mud Hens to third place. Toledo defeated first-place Richmond, three games to two, in the playoff opener, then won the Governors' Cup by downing Columbus in the finals, four games to one.

The next season Tighe led the Mud Hens to the pennant, receiving his second consecutive Manager of the Year award. A strong pitching staff featured strikeout champ Jim Rooker (14-8 with 206 Ks in 190 IP) and righthanders Dick Drago (15-8) and Mike Marshall (15-9 with a league-leading 211 IP and 16 CG). The offense was sparked by outfielder Robert Christian (.319) and Ron Woods (.292), and All-Star second baseman

Toledo is the hometown of Jamie Farr who won fame as Klinger on the long-running TV comedy M*A*S*H. Occasionally Klinger wore a Mud Hens cap and jersey on-screen, and one episode was centered around the Mud Hens' late-season pursuit of the IL pennant. The Mud Hens, of course, enjoyed an enormous publicity boost from Farr and M*A*S*H. (Courtesy Toledo Mud Hens)

David Campbell (.265 with 26 homers in just 96 games). The Mud Hens edged second-place Columbus by half a game for the flag, but lost the playoff opener to Jacksonville.

Ten seasons would pass before the Mud Hens reappeared in the playoffs. In 1972 righthander Joe Niekro fired a seven-inning perfect game over Tidewater, and three years later Wayne Simpson pitched a seven-inning no-hitter against Syracuse. Starter-reliever Chuck Seelbach recorded 10 consecutive victories in 1971 and won the percentage title (12-2). Catcher Bill Nahorodny (.255 with 19 homers) brought Toledo its first home run crown in 1975, and the next season first-sacker Joey Lis led the league in RBIs, runs, and total bases (306, 30 HR, 103 RBI).

In 1978 the Mud Hens, now affiliated with the Twins, finished third, although Pawtucket won the playoff opener, three games to two. Toledo finished last in team hitting, but outfielder Gary Ward was formidable at the plate (.294 with a league-leading 12 triples), along with infielder Dan Graham (.277 with 23 homers). Manager Cal Ermer fashioned another Toledo winner in 1980, this time guiding the Mud Hens to second place. Toledo boasted the IL's leading offense (.272) behind batting champ Dave Engle (.307), first-sacker Jesus Vega (.303), outfielder Greg Johnston (.296), third baseman Ron Washington (.287), and All-Star catcher Ray Smith (.277). The Mud Hens won the opening round of playoffs from Richmond but lost the finals to first-place Columbus.

Toledo dropped to last place the next year and rose only to seventh in 1982, even though first baseman Greg Wells was the '82 batting and RBI champ (.336, 28 HR, 107 RBI) and righthander Don Cooper won the strikeout title (12-10, 125 Ks). Although Dave Meier (.336), Mike Wilson (.325), and Tim Teufel (.323, 27 HR, 100 RBI) hit impressively in 1983, Toledo again suffered a losing season.

But the next year Mike Wilson led the league in stolen bases and walks (.287, 48 SB, 94 W), and the pitching staff included strikeout leader Brad Havens (11-10, 129 Ks), fellow lefty Keith Comstock (12-6), and righthander Dick Yett (12-9). Longtime field general Cal Ermer (1978-84) led the Mud Hens to third place, but the Maine Guides swept the playoff opener.

The 1984 Mud Hens proved to be Toledo's last playoff team for 18 years. During the intervening 17 seasons Toledo fans enjoyed only two winning teams, and in 1998 and 1999 there were back-to-back last-place finishes in a 14-team league. But Mud Hen fans, like those of the Chicago Cubs and the early New York Mets, were resolutely loyal to their "lovable losers."

These fans at least could enjoy stellar play from individual Mud Hens, such as the 1986 efforts of batting champ Andre David (.328)

and All-Star catcher Pat Dempsey (.300). Outfielder-first baseman Tim Tolman (.314), outfielder Bruce Fields (.305), and victory leader Paul Gibson (14-7) played well in 1987, and fellow lefty Steve Searcy was voted Most Valuable Pitcher of 1988 (13-7 with a league-leading 176 Ks in 170 IP). John De Silva was the 1993 strikeout leader with 136 Ks, while Shannon Penn stole 45 bases to lead the 1994 IL.

Two Mud Hen pitchers turned in classic performances in 1994. On May 4 Felipe Lira twirled a seven-inning no-hitter to beat Columbus, 4-0. Righthander Jose Lima was even better on August 17, firing a nine-inning no-hit gem to defeat Pawtucket, 3-0. On May 4, 1996, Randy Marshall and Mike Walker combined to pitch a seven-inning no-hitter in a 2-1 victory over Charlotte. Also in 1996 Phil Hiatt was named Most Valuable Player after leading the league with 42 homers, 119 RBIs, and 99 runs scored.

The next season Kimera Bartee was the stolen base champ with 33 thefts, while relief pitcher Eddie Gaillard led the IL with 28 saves. Billy McMillon (.345) won the hitting title in 2000.

Kirk Gibson spent six games with Toledo in 1987 on a rehab assignment. The next season, as a Dodger, he was the National League MVP and hit one of the most memorable home runs in World Series history. (Courtesy Toledo Mud Hens)

Home Plate entrance to Toledo's Fifth Third Field. (Photo by Karon O'Neal)

In 2002 Toledo moved into a downtown ballpark, Fifth Third Field, with a seating capacity of 8,943. The Mud Hens celebrated their new stadium with Toledo's first playoff club since 1994. Andres Torres won the stolen base crown with 33 steals, and the Mud Hens won the West Division. Toledo was swept by Durham in the playoff opener, but the drought was over.

Fifth Third Field has been instrumental in reviving downtown Toledo. (Photo by Karon O'Neal)

With Manager of the Year Larry Parrish at the helm, the 2005 Mud Hens vaulted from worst to first. In 2004 Toledo finished fourteenth, then drove to the league's best record (89-55) and the 2005 West Division crown. A franchise record 592,046 fans turned out to watch the IL's best club. The pitching staff led the league in ERA (3.71), shutouts (15), fewest home runs (116), fewest hits, fewest runs, and other categories. Kenny Baugh (12-8) and Jason Grilli (12-9) provided a solid starting duo, while closer Jason Karnuth (7-2, 23 saves, 2.13 ERA) headed a strong bullpen. The offense featured All-Star outfielder Curtis Granderson (.290, with 13 triples, 15 homers, and 22 stolen bases), outfielder Marcus Thames (.340 with 22 home runs), first baseman Carlos Pena (.311), and infielder Chris Shelton (.331

The century-old, six-story commercial building incorporated into the right field corner of Fifth Third Field is utilized by the Mud Hens for offices, storage, banquet halls, and a spacious gift shop. (Photo by Karon O'Neal)

before a callup to the Tigers). Third sacker Mike Hessman added 28 home runs to a hard-hitting lineup. In the playoff opener Toledo won the first game at Norfolk and at Fifth Third Field, then held on to a 5-3 lead in Game Five. Now on a roll, the Mud Hens swept Indianapolis to bring Toledo its first Governors' Cup since 1967.

Toledo's next Governors' Cup came just one year later. Manager Larry Parrish remained at the controls, and Mike Hessman returned to pound 24 home runs—along with four more in the playoffs. First baseman Josh Phelps (.308, 24 HR, 90 RBI) was a steady force in the lineup, along with outfielders Ryan Rayburn (.275, 20 HR, 79 RBI) and Ryan Ludwick (.266, 28 HR, 80 RBI). Also adding hits were third baseman Jack Hanahan (.282) and second sacker Kevin Hooper (.276). Strikeout king Chad Durbin (11-8, 149 Ks) and Jordan Tata (10-6) were solid pitchers. Indianapolis and Toledo had identical records in the West, but the Mud Hens won a single-game playoff and the division. Toledo beat Charlotte in the opening round of the playoffs. Facing Rochester in the finals, Toledo could win just one of the first three games, but evened the series with a 6-0 shutout. In Game Five the Mud Hens unleashed a 13-hit attack, including four home runs, and won 10-1. Toledo lost the first "Bricktown Showdown" to the PCL champion Tucson Sidewinders in Oklahoma City. But with back-to-back Governors' Cups in 2005 and 2006, the lovable losers may still

have been lovable, but they were losers no more.

Indeed, the Mud Hens won the West again in 2007, although they were beaten in the playoff opener. For their third consecutive division title the Mud Hens featured veteran

One of two banquet halls in the six-story building at the right field corner of Fifth Third Field. These halls are rented regularly for dinners, parties and other occasions. (Author photo)

"Who's Up?" Knothole Gang statuary outside center field at Toledo's Fifth Third Field. (Author photo)

In 2005 the Toledo Mud Hens won their division with the best record in the IL, then marched through the playoffs to claim the Governors' Cup. The Mud Hens won the Governors' Cup again in 2006. (Courtesy IL)

A Boy Scout sleepover courtesy of the Toledo Mud Hens, with tents set up across the outfield of Fifth Third Field. (Courtesy IL)

outfielder Timo Perez and a rock-solid pitching staff—Virgil Vasquez (12-5 with 2 shutouts), Ron Chiavecci (12-6), Dennis Tankersley (10-7), and Yorman Bazardo (10-6).

Year	Record	Pcg.	Finish
1889	54-51	.514	Fourth
1965	68-78	.466	Seventh
1966	71-75	.486	Sixth
1967	73-66	.525	Third (won opener and finals)
1968	83-64	.565	First (lost opener)
1969	68-72	.486	Sixth
1970	51-89	.364	Eighth
1971	60-80	.429	Seventh
1972	75-69	.521	Fifth
1973	65-81	.445	Seventh
1974	70-74	.486	Fifth
1975	62-78	.443	Seventh
1976	55-85	.393	Eighth
1977	56-84	.400	Eighth
1978	74-66	.529	Third (lost opener)
1979	63-76	.453	Seventh
1980	77-63	.550	Second (won opener, lost finals)
1981	53-87	.379	Eighth
1982	60-80	.429	Seventh
1983	68-72	.486	Fifth
1984	74-63	.540	Third (lost opener)
1985	71-68	.511	Sixth
1986	62-77	.446	Sixth
1987	70-70	.500	Fifth
1988	58-84	.408	Eighth
1989	69-76	.476	Sixth
1990	58-86	.403	Eighth
1991	74-70	.514	Fifth
1992	64-80	.444	Sixth
1993	65-77	.458	Seventh
1994	63-79	.444	Ninth
1995	71-71	.500	Sixth
1996	70-72	.493	Fifth
1997	68-73	.482	Seventh
1998	52-89	.369	Fourteenth
1999	57-87	.396	Fourteenth
2000	55-86	.390	Twelfth
2001	65-79	.451	Twelfth
2002	81-63	.563	Third (won West, lost opener)
2003	65-78	.455	Eleventh
2004	65-78	.455	Fourteenth
2005	89-55	.618	First (won West, opener and finals)
2006	76-66	.535	Fifth (won West, opener and finals, lost Bricktown Showdown)
2007	82-61	.573	Second (won West, lost opener)

Wilkes-Barre
(COAL BARONS, RED BARONS, YANKEES)

"This town has the reputation of having the toughest base ball audiences of any town in the league, and some go so far as to say in the United States." This critical observation was delivered in *The Sporting Life* just before the opening of the 1895 Eastern League (IL) season. *The Sporting Life* recommended that the club management pay one or two dollars to off-duty officers and station them throughout the bleachers to eject the most troublesome rowdies.

The coal miners of Wilkes-Barre began to develop their boisterous appreciation of the national pastime in 1865, when the Susquehanna Baseball Club became the first nine to represent the prosperous coal-mining community in northeastern Pennsylvania. It was another 20 years before the Wilkes-Barre Baseball Club provided the city with a team of professionals who played all comers, from exhibitions against National League teams to college clubs to crack amateur nines. Games were played at Lee Park, but attendance usually averaged only 200 or so kranks.

In 1887 the International League expanded to 10 teams, including Wilkes-Barre and neighboring Scranton. The natural rivalry amounted to little, however, as Wilkes-Barre staggered into ninth place with a 26-75 record, while Scranton occupied the cellar until throwing in the towel. The league returned to an eight-team format for 1888, and the two Pennsylvania cities dropped out—for the time being.

Wilkes-Barre rejoined the league in 1893. Earlier called the "Colts," the Wilkes-Barre team now was descriptively labeled the "Coal Barons," a nickname that later would be shortened to "Barons." The 1893 Coal Barons hit .306 as a team, and starred future big leaguers Frank Bonner (.368) and Candy Lachance (.357), along with 13-year major league veteran Dandy Wood (.335). The next season outfielder Dad Lytle posted the league's second highest batting average (.361).

In 1895 Scranton also joined the league, officially renewing the Coal Barons' best rivalry. Dad Lytle again hit impressively (.336) for Wilkes-Barre, and so did fellow outfielders Abel Lezotte (.332) and Sandy Griffin (.318), player-manager Dan Shannon (.346), and first-sacker Bill "Globetrotter" Earle (.329). This hard-hitting team finished third.

Abel Lezotte returned the following year to win the batting title and become the first of just four men in IL history to hit over .400 (.404). Frank Bonner (.337) also was back, along with Dad Lytle (.300), and there was a fine new outfielder named Betts (.353). But overall the Coal Barons were weaker and sank to seventh place. In 1897 Betts fell off by 60 points (.293), most of the other players were dealt to other clubs, and the pitching staff had two 20-game losers (Keenan, 10-26, and Odwell, 7-22), all of which doomed the Coal Barons to last place.

Wilkes-Barre fans were cheered by the play of native son Bill Goeckel, who broke in spectacularly with the Coal Barons in 1896 (.393 in 22 games as a first baseman). During the cellar year of 1897, Goeckel became the regular first-

Grandstand at PNC Field. (Author photo)

sacker, was the club's leading hitter (.330), and even pitched when called upon—turning in the only winning record (6-4) on the staff. In 1898 he led all first basemen in fielding and again hit well (.301 with 40 stolen bases), helping the Coal Barons to rise to second place and himself to the National League.

The 1898 Coal Barons finished just three games out of first, as outfielder Joe Wright posted the league's second-highest batting average (.371), and Bill Coughlin (.310) led all third basemen in fielding, en route to a long big league career. But the distractions of the Spanish-American War caused great disruption throughout professional baseball, and Wilkes-Barre was one of three teams that did not return to the IL for 1899.

During the next six seasons, the Coal Barons played in the Atlantic League and the Class B Penn State League, in which archrival Scranton also participated. Scranton joined the Class B New York State League in 1904, and Wilkes-Barre followed the next year. Both cities played until 1917, when the circuit disbanded because of the war. Wilkes-Barre won the pennant in 1910, and put together a 26-game winning streak in 1912.

In 1923 Wilkes-Barre and Scranton became charter members of the Class B New York-Pennsylvania League, which was elevated to Class A status in 1933, and four years later changed its name to Eastern League. For more than three decades the Wilkes-Barre Barons and Scranton Miners (later Red Sox) were cornerstone franchises of the circuit.

Since leaving nineteenth-century Lee Park, the Barons had played at Morgan B. Williams Park off Scott Street in the east end of town. In 1926 the Barons moved to beautiful Artillery Park on the west side of the Susquehanna River. Adjacent to a large colliery, Artillery Park was named because the 109th Field Artillery trained on the grounds, and eventually the State Armory Board pro-

vided a lighting system. In addition to professional baseball, Artillery Park also was the center of high school, college and pro football, as well as other athletic events.

Wilkes-Barre played in the inaugural game of the New York-Pennsylvania League, on May 9, 1923. The Barons finished first in 1930, 1932, 1941, 1950, 1951 and 1954, and added a postseason playoff championship in 1954. The only batting champs were Gene Woodling in 1943 (.344) and Joe Tipton in 1947 (.375), but righthander Red Embree set an Eastern League strikeout record in 1941 (21-5 with 213 Ks), and the next year Allie Reynolds twirled 11 shutouts while leading the league in ERA and strikeouts (18-7, 1.56 ERA, 193 Ks).

The left field corner at PNC Field. (Author photo)

Scranton/Wilkes-Barre infielder Danny Sandoval hit .331 and won the 2005 batting title. (Courtesy IL)

By the 1950s, however, the troubles plaguing all of minor league baseball were exacerbated in Wilkes-Barre (and in Scranton) by severe unemployment in the area coal mines. Despite back-to-back pennants in 1950 and 1951, attendance declined so badly that the parent Cleveland Indians moved the franchise to Reading following the 1951 championship. Backed by community ownership and the Detroit Tigers, Wilkes-Barre returned to the Eastern League in 1953 and won the pennant and playoffs the next year. But Detroit pulled out after 1954, and a partial agreement with the Giants proved inadequate. The franchise was transferred to Johnstown and a new stadium on July 1, 1955.

The grandstands at Artillery Park began to deteriorate and eventually were dismantled. Wilkes College continued to use the grounds for baseball, however, and tennis courts also were erected. Then, in the 1980s, Scranton interests began a movement to bring professional baseball back to the Wyoming Valley, and support was enlisted from Wilkes-Barre and Lackawanna County. Magnificent Lackawanna County Multi-Purpose Stadium, located alongside the Montage ski resort between Wilkes-Barre and Scranton, finally was ready in 1989, and an International League franchise moved in from Old Orchard Beach, Maine. The name of the team signified the new unity of the old rivals, the Wilkes-Barre Barons and the Scranton Red Sox—the Red Barons.

Water tower near the Scranton/Wilkes-Barre PNC Field. (Photo by Karon O'Neal)

Year	Record	Pcg.	Finish
1887	26-75	.257	Ninth
1893	40-65	.381	Eighth
1894	54-56	.495	Seventh
1895	61-49	.555	Third
1896	49-66	.426	Seventh
1897	28-87	.243	Eighth
1898	62-48	.564	Second
1989	64-79	.448	Seventh
1990	68-78	.466	Fifth
1991	65-68	.455	Seventh
1992	84-58	.592	Third (won Northern Division and opener, lost finals)
1993	62-80	.437	Eighth
1994	62-80	.437	Eighth
1995	70-72	.493	Eighth
1996	70-72	.493	Fifth
1997	66-76	.465	Eighth
1998	67-75	.472	Eleventh
1999	78-66	.542	Fourth (won North, lost opener)
2000	85-60	.586	Second (lost opener)
2001	78-65	.545	Fourth (lost opener)
2002	91-53	.632	First (won North, lost opener)
2003	73-70	.510	Sixth
2004	69-73	.486	Eighth
2005	69-75	.479	Ninth
2006	84-58	.592	First (won North, lost opener)
2007	84-59	.587	First (won North, lost opener)

International League Records

Annual Standings

From 1884 through 1932, with the exception of 1892, the team which compiled the best record over the regular schedule was declared the champion. The 1892 schedule featured a split season format, followed by a playoff series between the two winners. In 1933 Frank Shaughnessy, longtime International League executive, devised the postseason playoff scheme that would be permanently adopted by the IL (indeed, some version of the Shaughnessy Plan would become a fixture of almost all minor league schedules). In 1963, 1973, and 1974 the International League was organized into two divisions, but the Shaughnessy playoff continued to be staged in postseason play. In 1988, however, the International League created Eastern and Western divisions, with division winners engaging in a postseason playoff to determine the IL champ. When the league expanded to fourteen teams in 1998 there were three divisions: North, South, and West. The winners of each division and a Wild Card team would stage a post-season playoff for the Governors' Cup.

indicates playoff winners

1884

Trenton	46-38	.547
Lancaster	30-31	.492
Newark	32-40	.444
Allentown	30-41	.422
York	11-20	.355
Wilmington	49-12	.803
Richmond	30-28	.517
Reading	27-27	.500
Harrisburg	15-24	.385
Baltimore	3-10	.231

1885

Syracuse	45-32	.584
Rochester	40-36	.526
Utica	41-38	.518
Binghamton	36-42	.461
Oswego	32-46	.410
Albany	No record	

1886

Utica	62-34	.645
Rochester	56-39	.589
Toronto	53-41	.563
Hamilton	52-43	.547
Buffalo	50-45	.526
Syracuse	46-47	.491
Binghamton	37-58	.389
Oswego	23-72	.242

1887

Toronto	65-36	.643
Buffalo	63-40	.611
Syracuse	61-40	.604
Newark	59-39	.602
Hamilton	57-42	.575
Jersey City	48-49	.494
Rochester	49-52	.485
Binghamton	27-46	.369
Wilkes-Barre	26-75	.257
Scranton	19-55	.256

1888

Syracuse	81-31	.723
Toronto	77-34	.694
Rochester	64-43	.598
Hamilton	66-45	.595
London	53-53	.500
Buffalo	47-60	.439
Troy	28-80	.259
Albany	18-88	.170

1889

Detroit	72-39	.649
Syracuse	64-44	.593
Rochester	60-50	.545
Toledo	54-51	.514
Toronto	56-55	.505
London	51-55	.481
Buffalo	41-65	.404
Hamilton	35-74	.321

1890

Detroit	29-18	.617
Saginaw-Bay City	29-19	.604
Toronto	30-20	.600
Montreal	27-26	.509
Grand Rapids	14-27	.341
London	15-34	.306
Buffalo	6-12	.333
Hamilton	No record	

1891

Buffalo	72-27	.727
Albany	57-41	.582
Syracuse	56-42	.571
New Haven	48-39	.552
Troy	46-58	.442

Lebanon	37-60	.381
Rochester	36-60	.375
Providence	29-54	.349

1892

Binghamton	60-52	.536
Providence*	57-59	.491
	won first half	
Albany	60-58	.509
Rochester	68-57	.544
Elmira	33-27	.556
Troy	62-57	.521
Buffalo	53-60	.469
New Haven	20-17	.541
Philadelphia	12-26	.316
Utica	24-36	.400

1893

Erie	63-41	.606
Springfield	61-43	.587
Troy	66-49	.574
Buffalo	61-53	.535
Binghamton	48-55	.466
Albany	53-61	.465
Providence	44-69	.389
Wilkes-Barre	40-65	.381

1894

Providence	78-34	.678
Troy	43-32	.573
Syracuse	63-56	.529
Erie	57-49	.538
Springfield	57-54	.514
Buffalo	65-61	.512
Wilkes-Barre	54-56	.495
Binghamton	18-62	.225
Allentown	8-16	.333
Scranton	8-31	.205

1895

Springfield	79-36	.687
Providence	74-44	.627
Wilkes-Barre	61-49	.555
Syracuse	62-53	.539
Buffalo	63-61	.508
Scranton	44-72	.379
Rochester	47-82	.364
Toronto	43-76	.361

1896

Providence	71-47	.602
Buffalo	70-53	.569
Rochester	68-58	.540
Toronto	59-57	.509
Syracuse	59-62	.488
Springfield	54-64	.458
Wilkes-Barre	49-66	.426
Scranton	44-67	.396

1897

Syracuse	86-50	.632
Toronto	75-52	.591
Buffalo	74-58	.561
Springfield	70-56	.556
Providence	70-60	.538
Scranton	52-63	.452
Montreal	49-76	.392
Wilkes-Barre	28-87	.243

1898

Montreal	68-48	.586
Wilkes-Barre	62-48	.564
Toronto	64-55	.538
Buffalo	62-60	.508
Providence	58-60	.487
Syracuse	52-63	.452
Springfield	48-63	.432
Ottawa	53-70	.431

1899

Rochester	71-42	.628
Montreal	61-50	.550
Worcester	58-51	.532
Toronto	55-55	.500
Springfield	52-56	.481
Hartford	50-56	.472
Providence	54-62	.466
Syracuse	39-68	.364

1900

Providence	84-52	.623
Rochester	77-56	.579
Hartford	68-55	.556
Worcester	62-63	.496
Springfield	61-63	.492
Toronto	63-67	.485
Montreal	53-71	.427
Syracuse	43-84	.339

1901

Rochester	89-49	.645
Toronto	74-52	.587
Providence	73-58	.557
Hartford	58-56	.509
Worcester	62-64	.492
Montreal	64-66	.492
Buffalo	40-73	.354
Syracuse	45-87	.341

1902

Toronto	85-42	.669
Buffalo	88-46	.657
Jersey City	72-65	.526
Worcester	69-63	.523
Providence	67-68	.496
Montreal	59-77	.434
Rochester	57-76	.429
Newark	40-99	.288

1903

Toronto	85-42	.669
Buffalo	88-45	.662
Jersey City	72-65	.526
Worcester	69-63	.523
Providence	68-66	.507
Rochester	56-76	.424
Montreal	57-78	.422
Newark	40-100	.286

1904

Buffalo	88-46	.657
Baltimore	78-52	.600
Jersey City	76-57	.571
Newark	77-59	.566
Montreal	67-62	.519
Toronto	67-71	.486
Providence	52-81	.391
Rochester	28-105	.211

1905

Providence	83-47	.638
Baltimore	82-47	.636
Jersey City	81-49	.623
Newark	70-62	.530
Buffalo	63-74	.460
Montreal	56-80	.412
Rochester	51-86	.372
Toronto	48-89	.350

1906

Buffalo	85-55	.607
Jersey City	80-57	.584
Baltimore	76-61	.555
Rochester	77-62	.554
Newark	66-71	.482
Providence	65-75	.464
Montreal	57-83	.407
Toronto	46-88	.343

1907

Toronto	83-51	.619
Buffalo	73-59	.553
Providence	72-63	.533
Newark	67-66	.504
Jersey City	67-66	.504
Baltimore	68-69	.495
Rochester	59-76	.437
Montreal	46-85	.351

1908

Baltimore	83-57	.593
Providence	79-57	.581
Newark	79-58	.577
Buffalo	75-65	.536
Montreal	64-75	.461
Toronto	59-79	.428
Jersey City	58-79	.423
Rochester	55-82	.401

1909

Rochester	90-61	.596
Newark	86-67	.562
Providence	80-70	.533
Toronto	79-72	.523
Buffalo	72-79	.477
Montreal	68-83	.450
Baltimore	67-86	.438
Jersey City	63-87	.420

1910

Rochester	92-61	.601
Newark	88-66	.571
Baltimore	83-70	.542
Toronto	80-72	.526
Montreal	71-80	.470
Buffalo	69-81	.460
Jersey City	66-88	.432
Providence	61-92	.399

1911

Rochester	98-54	.645
Baltimore	95-58	.621
Toronto	94-59	.614
Buffalo	74-75	.497
Montreal	72-80	.474
Jersey City	63-88	.417
Newark	57-95	.375
Providence	54-98	.356

1912

Toronto	91-62	.595
Rochester	86-67	.562
Newark	80-72	.526
Baltimore	74-75	.497
Buffalo	71-78	.477
Montreal	71-81	.467
Jersey City	70-85	.451
Providence	64-87	.424

1913

Newark	95-57	.625
Rochester	92-62	.597
Baltimore	77-73	.513
Providence	78-75	.510
Montreal	74-77	.490
Buffalo	69-80	.463
Toronto	70-83	.458
Jersey City	53-101	.344

1914

Providence	95-59	.617
Toronto	89-61	.593
Buffalo	91-63	.591
Newark	74-70	.514
Baltimore	73-77	.487
Rochester	73-77	.487
Jersey City	60-80	.403
Montreal	48-106	.312

1915

Buffalo	86-50	.632
Providence	85-53	.616
Toronto	72-67	.518
Rochester	69-69	.500
Montreal	67-70	.489
Harrisburg	61-76	.445
Richmond	59-81	.422
Jersey City	52-85	.380

1916

Baltimore	82-58	.586
Providence	76-62	.551
Montreal	75-64	.539
Baltimore	74-66	.529
Toronto	73-66	.525
Richmond	64-75	.460
Rochester	60-78	.435
Newark	52-87	.374

1917

Toronto	93-61	.604
Providence	89-61	.596
Baltimore	88-61	.591
Newark	86-68	.558
Rochester	72-82	.468
Buffalo	67-84	.444
Montreal	56-94	.373
Richmond	53-94	.361

1918

Toronto	88-39	.693
Binghamton	85-38	.691
Baltimore	74-53	.583
Newark	64-63	.504
Rochester	60-61	.496
Buffalo	53-68	.438
Syr.-Hamilton	38-76	.333
Jersey City	30-94	.242

1919

Baltimore	100-49	.671
Toronto	92-57	.617
Buffalo	81-67	.548
Binghamton	75-71	.514
Newark	71-80	.470
Rochester	67-83	.447
Jersey City	56-93	.376
Reading	51-93	.354

1920

Baltimore	109-44	.712
Toronto	108-46	.701
Buffalo	96-57	.627
Akron	89-62	.589
Reading	65-85	.433
Jersey City	62-91	.407
Rochester	45-106	.298
Syracuse	33-116	.221

1921

Baltimore	119-47	.717
Rochester	100-68	.595
Buffalo	99-69	.589
Toronto	89-77	.536
Newark	72-92	.433
Syracuse	71-96	.425
Jersey City	59-106	.358
Reading	56-110	.337

1922

Baltimore	115-52	.689
Rochester	105-62	.629
Buffalo	95-72	.569
Jersey City	83-82	.503
Toronto	76-88	.463
Reading	71-93	.433
Syracuse	64-102	.386
Newark	54-112	.325

1923

Baltimore	115-53	.677
Rochester	101-65	.608
Reading	85-79	.518
Toronto	81-79	.506
Buffalo	83-81	.506
Syracuse	73-92	.442
Newark	60-101	.373
Jersey City	61-105	.367

1924

Baltimore	117-48	.709
Toronto	98-67	.594
Buffalo	84-83	.503
Rochester	83-84	.497
Newark	80-83	.491
Syracuse	79-83	.488
Reading	63-98	.391
Jersey City	53-111	.323

1925

Baltimore	105-61	.633
Toronto	99-63	.611
Rochester	83-77	.519
Buffalo	78-84	.481
Reading	78-90	.464
Syracuse	74-87	.460
Jersey City	74-92	.446
Providence	63-100	.387

1926

Toronto	109-57	.657
Baltimore	101-65	.608
Newark	99-66	.600
Buffalo	92-72	.561
Rochester	81-83	.494
Jersey City	72-92	.439
Syracuse	70-91	.435
Reading	31-129	.194

1927

Buffalo	112-56	.667
Syracuse	102-66	.607
Newark	90-77	.539
Toronto	89-78	.509
Baltimore	85-82	.509
Rochester	81-86	.485
Jersey City	66-100	.398
Reading	43-123	.259

1928

Rochester	90-74	.549
Buffalo	92-76	.548
Toronto	86-80	.518
Reading	84-83	.503
Montreal	84-84	.500
Baltimore	82-82	.500
Newark	81-84	.491
Jersey City	66-102	.393

1929

Rochester	103-65	.613
Toronto	92-76	.548
Baltimore	90-78	.536
Montreal	88-79	.527
Buffalo	83-84	.497
Newark	81-85	.488
Reading	80-86	.482
Jersey City	51-115	.307

1930

Rochester	105-62	.629
Baltimore	97-70	.581
Montreal	96-72	.571
Toronto	87-80	.521
Newark	80-88	.476
Buffalo	74-91	.448
Reading	68-98	.410
Jersey City	59-105	.360

1931

Rochester	101-67	.601
Newark	99-69	.589
Baltimore	94-72	.566
Montreal	85-80	.515
Toronto	83-84	.497
Reading	79-88	.473
Jersey City	65-102	.389
Buffalo	61-105	.367

1932

Newark	109-59	.649
Baltimore	93-74	.557
Buffalo	91-75	.548
Montreal	90-78	.536
Rochester	88-79	.527
Jersey City	73-94	.437
Albany	71-97	.423
Toronto	54-113	.323

1933

Newark	102-62	.622
Rochester	88-77	.533
Baltimore	84-80	.512
Buffalo*	83-85	.494
Toronto	82-85	.491
Montreal	81-84	.491
Albany	80-84	.488
Jersey City	61-104	.370

1934

Newark	93-60	.608
Rochester	88-63	.583
Toronto*	85-67	.559
Albany	81-72	.529
Buffalo	76-77	.497
Montreal	73-77	.487
Syracuse	60-94	.390
Baltimore	53-99	.349

1935

Montreal	92-62	.597
Syracuse*	87-67	.565
Buffalo	86-67	.562
Newark	81-71	.533
Baltimore	78-74	.513
Toronto	78-76	.506
Rochester	61-91	.401
Albany	49-104	.320

1936

Buffalo*	94-60	.610
Rochester	89-66	.574
Newark	88-67	.568
Baltimore	81-72	.529
Toronto	77-76	.503
Montreal	71-81	.467
Syracuse	59-95	.383
Albany	56-98	.364

1937

Newark*	109-42	.717
Montreal	82-67	.550
Syracuse	78-74	.513
Baltimore	76-75	.503
Buffalo	74-79	.484
Rochester	74-80	.481
Toronto	63-88	.417
Jersey City	50-100	.333

1938

Newark*	104-48	.684
Syracuse	87-67	.567
Rochester	80-74	.519
Buffalo	79-74	.516
Toronto	72-81	.471
Montreal	69-84	.451
Jersey City	68-85	.444
Baltimore	52-98	.347

1939

Jersey City	89-64	.582
Rochester*	84-67	.556
Buffalo	82-72	.532
Newark	82-73	.529
Syracuse	81-74	.523
Baltimore	68-85	.444
Montreal	64-88	.421
Toronto	63-90	.412

1940

Rochester	96-61	.611
Newark*	95-65	.594
Jersey City	81-78	.509
Baltimore	81-79	.506
Montreal	80-80	.500
Buffalo	76-83	.478
Syracuse	71-90	.441
Toronto	57-101	.361

1941

Newark	100-54	.649
Montreal*	90-64	.584
Buffalo	88-65	.575
Rochester	84-68	.553
Jersey City	74-76	.493
Syracuse	70-83	.458
Baltimore	58-94	.382
Toronto	47-107	.305

1942

Newark	92-61	.601
Montreal	82-71	.536
Syracuse*	78-74	.513
Jersey City	77-75	.507
Baltimore	75-77	.493
Toronto	74-79	.484
Buffalo	73-80	.477
Rochester	59-93	.388

1943

Toronto	95-57	.625
Newark	85-68	.556
Syracuse*	82-71	.536
Montreal	76-76	.500
Rochester	74-78	.487
Baltimore	73-81	.474
Buffalo	66-87	.431
Jersey City	60-93	.392

1944

Baltimore*	84-68	.553
Newark	85-69	.552
Toronto	79-74	.516
Buffalo	78-76	.506
Jersey City	74-79	.484
Montreal	73-80	.477
Rochester	71-82	.464
Syracuse	68-84	.447

1945

Montreal	95-58	.621
Newark*	89-64	.582
Toronto	85-67	.559
Baltimore	80-73	.523
Jersey City	71-82	.464
Buffalo	64-89	.418
Syracuse	64-89	.418
Rochester	64-90	.416

1946

Montreal*	100-54	.649
Syracuse	81-72	.529
Baltimore	81-73	.526
Newark	80-74	.519
Buffalo	78-75	.510
Toronto	71-82	.464
Rochester	65-87	.428
Jersey City	57-96	.373

1947

Jersey City	94-60	.610
Montreal	93-60	.608
Syracuse*	88-65	.575
Buffalo	77-75	.507
Rochester	68-86	.442
Newark	65-89	.422
Baltimore	65-89	.422
Toronto	64-90	.416

1948

Montreal*	94-59	.614
Newark	80-72	.526
Syracuse	77-73	.513
Rochester	78-75	.510
Toronto	78-76	.506
Buffalo	71-80	.470
Jersey City	69-83	.454
Baltimore	59-88	.401

1949

Buffalo	90-64	.584
Rochester	85-67	.559
Montreal*	84-70	.545
Jersey City	83-71	.539
Toronto	80-72	.526
Syracuse	73-80	.477
Baltimore	63-91	.409
Newark	55-98	.359

1950

Rochester	92-59	.609
Montreal	86-67	.562
Baltimore*	85-68	.556
Jersey City	81-70	.536
Springfield	74-78	.487
Syracuse	74-79	.484
Toronto	60-90	.400
Buffalo	56-97	.366

1951

Montreal*	95-59	.617
Rochester	83-69	.546
Syracuse	82-71	.536
Buffalo	79-75	.513
Toronto	77-76	.505
Baltimore	69-82	.457
Ottawa	62-88	.413
Springfield	63-90	.412

1952

Montreal	95-56	.629
Syracuse	88-66	.571
Rochester*	80-74	.519
Toronto	78-76	.506
Buffalo	71-83	.461
Baltimore	70-84	.455
Ottawa	65-86	.433
Springfield	65-88	.425

1953

Rochester	97-57	.630
Montreal*	89-63	.586
Buffalo	87-65	.572
Baltimore	82-72	.532
Toronto	78-76	.506
Ottawa	71-83	.461
Syracuse	58-95	.379
Springfield	51-102	.333

1954

Toronto	97-57	.630
Montreal	88-66	.571
Rochester	86-68	.558
Syracuse*	79-76	.510
Havana	78-77	.503
Buffalo	71-83	.461
Richmond	60-94	.390
Ottawa	58-96	.377

1955

Montreal	95-57	.617
Toronto	94-59	.614
Havana	87-66	.569
Rochester*	76-77	.497
Syracuse	74-79	.484
Buffalo	65-89	.422
Columbus	64-89	.418
Richmond	58-95	.379

1956

Toronto	86-66	.566
Rochester*	83-67	.553
Miami	80-71	.530
Montreal	80-72	.526
Richmond	74-79	.484
Havana	72-82	.468
Columbus	69-84	.451
Buffalo	64-87	.424

1957

Toronto	88-65	.575
Buffalo*	88-66	.571
Richmond	81-73	.526
Miami	75-78	.490
Rochester	74-80	.481
Havana	72-82	.468
Columbus	69-85	.448
Montreal	68-86	.442

1958

Montreal*	90-63	.588
Toronto	87-65	.572
Rochester	77-75	.507
Columbus	77-77	.500
Miami	75-78	.490
Richmond	71-82	.464
Buffalo	69-83	.454
Havana	65-88	.425

1959

Buffalo	89-64	.582
Columbus	84-70	.545
Havana*	80-73	.523
Richmond	76-78	.494
Rochester	74-80	.481
Montreal	72-82	.468
Miami	71-83	.461
Toronto	69-85	.448

1960

Toronto*	100-54	.649
Richmond	82-70	.539
Rochester	81-73	.526
Buffalo	78-75	.510
Jersey City	76-77	.497
Columbus	69-84	.451
Miami	65-88	.425
Montreal	62-92	.403

1961

Columbus	92-62	.597
Charleston	88-66	.571
Buffalo*	85-67	.559
Rochester	77-78	.497
Toronto	76-79	.490
Richmond	71-83	.461
Jersey City	70-82	.461
Syracuse	56-98	.364

1962

Jacksonville	94-60	.610
Toronto	91-62	.595
Atlanta*	83-71	.539
Rochester	82-72	.532
Columbus	80-74	.519
Buffalo	73-80	.477
Richmond	59-95	.383
Syracuse	53-101	.344

1963

NORTHERN DIVISION

Syracuse	80-70	.533
Toronto	76-75	.503
Rochester	75-76	.497
Richmond	66-81	.490

SOUTHERN DIVISION

Indianapolis*	86-67	.562
Atlanta	85-68	.556
Arkansas	78-73	.517
Columbus	75-73	.507
Jacksonville	56-91	.381

1964

Jacksonville	89-62	.589
Syracuse	88-66	.571
Buffalo	80-69	.537
Rochester*	82-72	.532
Toronto	80-72	.526
Columbus	68-85	.444-
Richmond	65-88	.425
Atlanta	55-93	.372

1965

Columbus*	85-61	.582
Atlanta	83-64	.565
Toronto	81-64	.556
Syracuse	74-73	.503
Rochester	73-74	.497

Jacksonville	71-76	.483
Toledo	68-78	.466
Buffalo	51-96	.347

1966

Rochester	83-64	.565
Columbus	82-65	.558
Toronto*	82-65	.558
Richmond	75-72	.510
Buffalo	72-74	.493
Toledo	71-75	.486
Jacksonville	68-79	.463
Syracuse	54-93	.367

1967

Richmond	81-60	.574
Rochester	80-61	.567
Toledo*	73-66	.525
Columbus	69-71	.493
Jacksonville	66-73	.475
Toronto	64-75	.460
Buffalo	63-76	.453
Syracuse	63-77	.450

1968

Toledo	83-64	.565
Columbus	82-64	.562
Rochester	77-69	.527
Jacksonville*	75-71	.514
Syracuse	72-75	.490
Louisville	72-75	.490
Buffalo	66-81	.449
Richmond	59-87	.404

1969

Tidewater	76-59	.563
Louisville	77-63	.550
Syracuse*	75-65	.536
Columbus	74-66	.529
Rochester	71-69	.507
Toledo	68-72	.486
Buffalo	58-78	.426
Richmond	56-83	.403

1970

Syracuse*	84-56	.600
Columbus	81-59	.579
Rochester	76-64	.543
Tidewater	74-66	.529

Richmond	73-67	.521
Louisville	69-71	.493
Buff.-Winnipeg	52-88	.371
Toledo	51-89	.364

1971

Rochester*	86-54	.614
Tidewater	79-61	.564
Charleston	78-62	.557
Syracuse	73-67	.521
Louisville	71-69	.507
Richmond	69-71	.493
Toledo	60-80	.429
Winnipeg	44-96	.314

1972

Louisville	81-63	.563
Charleston	80-64	.556
Tidewater*	78-65	.545
Rochester	76-68	.528
Toledo	75-69	.521
Richmond	65-78	.455
Syracuse	64-80	.444
Peninsula	56-88	.389

1973
AMERICAN DIVISION

Rochester	79-67	.541
Pawtucket*	78-68	.534
Syracuse	76-70	.521
Toledo	65-81	.445

NATIONAL DIVISION

Charleston	85-60	.586
Tidewater	75-70	.517
Peninsula	72-74	.493
Richmond	53-93	.363

1974
NORTHERN DIVISION

Rochester*	88-56	.611
Syracuse	74-70	.514
Toledo	70-74	.486
Pawtucket	57-87	.396

SOUTHERN DIVISION

Memphis	87-55	.613
Richmond	75-65	.536
Charleston	62-81	.434
Tidewater	57-82	.410

1975

Tidewater*	86-55	.610
Rochester	85-56	.603
Syracuse	72-64	.529
Charleston	72-67	.518
Memphis	65-75	.464
Richmond	62-75	.453
Toledo	62-78	.443
Pawtucket	53-87	.379

1976

Rochester	88-50	.638
Syracuse*	82-57	.590
Memphis	69-69	.500
Richmond	69-71	.493
Pawtucket	68-70	.493
Charleston	62-73	.459
Tidewater	60-78	.435
Toledo	55-85	.393

1977

Pawtucket	80-60	.571
Charleston*	78-62	.557
Tidewater	73-67	.521
Richmond	71-69	.507
Syracuse	70-70	.500
Rochester	67-73	.479
Columbus	65-75	.464
Toledo	56-84	.400

1978

Charleston	85-55	.607
Pawtucket	81-59	.579
Toledo	74-66	.529
Richmond*	71-68	.511
Tidewater	69-71	.493
Rochester	68-72	.486
Columbus	50-90	.357

1979

Columbus*	85-54	.612
Syracuse	77-63	.550
Richmond	76-64	.543
Tidewater	73-67	.521
Pawtucket	66-74	.471
Charleston	65-74	.468
Toledo	63-76	.453
Rochester	53-86	.381

1980

Columbus*	83-57	.593
Toledo	77-63	.550
Rochester	74-65	.532
Richmond	69-71	.493
Charleston	67-71	.486
Tidewater	67-72	.482
Pawtucket	62-77	.446
Syracuse	58-81	.417

1981

Columbus*	88-51	.633
Richmond	83-56	.597
Tidewater	70-68	.507
Rochester	69-70	.496
Charleston	67-72	.482
Pawtucket	67-73	.479
Syracuse	60-80	.429
Toledo	53-87	.379

1982

Richmond	82-57	.590
Columbus	79-61	.564
Tidewater*	74-63	.540
Rochester	72-68	.514
Pawtucket	67-71	.486
Syracuse	64-76	.457
Toledo	60-80	.429
Charleston	59-81	.421

1983

Columbus	83-57	.593
Richmond	80-59	.576
Charleston	74-66	.529
Tidewater*	71-68	.511
Toledo	68-72	.486
Rochester	65-75	.464
Syracuse	61-78	.439
Pawtucket	56-83	.403

1984

Columbus	82-57	.590
Maine	77-59	.566
Toledo	74-63	.540
Pawtucket*	75-65	.536
Tidewater	71-69	.507
Richmond	66-73	.475
Syracuse	58-81	.417
Rochester	52-88	.371

1985

Syracuse	79-61	.564
Maine	76-63	.547
Tidewater*	75-64	.540
Columbus	75-64	.540
Richmond	75-65	.536
Toledo	71-68	.511
Rochester	58-81	.417
Pawtucket	48-91	.345

1986

Richmond*	80-60	.571
Rochester	75-63	.543
Pawtucket	74-65	.532
Tidewater	74-66	.529
Syracuse	72-67	.518
Toledo	62-77	.446
Columbus	62-77	.446
Maine	58-82	.414

1987

Tidewater	81-59	.579
Columbus*	77-63	.550
Rochester	74-65	.532
Pawtucket	73-67	.521
Toledo	70-70	.500
Syracuse	68-72	.486
Maine	60-80	.429
Richmond	56-83	.403

1988

EASTERN DIVISION

Tidewater	77-64	.546
Richmond	66-75	.468
Pawtucket	63-79	.444
Maine	62-80	.437

WESTERN DIVISION

Rochester*	77-64	.546
Syracuse	70-71	.496
Columbus	65-77	.458
Toledo	58-84	.408

1989

EASTERN DIVISION

Syracuse	83-62	.572
Rochester	72-73	.497
Scranton/W-B	64-79	.448
Pawtucket	62-84	.425

WESTERN DIVISION

Richmond*	81-65	.555
Tidewater	77-69	.527
Columbus	77-69	.527
Toledo	69-76	.476

1990

EASTERN DIVISION

Rochester*	89-56	.614
Scranton/W-B	68-78	.466
Syracuse	62-83	.428
Pawtucket	62-84	.425

WESTERN DIVISION

Columbus	87-59	.596
Tidewater	79-67	.541
Richmond	71-74	.490
Toledo	58-86	.403

1991

EASTERN DIVISION

Pawtucket	79-64	.552
Rochester	76-68	.528
Syracuse	73-71	.507
Scranton/W-B	65-68	.455

WESTERN DIVISION

Columbus*	85-59	.590
Tidewater	77-65	.542
Toledo	74-70	.514
Richmond	65-79	.451

1992

EASTERN DIVISION

Scranton/W-B	84-58	.592
Pawtucket	71-72	.497
Rochester	70-74	.486
Syracuse	60-83	.420

WESTERN DIVISION

Columbus*	95-49	.660
Richmond	73-71	.507
Toledo	64-80	.444
Tidewater	56-86	.394

1993

EASTERN DIVISION

Rochester	74-67	.525
Ottawa	73-69	.574
Scranton/W-B	62-80	.437
Pawtucket	60-82	.423
Syracuse	59-82	.418

WESTERN DIVISION

Charlotte*	86-55	.610
Richmond	80-62	.563
Columbus	78-62	.557
Norfolk	70-71	.496
Toledo	65-77	.458

1994
EASTERN DIVISION

Pawtucket	78-64	.549
Syracuse	71-71	.500
Ottawa	70-72	.493
Rochester	67-74	.475
Scranton/W-B	62-80	.437

WESTERN DIVISION

Richmond*	80-61	.567
Charlotte	77-65	.542
Columbus	74-68	.521
Norfolk	67-75	.472
Toledo	63-79	.444

1995
NORTHERN DIVISION

Rochester	73-69	.514
Ottawa*	72-70	.507
Pawtucket	70-71	.496
Scranton/W-B	70-72	.493
Syracuse	59-82	.418

SOUTHERN DIVISION

Norfolk	86-56	.606
Richmond	75-66	.532
Columbus	71-68	.511
Toledo	71-71	.500
Charlotte	59-81	.421

1996
NORTHERN DIVISION

Pawtucket	78-64	.549
Rochester	72-69	.511
Scranton/W-B	70-72	.493
Syracuse	67-75	.472
Ottawa	60-82	.429

SOUTHERN DIVISION

Columbus*	85-67	.599
Norfolk	82-59	.582
Toledo	70-72	.493
Charlotte	62-79	.440
Richmond	62-79	.440

1997
NORTHERN DIVISION

Rochester*	83-58	.589
Pawtucket	81-60	.574
Scranton/W-B	66-76	.465
Syracuse	55-87	.387
Ottawa	54-86	.386

SOUTHERN DIVISION

Columbus	79-63	.556
Charlotte	76-65	.539
Norfolk	75-67	.528
Richmond	70-72	.493
Toledo	68-73	.482

1998
NORTH DIVISION

Buffalo*	81-62	.566
Syracuse	80-62	.563
Pawtucket	77-64	.546
Rochester	70-74	.486
Ottawa	69-74	.483
Scranton/W-B	67-75	.472

WEST DIVISION

Louisville	77-67	.535
Indianapolis	76-67	.531
Columbus	67-77	.465
Toledo	52-89	.369

SOUTH DIVISION

Durham	80-64	.556
Norfolk	70-72	.493
Charlotte	70-73	.490
Richmond	64-80	.444

1999
NORTH DIVISION

Scranton/W-B	78-66	.542
Pawtucket	76-68	.528
Syracuse	73-71	.507
Buffalo	72-72	.500
Rochester	61-83	.424
Ottawa	59-85	.410

WEST DIVISION

Columbus	83-58	.589
Indianapolis	75-69	.521
Louisville	63-81	.438
Toledo	57-87	.396

SOUTH DIVISION

| Durham | 83-60 | .580 |

Charlotte*	82-62	.569		Pawtucket	60-84	.417
Norfolk	77-63	.550		Rochester	55-89	.382
Richmond	64-78	.451		WEST DIVISION		
				Toledo	81-63	.563
2000				Louisville	79-65	.549
NORTH DIVISION				Indianapolis	59-83	.469
Buffalo	86-59	.593		Columbus	59-83	.415
Scranton/W-B	85-60	.586		SOUTH DIVISION		
Pawtucket	82-61	.573		Durham*	80-64	.556
Syracuse	74-66	.529		Richmond	75-67	.528
Rochester	65-79	.451		Norfolk	70-73	.490
Ottawa	53-88	.376		Charlotte	55-88	.385
WEST DIVISION						
Indianapolis*	81-63	.563		**2003**		
Columbus	75-69	.521		NORTH DIVISION		
Louisville	71-73	.493		Pawtucket	83-61	.576
Toledo	55-86	.390		Ottawa	79-65	.549
SOUTH DIVISION				Buffalo	73-70	.510
Durham	81-62	.566		Scranton/W-B	73-70	.510
Charlotte	78-65	.545		Rochester	68-74	.476
Norfolk	65-79	.451		Syracuse	62-79	.440
Richmond	51-92	.357		WEST DIVISION		
				Louisville	79-64	.552
2001				Columbus	76-68	.528
NORTH DIVISION				Toledo	65-78	.455
Buffalo	91-51	.641		Indianapolis	64-78	.451
Scranton/W-B	78-65	.545		SOUTH DIVISION		
Syracuse	71-73	.493		Durham*	73-67	.521
Ottawa	68-76	.472		Charlotte	74-70	.514
Pawtucket	60-82	.423		Norfolk	67-76	.469
Rochester	60-84	.417		Richmond	64-79	.448
WEST DIVISION						
Louisville*	84-60	.583		**2004**		
Columbus	67-76	.469		NORTH DIVISION		
Indianapolis	66-78	.458		Buffalo*	83-61	.576
Toledo	65-79	.451		Pawtucket	73-71	.507
SOUTH DIVISION				Rochester	73-71	.507
Norfolk	85-57	.599		Scranton/W-B	69-73	.486
Durham	74-70	.514		Ottawa	66-78	.458
Richmond	68-76	.472		Syracuse	66-78	.458
Charlotte	67-77	.465		WEST DIVISION		
				Columbus	80-64	.556
2002				Louisville	67-77	.465
NORTH DIVISION				Indianapolis	66-78	.458
Scranton/W-B	91-53	.632		Toledo	65-78	.455
Buffalo	87-57	.604		SOUTH DIVISION		
Ottawa	80-61	.567		Richmond	79-62	.560
Syracuse	64-80	.444		Durham	77-67	.535

Norfolk	72-72	.500
Charlotte	68-74	.475

2005

NORTH DIVISION

Buffalo	82-62	.569
Pawtucket	75-69	.521
Rochester	75-69	.521
Syracuse	71-73	.493
Ottawa	69-75	.479
Scranton/W-B	69-75	.479

WEST DIVISION

Toledo*	89-55	.618
Indianapolis	78-66	.542
Columbus	77-67	.535
Louisville	66-78	.458

SOUTH DIVISION

Norfolk	79-65	.549
Durham	65-79	.451
Charlotte	57-87	.396
Richmond	56-88	.389

2006

NORTH DIVISION

Scranton/W-B	84-58	.592
Rochester	79-64	.552
Buffalo	73-68	.518
Ottawa	74-69	.517
Pawtucket	69-75	.479
Syracuse	64-79	.448

WEST DIVISION

Toledo*	76-66	.535
Indianapolis	76-66	.535
Louisville	75-68	.524
Columbus	69-73	.436

SOUTH DIVISION

Charlotte	79-62	.560
Durham	64-78	.451
Norfolk	57-84	.404
Richmond	57-86	.399

2007

NORTH DIVISION

Scranton/W-B	84-59	.587
Rochester	77-67	.535
Buffalo	75-67	.528
Pawtucket	67-75	.472

Syracuse	64-80	.444
Ottawa	55-88	.385

WEST DIVISION

Toledo	82-61	.573
Louisville	74-70	.514
Indianapolis	70-73	.490
Columbus	64-80	.444

SOUTH DIVISION

Durham*	80-63	.559
Richmond	77-64	.546
Norfolk	69-74	.483
Charlotte	63-80	.441

Playoff Results

1892 Binghamton defeated Providence 4 games to 2.

1933 Rochester defeated Newark 3 games to 1. Buffalo defeated Baltimore 3 games to 0. *Finals*: Buffalo defeated Rochester 4 games to 2.

1934 Toronto defeated Newark 4 games to 3. Rochester defeated Albany 4 games to 1. *Finals*: Toronto defeated Rochester 4 games to 1.

1935 Montreal defeated Buffalo 4 games to 2. Syracuse defeated Newark 4 games to 0. *Finals*: Syracuse defeated Montreal 4 games to 3.

1936 Buffalo defeated Newark 4 games to 1. Baltimore defeated Rochester 4 games to 2. *Finals*: Buffalo defeated Baltimore 4 games to 2.

1937 Newark defeated Syracuse 4 games to 0. Baltimore defeated Montreal 4 games to 1. *Finals*: Newark defeated Baltimore 4 games to 0.

1938 Newark defeated Rochester 4 games to 3. Buffalo defeated Syracuse 4games to 0. *Finals*: Newark defeated Buffalo 4 games to 1.

1939 Newark defeated Jersey City 4 games to 2. Rochester defeated Buffalo 4games to 1. *Finals*: Rochester defeated Newark 4 games to 3.

1940 Newark defeated Jersey City 4 games to 0. Baltimore defeated Rochester 4games to 2. *Finals*: Newark defeated Baltimore 4 games to 3.

1941 Newark defeated Rochester 4 games to 1. Montreal defeated Buffalo 4games to 3. *Finals*: Montreal defeated Newark 4 games to 3.

1942 Jersey City defeated Newark 4 games to 2. Syracuse defeated Montreal 4games to 1. *Finals*: Syracuse defeated Jersey City 4 games to 0.

1943 Toronto defeated Montreal 4 games to 0. Syracuse defeated Newark 4games to 2. *Finals*: Syracuse defeated Toronto 4 games to 2.

1944 Baltimore defeated Buffalo 4 games to 3. Newark defeated Toronto 4games to 0. *Finals*: Baltimore defeated Newark 4 games to 3.

1945 Montreal defeated Baltimore 4 games to 3. Newark defeated Toronto 4games to 2. *Finals*: Newark defeated Montreal 4 games to 1.

1946 Montreal defeated Newark 4 games to 2. Syracuse defeated Baltimore 4games to 2. *Finals*: Montreal defeated Syracuse 4 games to 1.

1947 Buffalo defeated Jersey City 4 games to 9. Syracuse defeated Montreal 4games to 9. *Finals*: Syracuse defeated Buffalo 4 games to 3.

1948 Montreal defeated Rochester 4 games to 3. Syracuse defeated Newark 4games to 3. *Finals*: Montreal defeated Syracuse 4 games to 1.

1949 Buffalo defeated Jersey City 4 games to 1. Montreal defeated Rochester 4games to 0. *Finals*: Montreal defeated Buffalo 4 games to 1.

1950 Rochester defeated Jersey City 4 games to 2. Baltimore defeated Montreal 4 games to 3. *Finals*: Baltimore defeated Rochester 4 games to 2.

1951 Montreal defeated Buffalo 4 games to 0. Syracuse defeated Rochester 4games to 1. *Finals*: Montreal defeated Syracuse 4 games to 1.

1952 Montreal defeated Toronto 4 games to 3.

Rochester defeated Syracuse 4games to 0. *Finals*: Rochester defeated Montreal 4 games to 2.

1953 Rochester defeated Baltimore 4 games to 3. Montreal defeated Buffalo 4games to 2. *Finals*: Montreal defeated Rochester 4 games to 0.

1954 Syracuse defeated Toronto 4 games to 2. Montreal defeated Rochester 4games to 2. *Finals*: Syracuse defeated Montreal 4 games to 3.

1955 Rochester defeated Montreal 4 games to 1. Toronto defeated Havana 4games to 1. *Finals*: Rochester defeated Toronto 4 games to 0.

1956 Toronto defeated Montreal 4 games to 1. Rochester defeated Miami 4games to 1. *Finals*: Rochester defeated Toronto 4 games to 3.

1957 Miami defeated Toronto 4 games to 2. Buffalo defeated Richmond 4 gamesto 2. *Finals*: Buffalo defeated Miami 4 games to 1.

1958 Montreal defeated Columbus 4 games to 3. Toronto defeated Rochester 4games to 1. *Finals*: Montreal defeated Toronto 4 games to 1.

1959 Richmond defeated Buffalo 4 games to 1. Havana defeated Columbus 4games to 0. *Finals*: Havana defeated Richmond 4 games to 2.

1960 Toronto defeated Buffalo 4 games to 0. Rochester defeated Richmond 4games to 1. *Finals*: Toronto defeated Rochester 4 games to 1.

1961 Rochester defeated Columbus 4 games to 1. Buffalo defeated Charleston 4games to 0. *Finals*: Buffalo defeated Rochester 4 games to 1.

1962 Jacksonville defeated Rochester 4 games to 3. Atlanta defeated Toronto 4games to 2. *Finals*: Atlanta defeated Jacksonville 4 games to 3.

1963 Indianapolis defeated Syracuse 4 games to 1. Atlanta defeated Toronto 4 games to 0. *Finals*: Indianapolis defeated Atlanta 4 games to 1.

1964 Rochester defeated Jacksonville 4 games to 0. Syracuse defeated Buffalo 4games to 3. *Finals*: Rochester defeated Syracuse 4 games to 2.

1965 Columbus defeated Syracuse 4 games to 2. Toronto defeated Atlanta 4games to 0. *Finals*: Toronto defeated Columbus 4 games to 1.

1966 Richmond defeated Rochester 3 games to 1. Toronto defeated Columbus 3games to 2. *Finals*: Toronto defeated Richmond 4 games to 1.

1967 Toledo defeated Richmond 3 games to 2. Columbus defeated Rochester 3games to 1. *Finals*: Toledo defeated Columbus 4 games to 1.

1968 Jacksonville defeated Toledo 3 games to 1. Columbus defeated Rochester 3games to 2. *Finals*: Jacksonville defeated Columbus 4 games to 0.

1969 Columbus defeated Tidewater 3 games to 1. Syracuse defeated Louisville 3games to 2. *Finals*: Syracuse defeated Louisville 4 games to 1.

1970 Syracuse defeated Tidewater 3 games to 0. Columbus defeated Rochester 3 games to 2. *Finals*: Syracuse defeated Columbus 3 games to 1.

1971 Rochester defeated Syracuse 3 games to 1. Tidewater defeated Charleston 3 games to 0. *Finals*: Rochester defeated Tidewater 3 games to 2.

1972 Louisville defeated Rochester 2 games to 1. Tidewater defeated Charleston 2 games to 1. *Finals*: Tidewater defeated Louisville 3 games to 2.

1973 Charleston defeated Rochester 3 games to 0. Pawtucket defeated Tidewater 3 games to 2. *Finals*: Pawtucket defeated Charleston 3 games to 2.

1974 Rochester defeated Memphis 4 games to 2. Syracuse defeated Richmond 4 games to 2. *Finals*: Rochester defeated Syracuse 4 games to 3.

1975 Tidewater defeated Charleston 3 games to 0. Syracuse defeated Rochester 3 games to 1.

Finals: Tidewater defeated Syracuse 3 games to 1.

1976 Syracuse defeated Memphis 3 games to 0. Richmond defeated Rochester 3games to 1. *Finals*: Syracuse defeated Richmond 3 games to 1.

1977 Pawtucket defeated Richmond 3 games to 1. Charleston defeated Tidewa-ter 3 games to 1. *Finals*: Charleston defeated Pawtucket 4 games to 0.

1978 Richmond defeated Charleston 3 games to 1. Pawtucket defeated Toledo 3 games to 2. *Finals*: Richmond defeated Pawtucket 4 games to 3.

1979 Columbus defeated Tidewater 3 games to 1. Syracuse defeated Richmond 3 games to 2. *Finals*: Columbus defeated Syracuse 4 games to 3.

1980 Columbus defeated Richmond 3 games to 2. Toledo defeated Rochester 3games to 1. *Finals*: Columbus defeated Toledo 4 games to 1.

1981 Columbus defeated Rochester 3 games to 2. Richmond defeated Tidewater3 games to 2. *Finals*: Columbus defeated Richmond 2 games to 1.

1982 Rochester defeated Richmond 3 games to 0. Tidewater defeated Columbus 3 games to 0. *Finals*: Tidewater defeated Rochester 3 games to 0.

1983 Richmond defeated Charleston 3 games to 0. Tidewater defeated Columbus 3 games to 2. *Finals*: Tidewater defeated Richmond 3 games to 1.

1984 Pawtucket defeated Columbus 3 games to 1. Maine defeated Toledo 3 games to 0. *Finals*: Pawtucket defeated Maine 3 games to 2.

1985 Columbus defeated Syracuse 3 games to 1. Tidewater defeated Maine 3 games to 2. *Finals*: Tidewater defeated Columbus 3 games to 1.

1986 Richmond defeated Tidewater 3 games to 0. Rochester defeated Pawtucket 3 games to 1. *Finals*: Richmond defeated Rochester 3 games to 2.

1987 Columbus defeated Rochester 3 games to 0. Tidewater defeated Pawtucket 3 games to 0. *Finals*: Columbus defeated Tidewater 3 games to 0.

1988 Rochester defeated Tidewater 3 games to 1.

1989 Richmond defeated Syracuse 3 games to 1.

1990 Rochester defeated Columbus 3 games to 2.

1991 Columbus defeated Pawtucket 3 games to 1.

1992 Columbus defeated Richmond 3 games to 1. Scranton/Wilkes-Barre defeated Pawtucket 3 games to 1. *Finals*: Columbus defeated Scranton/Wilkes-Barre 3 games to 2.

1993 Rochester defeated Ottawa 3 games to 2. Charlotte defeated Rochester 3 games to 2. *Finals*: Charlotte defeated Rochester 3 games to 2.

1994 Syracuse defeated Pawtucket 3 games to 1. Richmond defeated Charlotte 3 games to 1. *Finals*: Richmond defeated Syracuse 3 games to 0.

1995 Ottawa defeated Rochester 3 games to 2. Norfolk defeated Richmond 3 games to 2. *Finals*: Ottawa defeated Norfolk 3 games to 1.

1996 Columbus defeated Norfolk 3 games to 0. Rochester defeated Pawtucket 3 games to 1. *Finals*: Columbus defeated Rochester 3 games to 0.

1997 Rochester defeated Pawtucket 3 games to 1. Columbus defeated Charlotte 3games to 1. *Finals*: Rochester defeated Columbus 3 games to 2.

1998 Buffalo defeated Syracuse 3 games to 0. Durham defeated Louisville 3 games to 0. *Finals*: Buffalo defeated Durham 3 games to 2.

1999 Durham defeated Columbus 3 games to 0. Charlotte defeated Scranton/Wilkes-Barre 3 games to 2. *Finals*: Charlotte defeated Columbus 3 games to 1.

2000 Scranton/Wilkes-Barre defeated Buffalo 3 games to 1. Indianapolis defeated Durham 3 games to 2. *Finals*: Indianapolis SWB 3 games to 2.

2001 Louisville defeated Norfolk 3 games to 2. Scranton/Wilkes-Barre Buffalo 3 games to 2. *Finals*: Louisville defeated SWB 1 games to 0.

2002 Buffalo defeated Scranton/Wilkes-Barre 3 games to 0. Durham defeated Toledo 3 games to 0. *Finals*: Durham defeated Buffalo 3 games to 0.

2003 Pawtucket defeated Ottawa 3 games to 2. Durham defeated Louisville 3 games to 1. *Finals*: Durham defeated Pawtucket 3 games to 0.

2004 Buffalo defeated Durham 3 games to 2. Richmond defeated Columbus 3 games to 2. *Finals*: Buffalo defeated Richmond 3 games to 1.

2005 Indianapolis defeated Buffalo 3 games to 2. Toledo defeated Norfolk 3 games to 2. *Finals*: Toledo defeated Indianapolis 3 games to 0.

2006 Toledo defeated Charlotte 3 games to 1. Rochester defeated Scranton/Wilkes-Barre 3 games to 1. *Finals*: Toledo defeated Rochester 3 games to 2.

2007 Richmond defeated Scranton/Wilkes-Barre 3 games to 1. Durham defeated Toledo 3 games to 1. *Finals*: Durham defeated Richmond 3 games to 2.

Little World / Junior World Series Results

This postseason classic was called the Little World Series through 1931, after which it was officially designated the Junior World Series. International League champs also participated in the Kodak World Series Baseball Classic in 1972, the AAA World Series in 1983, the Triple-A Classic from 1998 through 1991, the Las Vegas Triple-A World

Series from 1998 through 2000, and the Bricktown Showdown, beginning in 2006.

(International League team listed first; winner in CAPS; record in parentheses.)

1904 BUFFALO v. St. Paul (2-1)
1906 BUFFALO v. Columbus (3-2)
1907 TORONTO v. Columbus (4-1)
1917 Toronto v. INDIANAPOLIS (4-1)
1920 BALTIMORE v. St. Paul (5-1)
1921 Baltimore v. LOUISVILLE (5-3)
1922 BALTIMORE v. St. Paul (5-2)
1923 Baltimore v. KANSAS CITY (5-4)
1924 Baltimore v. ST. PAUL (5-4-1)
1925 BALTIMORE v. Louisville (5-3)
1926 TORONTO v. Louisville (5-0)
1927 Buffalo v. TOLEDO (5-1)
1928 Rochester v. INDIANAPOLIS (5-1-1)
1929 Rochester v. KANSAS CITY (5-4)
1930 ROCHESTER v. Louisville (5-3)
1931 ROCHESTER v. St. Paul (5-3)
1932 NEWARK v. Minneapolis (4-2)
1933 Buffalo v. COLUMBUS (5-3)
1934 Toronto v. COLUMBUS (5-4)
1936 Buffalo v. MILWAUKEE (4-1)
1937 NEWARK v. Columbus (4-3)
1938 Newark v. KANSAS CITY (4-3)
1939 Rochester v. LOUISVILLE (4-3)
1940 NEWARK v. Louisville (4-2)
1941 Montreal v. COLUMBUS (4-2)
1942 Syracuse v. COLUMBUS (4-1)
1943 Syracuse v. COLUMBUS (4-1)
1944 BALTIMORE v. Louisville (4-2)
1945 Newark v. LOUISVILLE (4-2)
1946 MONTREAL v. Louisville (4-2)
1947 Syracuse v. MILWAUKEE (4-3)
1948 MONTREAL v. St. Paul (4-1)
1949 Montreal v. INDIANAPOLIS (4-2)
1950 Montreal v. COLUMBUS (4-2)
1951 Montreal v. MILWAUKEE (4-2)
1952 ROCHESTER v. Kansas City (4-3)
1953 MONTREAL v. Kansas City (4-1)
1954 Syracuse v. LOUISVILLE (4-2)

1955 Rochester v. MINNEAPOLIS (4-3)
1956 Rochester v. INDIANAPOLIS (4-0)
1957 Buffalo v. DENVER (4-1)
1958 Montreal v. MINNEAPOLIS (4-0)
1959 HAVANA v. Minneapolis (4-3)
1960 Toronto v. LOUISVILLE (4-2)
1961 BUFFALO v. Louisville (4-0)
1962 ATLANTA v. Louisville (4-3)
1970 SYRACUSE v. Omaha (4-1)
1971 ROCHESTER v. Denver (4-3)
1973 PAWTUCKET v. Tulsa (4-1)
1975 Tidewater v. EVANSVILLE (4-1)
1988 Rochester v. INDIANAPOLIS (4-2)
1989 Richmond v. INDIANAPOLIS (4-0)
1990 Rochester v. OMAHA (4-1)
1991 Columbus v. DENVER (4-1)
1998 Buffalo v. NEW ORLEANS (3-1)
1999 Charlotte v. VANCOUVER (3-2)
2000 INDIANAPOLIS v. Memphis (3-1)
2006 Toledo v. TUCSON (1-0)
2007 Richmond v. SACRAMENTO (1-0)

International League Presidents

1884 Henry Diddlebock
1885 W. S Arnold
1886 F. R. Winne
1887 Frank T. Gilbert
1888 E. Strachen Cox
1889 Riley V. Miller
1890-1892 Charles D. White
1893-1905 Patrick Powers
1906 Harry L. Taylor
1907-1910 Patrick Powers
1911-1917 Ed Barrow
1918 John H. Farrell
1919 David L. Fultz
1920-1928 John C. Toole
1929-1936 Charles H. Knappe
1936 Warren Giles
1937-1960 Frank J. Shaughnessy
1961-1965 Thomas Richardson

1966-1976	George H. Sisler, Jr.
1977-1990	Harold M. Cooper
1991-	Randy Mobley

Batting Champions

1884	J.W. Coogan, Nwk.	.380
1985	Records unavailable	
1886	Jon Morrison, Tor.	.353
1887	Frank Grant, Buf.	.366
1888	Patsy Donovan, Lon.	.359
1889	Perry Werden, Tol.	.394
1890	Records unavailable	
1891	Buck West, Syr.	.336
1892	Willie Keeler, Bing.	.373
1893	Jack Drauby, Buf.	.379
1894	Joe Knight, W-B, Prov.	.371
1895	Judson Smith, Tor.	.373
1896	Able Lezotte, W-B	.404
1897	Dan Brouthers, Sprgfld.	.415
1898	Buck Freeman, Tor.	.347
1899	Jim Bannon, Tor.	.341
1900	Bill Bransfield, Wor.	.371
1901	Homer Smoot, Wor.	.356
1902	Bill Halligan, JC	.351
1903	Harry McCormick, JC	.362
1904	Joe Yeager, Mtl.	.332
1905	Frank LaPorte, Buf.	.331
1906	Jack Thoney, Tor.	.294
1907	Jack Thoney, Tor.	.329
1908	Elijah Jones, Mtl.	.309
1909	Myron Grimshaw, Tor.	.309
1910	Jack Slattery, Tor.	.310
1911	Hank Perry, Prov.	.343
1912	Eddie Murphy, Balt.	.361
1913	George Simmons, Roch.	.339
1914	Dave Shean, Prov.	.334
1915	Chris Shorten, Prov.	.322
1916	James Smyth, Mtl.	.344
1917	Nap LaJoie, Tor.	.380
1918	Howard McLarry, Bing.	.385
1919	Otis Lawry, Balt.	.364

1920	Merwyn Jacobson, Balt.	.404
1921	Jack Bentley, Balt.	.412
1922	Bob Fothergill, Roch.	.383
1923	Clarence Pitt, Roch-Balt.	.357
1924	Dick Porter, Balt.	.364
1925	James Walsh, Buf.	.357
1926	James Walsh, Buf.	.388
1927	Dick Porter, Balt.	.376
1928	Dale Alexander, Tor.	.380
1929	Dan Taylor, Rdg.	.371
1930	Rip Collins, Roch.	.376
1931	Ike Boone, Nwk.	.356
1932	George Puccinelli, Roch.	.391
1933	Julius Solters, Balt.	.363
1934	Ike Boone, Tor.	.372
1935	George Puccinelli, Balt.	.359
1936	Smead Jolley, Alb.	.373
1937	Charley Keller, Nwk.	.353
1938	Charley Keller, Nwk.	.365
1939	Johnny Dickshot, JC	.355
1940	Murray Howell, Balt.	.359
1941	Gene Corbett, Balt-Nwk.	.306
1942	Hank Majeski, Nwk.	.345
1943	Red Schoendienst, Roch.	.337
1944	Mayo Smith, Buf.	.340
1945	Sherm Lollar, Balt.	.364
1946	Jackie Robinson, Mtl.	.349
1947	Vernal Jones, Roch.	.337
1948	Coaker Triplett, Buf.	.353
1949	Bobby Morgan, Mtl.	.337
1950	Don Richmond, Roch.	.333
1951	Don Richmond, Roch.	.350
1952	Frank Carswell, Buf.	.344
1953	Sandy Amoros, Mtl.	.353
1954	Bill Virdon, Roch.	.333
1955	Rocky Nelson, Mtl.	.364
1956	Clyde Parris, Mtl.	.321
1957	Joe Caffie, Buf.	.330
1958	Rocky Nelson, Tor.	.326
1959	Frank Herrera, Buf.	.329
1960	Jim Frye, Roch.	.317
1961	Ted Savage, Buf.	.325
1962	Vick Davalillo, Jax.	.346
1963	Dan Buford, Ind.	.336

1964	Sandy Valdespino, Atl.	.337
1965	Joe Foy, Tor.	.302
1966	Reggie Smith, Tor.	.320
1967	Elvio Jimenez, Col.	.340
1968	Merv Rettenmund, Roch.	.331
1969	Ralph Garr, Rmd.	.329
1970	Ralph Garr, Rmd.	.386
1971	Bobby Grich, Roch.	.336
1972	Alonza Bumbry, Roch.	.345
1973	Juan Beniquez, Paw.	.298
1974	Jim Rice, Paw.	.337
1975	Mike Vail, Tdw.	.342
1976	Richard Dauer, Roch.	.336
1977	Wayne Harer, Paw.	.350
1978	Mike Easler, Col.	.330
1979	Gary Hancock, Paw.	.325
1980	Dave Engle, Tol.	.307
1981	Wade Boggs, Paw.	.353
1982	Greg Wells, Tol.	.336
1983	John Perconte, Chn.	.346
1984	Scott Bradley, Col.	.335
1985	Juan Bonilla, Col.	.330
1986	Andre David, Tol.	.328
1987	Randy Milligan, Tdw.	.326
1988	Steve Finley, Roch.	.314
1989	Hal Morris, Col.	.326
1990	Jim Eppard, Syr.	.310
1991	Derek Bell, Syr.	.346
1992	J.T. Snow, Col.	.313
1993	Jim Thome, Char.	.332
1994	Shawn Green, Syr.	.344
1995	Robert Perez, Syr.	.343
1996	Billy McMillon, Char.	.352
1997	Tommy Gregg, Rich.	.332
1998	Todd Haney, Nor.	.345
1999	Steve Cox, Dur.	.341
2000	Billy McMillon, Tol.	.345
2001	Toby Hall, Dur.	.335
2002	Endy Chavez, Ott.	.343
2003	Ferenando Seguignol, Col.	.341
2004	Jason Kubel, Roch.	.343
2005	Danny Sandoval, SWB	.331
2006	Norris Hooper, Lou.	.347
2007	Ben Francisco, Buf.	.318

Home Run Champions

1904	Frank LaPorte, Buff.	9
1905	Jim Murray, Buff.Tor.	9
1906	Jim Murray, Buff.	7
1907	Bill Abstein, Prov.	7
	Natty Nattress, Buff.	7
1908	William Phyle, Tor.	16
1909	Hack Simmons, Roch.	9
1910	Al Shaw, Tor.	11
1911	Tim Jordan, Tor.	20
1912	Tim Jordan, Tor.	19
1913	Del Paddock, Roch.	8
1914	Wally Pipp, Roch.	15
1915	Lucky Whiteman, Mtl.	14
1916	G. W. Twombly, Bait.	12
1917	H. R. Damrau, Mtl.	16
1918	Fred Lear, Tor.	5
1919	George Kelly, Roch.	15
1920	Frank Brower, Rdg.	22
	Mike Konnick, Rdg.	22
1921	Jack Bentley, Balt.	24
1922	Red Wingo, Tor.	34
1923	Max Bishop, Balt.	22
	Billy Webb, Buff.	22
1924	Billy Kelly, Buff.	28
1925	Joe Kelly, Tor.	29
1926	Billy Kelly, Buff.	44
1927	Del Bissonette, Buff.	31
1928	Dale Alexander, Tor.	31
1929	Rip Collins, Roch.	38
1930	Joe Hauser, Balt.	63
1931	Joe Hauser, Balt.	31
1932	Buzz Arlett, Balt.	54
1933	Buzz Arlett, Balt.	39
1934	Woody Abernathy, Balt.	32
	Vincent Barton, Nwk.	32
1935	Geo. Puccinelli, Balt.	53
1936	Woody Abernathy, Balt.	42
1937	Ab Wright, Balt.	37
1938	Ollie Carnegie, Buff.	45
1939	Ollie Carnegie, Buff.	29
1940	Bill Nagle, Balt.	37
1941	Frank Kelleher, Nwk.	37

1942	Les Burge, Mtl.	28	1984	Charles Keller, Syr.	28
1943	Ed Kobesky, Buff.	18	1985	Jim Wilson, Maine	26
1944	Howard Moss, Balt.	27	1986	Ken Gerhart, Roch.	28
1945	Francis Skaff, Balt.	38	1987	Jay Buhner, Col.	31
1946	Howard Moss, Balt.	38	1988	Dave Griffin, Rmd.	21
1947	Howard Moss, Balt.	53	1989	Glen Hill, Syr.	21
1948	Howard Moss, Balt.	33	1990	Phil Plantier, Paw.	33
1958	Rocky Nelson, Tor.	43	1991	Rich Lancellotti, Paw.	21
1981	Steve Balboni, Col.	33	1992	Hensley Meulens, Col.	26
1949	Russ Derry, Roch.	42	1993	Sam Horn, Char.	38
1950	Russ Derry, Roch.	30	1994	Jeff Manto, Nor.-Roch.	31
	Chet Laabs, Tor.-JC.	30	1995	Butch Huskey, Nor.	28
1951	Marv Rickert, Balt.	35	1996	Phil Hiatt, Tol.	42
1952	Frank Carswell, Buff.	30	1997	Russ Morman, Char.	33
1953	J. Wallaesa, Sprg.-Buff.	36	1998	Brian Daubach, Char.	36
1954	Rocky Nelson, Mtl.	31	1999	Luis Raven, Char.	33
1955	Rocky Nelson, Mtl.	37	2000	Chad Mottola, Syr.	33
1956	Luke Easter, Buff.	35	2001	Izza Alcantara, Paw.	36
1957	Luke Easter, Buff.	40	2002	Izzy Alcantara, Ind.	27
1959	Frank Herrera, Buff.	37	2003	Fernando Seguignol, Col.	28
1960	Joe Altobelli, Mtl.	31	2004	Earl Snyder, Paw.	36
1961	John Powell, Roch.	32	2005	John Ford Griffin, Syr.	30
1962	Frank Herrera, Buff.	32	2006	Kevin Witt, Dur.	36
1963	Dick Allen, Ark.	33	2007	Mike Hessman, Tol.	31
1964	Mark Jones, Syr.	39			
1965	Frank Herrera, Col.	21			
1966	Mike Epstein, Roch.	29			
1967	Jim Beauchamp, Rmd.	25			

RBI Leaders

1968	Dave Nicholson, Rmd.	34			
1969	Bob Robertson, Col.	34	1925	Billy Kelly, Buff.	125
1970	Hal Breeden, Rmd.	37	1926	Billy Kelly, Buff.	151
1971	Bobby Grich, Roch.	32	1927	Del Bissonette, Buff.	167
1972	Richard Zisk, Chn.	26	1928	Dale Alexander, Tor.	144
1973	James Fuller, Roch.	39	1929	Rip Collins, Roch.	134
1974	Jim Rice, Paw.	25	1930	Rip Collins, Roch.	180
1975	Bill Nahorodny, Tol.	19	1931	Jim Poole, Rdg.	126
1976	Jack Baker, Paw.	36	1932	Buzz Arlett, Balt.	144
1977	Terry Crowley, Roch.	30	1933	Julius Solters, Balt.	157
1978	Henry Small, Rmd.	25	1934	Fred Sington, Alb.	147
1979	Sam Bowen, Paw.	28	1935	Geo. Puccinelli, Balt.	172
1980	Marshall Brant, Col.	23	1936	Colonel Mills, Roch.	134
1982	Steve Balboni, Col.	32	1937	Ab Wright, Balt.	127
1983	Brian Dayett, Col.	35	1938	Ollie Carnegie, Buff.	136

1939	Ollie Carnegie, Buff.	112
1940	Nick Etten, Balt.	128
1941	Frank Kelleher, Nwk.	125
1942	Hank Majeski, Nwk.	121
1943	Geo. Staller, Balt.	98
1944	Howard Moss, Balt.	141
1945	Francis Skaff, Balt.	126
1946	Eddie Robinson, Balt.	123
1947	Hank Sauer, Syr.	141
1948	Clyde Vollmer, Syr.	104
1949	Steve Bilko, Roch.	125
1950	Russ Derry, Roch.	102
1951	Arch Wilson, Buff.	112
1952	Ed Stevens, Tor.	113
1953	Rocky Nelson, Mtl.	136
1954	Ed Stevens, Tor.	113
1955	Rocky Nelson, Mtl.	130
1956	Luke Easter, Buff.	106
1957	Luke Easter, Buff.	128
1958	Rocky Nelson, Tor.	120
1959	Frank Herrera, Buff.	128
1960	Joe Altobelli, Mtl.	105
1961	Frank Leja, Rich.-Syr.	98
1962	Frank Herrera, Buff.	108
	Bob Bailey, Col.	108
1963	Dick Allen, Ark.	97
1964	Mark Jones, Syr.	102
1965	Steve Demeter, Roch.	90
1966	Mike Epstein, Roch.	102
1967	Curt Motton, Roch.	70
1968	Dave Nicholson, Rmd.	86
1969	Roy Foster, Tdw.	92
1970	Roger Freed, Roch.	130
1971	Richard Zisk, Chn.	109
1972	Dwight Evans, Lou.	95
1973	James Fuller, Roch.	108
1974	Jim Rice, Paw.	93
1975	Roy Staiger, Tdw.	81
1976	Joey Lis, Tol.	103
1977	Dale Murphy, Rmd.	90
1978	Henry Small, Rmd.	101
1979	Sam Bowen, Paw.	75
	Charles Keller, Rmd.	75

1980	Marshall Brant, Col.	92
1981	Steve Balboni, Col.	98
1982	Greg Wells, Tol.	107
1983	Brian Dayett, Col.	108
1984	Scott Bradley, Col.	84
	Jim Wilson, Maine	84
1985	Jim Wilson, Maine	101
1986	Pat Dodson, Paw.	102
1987	Randy Milligan, Tdw.	103
1988	Ron Jones, Maine	75
1989	Tom O'Malley, Tdw.	84
1990	Len Gomez, Roch.	97
1991	Derek Bell, Syr.	93
1992	Hensley Meulens, Col.	100
1993	Jim Thome, Char.	102
1994	Jeff Manto, Nor.-Roch.	100
1995	Don Sparks, Col.	90
1996	Phil Hiatt, Tol.	119
1997	Randall Simon, Rich.	102
1998	Brian Daubach, Char.	124
1999	Steve Cox, Dur.	127
2000	Ozzie Timmons, Dur.	104
2001	Calvin Pickering, Roch-Lou	99
2002	Kevin Witt, Lou.	107
2003	Andy Abad, Paw.	93
2004	Earl Snyder, Paw.	104
2005	John Ford Griffin, Syr.	103
2006	Kevin Witt, Dur.	99
2007	Mike Hessman, Tol.	101

Stolen Base Leaders

1888	Ed Burke, Tor.	107
1889	Ed Burke, Tor.	97
1891	Herman Bader, Alb.	106
1892	Bob Wheelock, Elm.-Roch.	53
1893	Bill Eagan, Alb.	75
1895	W. J. Murray, Prov.	74
1896	W. J. Murray, Prov.	75
1897	William Lush, Tor.	70
1898	Doc Casey, Tor.	66

1900	Al Davis, Prov.	70	1944	Ora Burnett, Roch.	41
1901	Harold O'Hagan, Roch.	51	1945	Walt Cazen, Syr.	74
1903	Art Devlin, Nwk.	51	1946	Marv Rackley, Mtl.	65
1904	William Keister, JC	53	1947	Bob Wilson, Balt.	36
1905	William Keister, JC	68	1948	Sam Jethroe, Mtl.	18
1906	John Kelly, Balt.	63		John Welaj, Tor.	18
1907	William O'Hara, Balt.	63	1949	Sam Jethroe, Mtl.	89
1908	George Schirm, Buff.	61	1950	Pete Pavlick, JC	23
1909	Herbie Moran, Prov.	58	1951	Hector Rodriguez, Md.	26
1910	Dan Moeller, JC-Roch.	47	1952	Jim Gilliam, Mtl.	18
1911	Ward Miller, Md.	63	1953	Walt Rogers, Ott.	30
1912	Cozy Dolan, Roch.	78	1954	Don Nicholas, Hav.	37
1913	Fritz Maisel, Balt.	44	1955	John Brandt, Roch.	24
1914	Frank Gilhooley, Buff.	62		Sam Jethroe, Tor.	24
1915	Frank Gilhooley, Buff.	53		Joe Caffie, Syr.	24
1916	Merlin Kopp, Buff.	59	1956	Len Johnston, Rmd.	40
1917	Merlin Kopp, Buff.	57	1957	Len Johnston, Rmd.	26
1918	Otis Lawry, Balt.	35	1958	Len Johnston, Rmd.	37
1919	Ed Miller, Nwk.	87	1959	Larry Raines, Tor.	32
1920	Ray Dowd, Buff.	59	1960	Sol Drake, Buff.	16
1921	Sugar Kane, JC	68	1961	Ted Savage, Buff.	31
1922	Flash Archdeacon, Roch.	55	1962	Vic Davalillo, Jax	24
1923	Otis Lawry, Balt.	41	1963	Don Buford, Ind.	42
1924	Dan Silva, Syr.-Rdg.	41	1964	Ted Savage, Col.	26
1925	Ray Dowd, JC	38	1965	George Spriggs, Col.	66
1926	George Burns, Nwk.	38	1966	George Spriggs, Col.	34
1927	Harry Layne, Syr.	50	1967	Freddie Patek, Col.	42
1928	Joe Rabbitt, Tor.	42	1968	George Spriggs, Col.	46
1929	Joe Rabbitt, Tor.	46	1969	Ralph Garr, Rmd.	63
1930	Henry Haines, Mtl.	45	1970	Ralph Garr, Rmd.	39
1931	Dennis Sothern, Balt.	33	1971	John Jeter, Chn.	36
1932	John Neun, Nwk.	25	1972	Jose Mangual, Pen.	39
1933	L. F. Thompson, JC-Buff.	35	1973	Larry Lintz, Pen.	48
1934	Harvey Walker, Mtl.	33	1974	Jose Mangual, Mem.	46
1935	Ernie Koy, Nwk.	33	1975	Miguel Dilone, Chn.	48
1936	John Dickshot, Buff.	33	1976	Miguel Dilone, Chn.	61
1937	John Hopp, Roch.	33	1977	Mike Edwards, Col.	62
1938	George Myatt, JC	45	1978	Ed Miller, Rmd.	36
1939	Herman Clifton, Tor.	22	1979	Ed Miller, Rmd.	76
1940	Eddie Collins, Balt.	21	1980	Ed Miller, Rmd.	60
1941	Paul Campbell, Mtl.	24	1981	Dallas Williams, Roch.	51
1942	Geo. Stirnweiss, Nwk.	73	1982	Albert Hall, Rmd.	62
1943	Roland Harrington, Syr.	52	1983	Otis Nixon, Col.	94

1984	Mike Wilson, Tol.	48
1985	Dwight Taylor, Maine	52
1986	Albert Hall, Rmd.	72
1987	Roberto Kelly, Col.	51
1988	Eric Yelding, Syr.	59
1989	Tom Barrett, SWB	44
1990	Milt Cuyler, Tol.	52
1991	Jim Walewander, Col.	54
1992	Mike Humphries, Col.	37
1993	Eric Bullock, Nor.	45
1994	Shannon Penn, Tol.	45
1995	Jim Buccheri, Ott.	44
1996	Shannon Stewart, Syr.	35
1997	Kimera Bartee, Tol.	33
1998	Scott Pose, Col.	47
1999	Greg Martinez, Lou.	48
2000	Alex Sanchez, Dur.	52
2001	Henry Mateo, Ott.	48
2002	Nick Punto, SWB	42
	Andres Torres, Tol.	42
2003	Esix Snead, Nor.	61
2004	Esix Snead, Nor.	40
2005	Esix Snead, Rich.	46
2006	B. J. Upton, Dur.	46
2007	Bernie Castro, Col.	34

.400 Hitters

1896	.404	Abel Lezotte, W-B
1897	.415	Dan Brouthers, Sprgfld.
1920	.404	Merwyn Jacobson, Balt.
1921	.412	Jack Bentley, Bait.

50 Home Runs

1930	63	Joe Hauser, Balt.
1932	54	Buzz Arlett, Balt.
1935	53	George Puccinelli, Balt.
1947	53	Howie Moss, Balt.
1947	50	Hank Sauer, Syr.

Triple Crown Winners

1928	Dale Alexander, Tor.
	.380, 31 HR, 144 RBI
1935	George Puccinelli, Balt.
	.359, 53 HR, 172 RBI
1955	Rocky Nelson, Md.
	.364, 37 HR, 139 RBI
1958	Rocky Nelson, Tor.
	.326, 43 HR, 120 RBI
1959	Frank Herrera, Buff.
	.329, 37 HR, 128 RBI
1974	Jim Rice, Paw.
	.337, 25 HR, 93 RBI

Pitchers
—Most Victories—

1887	George Stovey, Nwk.	35
1888	Conny Murphy, Syr.	34
1889	Robert Barr, Roch.	29
1903	Pfanmiller, JC	28
1904	Malcolm Eason, JC	26
1905	John Cronin, Prov.	29
1906	Del Mason, Balt.	26
1907	Joe Lake, JC	25
1908	Doc Adkins, Balt.	29
1909	Joe McGinnity, Nwk.	29
1910	Joe McGinnity, Nwk.	30
1911	Rube Vickers, Balt.	32
1912	Dick Rudolph, Tor.	25
1913	Watty Lee, Nwk.	22
	Roth, Balt.	22
1914	Carl Mays, Prov.	24
1915	Fred Beebe, Buff.	27
1916	Leon Cadore, Mtl.	25
1917	Harry Thompson, Tor.	25
1918	Worrell, Balt.	25
1919	Rube Parnham, Balt.	28
1920	Red Shea, Tor.	27
	John Ogden, Balt.	27
1921	John Ogden, Balt.	31

1922	John Ogden, Balt.	24	1960	Al Cicotte, Tor.	16
1923	Rube Parnham, Balt.	33	1961	Ray Washburn, Chn.	16
1924	Lefty Grove, Balt.	26	1962	Joe Schaffernoth, Jax	18
1925	Al Thomas, Balt.	32	1963	Fritz Ackley, Ind.	18
1926	John Ogden, Balt.	24	1964	Bruce Brubaker, Syr.	15
1927	Al Mamaux, Nwk.	25	1965	Dick LeMay, Jax	17
1928	Harry Seibold, Rdg.	22	1966	Gary Waslewski, Tor.	18
1929	Elon Hogsett, Mtl.	22	1967	Dave Leonhard, Roch.	15
1930	Paul Derringer, Roch.	23	1968	Dave Roberts, Col.	18
1931	John Allen, JC-Tor.	21	1969	Fred Beene, Roch.	15
	Monte Weaver, Bait.	21		Gerard Janeski, Lou.	15
1932	Don Brennan, Nwk.	26		Ron Klimkowski, Syr.	15
1933	Jim Weaver, Nwk.	25	1970	Rob Gardner, Syr.	16
1934	Walter Brown, Nwk.	20	1971	Jim Bibby, Tdw.	15
1935	Pete Appleton, Mtl.	23		Roric Harrison, Roch.	15
1936	Bob Weiland, Roch.	23	1972	Craig Skok, Lou.	15
1937	Joe Beggs, Nwk.	21	1973	John Montague, Pen.	15
	Marv Duke, Mtl.	21	1974	Bill Kirkpatrick, Roch.	15
1938	Joe Sullivan, Tor.	18	1975	Odell Jones, Chn.	14
1939	Silas Johnson, Roch.	22		Mike Willis, Roch.	14
1940	Dominic Ryba, Roch.	24	1976	Dennis Martinez, Roch.	14
1941	Fred Hutchinson, Buff.	26	1977	Larry McCall, Syr.	16
1942	Charles Barrett, Syr.	20	1978	Dan Larson, Chn.	14
1943	Ed Klieman, Balt.	23		Gary Wilson, Chn.	14
1944	Charles Embree, Balt.	19	1979	Bob Kammeyer, Col.	16
1945	Jean Roy, Mtl.	25	1980	Bob Kammeyer, Col.	15
1946	Steve Nagy, Mtl.	17	1981	Ken Dayley, Rmd.	13
1947	Jim Prendergast, Syr.	20	1982	Craig McMurtry, Rmd.	17
1948	John Banta, Mtl.	19	1983	Mark Bomback, Syr.	13
1949	Al Widmar, Balt.	22		Dennis Rasmussen, Col.	13
1950	Tom Poholsky, Roch.	18	1984	Gerald Ujdar, Maine	14
1951	John Hetki, Tor.	19	1984	Gerald Ujdar, Maine	14
1952	Bob Keegan, Syr.	20	1985	Dennis Burtt, Tol.	14
	Charles Bishop, Ott.	20		Stan Clarke, Syr.	14
1953	Bob Trice, Ott.	21	1986	Charles Puleo, Rmd.	14
1954	Ed Roebuck, Mtl.	18	1987	Paul Gibson, Tol.	14
	Ken Lehman, Mtl.	18	1988	Scott Nielsen, Col.	13
1955	Ken Lehman, Mtl.	22		Steve Searcy, Tol.	13
1956	Lynn Lovenguth, Tor.	24	1989	Gary Eave, Rmd.	13
1957	H. V. Robinson, Tor.	18		Alex Sanchez, Syr.	13
	Walt Craddock, Buff.	18		Curtis Schilling, Roch.	13
1958	Tommy Lasorda, Mtl.	18	1990	Dave Eiland, Col.	16
1959	Bob Keegan, Roch.	18	1991	Blaine Beatty, Tdw.	12

	Mark Dewey, Tdw.	12
	Yorkis Perez, Tdw.	12
	John Shea, Syr.	12
	Anthony Telford, Roch.	12
	Mike Weston, Syr.	12
1992	David Nied, Rich.	14
1993	Mike Birlebeck, Rich.	13
	Chad Ogea, Char.	13
1994	Julian Tavarez, Char.	15
	Brad Woodall, Rich.	15
1995	Jimmy Hagnes, Roch.	12
	Jimmy Williams, Nor-Rich	12
1996	Mike Fyhrie, Nor.	15
1997	Brian Rose, Paw.	17
1998	Shannon Witham, Syr.	17
1999	Denny Harriger, Ind.	14
2000	Horacio Estrada, Ind.	14
2001	Brandon Duckworth, SWB	13
2002	Trey Hodges, Rich.	15
2003	Brian Cooper, Char.	15
2004	Dave Gassmer, Roch.	16
2005	Jason Scobie, Nor.	15
2006	Charlie Haegon, Char.	14
2007	Heath Phillips, Char.	13
	Mitch Talbot, Dur.	13

Pitchers
—Winning Percentage—

1889	Smith, Detroit	18-8	.692
1903	Jake Thielman, JC	23-5	.821
1904	Stan Yerkes, Buff.	10-3	.769
1905	Alex Lindaman, JC	24-7	.774
1906	Del Mason, Balt.	26-9	.743
1907	George McQuillan, Prov.	19-7	.731
1908	Mueller, Newark	18-7	.720
1909	John Cronin, Prov.	16-8	.667
1910	Buck Donnelly, Balt.	11-4	.733
1911	George McConnell, Roch.	30-8	.789
1912	Dick Rudolph, Tor.	25-10	.714
1913	Raleigh Aitchison, Nwk.	21-5	.808

1914	Carl Mays, Prov.	24-8	.750
1915	Fred Beebe, Buff.	27-7	.794
1916	Urban Shocker, Tor.	15-3	.833
1917	Bunny Hearne, Tor.	23-9	.719
1918	Beckersmith, Bing.	17-4	.810
1919	Harry Frank, Balt.	24-6	.800
1920	John Bentley, Balt.	16-3	.842
1921	John Bentley, Balt.	12-1	.923
1922	John Bentley, Balt.	13-2	.867
1923	Rube Parnham, Balt.	33-7	.825
1924	Lefty Grove, Balt.	26-6	.813
1925	Carl Yowell, Roch.	11-1	.917
1926	Clarence Fisher, Buf-Tor.	15-4	.789
1927	John Bentley, Nwk.	11-3	.786
1928	Harry Seibold, Rdg.	22-8	.733
1929	Phil Page, Tor.	10-3	.769
1930	Roy Buckaleu, Mtl.	13-4	.765
1931	Myles Thomas, Nwk.	18-6	.750
1932	Don Brennan, Nwk.	26-8	.765
1933	Harry Smythe, Balt.	21-8	.724
1934	Walter Brown, Nwk.	20-6	.769
1935	Pete Appleton, Mtl.	23-9	.719
1936	John Wilson, Buf.	14-7	.667
1937	Joe Beggs, Nwk.	21-4	.840
1938	John Haley, Nwk.	17-2	.895
1939	Roy Joiner, JC	21-8	.724
1940	Harold White, Buf.	16-4	.800
1941	John Lindell, Nwk.	23-4	.852
1942	Tommy Byrne, Nwk.	17-4	.810
1943	Joe Page, Nwk.	14-5	.737
1944	Ken Brondell, JC	13-6	.684
1945	Les Webber, Mtl.	11-3	.786
1946	Steve Nagy, Mtl.	17-4	.810
1947	Ed Heusser, Mtl.	19-3	.864
1948	Don Newcombe, Mtl.	17-6	.736
1949	Bob Hooper, Buf.	19-3	.864
1950	Ken Wild, Roch.	12-1	.923
1951	Mel Mallette, Mtl.	10-2	.833
1952	Mel Mallette, Mtl.	13-2	.867
1953	Milt Jordan, Buf.	12-1	.923
1954	Tony Jacobs, Roch.	13-1	.929
1955	Cliff Johnson, Tor.	12-2	.857
1956	Bob Spicer, Col.	12-4	.750

1957	Ray Semproch, Miami	12-4	.750
1958	Bob Tifenauer, Tor.	17-5	.773
1959	Al Jackson, Col.	15-4	.789
1960	Bob Tiefenauer, Tor.	11-4	.733
1961	Ray Washburn, Chn.	16-9	.640
1962	Jimmy Constable, Tor.	16-4	.800
1963	Willie Smith, Syr.	14-2	.875
1964	Ron Piche, Tor.	14-3	.824
1965	Bill Short, Roch.	13-4	.765
1966	Ed Barnowski, Roch.	17-8	.680
1967	Dave Leonhard, Roch.	15-3	.833
1968	Dave Roberts, Col.	18-5	.783
1969	Larry Bearnath, Tdw.	11-4	.733
1970	Frank Bertaina, Roch.	12-3	.800
	Dick Colpaert, Col.	12-3	.800
1971	Charles Seelbach, Tol.	12-2	.857
1972	Gene Garber, Chn.	14-3	.824-
1973	George Manz, Roch.	11-5	.688
	John Morlan, Chn.	11-5	.688
1974	Paul Mitchell, Roch.	14-6	.700
1975	Mike Flanagan, Roch.	13-4	.765
1976	Bob Galasso, Roch.	13-5	.722
1977	Allen Ripley, Paw.	15-4	.789
1978	Dan Larson, Chn.	14-6	.700
1979	Dick Anderson, Col.	13-3	.813
1980	Paul Hartzell, Roch.	10-4	.714
1981	Dave Wehrmeister, Col.	11-3	.786
1982	James Lewis, Col.	12-6	.667
	Mike Boddicker, Roch.	10-5	.667
	Neal Heaton, Chn.	10-5	.667
1983	Walt Terrell, Tdw.	10-1	.909
1984	Kelly Faulk, Col.	11-1	.917
1985	Stan Clarke, Syr.	14-4	.778
1986	Charles Puleo, Rmd.	14-7	.667
1987	Don Schultze, Tdw.	11-1	.917
1988	Dave West, Tdw.	12-4	.750
1989	Gary Eave, Rmd.	13-3	.813
1990	Mike Weston, Roch.	11-1	.917
1991	Mark Dewey, Tdw.	12-3	.800
	Yorkis Perez, Rmd.	12-3	.800
1992	Mike Williams, SWB	9-1	.900
1993	Mike Williams, SWB	9-2	.818
1994	Eric Hillman, Nor.	10-1	.909

1995	Jason Isringhausen, Nor.	9-1	.900
1996	Mike Gardiner, Nor.	13-3	.813
1997	Jim Dougherty, Nor.	10-1	.909
1998	Jason Jacome, Buff.	14-2	.875
1999	Alan Newman, Dur.	10-1	.000
2000	Jon Garland, Char.	9-2	.818
2001	Brandon Duckworth, SWB	13-2	.867
2002	Joe Roa, SWB	14-1	.000
2003	Jason Phillips, Buff.	10-1	.909
2004	Felix Diaz, Char.	10-2	.833
2005	Steve Watkins, Buff.	9-2	.818
2006	Jeremy Sowers, Buff.	9-1	.900
2007	Manny Acosta, Rich.	9-3	.750
	Aaron Laffey, Buff.	9-3	.750

Pitchers
—Most Strikeouts—

1888	Al Atkinson, Tor.	307
1889	Ed Cushman, Tol.	194
	Tom Vickery, Tor.	194
1904	Cy Falkenberg, Tor.	175
1905	Walt Clarkson, JC	195
1906	Fred Burchell, Balt.	183
1907	Joe Lake, JC	187
1908	Tom Hughes, Nwk.	161
1909	Joe McGinnity, Nwk.	195
1910	Lefty Russell, Balt.	219
1911	Jim Dygert, Balt.	218
1912	Bill Bailey, Prov.	169
1913	George Davis, JC	199
1914	Tom Hughes, Roch.	182
1915	Allen Russell, Rmd.	239
1916	William McTigue, Tor.	187
1917	Vean Gregg, Prov.	249
1918	Brogan, Roch.	157
1919	Rube Parnham, Balt.	187
1920	Zeke Barnes, Roch.	142
1921	Lefty Grove, Balt.	254
1922	Lefty Grove, Balt.	205
1923	Lefty Grove, Balt.	330

1924	Lefty Grove, Balt.	231	1966	Tom Phoebus, Roch.	208
1925	Al Thomas, Balt.	268	1967	Jerry Koosman, Jax	183
1926	Roy Chesterfield, Nwk.	141	1968	Jim Rooker, Tol.	206
1927	George Earnshaw, Balt.	172	1969	Mike Adamson, Roch.	133
1928	Guy Cantrell, Balt.	165	1970	Ernest McAnally, Wpg.	178
1929	Charles Fischer, Nwk.	191	1971	Roric Harrison, Roch.	182
1930	Paul Derringer, Roch.	164	1972	Jim McKee, Chn.	159
1931	Don Brennan, Nwk.	143	1973	Dick Pole, Paw.	158
1932	Beryl Richmond, Balt.	155	1974	Jim Burton, Paw.	146
1933	Jim Weaver, Nwk.	175	1975	Odell Jones, Chn.	157
1934	Darrell Blanton, Alb.	165	1976	Dennis Martinez, Roch.	140
1935	Bill Harris, Buff.	137	1977	Mike Parrott, Roch.	146
1936	Bob Weiland, Roch.	171	1978	Odell Jones, Col.	169
1937	Lloyd Moore, Syr.	149	1979	Tom Boggs, Rmd.	138
1938	Richard Donald, Nwk.	133	1980	Juan Berenguer, Tdw.	178
1939	John Tising, Balt.-Syr.	144	1981	Ken Dayley, Rmd.	162
1940	Geo. Washburn, Nwk.	145	1982	Don Cooper, Tol.	125
1941	Virgil Trucks, Buff.	204	1983	Dennis Rasmussen, Col.	187
1942	Jack Hallett, Tor.	187	1984	Brad Havens, Tol.	169
1943	Steve Gromek, Balt.	188	1985	Brad Havens, Roch.	129
1944	Charles Embree, Balt.	225	1986	Charles Puleo, Rmd.	124
1945	Jean Roy, Mtl.	139	1987	Odell Jones, Syr.	147
1946	Art Houttemand, Buff.	147	1988	Steve Searcy, Tol.	176
1947	John Banta, Mtl.	199	1989	Kent Mercker, Rmd.	144
1948	John Banta, Mtl.	193	1990	Manny Hernandez, Tdw.	157
1949	Dan Bankhead, Mtl.	176	1991	Pat Hentgen, Syr.	155
1950	Roger Bowman, JC	181	1992	David Nied, Rich.	159
1951	Bill Miller, Syr.	131	1993	Mike Birkbeck, Rich.	136
1952	Harry Markell, Tor.	120		John DeSilva, Tol.	136
1953	Don Johnson, Tor.	156	1994	Frank Rodriguez, Paw.	160
1954	John Meyer, Syr.	173	1995	Jimmy Haynes, Roch.	140
1955	Jim Owens, Syr.	161	1996	Jeff Suppan, Paw.	146
1956	Seth Morehead, Miami	168	1997	Nerio Rodruiguez, Roch.	160
1957	Jim Coates, Rmd.	161	1998	Juan Pena, Paw.	146
1958	Calvin Browning, Roch.	173	1999	Jeff Juden, Col.	151
1959	Joe Gibbon, Col.	152	2000	Brandon Knight, Col.	138
1960	Al Cicotte, Tor.	158	2001	Brandon Knight, Col.	173
1961	Bob Veale, Col.	208	2002	Doug Linton, Rich.	160
	Steve Shields, Rmd.	124	2003	Andy Pratt, Rich.	161
1962	Harry Fanok, Ad.	192	2004	Alex Gramman, Col.	129
1963	Frank Kreutzer, Ind.	157		Chuck Smith, Rich.	129
1964	Jim Merritt, Atl.	174	2005	Boof Bonser, Roch.	168
1965	Frank Bertaina, Roch.	188	2006	Chad Durbin, Tol.	149

2007	J.P. Howell, Dur.	145

Pitchers
Lowest-Earned Run Average

Year	Player	ERA
1888	Conny Murphy, Syr.	1.27
1889	Cannonball Titcomb, Tor.	1.29
1916	Urban Shocker, Tor.	1.31
1917	Vean Gregg, Prov.	1.72
1918	Habry Heitman, Roch.	1.32
1919	Ray Jordan, Buff.	1.43
1920	John Bendey, Balt.	2.11
1921	John Ogden, Balt.	2.01
1922	John Bentley, Balt.	1.73
1923	Joe Lucey, JC	2.73
1924	Walter Beall, Roch.	2.76
1925	Walter Stewart, Tor.	2.51
1926	Al Mamaux, Nwk.	2.22
1927	Al Mamaux, Nwk.	2.61
1928	Maurice Bream, JC	2.32
1929	Hub Pruett, Nwk.	2.43
1930	John Berly, Roch.	2.49
1931	Ray Starr, Roch.	2.83
1932	Don Brennan, Nwk.	2.79
1933	Fred Ostermueller, Roch.	2.44
1934	Walter Brown, Nwk.	2.56
1935	Joe Cascarella, Syr.	2.35
1936	Silas Johnson, Tor.	2.38
1937	Ben Cantwell, JC	1.65
1938	Charles Barrett, Syr.	2.34
1939	Roy Joiner, JC	2.53
1940	Harold White, Buff.	2.43
1941	John Lindell, Buff.	2.05
1942	Ray Coombs, JC	1.99
1943	Lou Polli, JC	1.85
1944	Woody Crowson, Tor.	2.41
1945	Les Webber, Md.	1.88
1946	Herb Karpel, Nwk.	2.41
1947	Luke Hamlin, Tor.	2.22
1948	Bob Porterfield, Nwk.	2.17
1949	Bubba Church, Tor.	2.35
1950	Tom Poholsky, Roch.	2.17
1951	Alex Konikowski, Otto	2.59
1952	Marion Fricano, Otto	2.26
1953	Don Johnson, Tor.	2.67
1954	Jim Owens, Syr.	2.87
1955	Jack Crimian, Tor.	2.10
1956	Ed Blake, Tor.	2.61
1957	Mike Cuellar, Hav.	2.44
1958	Bob Tiefenauer, Tor.	1.89
1959	Artie Kay, Miami	2.08
1960	Al Cicotte, Tor.	1.79
1961	Ray Washburn, Chn.	2.34
1962	Jim Constable, Tor.	2.56
1963	Fritz Ackley, Ind.	2.76
1964	Bruce Brubaker, Syr.	2.63
1965	Jack Hamilton, Syr.	2.42
1966	Wilbur Wood, Col.	2.41
1967	Tug McGraw, Jax.	1.99
1968	Galen Cisco, Lou.	2.21
1969	Ron Klimkowski, Syr.	2.18
1970	Rob Gardner, Syr.	2.53
1971	Buzz Capra, Tdw.	2.10
1972	Gene Garber, Chn.	2.26
1973	Dick Pole, Paw.	2.03
1974	Larry Gura, Syr.	2.14
1975	Pablo Torrealba, Rmd.	1.45
1976	Dennis Martinez, Roch.	2.50
1977	Tom Dixon, Chn.	2.25
1978	Frank Riccelli, Chn.	2.78
1979	Scott Holman, Tdw.	1.99
1980	Ken Clay, Col.	1.96
1981	Bob Ojeda, Paw.	2.13
1982	James Lewis, Col.	2.60
1983	Tom Brennen, Chn.	3.31
1984	Jim Deshaies, Col.	2.39
1985	Don Gordon, Syr.	2.07
1986	Doug Jones, Maine	2.09
1987	DeWayne Vaughn, Tdw.	2.66
1988	Dave.West, Tdw.	1.80
1989	Jose Nunez, Syr.	2.21
1990	Paul Marak, Rmd.	2.49
1991	Armando Reynoso, Rmd.	2.61
1992	Sam Militello, Col.	2.29

1993	Kevin McGehee, Roch.	2.96
1994	Brad Woodall, Rich.	2.38
1995	Jason Schmidt, Rich.	2.25
1996	Mike Fyhrie, Nor.	3.04
1997	Brian Rose, Paw.	3.02
1998	Terry Burrows, Roch.	2.92
1999	Ed Yarnell, Col.	3.47
2000	Tomo Ohko, Paw.	2.96
2001	Brandon Duckworth, SWB	2.63
2002	Luis de los Santos, Dur.	2.42
2003	Jeremy Griffith, Nor.	2.74
2004	Ben Hendrickson, Ind.	2.02
2005	Scott Baker, Roch.	3.01
2006	Brian Mazone, SWB	2.03
2007	Kevin Slowey, Roch.	1.89

30-Game Winners

1887	35-14	George Stovey, Nwk.
1888	34-15	Conny Murphy, Syr.
1910	30-19	Joe McGinnity, Nwk.
1911	32-14	Rube Vickers, Balt.
1911	30-8	Geo. McConnell, Roch.
1921	31-8	John Ogden, Balt.
1923	33-7	Rube Parhnam, Balt.
1925	32-12	Al Thomas, Balt.

Triple Crown Winners

1960   Al Cicotte, Tor.
      16-7, 158K, 1.79 ERA
1976   Dennis Martinez, Roch.
      14-8, 140K, 2.50 ERA

Most Valuable Players

Beginning in 1932, International League sportswriters selected a Most Valuable Player. Rocky Nelson was voted MVP in 1953, 1955, and 1958, and is the only athlete besides Roberto Petagine in 1997 and 1998 to have been honored more than once. In 1970 and 1979 two players shared the award, and in 1976 there was a three-way tie. In 1953 a separate award was established for the Most Valuable Pitcher, and in 1950 a Rookie of the Year became an annual selection.

1932	Marvin Owen, IF, Tor.-Nwk.
1933	Red Rolfe, SS, Nwk.
1934	Ike Boone, OF, Tor.
1935	George Puccinelli, OF, Balt.
1936	Frank McGowen, CF, Buff.
1937	Clyde Crouse, C, Buff.-Balt.
1938	Ollie Carnegie, LF, Buff.
1939	Mickey Witek, IF, Nwk.
1940	Dominick Ryba, P, Buff.
1941	Fred Hutchinson, P, Buff.
1942	Red Barrett, P, Syr.
1943	Red Schoendienst, SS, Roch.
1944	Howie Moss, OF, Balt.
1945	Sherm Lollar, C, Balt.
1946	Eddie Robinson, 1B, Balt.
1947	Hank Sauer, OF, Syr.
1948	Jimmy Bloodworth, 2B, Mtl.
1949	Bob Morgan, SS, Mtl.
1950	Tom Poholsky, P, Roch.
1951	Archie Wilson, OF, Buff.
1952	Jim Gilliam, 2B-OF, Mtl.
1953	Rocky Nelson, 1B, Mtl.
1954	Elston Howard, C-OF, Tor.
1955	Rocky Nelson, 1B, Mtl.
1956	Mike Goliat, 2B, Tor.
1957	Mike Baxes, SS, Buff.
1958	Rocky Nelson, 1B, Tor.
1959	Frank Herrera, 1B, Buff.
1960	Jim King, OF, Tor.
1961	Ted Savage, CF, Buff.
1962	Tony Martinez, SS, Jax
1963	Don Buford, 3B, Ind.

1964	Joe Morgan, 3B, Jax
1965	Joe Foy, 3B, Tor.
1966	Mike Epstein, 1B, Roch.
1967	Tom Aaron, 1B-OF, Rmd.
1968	Merv Rettenmund, OF, Roch.
1969	Luis Alvarado, SS, Lou.
1970	George Kopacz, 1B, Col.
	Roger Freed, OF, Roch.
1971	Bobby Grich, SS, Roch.
1972	Dwight Evans, OF, Lou.
1973	Jim Fuller, 1B-OF, Paw.
1974	Jim Rice, OF, Paw.
1975	Mike Vail, OF, Tdw.
1976	Rich Dauer, 2B, Roch.
	Mickey Klutts, SS, Syr.
	Joe Lis, 1B, Tor.
1977	Ted Cox, 3B, Paw.
1978	Gary Allenson, C, Paw.
1979	Bobby Brown, OF, Col.
	Dave Stapleton, 3B, Paw.
1980	Marshall Brant, 1B, Col.
1981	Brett Butler, OF, Rmd.
1982	Tucker Ashford, 3B, Col.
1983	Tim Teufel, 2B, Tol.
1984	Scott Bradley, C-OF, Col.
1985	Dan Pasqua, OF, Col.
1986	Pat Dodson, 1B, Paw.
1987	Randy Milligan, 1B, Tdw.
1988	Craig Worthington, 3B, Roch.
1989	Tom O'Malley, 3B, Tdw.
1990	Hensley Muelens, OF, Col.
1991	Derek Bell, OF, Syr.
1992	J.T. Snow, 1B-OF, Col.
1993	Jim Thorne, 3B, Char.
1994	Jeff Manto, 3B, Nor.-Roch.
1995	Butch Huskey, 3B-OF-1B, Nor.
1996	Phil Hiatt, 3B, Tol.
1997	Roberto Petagine, 1B, Nor.
1998	Roberto Petagine, 1B, Ind.
1999	Steve Cox, 1B, Dur.
2000	Chad Mottola, OF, Syr.
2001	Toby Hall, C, Dur.
2002	Raul Gonzalez, OF, Lou.

2003	Fernando Seguignol, 1B, Col.
2004	Jhonny Peralta, SS-3B, Buff.
2005	Shane Victorino, OF, SWB
2006	Kevin Whitt, 1B, Dur.
2007	Mike Hessman, 3B, Tol.

Rookie of the Year

1950	Ransom Jackson, 3B, Sprg.
1951	Hector Rodriguez, 3B, Mtl.
1966	Mike Epstein, 1B, Roch.
1952	Ray Jablonski, IF, Roch.
1967	Curt Motton, OF, Roch.
1953	Bob Trice, P, Ott.
1968	Merv Rettenmund, OF, Roch.
1954	Jim Owens, P, Syr.
1969	Luis Alvarado, SS, Lou.
1955	Jack Brandt, OF, Roch.
1970	Roger Freed, OF, Roch.
1956	Fred Kipp, P, Mtl.
1971	Rusty Torres, OF, Syr.
1957	Walter Craddock, P, Buff.
1972	Al Bumbry, OF, Roch.
1958	Rogelio Alvarez, 1B-OF, Hav.
1973	Otto Velez, OF, Syr.
1959	Charles James, OF, Roch.
1974	Jim Rice, OF, Paw.
1960	Bob Wine, SS, Buff.
1975	Mike Vail, OF, Tdw.
1961	Tom Tresh, SS, Rmd.
1976	Rich Dauer, 2B, Roch.
1962	Bob Bailey, IF, Col.
1977	Dale Murphy, C-1B, Rmd.
1963	Don Buford, 3B, Ind.
1978	Glenn Hubbard, 2B, Rmd.
1964	Jim Northrup, OF, Syr.
1979	Mookie Wilson, OF, Tdw.
1965	Joe Foy, 3B, Tor.
1980	Bob Bonner, SS, Roch.
1986	Orestes Destrade, 1B, Col.

1981	Cal Ripken, Jr., IF, Roch.
1987	Randy Milligan, 1B, Tdw.
1982	Brook Jacoby, 3B, Rmd.
1988	Steve Finley, OF, Roch.
1983	Brad Komminsk, OF, Rmd.
1989	Frank Cabrera, C, Syr.
1984	Scott Bradley, C-OF, Col.
1990	Phil Plantier, OF, Paw.
1985	Dan Pasqua, OF, Col.
1991	Luis Mercedes, OF, Roch.
1992	J.T. Snow, 1B-OF, Col.
1993	Chipper Jones, SS, Rich.
1994	Shawn Coreen, OF, Syr.
1995	Jason Isringhausen, P, Nor.
1996	Billy McMillon, OF, Char.
1997	Brian Rose, P, Paw.
1998	Marlon Anderson, 2B, SWB
1999	Kurt Bierek, 1B, Col.
2000	Aubrey Huff, 3B, Dur.
2001	Brandon Duckworth, P, SWB
2002	Carl Crawford, 1B, Durham
2003	Aaron Miles, 2B-3B, Char.
2004	Jason Kubel, OF, Roch.
2005	Francisco Liriano, P, Roch.
2006	Josh Fields, 3B, Char.
2007	Joey Votto, 1B-OF, Lou.

Most Valuable Pitcher

1953	Bob Trice, Ott.
1954	Tony Jacobs, Roch.
1955	Jack Crimian, Tor.
1956	Lynn Lovenguth, Tor.
1957	Don Johnson, Tor.
1958	Tom Lasorda, Mtl.
1959	Bill Short, Rmd.
1960	Al Cicotte, Tor.
1961	Diomedes Olivo, Col.
1962	Joe Schaffernoth, Jax
1963	Fred Ackley, Ind.
1964	Mel Stottlemyre, Rmd.

1965	Sam Jones, Col.
1966	Gary Waslewski, Tor.
1967	Dave Leonard, Roch.
1968	Dave Roberts, Col.
1969	Ron Klimkowski, Syr.
1970	Rob Gardner, Chn.
1971	Roric Harrison, Roch.
1972	Gene Garber, Chn.
1973	Dick Pole, Paw.
1974	Scott McGregor, Syr.
1975	Craig Swan, Tdw.
1976	Dennis Martinez, Tdw.
1977	Mike Parrott, Roch.
1978	Juan Berenguer, Tdw.
1979	Rick Anderson, Col.
1980	Bob Kammemeyer, Col.
1981	Bob Ojeda, Paw.
1982	Craig McMurtry, Rmd.
1983	Walt Terrell, Tdw.
1984	Brad Havens, Tol.
1985	Tom Henke, Syr.
1986	John Mitchell, Tdw.
1987	Brad Arnsberg, Col.
1988	Steve Searcy, Tol.
1989	Alex Sanchez, Syr.
1990	Dave Eiland, Col.
1991	Mike Mussina, Roch.
1992	Sam Militello, Col.
1993	Aaron Sele, Paw.
1994	Brad Woodall, Rich.
1995	Jason Isringhansen, Nor.
1996	Mike Fyhrie, Nor.
1997	Brian Rose, Paw.
1998	Shannon Withem, Syr.
1999	Ed Yarnell, Col.
2000	Jon Garland, Char.
2001	Brandon Duckworth SWB
2002	Joe Roa, SWB
2003	Branson Arroyo, Paw.
2004	Ben Hendrickson, Ind.
2005	Zach Duke, Ind.
2006	Heath Phillips, Char.
2007	Kevin Slowey, Roch.

National Baseball Hall of Fame —Hall of Famers Who Have Played, Managed or Umpired in the IL—

In 1936, when the "Select Five" were chosen as the first inductees into the National Baseball Hall of Fame, two of these five superstars once had worn flannel uniforms in the International League. As a nineteen-year-old phenom in 1914, Babe Ruth launched his fabled career with Baltimore and Providence. Following twenty-one seasons and 416 victories with the Washington Senators, Walter Johnson managed Newark of the IL in 1928, then returned to the majors as a manager for seven more years.

International League fans have watched the stellar performances of a parade of Hall of Famers for more than a century. As of this writing, a total of ninety-seven men who have played, managed or umpired in the IL have been honored with plaques at Cooperstown.

Walt Alston (Rochester, 1937, 1943-44; Mgr., Montreal, 1950-53)
Sparky Anderson (Montreal, 1956-58; Toronto, 1960-63; Mgr., Toronto, 1964)
Luke Appling (Mgr., Richmond, 1955)
John Baker (Baltimore, 1907)
Al Barlick (Umpire, 1940)
Ed Barrow (Owner-mgr., Toronto, 1900-02; IL pres., 1910-18)
Johnny Bench (Buffalo, 1966-67)
Chief Bender (Reading, 1922; Baltimore, 1923)
Yogi Berra (Newark, 1946)
Wade Boggs (Pawtucket, 1980-81)
Jim Bottomley (Syracuse, 1922)
Lou Boudreau (Buffalo, 1939)
Dan Brouthers (Springfield, 1896-99; Toronto, 1898; Rochester, 1899)
Jim Bunning (Buffalo, 1953, 1955)
Roy Campanella (Montreal, 1947)

Gary Carter (Peninsula, 1973; Memphis, 1974; Tidewater, 1989)
Jack Chesbro (Springfield, 1895)
Nestor Chylak (Umpire, 1952-53)
Roberto Clemente (Montreal, 1954)
Eddie Collins (Newark, 1907)
Jimmy Collins (Buffalo, 1893-94; Providence, 1910-11)
Jocko Conlan (Rochester, 1924-26; Newark, 1927-29; Montreal, 1931-32)
Leon Day (Toronto, 1951)
Bill Dickey (Buffalo, 1928)
Don Drysdale (Montreal, 1955)
Hugh Duffy (Hartford, 1886; Springfield, 1887; Providence, 1907-09)
Dennis Eckersley, Pawtucket, 1998)
Johnny Evers (Mgr., Albany, 1935)
Carlton Fisk (Louisville, 1971)
Jimmie Foxx (Providence, 1925)
Pud Galvin (Buffalo, 1894)
Charley Gehringer (Toronto, 1925)
Bob Gibson (Rochester, 1958, 1960)
Warren Giles (GM, Syracuse, 1934-36)
Frank Grant (Buffalo, 1886-88)
Burleigh Grimes (Mgr., Montreal, 1939; Toronto, 1942-44, 1947, 1952-53)
Lefty Grove (Baltimore, 1920-24)
Chick Hafey (Syracuse, 1925)
Billy Hamilton (Mgr., Springfield, 1914; Worcester, 1916)
Ned Hanlon (Owner, Baltimore, 1903-08)
Bucky Harris (Buffalo, 1918-19; Mgr., Buffalo, 1944-45)
Gabby Hartnett (Jersey City, 1943-44; Mgr., Buffalo, 1946)
Rogers Hornsby (Baltimore, 1938; Mgr., Baltimore, 1939)
Waite Hoyt (Montreal, 1917; Newark, 1918)
Cal Hubbard (Umpire, 1931-35)
Carl Hubbell (Toronto, 1926)
Monte Irvin (Jersey City, 1949-50)
Travis Jackson (Mgr., Jersey City, 1937-38)
Ferguson Jenkins (Buffalo, 1962; Arkansas, 1963)

Hughey Jennings (Baltimore, 1903-06)
Walter Johnson (Mgr., Newark, 1928)
Willie Keeler (Binghamton, 1892-93)
Joe Kelley (Toronto, 1907, 1909-10)
George Kelly (Rochester, 1917, 1919; Jersey City, 1932)
King Kelly (Player-Mgr., Allentown 1894)
Ralph Kiner (Toronto, 1943)
Nap Lajoie (Toronto, 1917)
Tom Lasorda (Montreal, 1950-55, 1958-60)
Tony Lazzeri (Player-Mgr., Toronto, 1939-40)
Bob Lemon (Baltimore, 1942; Mgr., Richmond, 1975)
Heinie Manush (Toronto, 1938-39)
Rabbit Maranville (Mgr., Montreal, 1937-38)
Rube Marquard (Baltimore, 1927)
Joe McCarthy (Buffalo, 1914-15)
Joe McGinnity (Newark, 1909-12; Mgr., 1909, 1911-12)
Bill McGowan (Umpire, 1916)
Johnny Mize (Rochester, 1933-35)
Eddie Murray (Rochester, 1976)
Stan Musial (Rochester, 1941)
Phil Niekro (Richmomd, 1966; Mgr., Richmond, 1991)
Satchel Paige (Miami, 1956-58)
Jim Palmer (Rochester, 1967-68)
Herb Pennock (Providence, 1915; Buffalo, 1916)
Kirby Puckett (Toledo, 1984)
Cal Ripken, Jr. (Rochester, 1981)
Jackie Robinson (Montreal, 1946)
Wilbert Robinson (Baltimore, 1903-04)
Babe Ruth (Baltimore-Providence, 1914)
Nolan Ryan (Jacksonville, 1967)
Ray Schalk (Mgr.-Buffalo, 1932-37, 1950)
Red Schoendienst (Rochester, 1943-44)
Tom Seaver (Jacksonville, 1966)
George Sisler, Sr. (Rochester, 1931)
Duke Snider (Montreal, 1948)
Tris Speaker (Player-Mgr., Newark, 1929-30)
Willie Stargell (Columbus, 1962)
Dazzy Vance (Rochester, 1918)

Bill Veeck (Executive, Miami, 1956)
Rube Waddell (Newark, 1910)
Ed Walsh (Newark, 1903)
Earl Weaver (Mgr., Rochester, 1966-67)
George Weiss (Executive, Rochester, 1929-31)
Mickey Welch (Troy, 1892)
Vic Willis (Syracuse, 1896-97)
Hack Wilson (Albany, 1935)
Ross Youngs (Rochester, 1917)

Lifetime Records

Best Lifetime Hitting

Average	Geo. Puccinelli	.334
Years	Eddie Onslow	17
Games	Eddie Onslow	2109
Runs	Fritz Maisel	1349
Hits	Eddie Onslow	2449
Doubles	Jimmy Walsh	405
Triples	Eddie Onslow	128
Home Runs	Ollie Carnegie	258
RBIs	Ollie Carnegie	1044
Stolen Bases	Fritz Maisel	384

Best Lifetime Pitching

Games	Clarence Fisher	524
Victories	Johnny Ogden	213
Losses	Clarence Fisher	143
Strikeouts	Tommy Thomas	1171
Shutouts	Rube Kisinger	31

Season Records

Best Individual Season Batting Records

Average	Dan Brouthers (Springfield, 1897)	.415
Runs	Joe Hauser (Baltimore, 1930)	173

Hits	Jack Bentley (Baltimore, 1921)	.246
Doubles	Jim Holt (Jersey City, 1924)	57
Triples	Guy Tutwiller (Providence, 1914)	29
Home Runs	Joe Hauser (Baltimore, 1930)	63
Extra Base Hits	Joe Hauser (Baltimore, 1930) 2B-39, 3B-11, HR-63	443
Consecutive Hits	George Quellich (Reading, 1929)	15
Hitting Streak (Games)	Brandon Watson (Columbus, 2007)	43
RBIs	Rip Collins (Rochester, 1930)	180
Stolen Bases	Mike Slattery (Toronto, 1887)	112
Walks	Blas Monaco (Baltimore, 1944)	167
Strikeouts	Dave Nicholson (Richmond, 1968)	199

Best Individual Season Pitching Records

Games	Bill Voiselle, (Richmond, 1955)	72
Victories	George Stovey (Newark, 1887)	35
Losses	George Keefe (Troy, 1888)	29
	Frank Leary (Rochester, 1903)	29
	Charles Swaney (Reading, 1926)	29
Winning Pcg.	Tony Jacobs (Rochester, 1954)	.929

Lowest ERA	Urban Shocker (Toronto, 1916)	1.31
Most Innings	Joe McGinnity (Newark, 1909)	422
Consecutive Wins	Jim Parnham (Baltimore, 1923)	20
Shutouts	Joe McGinnity (Newark, 1909)	11
Consecutive Shutout Innings	Urban Shocker (Toronto, 1916)	54
Strikeouts	Lefty Grove (Baltimore, 1923)	330
Walks	Lefty Grove (Baltimore, 1923)	186

Century Club

Winners

1921	Baltimore	119-47
1924	Baltimore	117-48
1922	Baltimore	115-52
1927	Buffalo	112-56
1923	Baltimore	111-53
1937	Newark	109-42
1920	Baltimore	109-44
1926	Toronto	109-57
1932	Newark	109-59
1920	Toronto	108-46
1925	Baltimore	105-61
1922	Rochester	105-62
1930	Rochester	105-62
1938	Newark	104-48
1929	Rochester	103-65
1933	Newark	102-62
1927	Syracuse	102-66
1923	Rochester	101-65
1926	Baltimore	101-65
1931	Rochester	101-67
1921	Rochester	100-68
1941	Newark	100-54

1946	Montreal	100-54	1923	Jersey City	61-105
1960	Toronto	100-54	1931	Buffalo	61-105
1919	Baltimore	100-49	1930	Jersey City	59-105
			1904	Rochester	28-105
			1933	Jersey City	61-104
	Losers		1935	Albany	49-104
1926	Reading	31-129	1922	Syracuse	64-102
1927	Reading	43-123	1931	Jersey City	65-102
1920	Rochester	33-116	1928	Jersey City	66-102
1929	Jersey City	51-115	1953	Springfield	51-102
1932	Toronto	54-113	1913	Jersey City	53-101
1922	Newark	54-112	1962	Syracuse	53-101
1924	Jersey City	53-111	1940	Toronto	57-101
1921	Reading	56-110	1923	Newark	60-101
1941	Toronto	47-107	1902	Newark	40-100
1921	Jersey City	59-106	1937	Jersey City	50-100
1914	Montreal	48-106	1925	Providence	63-100
1920	Rochester	45-106	1927	Jersey City	66-100

Index

BILL O'NEAL is the author of 32 books, including six volumes of baseball history. Recently Bill was named "Best Living Non-Fiction Writer, 2007," by *True West Magazine*. He has appeared on TV documentaries on The History Channel, TBS, The Discovery Channel, TNN, and A&E. A lifelong baseball fan, Bill taught history for 33 years at Panola College in Carthage, Texas, where he has spent decades as the Voice of Pony Baseball for KGAS Radio. At Panola Bill worked wth longtime Pony coach Jacke Davis, who played three seasons for Buffalo, and with such future International League stars as Todd Haney, the 1998 IL batting champ, and Robert Ellis, who fired a no-hitter in 2004 for Scranton/Wilkes-Barre. Bill's wife Karon teaches mathematics at Panola College, and she assisted with every aspect of this book.

Printed in the United States
108321LV00001B/111-1600/P